Nations and Firms in the Global Economy

This accessible introduction to the world economy and to the theory and practice of globalization argues that key topics in international economics cannot be understood without a knowledge of international business, and vice versa. It reviews and combines insights from both literatures and applies them to real-world issues, clearly explaining the main concepts of international economics and business in a uniquely integrated approach. Written in a lively and accessible style, this innovative textbook covers all the main issues, including international trade, capital mobility, comparative advantage, foreign direct investments, multinational behaviour, financial crises and economic growth. It includes carefully selected international examples and case studies, and special interest boxes which clearly explain more challenging economic concepts. The companion website includes additional case studies, exercises and answers to exercises, data, illustrations and links to other useful websites.

Steven Brakman is Professor of International Economics at the University of Groningen.

Harry Garretsen is Professor of International Economics at the Utrecht School of Economics, Utrecht University.

Charles van Marrewijk is Professor of Economics at Erasmus University Rotterdam.

Arjen van Witteloostuijn is Professor of International Economics and Business at the University of Groningen and Professor of Strategy at the University of Durham.

"This book is a remarkable achievement. It covers all the pressing international economic issues of our day in an accessible yet thorough manner. The authors adroitly combine illustrative data and essential theory to explain the how's and why's of trade and trade liberalisation, the delocation of firms and multinational activity, capital flows, currency and financial crises, and the role of international organisations such as the IMF and WTO. It is appropriate for students without an economics specialisation both at the undergraduate and non-specialists graduate level, e.g. MBA and Masters of Public Administration. The facts and real-world feel of the book make it interesting as a supplement for specialist students as well."

Richard Baldwin, *Professor of International Economics, Graduate Institute of International Studies, Geneva*

"International trade and international business have hitherto existed in two separate worlds – a world of nations and a world of firms – in academic teaching and even in research. This book gives us a welcome integration of the two at the level of teaching. Students who use it will develop a unified vision that will benefit them in their future careers, whether in business, government, international institutions, or academic research.

Avinash K. Dixit, *Department of Economics, Princeton University*

"This is a fascinating book with a practical approach to international economics that enhances our understanding of the globalisation process."

Hans-Werner Sinn, *President of the Ifo Institute for Economic Research, Munich*

"This book offers a valuable integration of the economics and business aspects of globalization. The integrated approach makes the book a unique and valuable resource for students of international economics and business studies."

Prof. Dr. Joseph Francois, *Tinbergen Institute, Rotterdam, and CEPR, London*

"Understanding the enormous changes taking place in the world economy requires the perspectives of many different disciplines, of which international economics and international business are two of the most relevant. Yet until now these two fields have interacted very little. This new text does a superb job of combining the insights of these two complementary academic fields. The authors present a lucid overview of theories of international economics, with an emphasis on recent contributions such as imperfect competition, multinational corporations, agglomeration and financial crises. In addition they present a wealth of relevant and insightful case-studies from the international business literature which helps bridge the gap between theory and reality. Students in a range of courses will benefit from this integration of different approaches, and researchers who want an overview of recent work in fields outside their own will learn a lot too."

J. Peter Neary, *Department of Economics, University College Dublin*

Nations and Firms in the Global Economy

An Introduction to International Economics and Business

Steven Brakman

Harry Garretsen

Charles van Marrewijk

Arjen van Witteloostuijn

CAMBRIDGE
UNIVERSITY PRESS

CAMBRIDGE UNIVERSITY PRESS
Cambridge, New York, Melbourne, Madrid, Cape Town, Singapore, São Paulo

Cambridge University Press
The Edinburgh Building, Cambridge CB2 2RU, UK

Published in the United States of America by Cambridge University Press, New York

www.cambridge.org
Information on this title: www.cambridge.org/9780521540575

First published 2006

Printed in the United Kingdom at the University Press, Cambridge

A catalogue record for this book is available from the British Library

ISBN-13   978-0-521-83298-4 hardback
ISBN-10   0-521-83298-5 hardback
ISBN-13   978-0-521-54057-5 paperback
ISBN-10   0-521-54057-7 paperback

Contents

Part IV Policy, dynamics and organization

Figures

Tables

Boxes

Preface

The title *Nations and Firms in the Global Economy: An Introduction to International Economics and Business* reflects our main motivations for writing this book. It contains the six core elements we address (i) introduction, (ii) the global economy, (iii) nations, (iv) firms, (v) international economics and (vi) international business. We briefly review these components and their interaction in this preface.

Introduction Our book is an introduction to the subject, indicating that our target audience consists of students interested in (international) economics and (international) business for whom this is the first structured encounter with the issues discussed, who wish to get acquainted with the facts and forces of the hotly debated globalization process. Depending on the background of the student and the type of programme (s)he is enrolled in, this first encounter could be in different parts of the curriculum, although it will usually be in the first or second year of an undergraduate programme. For other interested readers, this book offers an up-to-date introduction to what we know about globalization, its drivers and its consequences, particularly from an economics and business perspective. The preliminary requirements for a proper understanding of our book are limited. We assume that the reader has taken an introductory (micro and macro) economics course, and that (s)he has some grasp of elementary mathematics allowing him or her to understand simple graphs and equations. We also provide some technical material in boxes, as quick reminders of essential concepts.

The global economy We analyse the global economy–or, as it is more popularly known: the globalization process. As this is an introduction to the global economy, we define in chapter 1 what we mean by 'globalization' and what we will and will not analyze in the sequel. Throughout the book, we provide ample empirical information on the globalization process so that we may distinguish between fact and myth. In presenting the facts, we show longer time series than most textbooks or popular introductions. This enables readers to place current developments into their proper perspective, providing a better understanding of the developments giving rise to today's complex structure of the international economy. We address all the major economic components of the globalization process, both real and monetary. We discuss international trade and capital flows, foreign direct investments (FDI), multinational firms, exchange rates, financial crises, outsourcing, economic development, location and much more. In doing so, the emphasis will be more on international trade and capital mobility, and less on international labour mobility, which reflects the fact that in economic terms international trade and capital flows are much more important than international labour migration, as we shall show.

Nations   A proper understanding of the globalization process necessarily looks at the role of nations, governments and international organizations.

- Why do nations specialize in the export of certain types of goods and services, and import others?
- Is specialization always beneficial, or are there winners and losers from the globalization process?
- If so, who are these winners and losers?
- Why do governments adhere to particular policies regarding exchange rates, trade flows and capital mobility?

And so on and so forth. We address these and other issues from both a theoretical and a practical point of view by giving many empirical examples and discussing numerous case studies.

Firms   In many respects, the decisions by individual (multinational) firms produce the most important driving forces behind the globalization process, ultimately determining international trade, capital flows and FDI. Naturally, these firms react to the conditions of the economic environment in which they operate, which is determined to a considerable extent by governments and international organizations. Firms therefore both shape the global environment and are shaped by it. Throughout the book, we discuss the forces with which firms are confronted, the competitive forces they unleash and how the interaction of these powers influences the firm's organizational structure, human resource management (HRM), corporate governance and other issues internal to the firm. Here, our focus is on the multinational enterprise (MNE).

International economics   To some extent, it could be argued that the international economics literature tends to emphasize the role of nations (and comparative advantage) rather than the role of firms in the globalization process. This is, of course, not entirely accurate as the role of the industrial organization and international business literatures, and thus the factors influencing the organizational structure of individual firms, is becoming increasingly important in the international economics curriculum. We argue, therefore, that it is becoming increasingly clear that the latter type of analysis complements the former. Compared to other introductory textbooks on international economics, the primary goal of our book is not to cover the whole field, but to focus on those theories and insights that help us to understand the economic causes and consequences of globalization, as well as the role played by both nations and (multinational) firms. To give just one example, monetary policy is discussed in our analysis of international capital mobility, but we do not dwell on issues such as the conduct of monetary policy or the theory of monetary integration as such. We discuss such issues only if they are relevant within the context of the main theme of our book. This also means that when it comes to understanding the global economy, we cover a lot more ground than other introductory textbooks.

International business   It could be argued that the international business literature tends to emphasize the role of firms (and competitive advantage) rather than the role of nations in the globalization process. This, too, is not entirely accurate as the international economic environment in which the (multinational) firm operates is an increasingly important part of the international business curriculum. Once again, the latter type of analysis complements the former, which is the reason we combine these perspectives throughout the book. After all, MNEs do not operate in a vacuum – on the contrary, they must take account of all kinds of issues related to international economics, from exchange rate fluctuations and capital market restrictions to fiscal policies and labour market conditions.

To complement the material presented in this textbook, there is a website available providing additional information and supporting material. Its location is: www.charlesvanmarrewijk.nl.

The website provides: (i) background information on the structure of the book; (ii) background information on the authors; (iii) additional illustrations and data material, such as all the figures and tables used in the book; (iv) different types of exercises for self-study, as well as answers to (a subset of) these exercises; (v) other self-study material; and (vi) updates, and links to useful other sources of information. The choice of posting questions on a website rather than including them in the book itself is motivated by the important advantage that it allows us to integrate and respond to recent developments in the global economics and business environment in the questions posed.

Parts of this book were written during a visit by Brakman, Garretsen and van Marrewijk to the Department of Economics at Princeton University in June–July 2003, and during a visit by van Marrewijk to the School of Economics at the University of Adelaide in 2004. We are grateful to Princeton University and the University of Adelaide for their hospitality. In particular, we would like to thank Avinash Dixit, Gene Grossman and Ian McLean for making these visits possible. Moreover, we are grateful for financial support from the University of Groningen (Brakman and van Witteloostuijn), Utrecht School of Economics (Garretsen), the Erasmus University Trust Fund (van Marrewijk), the University of Adelaide (van Marrewijk) and the University of Durham (van Witteloostuijn).

We would also like to thank Bart van Ark, Gerrit Faber Karl Farmer, Peter Kenen, Henryk Kierzkowski and Chris Harrison for help in finding relevant data, and for providing useful comments and suggestions. Steven Poelhekke provided able research assistance for parts of this book. Harry Garretsen would also like to thank Hans van

Ees, Hans Groeneveld and Ralph de Haas for the opportunity to make use of previous mutual work.

Steven Brakman
Harry Garretsen
Charles van Marrewijk and
Arjen van Witteloostuijn

Groningen, Utrecht, Rotterdam and
Groningen–Durham
February 2005

Glossary

ASEAN	Association of Southeast Asian Nations
BCG	Boston Consulting Group
BIS	Bank of International Settlements
boe	barrels of oil equivalent
BPR	business process re-engineering
CEE	Central and Eastern European
CEO	chief executive officer
CFO	chief financial officer
CIF	cost, insurance, freight
CIS	Confederation of Independent States
COMESA	Common Market of Eastern and Southern Africa
CPE	centrally planned economy
FDI	foreign direct investment
EADS	European Aeronautic Defence and Space Company
EFTA	European Free Trade Association
EIC	East India Company
EITF	Emerging Issues Task Force
EMS	European Monetary System
EMU	European Monetary Union
EMBI	Emerging Market Bond Index
ERM	Exchange Rate Mechanism (EU)
EU	European Union
EVA	economic value added
FOB	free on board
FSU	former Soviet Union
FTA	free trade area
GAAP	Generally Accepted Accounting Principles (US)
GATT	General Agreement on Tariffs and Trade
GCI	gross capital income
GDP	gross domestic product
GGDP	Groningen Growth and Development Centre
GNP	gross national product
HGB	German Commercial Code

HRM	human resource management
IB	international business
ICP	International Comparison Project (UN)
ICRG	International Country Risk Guide
ICT	information and communication technology
IE	International economics
IFI	international financial institution
IFS	*International Financial Statistics* (IMF)
IMF	International Monetary Fund
IO	industrial organization
IPO	initial public offering
IT	information technology
ITC	International Trade Commission (US)
JIT	just-in-time
JV	joint venture
M&As	mergers and acquisitions
MC	marginal costs
MERCOSUR	Southern Common Market
MFN	most-favoured-nation
MITI	Ministry of International Trade and Industry (Japan)
MNC	multinational corporation
MNE	multinational enterprise
MPC	marginal productivity of capital
MR	marginal revenue
NAFTA	North American Free Trade Agreement
NIC	newly industrializing country
NIO	New International Order
NTB	non-tariff barrier
NW	Net worth
NYSE	New York Stock Exchange
OECD	Organization for Economic Cooperation and Development
OLI	Ownership, Location and Internalization (Dunning)
PPC	production possibility curve
PPP	purchasing power parity
PTA	preferential trade agreement
PWT	Penn World Tables
R&D	Research and Development
SAR	special administrative region (Hong Kong)
SDR	Special Drawing Rights (IMF)
SDRM	sovereign debt restructuring mechanism

SEC	Securities and Exchange Commission (US)
S–I	savings–investment (model)
SITC	Standard International Trade Classification
SOE	state-owned enterprise
SSA	Sub-Saharan Africa
TFP	total factor productivity
TNE	transnational enterprise
TNI	TransNationality Index
UDROP	universal debt rollover option with a penalty
UIP	uncovered interest parity
UN	United Nations
UNHCR	United Nations High Commissioner for Refugees
USTR	United States Trade Representative
VMPL	value marginal product of labour
VOC	Verenigde Oostindische Compagnie
WB	World Bank
WTO	World Trade Organization

Suggested course structure

Our book consists of five parts – *Introduction* (part I), *Firms, trade and location* (part II), *Capital, currency and crises* (part III), *Policy, dynamics and organization* (part IV) and *Conclusion* (part V). As the name suggests, part I provides an introduction into the world economy. We recommend that any course based on this book should always start with studying chapters 1 and 2. Part II concentrates on the *real* aspects of the global economy and analyzes, for example, production structure, trade flows, multinational firms and migration. Part III concentrates on the *monetary* aspects of the global economy and analyzes, for example, exchange rates, capital flows, investments, risk and uncertainty and financial crises. Depending on the focus of the course and the available time, either part II or part III can be skipped. We recommend that any course focusing on the real aspects of the global economy should study chapters 3–5 in sequence. Similarly, we recommend that any course focusing on the monetary aspects of the global economy should study chapters 6–9 in sequence. The first two chapters of part IV present important topics with a real–monetary combination. Both could be dealt with in a course skipping either part II or part III of the book, although a more complete comprehension is obtained when both parts are studied before turning to these chapters. Independently of the details of the course structure, we always recommend that any course should conclude by studying chapter 12 (on the organizational implications for the firm of operating in a global environment) and the two chapters of the concluding part V (an evaluation of globalization, from both a macro and micro perspective).

Part I

Introduction

The global economy

KEYWORDS

population	GDP in history	barriers to trade
distribution of population	GDP and GNP	GDP *per capita*
globalization	global market integration	capital flows
history of globalization	migration	

1.1 Introduction

Numerous factors active in the global economic environment affect the decisions that managers of firms have to make regarding the price to charge for their products, how much to produce, how much to invest in R&D, how much to spend on advertising and so on. Some of these factors are the number of firms competing in a market, the relative size of firms, technological and cost considerations, demand conditions and the ease with which competing foreign firms can enter or exit the market. The *economic globalization process* – that is, the increased interdependence of national economies, and the trend towards greater integration of goods, labour and capital markets (see section 1.4) – influences all these factors, and thus indirectly affects managerial decisions and market organization.

International economics analyses the *interactions in the global economic environment*. International business analyses the managerial decisions taken on the basis of a *cost–benefit analysis* in this global economic environment. In view of the above, we argue that central topics in international finance, business and public policy cannot be understood without a knowledge of international economics. Similarly, we conclude that the central topics in international economics cannot be fully understood without insights from international business.

This book provides an introduction to the global economy: what it is, how big it is, how it functions and how participants interact. Throughout the book, we analyse how international businesses are affected by the global economic environment and discuss the role played by firms in this process, thus allowing businesses to make better decisions. This is our primary perspective. In addition, we discuss examples of the other causality: from international businesses to (inter)national economies.

Before we can begin to analyse the global economy in chapter 2 and beyond, however, this chapter provides and evaluates some basic theoretical and empirical background information about the global economy concerning population, income, international trade, capital flows and the phenomenon of globalization. According to OECD Secretary-General Donald Johnston (see Maddison, 2001, p. 3), John Maynard Keynes argued that the master economist should 'examine the present in light of the past, for the purposes of the future'. We concur with this view, and shall not only pay attention to the current structure of the global economy, but also discuss how the economy has evolved over time – in particular, how globalization in its two basic manifestations (international trade and factor mobility) has progressed and culminated in the two waves of globalization of the nineteenth and twentieth centuries.

1.2 A sense of time: the universe and population

Some knowledge of the roles of time and history is helpful if we are to appreciate the modest position of the human species on a cosmic scale, relative to its current dominant position on our planet, to which we have become so accustomed. It all started with a 'Big Bang' which created the ever-expanding universe about 13.7 billion years ago: at least, that is the most recent and accurate estimate of NASA's cosmic background explorer (COBE) programme, based on measurements of minuscule differences in temperature. The first stars were formed some 200 million years later (earlier than initially anticipated). Our galaxy was formed some 10 billion years ago and our solar system some 5 billion years later. As further summarized in figure 1.1, the formation of planet earth took some 1.5 billion years, so the geologic eras started 3.5 billion years ago. The atoms gave way to molecules, the molecules to cells and the cells to life – the oldest known fossils (worms and algae) date back 3 billion years. The process of photosynthesis by plants began some 2 billion years ago. Mankind appeared on the scene 'only' 1.8 million years ago, taking *homo erectus* who invented tools as the starting point. In short, on a cosmic time scale mankind barely exists and our formidable achievements have not made a lasting impression.

Population size

Estimates of the size of the global population prior to 200 BC are based on archaeological and anthropological evidence, see Deevey (1960). In the nomadic period (before

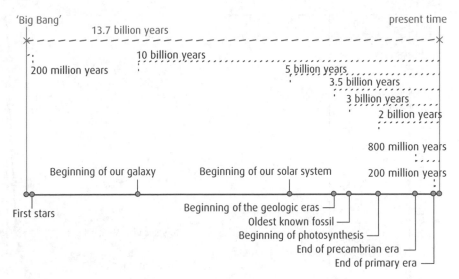

Figure 1.1 'Big Bang' and beyond
Data sources: Louis Henri Fournet (1998) and the website http://www.nasa.gov, 'A baby picture of the universe tells its age', 11 February 2003.

8000 BC), Fournet (1998, p. 5) notes that: 'the population subsisted primarily on gathering berries . . . and . . . it takes about five square kilometres to feed a human being.' Population growth rates were very low for a very long time period. According to the data sources in Kremer (1993), there were about 125,000 people 1 million years ago. Their number quadrupled to 1 million in the next 700,000 years and reached about 170 million when Christ was born. The estimates become more reliable after this, as they are based on Roman and Chinese censuses.

The developments in world population over the last 2,500 years are illustrated in figure 1.2. Despite the general upward trend there are periods of stagnation or decline in world population, for example as a result of the Mongol invasions in the thirteenth century, the bubonic plague (or 'Black Death', which wiped out a third of the European population in the sixth century and again in the fourteenth), the Thirty Years War (which raged throughout central Europe from 1618 to 1648) and the collapse of the Ming dynasty in China. A significant increase in the population growth rate began in the seventeenth century and reached a peak in the 1960s, leading to dramatic increases in population. There were 1 billion people in 1830, 2 billion in 1930 and more than 6 billion in 2000. The growth in world population is projected to fall significantly in the twenty-first century, partly as a result of a more rapid demographic transition process in many developing nations than originally anticipated and partly as a result of the raging AIDS epidemic, specifically in Africa.

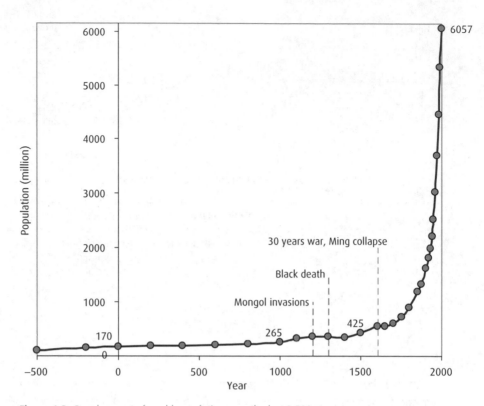

Figure 1.2 Development of world population over the last 2,500 years
Data sources: Kremer (1993, table 1) and UN Population Division (2001) (for the estimate of 2000), see http://www.un.org/popin.data.html.

Nonetheless, since demographic transition processes move as slowly as an oil tanker in the Thames, the world population is expected by the United Nations (UN) to increase to about 8.9 billion in 2050 (see figure 1.3).

According to the 2002 revision of the UN population division there were 6 billion 70 million 581 thousand people alive on our planet on 1 July 2000. Of course, given the inaccuracy of the data, the UN could have been off by a couple of million. Out of every 100 people alive more than twenty live in China and almost seventeen live in India. As the only two countries with more than 1 billion inhabitants, China and India are by far the most populous nations (see table 1.1). The world population is very unevenly divided, as indicated by the second part of table 1.1. The city-state of Singapore has the highest population density (6,587 people per km^2), followed by two other small countries (Bermuda and Malta). Only three of the twenty most populous nations, all located in Asia (Bangladesh, India, and Japan), are also among the twenty most densely populated nations.

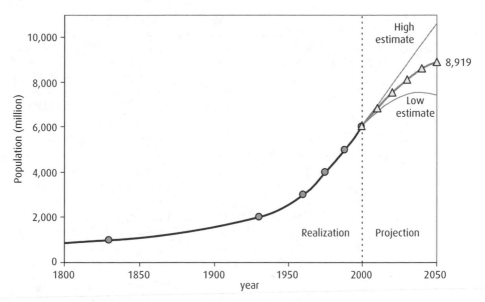

Figure 1.3 Developments in world population, 2000–2050, UN projection
Data sources: Kremer (1993, table 1) and UN Population Division (2001), see http://www.un.org/
popin.data.html.

Population projections

In 2000, eleven of the twenty most populous nations were located in Asia, which is home to almost 3.7 billion people, or about 60 per cent of the world total (table 1.2). Although the Asian population is expected to increase to 5.4 billion by 2050, its share is slightly falling to 58 per cent. The population of Africa is expected to increase most dramatically, from 796 million to 2 billion (from 13 to 22 per cent), while the only decline is expected in Europe, from 727 to 603 million (or from 12 to 7 per cent). This can be explained by the much higher total fertility rate – the average number of children per woman – in Africa (5.27) than in Europe (1.41). Total fertility is generally higher in the developing countries than in the developed countries. It is, for example, below the replacement level of 2.1 children per woman in Europe and Northern America. Total fertility will decline for all continents except for Europe, where it will rebound slightly from its current low level.

As a result of better health care systems, sufficient availability of food, and access to safe water supplies, life expectancy at birth is higher in the developed countries than in the developing countries (75 years versus 63 years in 2000). This gap will remain high, although it is expected to narrow over the next fifty years (82 years versus 75 years). Life expectancy is particularly low in Africa (51.4 years), which has been

Table 1.1 The twenty countries with highest population and population density, 2000

Rank	Country	Population	Country	Population density
1	China	1,262	Singapore	6,587
2	India	1,016	Bermuda	1,260
3	USA	282	Malta	1,219
4	Indonesia	210	Bangladesh	1,007
5	Brazil	170	Bahrain	1,001
6	Russian Federation (CIS)	146	Maldives	920
7	Pakistan	138	Barbados	621
8	Bangladesh	131	Mauritius	584
9	Nigeria	127	Aruba	532
10	Japan	127	Korea, Rep.	479
11	Mexico	98	Netherlands	470
12	Germany	82	San Marino	450
13	Vietnam	79	Puerto Rico	442
14	Philippines	76	Lebanon	423
15	Turkey	65	Virgin Islands (US)	356
16	Ethiopia	64	Japan	348
17	Egypt, Arab Rep.	64	Rwanda	345
18	Iran, Islamic Rep.	64	India	342
19	Thailand	61	American Samoa	327
20	UK	60	Belgium	312

Data source: World Bank (2002).
Notes: Population in millions, population density in people per km^2.

Table 1.2 Population projections, 2000–2050, the world and continents

	Population		Total fertility		Life expectancy		Median age	
	2000	2050	2000	2050	2000	2050	2000	2050
World	6,057	9,322	2.82	2.15	65.0	76.0	26.5	36.2
Africa	794	2,000	5.27	2.39	51.4	69.5	18.4	27.4
Asia	3,672	5,428	2.70	2.08	65.8	77.1	26.2	38.3
Latin America[a]	519	806	2.69	2.10	69.3	77.8	24.4	37.8
Europe	727	603	1.41	1.81	73.2	80.8	37.7	49.5
Northern America	314	438	2.00	2.08	76.7	82.7	35.6	41.0
Oceania	31	47	2.41	2.06	73.5	80.6	30.9	38.1

[a] Unless otherwise specified, the term 'Latin America' includes the Caribbean throughout this book.
Data source: UN Population Division (2001).
Notes: Population in millions, total fertility in average number of children per woman. Data for total fertility and life expectancy at birth are five-year estimates (for 1995–2000 and 2045–50). The projections for 2050 are based on the UN's medium variant.

struck hard by the HIV/AIDS epidemic.[1] The most affected countries – Botswana, South Africa, Swaziland and Zimbabwe – are all in Africa. The toll of AIDS in terms of increased mortality and population loss can be devastating. In the thirty-five most highly affected countries of Africa, for example, life expectancy at birth is estimated to be 6.5 years less than it would have been in the absence of AIDS, and the population is projected to be 10 per cent less in 2015 than it would have been without AIDS. Life expectancy at birth at the world level is estimated to increase from 65 years in 2000 to 76 years in 2050. Although it will probably remain the world's laggard, the UN expects a huge increase in African life expectancy (from 51 years in 2000 to 70 years in 2050).

Population ageing will be the major demographic trend for the next fifty years. The rise in life expectancy at birth combined with the decline in fertility rates around the world will lead to rapid increases in the share of older people. The median age – the age that divides the population into two equal halves – is used as an indicator of the shift of the population age distribution towards older ages. In 2000 the median age was 26.5 years, indicating that half of the world population was younger, and half the world population was older, than 26.5 years. By 2050 the median age will have increased to 36.2 years. Currently, Africa has the youngest and Europe has the oldest population (a median age of 18.4 years versus 37.7 years). The most rapid increases in the median age will occur in Latin America and Europe (the '50–50–50' rule: by 2050 roughly 50 per cent of the European population will be above 50 years old).

Population and business

Do managers of international firms care about the population distribution, the age profile, demographic trends and projected developments? Yes, they do. In fact, firms study such trends closely (and many more trends not discussed above) and try to predict the implications that these trends are likely to have for their core activities and strategies. A few examples may illustrate this:

- First, many automobile firms have started production and assembly plants in China since 2000, all with the intention of benefiting from the potentially large and rapidly growing Chinese market: almost 1.3 billion customers! In case you are wondering why they have not done the same in India, the answer is that automobile firms have invested only modest amounts there because the Indian income levels (see p. 13) are too low to generate a substantial demand for cars despite having more than 1 billion customers.

---

[1] AIDS = acquired immunodeficiency syndrome; HIV = human immunodeficiency virus.

- Second, all major investment firms are increasing the share of their investments in firms and activities that will benefit from the population ageing process, such as health care, travel and entertainment and retirement projects.
- Third, inspired by their marketing departments, firm R&D centres are being given instructions to find user-friendly solutions for an ageing population, such as milk cartons that do not spill, bottles and jars that can be opened without using pneumatic equipment and digital versatile disc (DVD) players that can be operated without reading the 150-page instruction book.

Business and population

Businesses are also important drivers of much that happens at the population level, both nationally and internationally. Clearly, policy-makers are keen to take account of business developments and try to influence them so that the advantages for society at large are maximized (or, for that matter, any disadvantages are kept within workable bounds). Again, a few examples may illustrate this:

- According to standard economics logic, businesses are the key drivers of macroeconomic performance, such as employment and growth, particularly in capitalist societies. Within the business world, the production of goods and services is extensive; many innovations are developed and commercialized. Macroeconomic developments are thus heavily influenced by microeconomic businesses.
- The allocation of jobs across the globe, for example, cannot be understood without insights into the location decision of multinationals. In the late twentieth and early twenty-first century, much industrial employment moved out of the Western high-wage region into low-wage developing countries.
- Many other examples are industry-specific. The pharmaceutical industry, for instance, is the key producer of new medicines. Because most money is to be earned in the rich West, the multi-billion R&D efforts of the multinational pharmaceutical companies are heavily biased toward the invention, development and commercialization of drugs that can help to prevent or cure Western 'welfare diseases' (e.g. cancer), rather than the much more common Third World plagues (e.g. malaria).

1.3 Income levels: GNP and GDP

The best indicator of the economic power of a nation is, of course, obtained by estimating the *total value of the goods and services produced* in a certain time period. Actually doing this and comparing the results across nations is a formidable task, which conceptually requires taking three steps:

- First, a well-functioning statistics office in each nation must gather accurate information on the value of millions of goods and services produced and provided by the firms in the economy. This will be done, of course, in the country's local currency – that is, dollars in the USA, pounds in the UK, yen in Japan, etc.
- Second, we have to decide what to compare between nations: gross *domestic* product or gross *national* product.
- Third, we have to decide *how* to compare the *outcome* for the different nations.

Domestic or national product?

As mentioned above, we can either compare GDP or GNP between nations. *GDP* is defined as the market value of the goods and services produced by labour and property *located* in a country. *GNP* is defined as the market value of the goods and services produced by labour and property of *residents* of a country. If, for example, a Mexican worker is providing labour services in the USA, these services are part of American GDP and Mexican GNP. The term 'located in' sometimes needs to be interpreted broadly – for example, if a Filipino sailor is providing labour services for a Norwegian shipping company, this is part of Norwegian GDP despite the fact that the ship is not actually located in Norway most of the time. The difference between GNP and GDP does not hold only for labour services, but also for other factors of production, such as capital

$$GDP + Net\ receipts\ of\ factor\ income = GNP \qquad\qquad (1.1)$$

So does it really matter whether we compare countries on the basis of GDP or GNP? No, for most countries it does not. This is illustrated for 2000 in figure 1.4, where the GDP and GNP values are measured in current US dollars. Since almost all observations are very close to a straight 45° line through the origin, the values of GDP and GNP are usually very close to one another. For example, British GDP was $1,415 billion, only 0.2 per cent below its GNP of $1,417 billion. Only two of the thirty-six countries with an income level above $100 billion have a deviation between GDP and GNP exceeding 5 per cent, namely Switzerland (where GNP is 5.8 per cent higher than GDP) and Indonesia (where GNP is 6.9 per cent lower than GDP). For some of the smaller countries the difference between GDP and GNP can be substantial in relative terms. For example, capital income from abroad ensures that Kuwait's GNP is 18.3 per cent higher than its GDP, while payments to capital reduce Ireland's GNP by 14.5 per cent compared to GDP. Unless indicated otherwise, we will use GDP throughout this book.

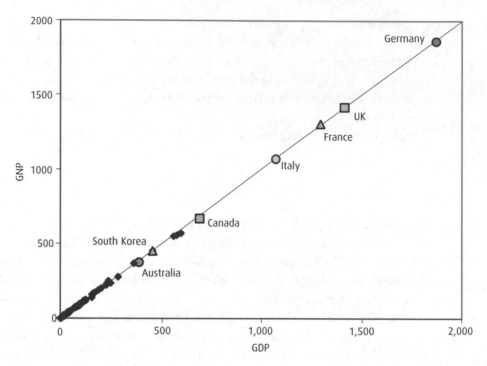

Figure 1.4 GDP and GNP, current $, 2000
Data source: World Bank (2002).
Note: Data are for 177 countries; observations for Japan and the USA are outside the shown range; the thin line is a 45° line.

Comparison

When the GDP level for each nation in local currency is simply converted to the same international standard currency (usually the US dollar, US $) on the basis of the average exchange rate in the period of observation (the current period), it comes as no surprise that the USA has the world's largest economy, with a total production value of $9.8 trillion (i.e. $9,800 billion) in 2000.[2] Since the total value of all goods and services produced in the world was estimated to be $30.8 trillion, measured this way the US economy would account for 31.9 per cent of world production, about double the share of Japan, and five times the share of Germany (see table 1.3). However, a ranking of the world's most powerful economies based on production values measured in current US $ would be deceptive because it would tend to over-estimate production in the high-income countries relative to the low-income countries. To understand this, we have to distinguish between *tradable* and *non-tradable* goods and services:

[2] Henceforth the $ sign always refers to the US $, unless stated otherwise.

Table 1.3 The twenty most powerful economies, 2000

	Country	GDP ppp		GDP		GDP *per capita*	
		Curr. int. $, billion		Current US $		PPP, curr. int. $	
		GDP	% of total	GDP	% of total	GDP *per capita*	Rank
1	USA	9,613	21.9	9,837	31.9	34,142	2
2	China	5,019	11.4	1,080	3.5	3,976	90
3	Japan	3,394	7.7	4,842	15.7	26,755	11
4	India	2,395	5.5	457	1.5	2,358	116
5	Germany	2,062	4.7	1,873	6.1	25,103	15
6	France	1,427	3.2	1,294	4.2	24,223	18
7	UK	1,404	3.2	1,415	4.6	23,509	20
8	Italy	1,363	3.1	1,074	3.5	23,626	19
9	Brazil	1,299	3.0	595	1.9	7,625	57
10	Russian Federation (CIS)	1,219	2.8	251	0.8	8,377	55
11	Mexico	884	2.0	575	1.9	9,023	52
12	Canada	856	1.9	688	2.2	27,840	7
13	South Korea	822	1.9	457	1.5	17,380	29
14	Spain	768	1.7	559	1.8	19,472	27
15	Indonesia	640	1.5	153	0.5	3,043	105
16	Australia	493	1.1	390	1.3	25,693	12
17	Argentina	458	1.0	285	0.9	12,377	41
18	Turkey	455	1.0	200	0.6	6,974	63
19	Netherlands	408	0.9	365	1.2	25,657	13
20	South Africa	402	0.9	126	0.4	9,401	48

- As the name suggests, tradable goods and services can be transported or provided in another country, perhaps with some difficulty and at some cost. In principle, therefore, the providers of tradable goods in different countries compete with one another fairly directly, implying that the prices of such goods are related and can be compared effectively on the basis of observed (average) exchange rates.
- In contrast, non-tradable goods and services have to be provided locally and do not compete with international providers. Think, for example, of housing services, getting a haircut, or going to the cinema.

Since (i) different sectors in the same country compete for the same labourers, so that (ii) the wage rate in an economy reflects the average productivity of a nation and (iii) productivity differences between nations in the non-tradable sectors tend to be smaller than in the tradable sectors, converting the value of output in the non-tradable sectors on the basis of observed exchange rates tends to under-estimate the value of production in these sectors for the low-income countries, as explained in box 1.1. For example, on the basis of observed exchange rates, getting a haircut in the

Box 1.1 Purchasing power parity (PPP) corrections

Suppose there are two countries (Australia and Botswana), each producing two types of goods (traded goods and non-traded goods) using only labour as an input in the production process. All labourers are equally productive within a country (homogeneous labour and constant returns to scale), but there are differences in productivity between countries. As illustrated in table 1.4, we assume Australian

Table 1.4 Assumed labour productivity, Australia and Botswana

	Number of products produced per working day	
	Traded goods	Non-traded goods
Australia	20	20
Botswana	4	10

workers to be five times more productive in the traded goods sector and only twice as productive in the non-traded goods sector:

- *Between-country arbitrage* Assuming that there are no transport costs or other trade restrictions, arbitrage in the traded goods sector will ensure that the wage rate in Australia will be five times as high as the wage rate in Botswana, because Australian workers are five times more productive. Taking this as the basis for international income comparisons leads us to think that *per capita* income is 400 per cent higher in Australia than it is in Botswana.

- *Within-country arbitrage* Assuming labour mobility between sectors within a country, arbitrage for labour between the traded and non-traded goods sector will ensure that the price of traded goods in local currency is the same as the price of non-traded goods in Australia (because labour is equally productive in the two sectors), whereas the price of traded goods in local currency is 2.5 times as high as the price of non-traded goods in Botswana (because labour is 2.5 times less productive in the traded goods sector than in the non-traded goods sector). In local currency, therefore, non-traded goods are much cheaper compared to traded goods in Botswana than in Australia.

- *Real income comparison* Suppose that 40 per cent of income is spent on non-traded goods in both countries. Some calculations (based on a 'Cobb–Douglas' welfare function) then show that the real *per capita* income is 247 per cent higher in Australia than in Botswana. Although substantial, this is significantly lower than our earlier estimate of 400 per cent because non-traded goods are relatively much cheaper in Botswana than in Australia. The 153 per cent (= 400 − 247 per cent) over-estimated difference between income in current dollars and real income is larger, (i) the larger the share of income spent on non-traded goods and (ii) the larger the international deviation between productivity in traded compared to non-traded goods.

USA may cost you $10 rather than the $1 you pay in Tanzania, while going to the cinema in Sweden may cost you $8 rather than the $2 you pay in Jakarta, Indonesia. In these examples, the value of production in the high-income countries relative to the low-income countries is over-estimated by a factor of 10 and 4, respectively.

To correct for these differences, the UN International Comparison Project (ICP) collects data on the prices of goods and services for virtually all countries in the world and calculates 'purchasing power parity' (PPP) exchange rates, which better reflect the value of goods and services that can be purchased in a country for a given amount of dollars (box 1.1). Reporting PPP GDP levels therefore gives a better estimate of the actual value of production in a country, which is the basis for the ranking of the most powerful economies in table 1.3. The USA is still the world's dominant economy, even though its estimated share of the world total has dropped from 31.9 per cent to 21.9 per cent. After correcting for purchasing power, China is the world's second largest economy (11.4 per cent of the world total), followed by Japan (7.7 per cent) and India (5.5 per cent). The relative production of China is more than three times as high after the PPP correction. Similarly for India, Russia and Indonesia. The reduction in the estimated value of output is particularly large for Japan (falling from 15.7 per cent to 7.7 per cent), reflecting the high costs of living in Japan.

Income *per capita*

For an individual inhabitant of a country, the country's total production value is hardly relevant. More important is the *production value per person* (= *per capita*). It should be noted that income per capita gives an idea of the well-being for the 'average' person in the country, but gives no information on the distribution of the income level within the country. If Jack and Jill together earn $100 the average income level is $50, which holds if they both earn $50 *and* if Jack earns $1 while Jill earns $99. The average income level is therefore a poor indicator of the 'representative' situation in a country if the distribution of income is more skewed. In general, the income level is more evenly distributed in Europe and Japan than in the USA, where it is in turn more evenly distributed than in many low-income countries.

Table 1.3 also lists the *per capita* income levels (corrected for purchasing power) in 2000 for the most powerful economies. The average income level in the world was 7,415 current international dollars (CID) per person. The highest income level, almost seven times the world average, was generated in the tiny country of Luxembourg. The lowest income level ($480 *per capita*) was measured in Sierra Leone, a small African nation. High income levels *per capita* are generated in North America (the USA and Canada), Australia, Japan, Western Europe, and in some oil producing nations in the Middle East (e.g. Bahrain, Saudi Arabia, the United Arab Emirates). As

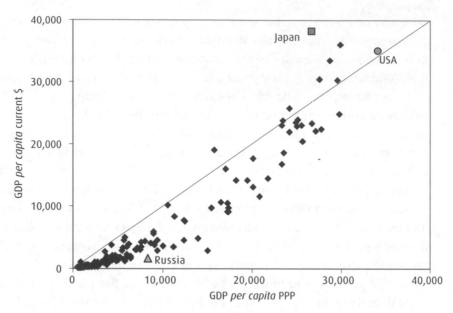

Figure 1.5 Correction of GDP *per capita* for purchasing power, 2000

argued above and illustrated in figure 1.5, the correction generally leads to a downward revision of *per capita* income for high-income countries such as Japan and to an upward revision for low-income countries such as Russia. Note, in particular, that close to the origin in figure 1.5 all observations are clustered significantly below the 45° line.

Income and business

Analogous to the question posed on p. 9 for population distributions and trends, we may ask: do managers of international firms care about the (dynamic trends of the) income levels generated in countries, corrections for purchasing power, the distinction between aggregate and *per capita* income levels and the distribution of income? Again, the answer is clear: yes, they do. One of the most crucial questions a firm asks is: how large will the demand be for this product in a particular region or country? To answer this question, the total size of the population and the population density is important, but the total income level and the *per capita* income level generated by this population and its distribution across the population is even more important. Some examples may illustrate this.

In section 1.2 we noted that many automobile firms are investing in China but not in India, despite the fact that both countries have more than 1 billion inhabitants. This can be explained by the higher income levels generated in China, where *per capita* income is double that in India measured in current dollars and 70 per cent higher after correcting for purchasing power, leading to a total income level in China which is at least double the total income level in India. Together with the more dynamic developments in China (to be discussed on p. 332) this double income level makes the Chinese car market much more interesting for automobile companies than the Indian car market.

To illustrate the importance of *per capita* income levels for some goods and services we continue with our China–India example. Since all human beings require the consumption of food and drink to survive, everyone spends money on those items, no matter how low their income level is. Obviously, the higher the income level, the more you can afford to spend on food and drink and the more luxurious the items you will buy. Total spending on food and drink will therefore rise quite gradually as total income level increases. This is not the case, however, for many other goods and services which people will start to purchase only once their individual income level has passed a certain threshold level. In the extreme, this holds for the 'conspicuous consumption' items such as luxury yachts and private jets which only the happy few can afford.[3] A less extreme example is provided by mobile telephones, which people will buy once their personal income passes a certain level. We noted above that, after correcting for purchasing power, Chinese *per capita* income was 70 per cent higher than Indian *per capita* income ($3,976 versus $2,358). Apparently, people start to buy mobile telephones somewhere in between those levels: in 2000 there were 65.8 mobile telephones per 1,000 inhabitants in China, compared to 3.5 in India. The market for mobile telephones in China is therefore not twice as large as in India (the total income comparison), but more than 23 times as large (83 million mobile phones compared to 3.5 million mobile phones).

Business and income

Again, causalities also run the other way around: from business to income. For one thing, business developments are a key determinant of any country's GDP *per capita*. If a nation's businesses prosper, so does GDP *per capita*. Profitable businesses create jobs, and profitable businesses can pay well. Loss-making businesses cut jobs, and additional unemployed put a downward pressure on wages. Without a large and well-performing business sector, a country will face great difficulty in producing and sustaining employment and income, as is clear from the economic history of developing, socialist and former socialist countries that are in the middle of the transition towards market economies. In an international context, the location decisions

---

[3] The income distribution is important here. Very poor countries may still purchase luxury items if the income distribution is so skewed that a few very rich people can afford to buy yachts and jets.

of multinationals influence the cross-country distribution of income, and hence of GDP *per capita*. For example, by investing abroad, multinationals stimulate macro-economic developments in the host countries by creating jobs and paying wages. Such FDI have a direct impact on the host countries' GDP *per capita*, as well as on within-country income distribution.

A nice example is the highly publicized development of top salaries in large (multi-national) enterprises in the late twentieth and the early twenty-first century. Under the influence of economic and political developments, particularly US large enter-prises started to pay their top managers extremely well. Economically, the prosperous 1990s produced a tail wind: profit levels skyrocketed, as did share prices. Politically, the Reaganesque and Thatcherite wave of neo-liberalism, stimulated further by the collapse of the Soviet communist empire, set the tone for a new *Zeitgeist*. In many multinationals across the globe, following the US lead, this was translated into a shareholders' value philosophy. To align the shareholders' interests with those of the managers, managerial remuneration packages became more and more performance-related by including shares and share options. As a result, with escalating share prices, the income of many top managers went through the roof. Clearly, this had impli-cations for the distribution of income, which became more unequal, particularly because the rise in the employees' wages lagged far behind the increase in the top managers' incomes.

1.4 What is the global economy?

The short and uninformative – but correct – answer to the question 'what is globalization?' is: everything you want it to be. Many of the heated disputes on the streets and in the media about the advantages and disadvantages of the global-ization process arise from the fact that this phrase means different things to different people. At the 1999 meeting of the WTO in Seattle, the environmentalists dressed in sea-turtle outfits cared about different issues than the French farm leaders protesting against the 'McDonaldization' driving out the consumption of Roquefort cheese. Similarly for the trade unionists and the human right activists. We can consider five key issues here:[4]

- *Cultural globalization*   This pertains to the debate whether there is a global culture or a set of universal cultural variables, and the extent to which these displace embedded national cultures and traditions. The first version of this section was written in the week in which the fifth Harry Potter book (entitled *Harry Potter and the Order of the Phoenix*) went on sale and set new selling records around the globe.

[4] See also McDonald and Burton (2002).

To an unprecedented extent we can have similar cultural experiences in virtually all countries of the world: we see similar (American) movies, listen to similar (American and British) music, eat at McDonald's, drink Coca Cola, drive Toyotas, etc. Often, the carriers of culture globalization are argued to be large multinationals, which triggered the saying that the world is facing 'McDonaldization'. Some people are afraid that this will lead to a boring, homogeneous global culture at the expense of local cultures and traditions. Others are not so gloomy, and see enough room for local traditions and new developments against a globally oriented background. After all, there is great regional cultural variety in China even after thousands of years of common experiences, and similarly for Europe. Be that as it may, cultural globalization is not the focus of this book. To avoid confusion in this respect from the start, the title of the book and the title of this section does not use the term 'globalization', but 'global economy'.

- *Economic globalization*   This centres on the decline of national markets and the rise of global markets as the firm's focal point, be it for the production and sale of final and intermediate goods and services or for the procurement of inputs (labour and capital). Driven by fundamental changes in technology which permit new, complicated and more efficient ways of internationally organizing production processes, the rules of competition are being redefined along the way and firms and governments will have to learn how to adapt. As suggested by the title of this book, we focus on the consequences of economic globalization, as defined by Neary (2003): the increased interdependence of national economies, and the trend towards greater integration of goods, labour and capital markets. Here, businesses play a key role, by engaging in FDI and cross-border acquisitions, for example.

- *Geographical globalization*   This refers to the sensation of compressed time and space as a result of reduced travel times between locations and the rapid (electronic) exchange of information. Knowledge and production previously confined to certain geographical areas may now cross borders and be made available because of the rapid transfer of information and transport innovations. Some neo-liberals claim this has led to the 'end of geography' in which location no longer matters and 'footloose' global capital can quickly cross borders. In a similar vein, global business players are said to emerge, without any national roots. This development is reflected in important cross-border acquisitions and mergers, such as that of Daimler Benz and Chrysler. Others, notably Porter (1990) and Krugman (1991), argue that local production processes and their intricate interconnections are required to gain a competitive advantage. Since the advances in information technology (IT) and transportation possibilities enable interconnections hitherto impossible, geography is becoming more, not less, important. Think, for example, of the clustering of international finance, with three global centres (London, New York and Tokyo). As this is at the core of many of the economic consequences of globalization, it will be discussed and evaluated throughout the remainder of the book.

- *Institutional globalization*   This relates to the spread of 'universal' institutional arrangements across the globe. In the aftermath of US President Reagan and UK Prime Minister Thatcher's influential programme – or 'revolution' – of neo-liberalism, in combination with the collapse of communist Soviet-type economic systems, more and more countries adopted similar reforms (Albert, 1993). These reforms share an emphasis on making markets more flexible, privatizing many former state-owned organizations (SOEs), reducing the size of welfare arrangements, etc. In an international context, these neo-liberal policies were and are promoted by such institutions as the International Monetary Fund (IMF) and the World Bank, which are often said to have forced the 'Washington Consensus' upon the developing world (Stiglitz, 2002). Another example is the WTO, which seeks to demolish international barriers to trade, and to the free movement of factors of production. In a similar vein, micro-level business institutions are influenced by global trends. Multinationals adopt similar policies under the pressure of competition and regulation. For instance, benchmarking practices are promoted by global consultancy businesses such as the Boston Consulting Group (BCG) and McKinsey, and the regulations of the New York Stock Exchange (NYSE) are imposed upon many non-American enterprises (Sorge and van Witteloostuijn, 2004). As institutions, both at the macro level of countries and at the micro level of firms, are key determinants of economic processes, we will deal with issues of institutional globalization throughout the book.

- *Political globalization*   This refers to the relationship between the power of markets and (multinational) firms versus the nation-state, which is undergoing continuous change and updating in reaction to economic and political forces – from counter-cyclical national demand policies and international cooperation after the Second World War to the renaissance of the belief in the power of the price mechanism and market forces for efficient allocation of resources in the 1970s. The globalization process is conditioned by the (financial) institutions and the dominant market players, such as multinational corporations (MNCs) and large investment firms. Some argue that the competitive pressure of international markets will 'hollow out' the functions of the nation-state and lead to an erosion of sovereignty and a race-to-the-bottom (be it in corporate tax rates or environmental policies). Popular anti-globalist rhetoric argues that large multinationals become more and more powerful, out-powering the majority of nation-states. Others point out that empirical evidence for these fears is lacking because of the undiminished importance of the nation-state for providing security, a legal system, education and infrastructure, all of which are vitally important for attracting the economic activity required for national prosperity. These issues are also at the core of many of the economic consequences of globalization and will therefore be discussed and evaluated throughout the remainder of this book.

Recall Keynes' quote from section 1.1 that the master economist should 'examine the present in light of the past, for the purposes of the future'. In this respect, it was argued for quite some time that economic globalization was a totally new phenomenon, so overwhelming in its power that traditional production and organization patterns would have to succumb to the new realities (Drucker, 1990) and multinational firms would create tight-knit international economic relationships (Ohmae, 1995). Extensive research in the 1990s, however, has shown that economic globalization – meaning increased interdependence of national economies and greater integration of goods, labour and capital markets, is not a new phenomenon in history at all (see O'Rourke and Williamson, 1999; Maddison, 2001; Bordo, Taylor and Williamson, 2003). Before analysing the global economy in section 1.7 and beyond, we shall therefore first give a brief historical overview of some aspects of the globalization process.

1.5 Globalization and income

In his impressive work full of historical detail entitled *The World Economy: A Millennial Perspective* (2001), Angus Maddison collects detailed statistics on a wide range of economic variables – such as income, population, international trade and capital flows – for all the major regions and countries in the world over the past 2,000 years. To describe the evolution of income over time Maddison uses so-called '1990 international dollars', which correct for PPP, and takes great care to ensure transitivity, base-country invariance and additivity. He collects data for twenty different countries and eight separate global regions: Western Europe, Eastern Europe, the Former USSR, Western Offshoots (including the USA and Australia), Latin America, Japan, Asia (excluding Japan) and Africa.

The development of world *per capita* income is illustrated in figure 1.6 using a logarithmic scale. As explained in Box 1.2, the advantage of using a logarithmic scale is the simultaneous depiction of the *level* of a variable (measured by its vertical height) and the *growth rate* of that variable (measured by the slope of the graph) in one figure. Average world *per capita* income in year zero was estimated to be $444. The subsistence income level is $400. Where the governing elite could maintain some degree of luxury and sustain a relatively elaborate system of governance, Maddison estimates the income level in year zero to be $450, as was the case for the Roman empire, China, India, other Asia, and the Northern part of Africa. As indicated in figure 1.6, there was no advance in *per capita* income on a global scale in the first millennium (the small advance in Japan was compensated by a decline in Western Europe). From the year 1000 to 1820, global *per capita* income started to increase

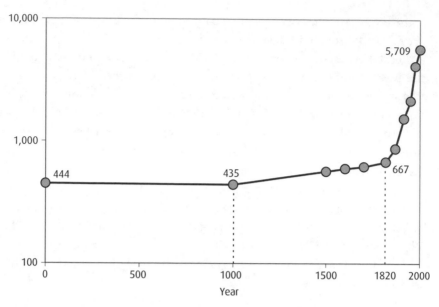

Figure 1.6 Development of world *per capita* income over the last 2,000 years, 1999 international $, logarithmic scale
Data source: Maddison (2001, table B-21).

Box 1.2 Logarithmic graphs

To graphically analyse the impact of economic growth on the *per capita* income level we use a logarithmic scale for the vertical axis in figure 1.6. As can be seen in the figure, such a scale divides the vertical axis in 'steps' of tenfold increases: the first step in the figure is the tenfold increase in income from 100 to 1,000 dollars, while the second step is the tenfold increase from 1,000 to 10,000 dollars. Compared to graphs with a regular scale, logarithmic graphs have both an important advantage and an important disadvantage, as illustrated in figure 1.7.

The important advantage of a logarithmic graph is that it can simultaneously depict developments in the level of a variable and in the growth rate of a variable because in such graphs the *slope* of the line reflects the *growth rate* of the variable. Suppose that:

- Variable *A* starts at the level '10' in 1950 and grows constantly by 14.7 per cent per year for fifty years.
- Variable *B* starts at the level '100' in 1950, has a negative growth rate of 5 per cent per year for thirty years, and a positive growth rate of 8 per cent per year for twenty years.
- Variable *C* is stagnant at the level '1,000' from 1950 to 2000.

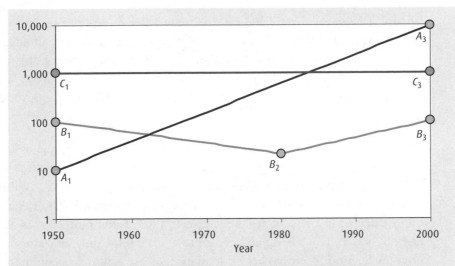

Figure 1.7 Advantages and disadvantages of logarithmic graphs

Figure 1.7 depicts the evolution of the three variables in a logarithmic graph. Because variables A and C have constant growth rates throughout the period (14.7 per cent and 0 per cent, respectively), they are represented as straight lines in figure 1.7, where the slope is a measure of the growth rate. Since variable B has constant negative growth for the first thirty years and constant positive growth for the next twenty years it is represented as a combination of two straight lines with a kink occurring in 1980 (at the point B_2). One graph therefore gives us information both of the *level* of the variables and their *growth rates*. This is an important advantage.

The important disadvantage of logarithmic graphs of which one should be acutely aware is that they can be deceptive concerning the difference in levels for variables at the same point in time and for the same variable at different points in time. In 1950, for example, variable B is ten times as high as variable A (point B_1 compared to A_1). Similarly, variable C is ten times as high as variable B (point C_1 compared to B_1). Now note that it *appears* in figure 1.7 that the difference between variables A and C is about twice that between variables B and C because the vertical difference is twice as large. However, since this is a logarithmic graph these differences are *multiplicative*. Variable A is ten times lower than variable B, which is in turn ten times lower than variable C. The level of variable C is therefore a staggering 100 times higher than the level of variable A. The same holds for 2000 with respect to points A_3, C_3 and B_3 (again, each time a tenfold difference). The developments of a variable over time can also be deceptive. Obviously, if the variables in figure 1.7 measure something positive, variable A has fared better than variables B and C. But just how much better? This is hard to tell from the figure. The indeed formidable growth rate of 14.7 per cent per year for variable *A*, when continued for fifty years, has led to an enormous thousandfold increase in variable *A*'s level! Variable *A* has gone from 100 times below variable *C* to ten times above it, and from ten times below variable *B* to 100 times above it. These are dramatic changes, perhaps not quite accurately reflected in a logarithmic graph.

in what we now consider a slow crawl – the world average rose by about 50 per cent in 820 years, to $667. A clear increase in the global economic growth rate started in 1820 with the industrial revolution. Since then, *per capita* income rose more than eightfold in a period of 180 years! The nineteenth and twentieth centuries have been unprecedented in terms of economic growth rates. Note, moreover, as Maddison argues (2001, p. 17): '*Per capita* income growth is not the only indicator of welfare. Over the long run, there has been a dramatic increase in life expectation. In the year 1000, the average infant could expect to live about 24 years. A third would die in the first year of life, hunger and epidemic disease would ravage the survivors . . . Now the average infant can expect to survive 66 years.'

Leaders and laggards: a widening perspective

We have already seen above that the spectacular almost thirteenfold increase in our average welfare in the last two millennia (from $444 to $5,706) occurred mainly in the nineteenth and twentieth century, as the world GDP *per capita* growth rate began to increase substantially in 1820. More specifically: *per capita* income was stagnant in the first millennium, there was a 50 per cent increase in the next 820 years, followed by an 850 per cent increase from 1820 until 1998. In the remainder of this section we concentrate on the leading and lagging nations and regions in *relative* terms, by calculating an index of GDP *per capita* relative to the world average GDP *per capita*.

At the beginning of our calendar (year zero), the wealthy regions were Western Europe (the Roman Empire), China, India and the rest of Asia (excluding Japan). Since these were also the most populous areas, their estimated GDP *per capita* was only 1 per cent above the world average. The lagging regions at that time were Eastern Europe, the former USSR (FSU), the Western Offshoots, Latin America and Japan, with an estimated GDP *per capita* 10 per cent below the world average.

At the turn of the first millennium (the year 1000), the steady developments in China, India and the rest of Asia (excluding Japan, where GDP *per capita* did not change over a period of 1,000 years) kept these regions in the lead, with an estimated GDP *per capita* 3 per cent higher than the world average. The collapse of the Roman Empire and subsequent developments in Western Europe decreased prosperity there

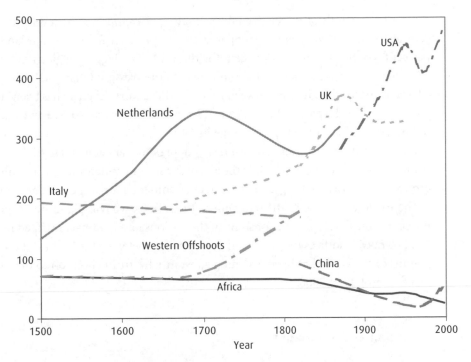

Figure 1.8 Leaders and laggards in GDP *per capita*: a widening perspective
Data source: Own calculations based on Maddison (2001, table B-21).
Note: Index relative to world average.

and ensured that this region joined the previous group of laggards, with an estimated GDP *per capita* 8 per cent below the world average.

In the next 500 years (from 1000 to 1500) world *per capita* GDP grew by about 30 per cent. More detailed statistical data at the level of individual nations are available, which makes it possible to pinpoint more specific wealthy regions. The rise of the Italian city-states – Florence, Genoa, Milan, Pisa and Venice – made Italy the leading region in the world, with an estimated GDP *per capita* 95 per cent higher than the world average. The stagnant developments in the Western Offshoots and the deterioration in Africa made these the lagging regions, with an estimated GDP *per capita* 29 per cent below the world average. From then on, Maddison's data set is complete, with estimates for twenty countries and eleven regions for the years 1500, 1600, 1700, 1820, 1870, 1913, 1950, 1973 and 1998. Figure 1.8 depicts the relative positions for the leading and lagging nations and regions since 1500.[5]

The leading nations in terms of GDP *per capita* were Italy, the Netherlands, the UK and the USA, in chronological order. As is clear from figure 1.8 and the discussion above, the gap between the world leader and the world average tends to increase over

[5] For clarity, the figure ignores the fact that around 1973 Switzerland had the highest GDP *per capita*.

time. At the zenith of its relative power, Italy's *per capita* income level was 95 per cent above the world average, compared to 234 per cent for the Netherlands, 268 per cent for the UK and 379 per cent for the USA. The lagging regions in terms of GDP *per capita* were Africa (initially jointly with the Western Offshoots), China, and Africa, respectively. The gap between Africa and the world average has been steadily increasing over the past 500 years, from 29 per cent below the world average in 1500 to 76 per cent below the world average in 1998. The developments in China in the twentieth century (wars and communism) depressed *per capita* GDP to 80 per cent below the world average in 1973. At the end of the second millennium, as a result of the economic reforms starting in 1979, China has embarked on a spectacular comeback in the world economy. In the remainder of this book we will dig more deeply into the economic developments for some of the nations and regions illustrated in figure 1.8. For now, it suffices to note that the income gap between the leading and lagging regions of the world has been widening substantially, from about 0.125 in year zero to a factor of 20 in 2000.

1.6 Globalization and international trade[6]

The most notable manifestation of the global economy is the rise in international trade and capital flows. This is not something new, as such flows have always been central in economic interactions: for the ancient cultures of Egypt and Greece as well as for China, India and Mesopotamia. According to Maddison, however, they have been most important for the economic rise of Western Europe in the past millennium. Based on improved techniques of shipbuilding and navigation (the compass), Venice played a key role from 1000 to 1500 in opening up trade routes within Europe, the Mediterranean and to China via the caravan routes, bringing in silk and valued spices as well as technology (glassblowing, also used for making spectacles, the cultivation of rice and sugar cane cutting). Venice's role in the development of banking, accounting and foreign exchange and credit markets was equally important, thus establishing a system of public finance which made it the lead economy of the period. The fall of Byzantium and the rise of the Ottoman empire eventually blocked Venetian contacts with Asia.

Portugal began more ambitious interactions between Europe and the rest of the world in the second half of the fifteenth century by opening up trade and settlement in the Atlantic islands and developing trade routes around Africa, to China, Japan and India. It took over the role of Venice as the major shipper of spices. Portugal's location on the South Atlantic coast of Europe enabled its fishermen to gather

---

[6] Unless indicated otherwise, all data in this section are from Maddison (2001).

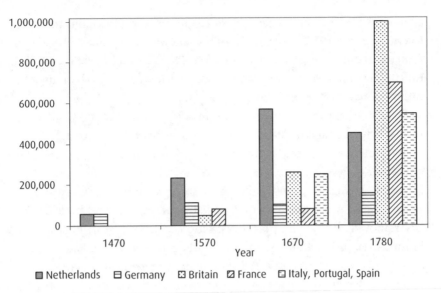

Figure 1.9 Carrying capacity of European merchant fleets, 1470–1780, metric tons
Data source: Maddison (2001, p. 77).
Note: Absence of a bar in a year for a particular country or group of countries indicates that no data are available.

knowledge of Atlantic winds, weather and tides. Combined with maritime experience, the development of compass bearings, cartography and adjustments in ship design to meet Atlantic sailing conditions, this allowed the Portuguese (e.g. Vasco da Gama) to embark on their explorations and play a dominant role in intercontinental trade. As Maddison (2001, p. 19) puts it: 'Although Spain had a bigger empire, its only significant base outside the Americas was the Philippines. Its two most famous navigators were Columbus who was a Genoese with Portuguese training, and Magellan who was Portuguese.' Portugal was able to absorb Jewish merchants and scholars, who were required to undergo a *pro forma* conversion and who played an important role in science, as intermediaries in trade with the Muslim world and in attracting foreign capital (Genoese and Catalan) for business ventures.[7]

From 1400 to the middle of the seventeenth century the Netherlands were the most dynamic European economy, using power from windmills and peat, creating large canal networks and transforming agriculture into horticulture, but most of all developing shipping, shipbuilding and commercial services. As illustrated in figure 1.9, by 1570 the carrying capacity of Dutch merchant shipping was about the same as the combined fleets of Britain, France and Germany. The Dutch were then able to maintain this lead for a century by more than doubling this capacity. Holland

---

[7] Unfortunately, Portugal also initiated the slave trade to the New World and carried about half of the slaves from Africa to the Americas between 1500 and 1870.

created a modern state which provided property rights, education and religious tolerance and had only 40 per cent of the labour force in agriculture. This attracted a financial and entrepreneurial elite from Flanders and Brabant, which emigrated to Holland on a large scale and made it the centre for banking, finance and international commerce.

Britain became the leading economy in the eighteenth century, initially by improving its financial, banking, fiscal and agricultural institutions along the lines pioneered by the Dutch, and subsequently by a surge in industrial productivity. The latter was based not only on the acceleration of technical progress and investments in physical capital, education and skills, but also on commercial trade policy, which in 1846 reduced protective duties on agricultural imports and by 1860 had unilaterally removed all trade and tariff restrictions. The British willingness to specialize in industrial production and import a large part of its food had positive effects on the world economy and diffused the impact of technical progress, but most of all it allowed Britain to achieve unprecedented rates of economic growth and establish itself as a global economic and political power by taking over the lands that the French and Dutch had lost in Asia and Africa. The soundness of its monetary system (the gold standard) and public credit gave Britain an important role in international finance. At the end of the nineteenth and the beginning of the twentieth century there was a massive outflow of European capital (French, Dutch and German, but most of all British – up to half of British savings) for overseas investment, mostly in the Americas and Russia. The famous British economist John Maynard Keynes (1919, ch. 2) summarized the high degree of global economic progress and development in this epoch as follows:

What an extraordinary episode in the economic progress of man that age was which came to an end in August 1914! . . . The inhabitant of London could order by telephone, sipping his morning tea in bed, the various products of the whole earth, in such quantity as he might see fit, and reasonably expect their early delivery upon his doorstep . . . But, most important of all, he regarded this state of affairs as normal, certain, and permanent, except in the direction of further improvement, and any deviation from it as aberrant, scandalous, and avoidable.

The old liberal order came to end, as indicated by Keynes' quote, as a result of two world wars (1914–18 and 1939–45) and the Great Depression in the 1930s, with its beggar-thy-neighbour policies, which drastically raised trade impediments and led to a collapse of trade, capital and migration flows. As a consequence, the world economy grew much more slowly from 1913 to 1950 than it had from 1870 to 1913.[8] The institutional arrangements with codes of behaviour and cooperation

---

[8] That is, 0.91 per cent per annum rather than 1.30 per cent. Although this difference might seem to be small, world income would have been 15 per cent higher in 1950 if the slowdown had not occurred and the economy would have maintained its 1.30 per cent growth rate.

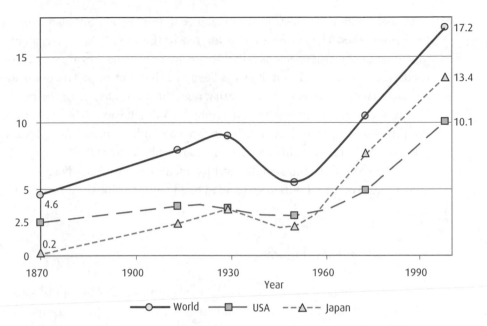

Figure 1.10 Two 'waves' of globalization, merchandise exports, per cent of GDP in 1990 prices
Data source: Maddison (2001, table F-5).

set up after the Second World War, such as GATT, the IMF, the Organization for Economic Cooperation and Development (OECD) and the World Bank, created a new liberal international order which abolished beggar-thy-neighbour policies in favour of liberal trading. In the post-Second World War period, this contributed to remarkable growth rates of income *per capita* (3 per cent per year), total world income (5 per cent per year) and world trade flows (8 per cent per year). At the same time, the world economy became more closely connected than ever before, as illustrated in figure 1.10.

International trade and MNEs

This type of globalization is not a monotone process, as clearly illustrated in figure 1.10, which depicts the development of merchandise exports relative to GDP for the world as a whole, the USA and Japan from 1870 to 2000. It is now customary to identify two 'waves' of globalization: the first wave at the end of the nineteenth and the beginning of the twentieth century and the second wave after the Second World War. Evidently, international trade rose much more rapidly than output for the period as a whole, but there was a long and substantial interruption as a result of two major international conflicts and economic policy changes. Some people fear that the same could happen again, which would lead to large losses, economic and otherwise.

Globalization is not restricted to macroeconomic issues, but also affects micro-level enterprises. The key example is the rise of the MNE. Commercial enterprises in the hands of private persons rather that royal or state parties are very common in modern economies. It has not always been like that, however. The first substantial commercial *multinational* enterprise that resembled a modern firm was probably the Dutch 'Verenigde Oostindische Compagnie', or VOC. It was established in 1602 with the aim of sending ships to Asia to buy pepper and other spices. The VOC developed into an MNE with branches in a dozen Asian countries (see Box 11.5, p. 329). The industrial revolution triggered the establishment of many VOC-like multinationals: globalization of trade tends to go hand in hand with the globalization of enterprises.

1.7 Analysing the global economy

In sections 1.5 and 1.6 we have shown that economic globalization is not a new phenomenon, but has been a fundamental force in economic history for a long time. This argument was based on the rising importance of international trade and capital flows, relative to world income. In the rest of the book, we will provide other supporting information – for example, concerning the rising importance of FDI and multinational firms. Recalling our definition of economic globalization: 'the increased interdependence of national economies and the trend towards greater integration of goods, labour and capital markets', we can now argue that focusing attention only on the *volume* of these flows (to be further discussed in chapter 2) gives a biased view of the degree of globalization. In this section, we give two examples to illustrate this point: the price wedge and fragmentation.

The price wedge

The most basic economic picture in (quantity, price) space consists of a downward-sloping demand curve (on the assumption that people buy less of a good if its price is higher) and an upward-sloping supply curve (on the assumption that firms produce more of a good if its price rises). As shown in figure 1.11, international trade flows can also be depicted in this most basic framework, with two twists. Suppose there are two countries, Home and Foreign, and we investigate Home's import market. The first twist is that Home's downward-sloping demand curve for *imports* actually consists of Home's demand for the good *not* provided by Home's domestic suppliers (it is therefore also called Home's *net* demand curve). This applies, similarly, to Foreign's export supply curve (or net supply curve). The second twist is that there may be a number of reasons for a deviation between Home's and Foreign's price, which is called

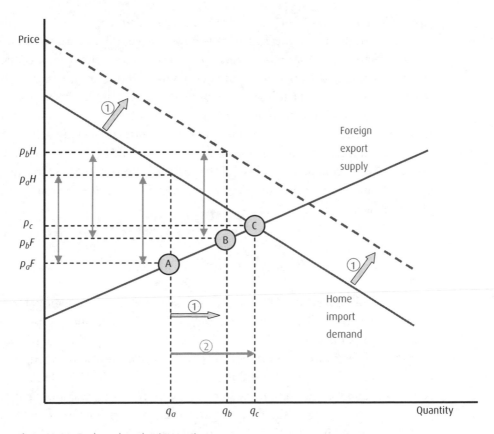

Figure 1.11 Trade and market integration

a *price wedge* – for example, because Foreign firms have to overcome transport costs, tariffs, trade impediments, cultural differences and all sorts of other extra costs before they can export the good to Home's market. This is illustrated in figure 1.11, where international trade results from the intersection of the downward-sloping domestic import demand curve and the upward-sloping foreign export supply curve. Suppose the world economy is initially at point A, where the price wedge results in a deviation between Home's price p_aH and Foreign's price p_aF (price wedge $= p_aH - p_aF > 0$), resulting in a volume of international trade equal to q_a.

As illustrated in figure 1.11, a rise in international trade flows can now occur, for two basic reasons. First, a shift to the right in either Foreign's export supply curve or Home's import demand curve at a constant price wedge will result in increasing trade flows – for example, as shown in figure 1.11, if Home's import demand curve shifts to the right due to a demand shock and the international economy moves to point B, such that international trade flows increase from q_a to q_b (at a constant price wedge $p_aH - p_aF = p_bH - p_bF$). As causes for this shift, one might think of changing preferences, or population growth. It is customary to argue that there is increased globalization if this rise in trade flows is larger than the rise in production (see also section 1.6). A second basic reason for a rise in trade flows occurs if the price wedge diminishes – for example, resulting from lower tariffs or lower transportation costs. Suppose, for argument's sake, that the price wedge completely disappears. This would take the international economy to point C in figure 1.11, leading to an increase in trade flows from q_a to q_c. At that point, international commodity markets would be perfectly integrated and the price of a commodity would be the same in Home and Foreign. This discussion illustrates that the volume of flows is only a partial indicator of globalization, prices are important, too. We shall keep this in mind when we illustrate the effects of globalization.

The price wedge in history

Trade

O'Rourke and Williamson (2002) argue that early growth of international trade was mostly of the first kind: rising trade in non-competing goods, such as spices, special dyes (indigo), coffee, tea and sugar, which could not be produced in substantial amounts in the importing countries themselves. Usually, these were expensive luxury items and their buyers could afford to pay for the price wedge. The discovery of the New World and its commodities created a market for these goods, shifting the home import demand curve to the right without necessarily reducing the price wedge. O'Rourke and Williamson (2002) provide evidence that the post-1492 trade boom was most likely caused by the demand for luxury items and population growth and hardly reduced the price wedge on traded goods, as measured by changes in the mark-up. Moreover, there is some evidence that the retreat of China and Japan from world markets from the mid-fifteenth century to the mid-nineteenth century further stimulated European–Asian trade.

The two waves of globalization illustrated in figure 1.10 provide examples of the second kind of growth in international trade. During the first wave of the nineteenth century there was an increase of trade in basic and homogeneous commodities. During the second wave after the Second World War there was an increase of trade in basic and differentiated manufactured products. Decreases in transports costs, technology improvements, falling trade restrictions, international cooperation and improved communication possibilities have all been important underlying forces in these two waves of globalization. The spectacular decline in transportation costs in the nineteenth century is considered to be the most important cause for increased trade. The railway and the steamship revolutionized the means of transportation, while the opening of the Suez canal and the Panama canal dramatically cut travel times and meant that traders could avoid the dangerous routes around the Cape

Table 1.5 Price convergence and declining transport cost, 1870–1913

Transport cost reductions (index)		
American export routes, deflated freight cost	1869/71–1908/10	100 to 55
American east coast routes, deflated freight cost	1869/71–1911/13	100 to 55
British tramp, deflated freight cost	1869/71–1911/13	100 to 78
Commodity price convergence at selected markets (% deviation)		
Liverpool–Chicago, wheat price gap	1870–1912	58 to 16
London–Cincinnati, bacon price gap	1870–1913	93 to 18
Philadelphia–London, pig iron price gap	1870–1913	85 to 19
London–Boston, wool price gap	1870–1913	59 to 28
London–Buenos Aires, hides price gap	1870–1913	28 to 9

Source: O'Rourke and Williamson (2000, table 1).

of Good Hope and Cape Horn.[9] Technological inventions, such as effective means of refrigeration which enabled the transportation of perishable goods (meat and fruit) across the Equator, further stimulated trade, as did reductions in protectionist measures (see p. 34). Table 1.5 provides empirical estimates from O'Rourke and Williamson (2002) for both the declining transport costs and the reduction in the price wedge for commodities produced in different markets, indicating closer market integration.

The rise in trade during the first wave of globalization was also caused by reductions in protectionist measures. Under the influence of Adam Smith's doctrine of free trade, many restrictions to trade were removed during the nineteenth century. By 1860 the UK and the Netherlands had unilaterally virtually removed all trade restrictions. Special bilateral arrangements were made between the UK and France (the Cobden–Chevalier Treaty of 1860).[10] Other bilateral arrangements involving other countries soon followed. Table 1.6 shows that tariffs were very high at the beginning of the nineteenth century and declined considerably until 1875. Around the 1880s, the tariff reductions more or less came to a stop. Cheap Russian grain increased competition in agricultural markets and real earnings of British farmers, for example, declined by more than 50 per cent between 1870 and 1913 (Findlay

---

[9] The size and speed of Atlantic liners, for example, increased spectacularly: it took the *Britannic* (using a combination of steam power and sails) 8 days and 20 hours to cross the Atlantic with 5,000 tons of pay load in 1874, whereas it took the *Mauritania* (using steam power only) 4 days and 10 hours to cross the Atlantic with 31,000 tons of pay load in 1907. During the same period railway mileage also increased dramatically: from 1850 to 1910 railway mileage in the UK increased from 6,621 to 23,387 miles, in the USA from 9,021 to 249,902 miles and in Germany from 3,637 to 36,152 miles (O'Rourke and Williamson, 1999).

[10] The treaty was also important because it introduced the most-favoured-nation (MFN) principle as the cornerstone of European trade policies (Findlay and O'Rourke, 2001).

Table 1.6 Tariffs on manufactures for selected countries, 1820–1950, per cent

	1820[a]	1875[a, b]	1913[a, b]	1931[c]	1950[c]	1998–1999[c]
Denmark	30	15–20	14	–	3	4.1 (EU)
France	Prohibition	12–15	20	30	18	4.1 (EU)
Germany	–	4–6	13	21	26	4.1 (EU)
Italy	–	8–10	18	46	25	4.1 (EU)
Russia	Prohibition	15	84	Prohibition	Prohibition	13
Spain	Prohibition	15–20	41	63	–	4.1 (EU)
Sweden	Prohibition	3–5	20	21	9	4.1 (EU)
Netherlands	7	3–5	4	–	11	4.1 (EU)
UK	50	0	0	–	23	4.1 (EU)
USA	45	40	44	48	14	4.5

Sources: [a] Baldwin and Martin (1999, table 8); [b] O'Rourke and Williamson (1999, table 6.1); [c] Findlay and O'Rourke (2001, table 5); – = data unavailable.

and O'Rourke, 2001). Soon Britain, France, Germany, Sweden and other countries returned to protectionist practices and tariffs were raised again. It seems that the integration of product markets, due to better transport systems, was so successful that it undermined its own success. In general, it seems that the transport revolution could flourish in an environment that already tended towards free-er trade, but that the income consequences led to adverse reactions.

Capital

The reduction in the price wedge during the first wave of globalization and the increase in the inter-war years is also visible on the capital market. This is illustrated in figure 1.12, depicting the mean bond spread for fourteen core and empire[11] countries surrounded by a measure of dispersion (a band equal to ± 2 standard deviations). The figure is based on Obstfeld and Taylor's (2003) work. They study government bonds traded in London for the entire period, focusing exclusively on bonds denominated in gold or in sterling so as to isolate the effects of default risk. The interest rate spread for these countries was small, usually within 1 or 2 percentage points of Britain's. Moreover, there was a convergence in bond spreads up to 1914, and a widening in spreads and increased volatility in the inter-war years. As with international trade flows, it is customary to identify two 'waves' of globalization for capital flows as well. This is illustrated in figure 1.13, where foreign capital stocks relative to world GDP are relatively high towards the end of the nineteenth and the beginning of the twentieth century, then drop dramatically in the inter-war

---

[11] The core and empire countries are Australia, Belgium, Canada, Denmark, France, Germany, India, the Netherlands, New Zealand, Norway, South Africa, Sweden, Switzerland, and the USA.

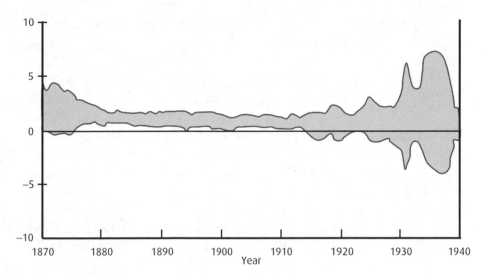

Figure 1.12 London external bond spread, 1870–1940, fourteen core and empire bonds
Source: Based on Obstfeld and Taylor (2003).
Note: The units are percentage points.

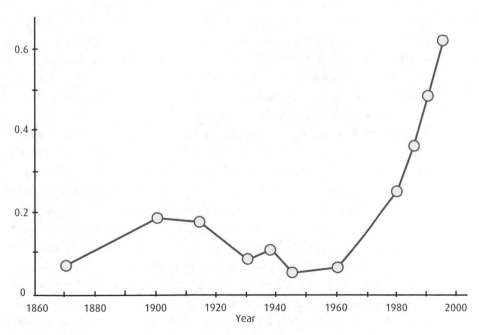

Figure 1.13 Foreign capital stocks; assets/world GDP, 1860–2000
Source: Based on Obstfeld and Taylor (2003).

years, only to reach unprecedented heights after the capital market liberalizations beginning in the 1960s.

Migration

We can also apply the idea of the wedge with respect to migration. In principle, real wage differences between countries explain the direction of migration flows to a large extent. Still large wage differences between countries exist. These are caused, for example, by a migration quota, the perceived probability of actually finding a job in the destination country, or lack of knowledge of foreign countries. Factors such as these contribute to the size of the wedge and to the absence of labour market integration.

UN evidence indicates that although the absolute numbers have increased, world migrants – i.e. foreign-born – comprise between 2 and 3 per cent of the world population. These low numbers seem inconsistent with popular opinion that the level of migrants is much larger, primarily as a result of the low number of migrants in developing countries. Indeed, in some individual countries these numbers are much larger. The share of foreign-born as a percentage of the labour force is relevant, as this number gives an impression of competition on the labour markets. In Australia, for example, 25 per cent of the labour force in 1999 was foreign-born, in Canada this number was 19 per cent, in the USA 11 per cent, in Germany 9 per cent and in the Netherlands 4 per cent. The United Nations High Commissioner for Refugees (UNHCR) estimates that 300,000 illegal immigrants enter the USA each year, while 500,000 enter the EU each year. In 2000, the UNHCR estimated that there were 560,000 asylum seekers in twenty-eight developed countries with about 1 million awaiting a decision on earlier applications.

Historians have identified two modern 'waves' of migration. The first took place between 1820 and 1913. More than 50 million migrants departed (mostly) from Europe to Australia, Canada, South America and the USA. Almost 60 per cent of the migrants went to the USA. Most were young, and relatively low-skilled. After 1850, most migrants came from Ireland. The second 'wave' started after the Second World War, and has not yet ended. Because of the rising population levels, this wave is smaller in relative terms (see figure 1.14). Between 1913 and 1950 migration was only a fraction of what it had been during the nineteenth century. The USA remained the main destination country. Immigration grew from a low of 252,000 per year in the 1950s to 916,000 in the 1990s, but the source countries changed dramatically. Before the 1950s most immigrants came from Europe, in the 1990s most came from Asia and, from 1990 onwards, also from the former eastern European countries. During this second wave immigration restrictions became more binding than before. Many countries use a quota, and allow in migrants for reasons such as a family reunion or specific labour needs. Within Europe, most migration flows are in the form of

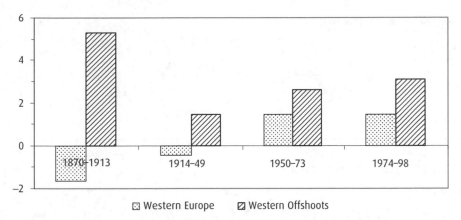

Figure 1.14 Relative migration flows, Western Europe and Western Offshoots, 1870–1998, per 1,000 inhabitants
Data source: Net migration in the period (Maddison, 2001, table 2-4) is divided by the (simple) average population and length of the period, normalized per 1,000 inhabitants.

intra-EU migration; however, between 1950 and 1998 Europe absorbed almost 20 million people, and the Western Offshoots 34 million. Immigration from Africa and Eastern Europe is relatively small compared to intra-EU migration: the evidence suggests that a typical European country has an inverted U-shaped pattern of emigration. Emigration first rose, and then declined. In contrast to globalization with respect to trade and capital, labour markets are less globally integrated.

Fragmentation

As a second illustration – besides the declining price wedge – of the fact that rising relative trade flows may under-estimate the degree of globalization and market integration, we briefly discuss a phenomenon known as 'fragmentation'. Part I of figure 1.15 depicts a traditional production process in which firm 1 located in country *A* uses inputs to produce a final good. As discussed later, international economics and business can help to clarify under what circumstances the firms of a country will have a comparative advantage in the production of a certain type of good, which will then be exported. However, technological and communication advances have enabled many production processes to be subdivided into various phases which are physically separable, a process known as fragmentation. This enables a finer and more complex division of labour, as the different phases of the production process may now be spatially separated and undertaken at locations where costs are lowest.

Part II of figure 1.15 shows an example of fragmentation in which the production process consists of four phases, performed in three countries by two firms. Service links – such as transportation, telecommunications, insurance, quality control and

I Traditional production process

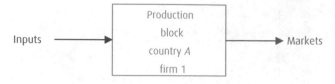

II Globalized fragmented production process

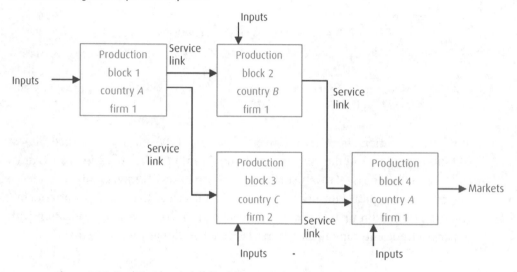

Figure 1.15 Traditional and globalized fragmented production processes

management control – facilitate the fragmentation process. International economics and business can also help to clarify in this more complex setting why the firms in a country will have a comparative advantage in a phase of the production process, where the coordination (service links) will take place, why some phases of the production process will be internally organized (phases 1, 2 and 4 in part II of figure 1.15) and why outsourcing is better for some other phase of the production process (phase 3 in part II of figure 1.15). It is clear that these more complex production processes lead to increased *interdependence* of national economies and more intricate international connections, as well as to large exports (and re-imports) of parts of products (as holds, for example, for country A in part II of figure 1.15). An example for the hard disk drive industry is discussed in Brakman, Garretsen and van Marrewijk (2001: 10–12).

1.8 Conclusions

We have provided a brief introduction to the evolution of the world economy. World population levels have risen drastically since 1800, in conjunction with (*per capita*) world income levels. We have stressed that economic leadership regularly shifts from one country to another and that wealthy countries are usually well connected with the rest of the world economy in terms of international trade, contacts, investments, migration and capital flows. Historians have identified two big 'waves' of economic globalization: at the end of the nineteenth century and following the end of the Second World War. These have episodes coincided with drastic decreases in international price gaps for goods and services and drastic increases in relative international trade and capital flows. The conclusions with respect to migration are less clear-cut. The 'fragmentation' process, in which different parts of goods and services are provided in different nations before they are combined in final goods, is a relatively new phenomenon. Part II of this book explains why this occurs and what is the role of national and international firms in this process.

Before we can analyse these issues, however, we need to have a firm grip of international accounting principles and practices, at the level of both nation-states and MNEs, to understand the interconnections between goods and services flows on the one hand and international capital flows on the other. This knowledge, provided in chapter 2, is also crucial for understanding the intricacies of international capital mobility and financial crises analysed in part III of this book.

International accounting practices

KEYWORDS

balance of payments	trade balance	capital account
firms' annual reports	current account	accounting principles
debit and credit entries	capital account	exchange rate risk
micro–macro accounting	assets and liabilities	value added versus sales

2.1 Exciting accounting?

Is accounting boring? Well, yes, according to many, it is. Of course, if you are an accountant at PriceWaterhouseCoopers or a head statistician at a country's Statistical Office, you are very likely to disagree. Most of us are not in the accounting business. However, we need accounting and its products, such as a country's balance of payments or a firm's annual report, as a platform on which to build many other activities. It helps us, as researchers and policy-makers, for example, to get a better perspective on the *de-industrialization debate*. Take the following story, which is being told time and again, by anti-globalists, journalists and politicians alike. Trade with low-wage countries is harmful for the high-wage OECD world, because 'they' can sell more to 'us' than 'we' to 'them'. Furthermore, MNEs will find it attractive to invest in those low-wage countries to take advantage of the low wages (and low work and environmental standards). For both reasons, the de-industrialization of many OECD countries is inevitable.

It is this type of story that appeals to many voters in the Western world, to which politicians react by promoting protectionist ideas. To prevent de-industrialization from happening, with the associated job losses, they argue that protectionist measures must be launched to save industries and jobs, and hence to promote national welfare. For example, this argument tends to pop up in each US presidential election. It did so in the 2004 Bush–Kerry presidential race. Building on the balance of payments analysis, as introduced below, this chapter uses sound accounting principles to show that the above reasoning is simply wrong. Its underlying logic is fundamentally flawed (see box 2.3, p. 59). Moreover, we shall illustrate how the complexity of international accounting practices materializes in the annual report of an MNE, taking advantage of international transfer-pricing opportunities, cross-country fiscal optimization, exchange rate risk-hedging policies and other tools of international financial management. In so doing, this chapter will provide the definitional basis for analysing financial capital flows in part III of the book. More generally, the chapter will introduce a number of basic definitions and principles of accounting at the macro level of nation-states (the balance of payments) and the micro level of the MNE (the annual report) – all of this is necessary for understanding many other issues in the international economics and business domain.

As an important by-product, this chapter will clarify two widespread misunderstandings, both relating to the aggregation fallacy. In the first place, in the context of the anti-globalization debate figureheaded by authors such as Noreena Hertz (2001) and Naomi Klein (2001), a standard piece of rhetoric is the argument that powerful multinationals are larger than many – if not most – nation-states. Indeed, this is rhetoric. The aggregation mistake made here is that micro-level data (from firms' annual reports) are wrongly compared with macro level ones (from national accounts). In the second place, transactions that are regarded as investments by individual firms – such as acquisitions and mergers – are frequently argued to be macro-level investments as well. In many cases, however, they are not. From a macro perspective, for instance, an acquisition simply involves the neutral shift of money from one firm to another. The aggregation mistake here is that micro-level firm data are erroneously aggregated to the macro level of the country.

2.2 Macro-level accounting: a country's balance of payments[1]

This section is subdivided into three parts. First, we briefly review some accounting principles. Second, we focus on some accounting identities at the macro level based on these principles. Third, we illustrate the usefulness of such identities for analysing, for example, capital flows between countries.

Accounting principles

The balance of payments records a country's transactions with other countries on the basis of a set of agreed-upon accounting definitions and principles. The balance of payments thus involves macro-level accounting for nation-states. As is the case for any individual firm, it is based on the rules of double-entry bookkeeping, with matching credit and debit entries. By definition, the balance of payments is therefore

---

[1] All this is explained in greater detail in any textbook on international finance or international financial management, such as Eun and Resnick (2001). A classic on this topic is Stern (1973).

Current account
    Goods   ⎫
               ⎬ Trade balance
    Services ⎭
    Income
    Current transfers
Capital and financial account
    Capital account
    Financial account
        Direct investment
        Portfolio investment
        Other investment
        Reserve assets

Figure 2.1 A country's balance of payments
Source: IMF (1996).

equal to zero. We distinguish between the two main parts of the balance of payments, namely the current account on the one hand and the capital and financial account on the other, each with subdivisions, as summarized in figure 2.1 (see also box 2.1).

Box 2.1 The balance of payments for Germany and the USA

Table 2.1 gives, by way of illustration, the summary statistics of the balance of payments accounts for Germany and the USA in 2002, providing somewhat more detail than given in figure 2.1. Clearly, Germany's balance of payments was in a different shape to the USA's. For example, the American balance on goods deficit of $479.38 billion is impressive, *vis-à-vis* the German balance on goods surplus of $122.18 billion.[a] This is only partly compensated by the American surplus and the German deficit on services trade. The income flows are virtually balanced for both countries, while both countries also, not surprisingly, run a current (unilateral) transfer deficit. Taken together, these flows translate into a modest current account surplus for Germany ($46.59 billion) and a large current account deficit for the USA ($480.86 billion). German net claims on the outside world must therefore in principle increase by $46.59 billion and American net claims on the outside world must decrease by $480.86 billion. This is largely caused by changes in other investment assets for Germany and by portfolio investments for the USA. To ensure that the double-entry bookkeeping properties hold – that is, to make sure that the overall balance of the balance of payments is indeed zero – both countries have

[a] This shows, by the way, that running a trade surplus is not necessarily a sign of economic strength, as is often suggested in the context of protectionist rhetoric. After all, the US economy in this period was performing much better than the German economy.

Table 2.1 Analytic presentation: balance of payments, 2002, billion US dollars

	Germany	USA
A Current account	46.59	−480.86
Goods: exports fob	615.02	685.38
Goods: imports fob	−492.84	−1,164.76
Balance on goods	*122.18*	*−479.38*
Services: credit	106.00	288.72
Services: debit	−150.49	−227.38
Balance on goods and services	*77.69*	*−418.04*
Income: credit	103.26	255.54
Income: debit	−109.26	−259.51
Balance on goods, services, and income	*71.69*	*−422.01*
Current transfers: credit	15.83	11.50
Current transfers: debit	−40.94	−70.35
B Capital account	−0.23	−1.29
Capital account: credit	2.09	1.11
Capital account: debit	−2.32	−2.39
Total: groups A plus B	*46.36*	*−482.14*
C Financial account	−77.08	531.68
Direct investment abroad	−25.30	−137.84
Direct investment in Germany/USA	37.30	39.63
Portfolio investment assets	−63.32	15.80
Portfolio investment liabilities	98.70	421.44
Financial derivatives	−0.79	. . .
Other investment assets	−151.21	−53.27
Other investment liabilities	27.55	245.91
Total: groups A through C	*−30.72*	*49.54*
D Net errors and omissions	28.74	−45.84
Total: groups A through D	*−1.98*	*3.69*
E Reserves and related items	1.98	−3.69
Overall balance	0.00	0.00

Source: IMF (2003).

to enter a substantial 'net errors and omissions' term ($28.74 billion for Germany and −$45.84 billion for the USA). The net change in 'reserves and related items' (mostly reserve assets) is rather modest for both countries ($1.98 billion for Germany and −$3.69 billion for the USA), as is usually the case in this period.

The transactions on the current account are *income-related*, pertaining to produced goods, provided services (also known as invisibles), income (from investment) and unilateral transfers. Exports are recorded as credit items (+) and imports as debit items (−). After all, with exports money is *earned*, and with imports it is *spent*. The sum of the merchandise and services balance is called the trade balance, indicating the net money earned from trade (exports minus imports), which may of course be negative in terms of money value if more is imported than exported. More important, however, is the current account balance, which also includes income and unilateral transfers because investment income, such as dividend payments, reflects the remuneration for the use of capital, a factor of production, by another country. It is therefore essentially the payment for trade in (capital) services. Unilateral transfers, such as foreign aid to a developing nation, remittances or military aid, are included as they represent income transfers to another country and not claims on another country. As a result, the current account balance measures the net change in claims on the outside world, which is recorded on the capital and financial account, which includes (in the capital account) capital transfers and transactions (purchases/sales) in an economy's non-produced, non-financial assets (such as patents and copyrights) and (in the financial account) transactions in an economy's external financial assets and liabilities.

Accounting identities

The transactions on the capital and financial account are asset-related. An increase in claims on foreigners is a *capital outflow* and appears as a debit. An increase in claims by foreigners on our country is a *capital inflow* and appears as a credit. If the claim is longer than one year, it is called long-term capital – for example, FDI and long-term portfolio investment, such as securities and loans. Otherwise, it is called short-term capital. Sometimes, the classification is difficult. Purchasing foreign stocks is a short-term capital flow, unless you buy so much of the company that it becomes an FDI. Changes in reserve assets may refer to changes by the central banking system in gold stocks, IMF credits, Special Drawing Rights (SDRs), or foreign exchange reserves.

As mentioned above, the balance of payments is zero by definition such that

Current account balance + Capital and financial account balance = 0   (2.1)

Suppose there is a surplus on the current account. This implies, roughly speaking, that the value of our exports (credit) is higher than the value of our imports (debit) – that is, the current account represents a net credit item. By the rules of double-entry accounting this must be matched by a net debit item on the capital account, and thus a net capital outflow, that is

Surplus current account ⇔ Net capital and financial outflow   (2.2)

To see how the current account and capital account are related and how the 'books are balanced', consider the following example. Suppose a country exports goods for €1 billion (net proceeds) and imports no goods at all. The country has a current account *surplus* and if the exporting firms decide to spend their proceeds on buying financial assets abroad, such as foreign shares or bonds, this constitutes a capital outflow and hence a debit because by buying these assets the country has *imported claims* (on future production) *on foreigners*. This means that the capital account will display a *deficit* because of the capital outflow of €1 billion. Of course, the net export proceeds do not have to be spent on foreign financial assets. The exporting firms may simply put their money on deposit with their bank. But in that case the reserve asset position of this country will increase by 1 billion and the result will be the same as with the acquisition of foreign shares or bonds. To see this, note that our exporting firms will have to be paid in local currency, which means that the foreigners who have bought the goods will first have to go to the bank to exchange their currency for that of the exporting firms, leading to an increase in the foreign exchange reserves of the exporting country (see the item reserve assets in figure 2.1, p. 42). A similar line of reasoning helps to explain why a net capital inflow is booked as a credit.

The principle underlying the balance of payments is exactly the same as that related to an individual's budget constraint.[2] If the income you earn this month (export of labour services, your only factor of production) is higher than the money you spend on consumption (import of goods and services), this will increase your claims on the outside world (for example, by an increase of the balance on your checking account). If your income is less than your consumption spending this month, this will decrease your claims on the outside world (see box 2.1).

Capital and financial flows

More interesting than a country's balance of payments specification in a given year is the development of a nation's balance *over time*. After all, any balance of payments' figure in year *t* may be a one-shot accident or a windfall. As explained above, the balance of payments is a direct source of information about a nation's transactions with the rest of the world in terms of traded goods and services, and a source of information for (net) international capital and financial flows. As is clear from (2.1), analysing a country's current account balance over a somewhat longer period of time gives a good idea of the net change in claims on the rest of the world. In fact, in many studies the current account balance is therefore used as an indicator of the

---

[2] In fact, budget constraints are additive, so we can do this for individuals in a country.

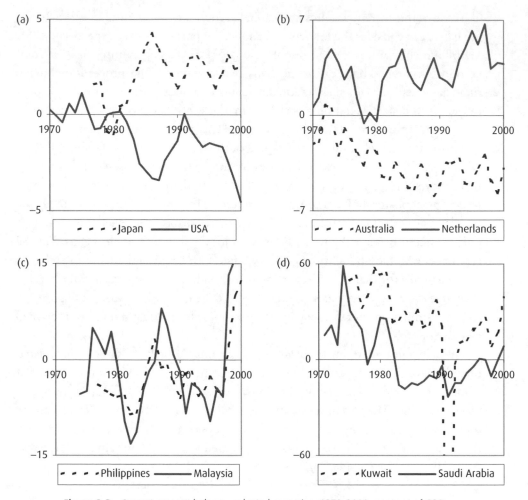

Figure 2.2 Current account balance, selected countries, 1970–2000, per cent of GDP
a Japan and the USA
b Australia and the Netherlands
c The Philippines and Malaysia
d Kuwait and Saudi Arabia

capital flows between the country under consideration and the rest of the world (see chapter 6).

Figure 2.2 illustrates the evolution of the current account balance over time for a selection of countries, where this balance is measured relative to GDP. Note that the scale on the vertical axis is not the same for the various panels in the figure. The USA, which used to be a net creditor, has accumulated such large current account deficits since the 1980s that it is now the world's largest debtor. Considering the enormous size of the US economy, the recent current account deficit of almost 5 per cent is very large. In the aftermath of the Iraq war and the expansionist policies of the

Bush administration (such as huge military expenditures and tax reductions, which produced large federal budget deficits), the account deficit deteriorated even further.

Japan has had a current account surplus fluctuating around 2 per cent of GDP, and has thus accumulated claims on the rest of the world, becoming a large creditor. Similar observations on a (relatively) somewhat larger scale hold for the Netherlands (which is consistently accumulating claims on the outside world) and Australia (which is borrowing from the rest of the world). Developments are more dramatic for the small Southeast Asian nations involved in the Asian crisis of 1997, as illustrated for Malaysia and the Philippines in figure 2.2. Both countries were borrowing on a large scale in the 1990s, in part to finance their rapid development processes and in part to finance their consumption. There was an abrupt break in the capital inflow as a result of the Asian crisis, which forced both countries to repay part of their debt, which in turn forced them to generate large current account surpluses. In chapters 8 and 9 we shall detail extensively these kind of crises and the role of capital flows in them. In terms of relative magnitude, the oil-producing nations, such as Kuwait and Saudi Arabia, are in a class of their own, with years in which 60 per cent of GDP was recorded as a capital or financial outflow. In the case of Kuwait, the impact of the Gulf war in the early 1990s is immediately evident (the current account deficit was 240 percent of GDP in 1991).

2.3 Micro-level accounting: a firm's annual report[3]

Micro-level accounting for an individual firm also follows the rules of double-entry bookkeeping.[4] It is defined as 'the process of identifying, measuring and communicating economic information about an organization or other entity, in order to permit informed judgements by users of the information' (American Accounting Association, 1966), where users range from employees and investors to customers and the public at large. The key accounting event for any firm is the publication of the annual report. Similar to what the balance of payments does at the level of a nation-state, an annual report records the firm's (financial) performance over a book year.

The construction of the annual report is subject to country-specific regulations. So, in the international business area, micro-level accounting is complicated in three ways:

---

[3] Again, more details can be found in any textbook on international accounting (see, e.g., Eiteman, Stonehill and Moffett, 2004) or international business (e.g. Daniels and Radebaugh, 2001).

[4] Strictly speaking, there are two types of micro-level accounting practices: *financial accounting* and *management accounting*. The former deals with issues of financial reporting to the outside world (such as in annual reports), whereas the latter has to do with firm internal accounting and control systems. This chapter deals only with the former.

- First, an internationally operating firm must decide how to account for *foreign currency transactions*. In this context, for example, the financial figures of foreign subsidiaries must be consolidated in some way in the annual report.
- Second, a firm with international operations must take care of *cross-country financial management*, involving such issues as exchange rate risk management and fiscal optimization. For instance, many hedging strategies can be used to manage a multinational's foreign exchange rate exposure.
- Third, an international firm is confronted with diverging *country-specific accounting regulations*. For example, the American so-called Generally Accepted Accounting Principles (GAAP) system is quite different from Germany's much more conservative accounting tradition.

In the context of this book, we restrict our discussion of firm-level international accounting issues to the basic definitions and principles, and a small number of examples that illustrate how operating internationally can complicate accounting matters. As is the case for any country's balance of payments, a firm's accounting system, as reflected in the balance sheet, is based on the rules of double-entry bookkeeping, with matching credit and debit entries. In annual reports, two main parts are distinguished: the statement of income (or profit and loss account) and the balance sheet, as illustrated in table 2.2 and table 2.3, respectively.

The statement of income is a description of the costs and benefits of the firm's operations in a book year, and hence of the resulting financial performance, reflecting an account of the enterprise's financial flows. Such a statement of income includes variable costs and revenues (such as wages and value added taxes), as well as amortized fixed costs and one-shot revenues (such as acquisitions and divestments). Although this may not sound problematic at first sight, it is anything but straightforward, as many accounting conventions are needed in order to be able to allocate intertemporal costs and benefits to a specified period – the book year – whether or not cash has been received or paid in that specified period. This implies, for instance, that goodwill benefits or re-organization costs must in some way be attributed to a specific book year. A classic example of this allocation principle is the way in which fixed assets, such as buildings and machineries, are amortized. This may be done, for example, on the basis of historical or replacement value.[5]

The balance sheet is a description of a firm's assets and liabilities, as measured in a particular book year, reflecting an account of the money value of the company's stocks. A balance sheet's main categories are current assets, fixed assets, current liabilities and long-term liabilities. *Current assets* include items that can change value

---

[5] As a result, the profit concept, so widely used in economics, is much less unambiguous than one might think. This is perhaps one of the reasons why performance measures are subject to such hype. For instance, with the rise of the fashion for shareholder value, the so-called 'economic value added' (EVA) notion gained popularity, while in the absence of actual profits dot-commers in the Internet era of the late 1990s were judged on the basis of sales-related yardsticks.

Table 2.2 A firm's statement of income[a] .

Revenue
Cost of sales
Gross profit
Selling, administrative, and other expenses
Research and development
Other income
Other expenses
Operating profit
Interest income
Interest expenses
Currency exchange gains or losses
Income before taxation
Taxation
Minority interests
Income after taxation
Income from discontinued operation (net of taxes)
Income on disposal of discontinued operations (net of taxes)
Cumulative effects of changes in accounting principles
Net income

[a] Neither the terminology nor the complete set-up needs to be similar across countries, firms and periods. For example, gross profit is often referred to as gross margin, and many firms list special items (such as merger or reorganization costs). In table 2.2, we list a 'common denominator'.

quickly, such as cash and inventories. *Fixed assets* are owned by the firm for the longer term, such as goodwill (an intangible asset) or machinery (a tangible asset). *Current liabilities* are short-term financial obligations, such as bank overdrafts and dividend payments. *Long-term liabilities* imply similar financial commitments, which include long-run loans and deferred tax payments. For many firms, much balance sheet information involves stockholders' equity.

From tables 2.2 and 2.3 it is immediately clear how international operations and transactions may affect the statement of income and the balance sheet. For example, the statement of income includes the item 'Currency exchange gains or losses', and the balance sheet has an item called 'Trade liabilities'. But apart from such visible items, much else may happen that has an impact on other items. For instance, a firm may decide to discontinue a foreign operation (the item 'Income from discontinued operations' on the statement of income) or acquire a foreign organization (the item 'Goodwill' on the balance sheet). To deal with such issues, internationally operating firms frequently (have to) employ financial management tools, such as hedging, transfer-pricing and tax-reduction strategies. With hedging, financial derivatives

Table 2.3 A firm's balance sheet[a]

Assets	Liabilities
Fixed assets	Stockholders' equity
Goodwill	Capital stock
Other intangible assets	Additional paid-in capital
Property, plant and equipment	Retained earnings
Investment and long-term fin. assets	Acc. other comprehensive income
Equipment on operating leases	Treasury stock
Current assets	Minority interests
Inventories	Accrued liabilities
Trade receivables	Financial liabilities
Receivables from fin. services	Trade liabilities
Other receivables	Other liabilities
Securities	Liabilities
Cash and cash equivalents	Deferred taxes
Deferred taxes	Deferred income
Pre-paid expenses	
Total assets	Total liabilities

[a] Although the main categories of a balance sheet are consistent across firms (e.g. current *vis-à-vis* fixed assets), the specific items are not, being industry- or even firm-specific. In table 2.3, we list an example derived from DaimlerChrysler's 2003 annual report.

(such as options and swaps) are used to 'hedge' against unpredictable moves in exchange rates. International transfer pricing is needed if the organization is involved in internal cross-border transactions. Tax-reduction strategies exploit differences in international tax regimes by 'moving money' to low-tax countries. Of course, the different tools are inter-related. For example, transfer prices can be set such that profit is moved to a country with low corporate tax rates (see also box 2.2).

Box 2.2 Annual reports for DaimlerChrysler and Royal Dutch Shell

As an illustration, we provide abstracts of the annual reports for 2003 and 2002/3 of two really international enterprises, namely DaimlerChrysler (table 2.4) and Royal Dutch Shell (table 2.5).[a] These are both discussed in more detail in the main text.

[a] Comparing tables 2.2 and 2.3 with tables 2.4 and 2.5 immediately confirms the observation expressed in the notes to tables 2.2 and 2.3. In the world of firm-level accounting, non-matches rather than matches are the rule. This is quite different in the macro-level accounting domain, where definitions and principles are shared across the globe. Note that for DaimlerChrysler, for the sake of brevity, we indicate $ figures only for the statement of income, and not for the balance sheet. For both firms, for the same reason, we have not reproduced the many explanatory note references that are routinely included in any annual report.

Table 2.4 Abstracts from the annual report of DaimlerChrysler, 2003

Income statement (million)	$	€
Revenues	171,870	136,437
Cost of sales	(135,474)	(109,926)
Gross profit	33,396	26,511
Selling, administrative and other expenses	(22,388)	(17,772)
Research and development	(7,018)	(5,571)
Other income	899	713
Turnaround plan expenses Chrysler Group	(591)	(469)
Income (expense) before financial income	4,298	3,412
Impairment of investment in EADS	(2,469)	(1,960)
Other financial income (expense)	(1,078)	(856)
Financial income (expense)	(3,547)	(2,816)
Income (loss) before income taxes	751	596
Income tax benefit (expense)	(1,234)	(979)
Minority interests	(44)	(35)
Income (loss) from continuing operations	(527)	(418)
Income from discontinued operations (net of taxes)	18	14
Income on disposal of discontinued operations (net of taxes)	1,111	882
Cumulative effects of changes in accounting principles	(38)	(30)
Net income	564	448

Balance sheet	
Assets	€
Goodwill	1,816
Other intangible assets	2,819
Property, plant & equipment	32,917
Investments & long-term financial assets	8,748
Equipment on operating leases	24,385
Fixed assets	70,685
Inventories	14,948
Trade receivables	6,081
Receivables from financial services	52,638
Other receivables	15,848
Securities	3,268
Cash and cash equivalents	11,017
Non-fixed assets	103,800
Deferred taxes	2,688
Pre-paid expenses	1,095
Total assets	178,268
Liabilities and stockholders' equity	
Capital stock	2,633
Additional paid-in capital	7,915
Retained earnings	29,085
Accumulated other comprehensive income	(5,152)
Stockholders' equity	34,481
Minority interests	470
Accrued liabilities	39,172
Financial liabilities	75,690
Trade liabilities	11,583
Other liabilities	8,805
Liabilities	96,078
Deferred taxes	2,736
Deferred income	5,331
Total liabilities and stockholders' equity	178,268

Table 2.5 Abstracts from the annual report of Royal Dutch Shell, 2002 and 2003

Income statement ($ million)	2003	Restated 2002
Sales proceeds	268,892	222,768
Sales taxes, excise duties and similar levies	67,164	65,167
Net proceeds	201,728	166,601
Cost of sales	167,500	137,997
Gross profit	43,228	28,604
Selling and distribution expenses	11,941	9,954
Administrative expenses	1,903	1,601
Exploration	1,476	1,073
Research and development	584	472
Operating profit of Group companies	18,324	15,504
Share of operating profit of associated companies	3,484	2,822
Operating profit	21,808	18,326
Interest and other income	1,973	758
Interest expense	1,381	1,364
Currency exchange gains or losses	(222)	(23)
Income before taxation	22,178	17,697
Taxation	9,572	7,796
Income after taxation	12,606	9,901
Income applicable to minority interests	365	179
Cumulative effects of changes in accounting principles	255	–
Net income	12,496	9,722

Balance sheet	2003	Restated 2002
Tangible assets	87,701	78,687
Intangible assets	4,735	4,696
Investments associated companies	19,384	17,948
Investments securities	2,317	1,719
Other investments	1,086	1,420
Total fixed assets	115,223	104,470
Other long-term assets	9,257	7,333
Inventories	12,690	11,338
Accounts receivable	28,969	28,761
Cash and cash equivalents	1,952	1,556
Total current assets	43,611	41,655
Short-term debt	11,027	12,874
Accounts payable and accrued liabilities	32,347	32,189
Taxes payable	5,927	4,985
Dividends payable to parent companies	5,123	5,153
Total current Liabilities	54,424	55,201
Long-term debt	9,100	6,817
Other long-term liabilities	6,054	6,174
Total long-term liabilities	15,154	12,991
Deferred taxation	13,355	12,696
Pensions and similar obligations	4,927	5,016
Decommissioning and restoration costs	3,955	3,528
Minority interests	3,428	3,582
Net assets	72,848	60,444

DaimlerChrysler is an MNC that emerged in the late 1990s from the acquisition of the American Chrysler Group by the German DaimlerBenz conglomerate. Royal Dutch Shell is a combination of the British Shell (40 per cent) and the Dutch Royal Petroleum (60 per cent) organizations, established in the early twentieth century. Examining all the details of both annual report abstracts (see box 2.2) would take too much space.[6] Rather, we discuss a number of key issues that illustrate the accounting implications of operating internationally. First, as both firms operate in different accounting systems, the formats of their balance sheets are different. DaimlerChrysler, applying US GAAP, uses

$$Assets = Liabilities + Shareholders' equity \qquad (2.3)$$

Royal Shell, adopting British rules, has

$$Fixed\, assets + Current\, assets - Current\, liabilities - Long\text{-}term\, liabilities$$
$$= Net\, assets \qquad (2.4)$$

This definitional dissimilarity already indicates that, notwithstanding the trend of convergence to the US system,[7] cultural differences remain an issue. By and large, cultural differences occur along two axes (Radebaugh and Gray, 1997): the extent of disclosure and the degree of conservatism. Take the examples of Germany and the USA, again. On the one hand, Germany's financial system is primarily bank-based, whereas the USA relies heavily on shareholders' equity. As a consequence, public disclosure is not so much an issue in Germany, but is radically different for the USA's equity-biased regime. In the US case, a large number of shareholders need to be informed (and protected, for that matter), while in the bank-driven system in Germany close personal ties can perform this job. As a result, US annual reports tend to be full of extensive footnote disclosures, much more so than in Germany. On the other hand, the German accounting culture is much more conservative than the USA's. In Germany, therefore, assets and income are relatively under-stated, to serve the liquidity interests of banks and to reduce the tax bill. Conversely, US firms want to impress the stock exchange, triggering 'optimistic' asset and income valuations.[8]

---

[6] Again, a proper analysis would require comparative time series data, where a firm like DaimlerChrysler is compared over time with its competitors.

[7] Together, however, both cases illustrate a global trend toward converging accounting practices, where the US GAAP (and the complementary Securities and Exchange Commission (SEC rules) is the modern yardstick. After all, DaimlerChrysler's dominant system is US GAAP, rather than its German counterpart, and Royal Dutch Shell re-stated its income statement and balance sheet to comply with US pressures. Largely, this is because the NYSE is so dominant that multinationals across the world are forced to adopt US guidelines.

[8] As a consequence, DaimlerChrysler must comply with different sets of rules. As they point out in their 2003 annual report, 'The accompanying consolidated financial statements . . . were prepared in accordance with generally accepted accounting principles in the United States of America (US GAAP). In order to comply

DaimlerChrysler is a good example of a modern 'global' firm, trying to adopt a worldwide rather than home-country identity, particularly since the merger of the very German DaimlerBenz with the equally very American Chrysler. In effect, in 1998 DaimlerChrysler became the first company in the world to introduce a 'global share', registered on twenty-one stock exchanges all over the world. Indeed, Daimler-Chrysler is active in basically all the countries of the world. This implies that international financial management is a real issue. According to a comment in the annual report:

[t]he global nature of DaimlerChrysler's business activities results in cash receipts and payments denominated in various currencies . . . Within the framework of central currency management, currency exposures are regularly assessed and hedged with suitable financial instruments according to exchange rate expectations . . . The effects of transaction risk on operating profit for the year 2003 were of minor significance compared with the prior year due to derivative currency-hedging transactions.

These types of issues really set multinationals apart from firms that operate only locally.

Royal Dutch Shell has experienced a reserves valuation crisis, which nicely illustrates the key role of pressures by authorities and shareholders, inside and outside the home countries (see table 2.5). The American authorities are particularly powerful, as is clear from two quotes from the annual report:

Certain prior period amounts have been reclassified, resulting in a reduction in sales proceeds and a corresponding reduction in cost of sales, following the implementation of US accounting guidance EITF Issue no. 02–03; [and] On January 9, 2004, the Group announced the removal from proved reserves of approximately 3.9 billion barrels of oil equivalent (boe) of oil and gas that were originally reported as of December 31, 2002 . . . The effect of the restatement was to reduce net income in 2002 by $108 million (2001: $42 million), of which additional depreciation in 2002 was $166 million (2001: $84 million), and to reduce the previously reported net assets as to December 31, 2002 by $276 million.

In the aftermath of the reserves valuation crisis, Royal Dutch Shell decided to demolish the dual British–Dutch structure that had served the company so well for so long, by announcing a transformation into a British public liability company, with a single London-type of share, an American-style board of directors, a single headquarter in The Hague and a fiscal domicile in the Netherlands.

with Section 292a of the HGB (German Commercial Code), the consolidated financial statements were supplemented with a consolidated business review report and additional explanations. Therefore, the consolidated financial statements . . . comply with the Fourth and Seventh Directive of the European Community.'

2.4 The importance of distinguishing between micro and macro

The above short introduction to macro- and micro-level accounting systems may seem to suggest that both are largely similar, as they rely on the shared key principle of double-entry bookkeeping. However, simply comparing the outcomes of both accounting systems is likely to produce conclusions that look very appealing at first sight, but that are actually plain wrong. Three examples may illustrate this observation:

- First, a micro-level investment, as reported in a firm's annual accounts, does not necessarily translate into a macro-level investment that materializes in a country's balance of payments or any other macroeconomic statistic. Much of what is called an 'investment' at the firm level, is no investment at all at the macro level of a country. DaimlerChrysler's annual report for 2003 (table 2.4), for example, includes a large item called 'Impairment of investment in EADS'. EADS is the so-called European Aeronautic Defence and Space Company. If DaimlerChrysler's investment in EADS were to be counted as a macro-level investment as well, double counts would contaminate the macro-level statistics. In the system of macro-level accounting, a firm-level investment is counted only once, depending upon the money's origin and destination, here at the level of EADS.

- Second, consider the very popular firm-level investments in mergers and acquisitions (M&As). Each year, multi-billions of dollars and euros are 'invested' in buying other companies, or parts of other companies. The annual report of the acquirer will then account for this transaction by increasing the 'Goodwill' item. Such firm-level 'investments' are neutral from a macro perspective, however. They simply imply that money is shifted from one firm or shareholder to another in order to restructure ownership, but without any productive investment taking place. In the case of a national acquisition, where both the acquiring and the acquired firm are from the same country, nothing happens to the balance of payments. If the acquisition involves firms from two different countries, though, the balance of payments is affected. Take the example of DaimlerBenz acquiring Chrysler. Assume that this transaction implied a shift of $2 billion from DaimlerBenz's to Chrysler's shareholders. The German balance of payments will then report a (then) German Mark equivalent of $2 billion as a capital outflow (debit) in the form of an FDI, increasing the long-term claim on the USA. However, although this reflects a (foreign direct) investment from the perspective of a specific country (Germany), this is not so from the viewpoint of the world as a whole.

- Third, and related to the above, consider the standard rhetoric in the context of the anti-globalization debate that the powerful multinationals are larger than many – if not most – nation-states. Noreena Hertz (2001) and Naomi Klein (2001), for instance, passionately oppose the increased power of large multinationals, referring to lists that rank countries and multinationals, in their order of size, in which many multinationals are much larger than many countries. In such ranking lists, the size measures used are GDP for countries and sales for firms. Table 2.6 constructs such a list for 2002. Indeed, in *sales* terms, multinationals are massive economic entities, frequently larger than economies populated with millions and millions of people (see the shaded entries in table 2.6). There are thirteen multinationals in the top 50 and forty-six in the top 100, with the highest-ranking firm (Wal-Mart) at number 19, above such countries as Sweden, Poland, Turkey and Indonesia. Indeed, in sales terms no less than sixteen firms rank higher than the Philippines, an economy with about 80 million inhabitants.

Table 2.7 gives a different ranking of firms and countries, using value added as the appropriate measure for comparing firm size with a country's GDP, as explained by De Grauwe and Camerman (2003).[9] In this case only two multinationals – Wal-Mart and Exxon – make it into the top 50 list.[10] Using sales as a size measure inflates firm size by cumulating double counts. After all, many expenses of a multinational relate to intermediate transactions. For instance, DaimlerChrysler must pay billions of dollars or euros to suppliers of raw materials (such as steel) and intermediate products (such as tyres). Therefore, a multinational's sales cannot be compared with a country's GDP, which is a value added measure. For a true comparison, only *value added* matters: that is, the value that is really produced by the multinational itself, and not by its large set of suppliers. In table 2.8, value added was approximated for an illustrative set of five multinationals by the sum of total wages, depreciation and amortization expenses and profits before taxes, as derived from their annual reports. Table 2.8 illustrates that the 'GDP-comparable' value added size of multinationals drastically decreases their estimated importance by about 75 per cent.

2.5 Accounting principles as a platform

This chapter offered an overview of key accounting definitions and principles. Not overly exciting, perhaps, at least for non-accountants and non-statisticians, but badly needed to understand wider issues of international economics and business, as will become clear in later chapters (see box 2.3). Moreover, although both macro and micro-level accounting principles are based upon double-entry bookkeeping,

---

[9] Such lists are a party game anyway, particularly as far as firms are concerned. After all, not only are unambiguous measures missing, but also the fluctuations over time are large. For instance, note that Enron figures prominently on the list! The sources are the World Bank and *Fortune Magazine*.

[10] Still, multinationals are very large. Wal-Mart, for example, is larger than such countries as the Czech Republic, Pakistan or the Ukraine. Moreover, thirty-seven multinationals are still listed among the 100 largest economic entities of the world. This offers further evidence as to why a book like this makes sense, linking issues of international economies and enterprises.

Table 2.6 Top 100 based on a sales – GDP ranking, 2002

Rank	Firm or country	Rank	Firm or country
1	USA	51	Venezuela, RB
2	Japan	52	Egypt, Arab Rep.
3	Germany	53	Singapore
4	UK	54	Volkswagen Group
5	France	55	IBM
6	China	56	Colombia
7	Italy	57	Philip Morris Companies Inc.
8	Canada	58	Philippines
9	Spain	59	Siemens AG
10	Mexico	60	United Arab Emirates
11	India	61	Czech Rep.
12	South Korea	62	Verizon Communications
13	Brazil	63	Hitachi Ltd
14	Netherlands	64	Hungary
15	Australia	65	Honda Motor Co Ltd
16	Russian Federation (CIS)	66	Carrefour SA
17	Switzerland	67	Chile
18	Belgium	68	Sony Corporation
19	Wal-Mart Stores	69	Matsushita Electric Industrial Co.
20	Sweden	70	Royal Ahold NV
21	Austria	71	Pakistan
22	Exxon Mobil Corporation	72	New Zealand
23	Norway	73	Nestlé
24	Poland	74	Conoco Phillips
25	Saudi Arabia	75	Hewlett-Packard
26	General Motors	76	Peru
27	Turkey	77	Algeria
28	British Petroleum Co. Plc	78	Vivendi Universal
29	Royal Dutch/Shell Group	79	Fiat Spa
30	Denmark	80	Merck & Co
31	Indonesia	81	Metro AG
32	Ford Motor Company	82	Samsung Electronics Co., Ltd.
33	Hong Kong, China	83	Bangladesh
34	DaimlerChrysler AG	84	Unilever
35	Greece	85	Romania
36	General Electric	86	Electricité de France
37	Finland	87	ENI Group
38	Toyota Motor Corporation	88	RWE Group
39	Thailand	89	France Telecom
40	Portugal	90	Suez
41	Ireland	91	Nigeria
42	Mitsubishi Corporation	92	Procter & Gamble
43	Mitsui & Co Ltd	93	Vodafone Group Plc
44	Iran, Islamic Rep.	94	Ukraine
45	South Africa	95	AOL Time Warner Inc.
46	Israel	96	BMW AG
47	Argentina	97	Motorola Inc.
48	ChevronTexaco Corp.	98	DeutschePostWorldNet
49	Total Fina Elf	99	BritishAmericanTobaccoGroup
50	Malaysia	100	Johnson & Johnson

Source: Calculations based on World Bank (2004) and UNCTAD (2004).

Table 2.7 Top 100 based on a value added–GDP ranking, 2000

Rank	Firm or country	Rank	Firm or country
1	USA	51	Bangladesh
2	Japan	52	United Arab Emirates
3	Germany	53	General Motors
4	UK	54	Hungary
5	France	55	Ford Motors
6	China	56	Mitsubishi
7	Italy	57	Mitsui
8	Canada	58	Nigeria
9	Brazil	59	Citigroup
10	Mexico	60	Itochu
11	Spain	61	DaimlerChrysler
12	India	62	Royal Dutch Shell
13	South Korea	63	British Petroleum
14	Australia	64	Romania
15	The Netherlands	65	Nippon T & T
16	Argentina	66	Ukraine
17	Russia	67	Morocco
18	Switzerland	68	AXA
19	Belgium	69	General Electric
20	Sweden	70	Sumitomo
21	Turkey	71	Vietnam
22	Austria	72	Toyota Motors
23	Hong Kong	73	Belarus
24	Poland	74	Marubeni
25	Denmark	75	Kuwait
26	Indonesia	76	Total Fina Elf
27	Norway	77	Enron
28	Saudi Arabia	78	ING Group
29	South Africa	79	Allianz Holding
30	Thailand	80	E.ON
31	Venezuela	81	Nippon LI
32	Finland	82	Deutsche Bank
33	Greece	83	AT&T
34	Israel	84	Verizon
35	Portugal	85	US Postal Service
36	Iran	86	Croatia
37	Egypt	87	IBM
38	Ireland	88	CGNU
39	Singapore	89	JP Morgan Chase
40	Malaysia	90	Carrefour
41	Colombia	91	Crédit Suisse
42	Philippines	92	Nissho Iwai
43	Chile	93	Bank of America
44	Wal-Mart	94	BNP Paribas
45	Pakistan	95	Volkswagen
46	Peru	96	Dominicans
47	Algeria	97	Uruguay
48	Exxon	98	Tunisia
49	Czech Rep.	99	Slovakia
50	New Zealand	100	Hitachi

Source: de Grauwe and Camerman (2002).

Table 2.8 The size ranking of firms in terms of sales *vis-à-vis* value added, 2000

Firm	Sales ($ billion)	Value added ($ billion)	Value added/ sales (%)
General Motors	184,632	42,175	22.8
Ford	170,064	46,802	27.5
DaimlerChrysler	162,384	44,438	27.4
Royal Dutch Shell	149,146	36,294	24.3
British Petroleum	148,062	33,536	22.6
Average			24.9

country and firm figures cannot be compared without a careful adaptation of the underlying calculus, to avoid falling into the trap of the aggregation fallacy. For example, firm-level investments are often irrelevant from a nation-state's perspective, and the anti-globalists' rhetoric about huge multinationals must be put in perspective of the double-counting flaw.

Box 2.3 Why accounting is useful and why accounting is not explaining

To illustrate the usefulness of basic accounting principles we return to the de-industrialization debate mentioned in section 2.1. Recall the anti-globalist rhetoric on the harmfulness of trade with low-wage countries, because (i) 'they' can sell more to 'us' than 'we' to 'them' and (ii) multinationals invest heavily in low-wage countries to take advantage of these low wages (and low work and environmental standards) to lower the costs of production, which inevitably leads to de-industrialization in the OECD countries. Using accounting principles, it is straightforward to show that observations (i) and (ii) are inconsistent.

The national income level is derived from the production of consumption goods C, investment goods I and export goods X. Earned income can be spent on consumption C, import goods M and (the remainder) savings S. Since whatever is earned must also be spent, we get[a]

$$C + M + S = I + X + C \quad \text{or} \quad S - I = X - M \tag{2.5}$$

The national savings surplus $S - I$ must therefore necessarily be equal to the current account surplus $X - M$. This shows why the above rhetoric must be wrong. If we are swamped by imports from low-wage countries (argument (i) above), we must have a current account deficit, that is $X - M < 0$. If massive amounts of capital are flowing to low-wage countries (argument (ii) above), our

[a] For simplicity, we do not take the government into consideration separately.

savings must be higher than our domestic investments, that is $S - I > 0$. Clearly, on the basis of (2.5) both observations *cannot* hold simultaneously (a negative number cannot be equal to a positive number), and the rhetoric above must be flawed.

This example is also useful in another way. It is a strong reminder that accounting, either on the firm or the national level, does not offer an explanation as to how a certain outcome came about. It does not offer a model as to how A may have led to B. If a country has, for instance, a current account deficit, we know that it is matched by a national savings deficit but we cannot without further information or analysis conclude that the former has 'caused' the latter. Nor can we conclude whether the current account deficit is a good or a bad thing. It may matter very much, however, for our judgement whether the deficit is somehow the result of private consumption outstripping national savings or of private investment exceeding national savings.

Firms, trade and location

Trade and comparative advantage

KEYWORDS

comparative advantage   Heckscher–Ohlin–Samuelson model
competitive advantage   Lerner diagram   outsourcing/fragmentation
productivity differences   technology differences   tests of trade theories
price equalization

3.1 Introduction

We now turn to the most salient and visible aspect of international interaction: international trade of commodities and services.[1] International trade increases the degrees of freedom for an economy. Without trade, all domestic consumption must be supplied by domestic producers. Trade allows consumers to buy from foreign sources and also enables them to compare prices internationally, instead of only domestically. This, by itself, increases the arbitrage possibilities for consumers. For firms, being exposed to international trade implies, on the one hand, that they are exposed to more competitors (foreign as well as domestic, where the former might be able to produce at lower costs). On the other hand, global markets increase the potential (export) market for domestic firms (which could have a competitive edge over foreign competitors in certain markets). Additional options arise if firms choose to re-locate to foreign markets in order to increase their competitive position by avoiding trade barriers and transportation costs, or by benefiting from local resources.

Trade thus creates both threats and opportunities, for both local and multinational firms. To analyse these, we investigate if trade patterns are systematically related to certain country-specific characteristics. Can we say anything specific about trading patterns between countries? The answer is yes. We start with the most famous part of the answer, by introducing the concept of *comparative advantage*. We also discuss the notion of *competitive advantage*. Countries are often said to benefit from competitive

---

[1] Not only commodities and services can be traded, but also capital. In this chapter, we focus on international trade in commodities and services, as listed on the current account (see chapter 2). In part III of this book we turn to capital flows.

advantages, or to suffer from a lack of them. Does this firm-level concept make any sense at the macro level of nation-states? Finally, as MNEs are carriers of trade, we briefly reflect on the theories that explain their very existence. Here, Dunning's (1977, 1981) international business theory of the MNE will prove very useful.

3.2 Comparative advantage: David Ricardo's fundamental insight

The theory of comparative advantage is one of those ideas that separates economists from other people: it is a remarkable insight that, once understood, should remain in the toolbox of every economist. In the words of Paul Samuelson 'comparative advantage is one of the few ideas in economics that is true without being obvious'.[2] To avoid unnecessary complications we make a number of simplifying assumptions. There is only one factor of production: labour. This factor of production is perfectly mobile within countries, but cannot migrate across borders. The factor reward, in this case the wage rate, is therefore the same in different sectors within a country, but may differ between countries. Furthermore, markets are characterized by perfect competition.[3] This implies that we do not have to deal with strategic interactions between firms or consumers. In imperfect markets, the action of one firm might trigger a reaction by other firms, which may result in, for example, price cartels or price wars. In the perfect competition case, individual firms are too small relative to the whole market to affect the behaviour of others. For the most simple international trade model, we need at least two commodities, one to export and one to import, and two countries; otherwise there could be no *international* trade.

The famous British economist David Ricardo (1772–1823) focused on technology differences as a prime reason for countries to engage in international trade. Given the set-up so far, table 3.1 summarizes the hypothetical state of technology for two countries, the USA and the EU, each able to produce two goods, cloth and wine. Table 3.1 measures labour productivity by indicating how much cloth and wine can be produced in both countries with one hour of labour.[4] In the USA, 1 hour of labour can be used to produce 6 units of cloth or 4 bottles of wine. In the EU, 1 hour of

---

[2] As cited in Krugman (1992).

[3] Perfect competition and constant returns to scale production go hand in hand: no matter if firms are small or large, unit costs are the same. In the hypothetical case of positive market profits, it is always possible to start a new firm. However small, a new firm has the same unit costs as incumbent firms, and this firm might try to capture some of the profits (by slightly undercutting the market price). This increases supply, and forces other firms to lower their prices as well (otherwise they would lose all sales). This process continues until market profits are zero. Increasing returns to scale would mean that larger firms have lower unit costs than smaller ones, and thus have a competitive edge over smaller firms. We return to imperfect competition later.

[4] All labourers in a country are therefore equally productive – or, if they are not and labour is measured in efficiency units, at least their relative productivity for producing cloth and wine is the same.

Table 3.1 Hypothetical labour
productivity, production per hour

	USA	EU
Cloth	6	1
Wine	4	2

labour can be used to produce 1 unit of cloth or 2 bottles of wine. Note that the USA is more efficient than the EU in the production of both cloth and wine – that is, the USA has a higher labour productivity for both sectors. We say that the USA has an *absolute* cost advantage for both sectors. Given that the USA is more efficient in the production of both goods, one might wonder why the USA would engage in international trade at all: why import products from another country if you can produce these more efficiently yourself? The answer is surprising: by focusing on the production of those goods in which a country is *relatively* more efficient both countries can gain from international trade, even if goods are imported from a less productive trade partner.

To see this, first note that in a relative sense the USA is six times more efficient in the production of cloth (6/1) and two times more efficient in the production of wine (4/2) than the EU. We say that the USA has a *comparative* advantage in the production of cloth, where it is relatively the most efficient. We also say that the EU has a comparative advantage in the production of wine, where it is least disadvantaged compared to the USA. The next step is to show that if countries start trading with each other according to their comparative advantages, this is beneficial for both countries.

Suppose that the USA has 4 hours of labour available for the production of wine or cloth and the EU 12 hours of labour (you might assume several billion labour hours to increase the reality of the example, but this does not change the underlying principles). In autarky (that is, without international trade), the USA could, for example, use 2 hours of labour for the production of cloth and 2 hours of labour for the production of wine. Similarly, the EU could, for example, use 8 hours of labour for the production of cloth and 4 hours of labour for the production of wine. As indicated in table 3.2a, this implies that the USA produces 12 units of cloth and 8 bottles of wine, while the EU produces 8 units of cloth and 8 bottles of wine. Total world production is therefore 20 units of cloth and 16 bottles of wine.

Now suppose that both countries specialize their production processes according to their comparative advantages: that is, the USA starts producing only cloth and the EU starts producing only wine. As we can see from table 3.2b, this implies that the USA produces 24 units of cloth and 0 bottles of wine, while the EU produces 0 units of cloth and 24 bottles of wine. Total world production for *both* goods has therefore increased: from 20 to 24 units of cloth and from 16 to 24 bottles of wine. This extra production of both cloth and wine in the world economy can be used, in

Table 3.2 Production of cloth and wine in the EU and the USA

a Autarky

	USA (4 labour hours)	EU (12 labour hours)	World production
Cloth	12	8	20
Wine	8	8	16

b Specialization according to (against) comparative advantage

	USA	EU	World production
Cloth	24 (0)	0 (8)	24 (16)
Wine	0 (16)	24 (0)	24 (12)

principle, to ensure that both countries gain from international trade. Specialization according to comparative advantage is therefore, in principle, beneficial for both trading partners, even if one country is less efficient than the other country for the production of all goods. Finally, note that if the countries were to specialize *against* their comparative advantage – that is, the USA started to produce only wine and the EU started to produce only cloth – the world production level for both goods would fall, as indicated by the production figures between brackets in table 3.2b.[5]

Although we have demonstrated above that the world welfare level can increase if countries specialize according to their comparative advantages, we have not answered the crucial question why comparative advantage works in practice: consumers are in general not familiar with the theory of comparative advantage when they go shopping, so how can we be sure that specialization takes place according to comparative advantage? The answer can be given by looking directly at something consumers do care about: *prices*. Under perfectly competitive conditions, with constant returns to scale and only one factor of production (labour), it follows that

$$Price\ of\ a\ commodity\ =\ \frac{Wage\ rate\ (per\ hour)}{Labour\ productivity\ (per\ hour)} \tag{3.1}$$

Consumers considering the purchase of a unit of cloth compare the price for a unit of cloth from the USA with the price of a unit of cloth from the EU. Since labour productivity in the USA is 6 units of cloth per hour worked (see table 3.1), only 1/6 hours of labour are needed to produce a unit of cloth in the USA, implying a price equal to 1/6 times the wage rate in the USA. Similarly, labour productivity in the EU is 1 unit of cloth per hour worked, implying a price for a unit of cloth produced in the EU equal to the wage rate in the EU. If we let p denote the price of a good, w the wage rate per hour worked and if we use subindices US, EU, cloth and wine to

---

[5] This fact depends, however, on the initially chosen autarky production levels.

identify the various possibilities, we see that consumers buy cloth produced in the USA if the price there is lower. That is

$$p_{US,cloth} < p_{EU,cloth} \quad \text{or} \quad \frac{1}{6} \times w_{US} < \frac{1}{1} \times w_{EU} \tag{3.2}$$

Clearly, if this inequality did not hold, the production of cloth would be cheaper in the EU and consumers would buy their cloth there. Note in particular that this holds if the wage rate in the EU is sufficiently low. Similarly, consumers purchasing wine will buy wine from the EU only if it is cheaper to produce there

$$p_{EU,wine} < p_{US,wine} \quad \text{or} \quad \frac{1}{2} \times w_{EU} < \frac{1}{4} \times w_{US} \tag{3.3}$$

Again, if this inequality does not hold, the production of wine would be cheaper in the USA and consumers would buy their wine there. Combining the two inequalities for the wage rates in the EU and the USA, which ensures that production takes place according to comparative advantage as given in (3.2) and (3.3), leads to a range of possibilities for the wage rate in the EU relative to the wage rate in the USA:

$$\frac{1}{6} = \frac{(1/1)}{(1/6)} < \frac{w_{EU}}{w_{US}} < \frac{(1/4)}{(1/2)} = \frac{1}{2} \tag{3.4}$$

Equation (3.4) informs us that the wage rate in the USA can be two to six times higher than the wage rate in the EU for production to take place in accordance with comparative advantage. If the relative wage is within the indicated range, consumers can simply enforce specialization according to comparative advantage by comparing prices and buying from the cheapest source.[6] The fact that the wage rate in the USA will be higher than in the EU reflects the fact that the USA is more efficient in all lines of production.[7]

What happens if wages are not in this range – for example, if wages in the USA are eight times higher than in the EU? This implies that the EU will attract all consumers, because both commodities will be cheaper in the EU than in the USA. The massive demand for EU products and the reduction of demand of USA products will increase labour demand and thus wages in the EU and will force wages down in the USA, until wages are in the range described by the inequality above. So, in the end, international trade will stimulate specialization according to comparative advantage. As long as this is not the case, profitable alternatives exist for both consumers and firms. The conclusion is that countries can always compete in world markets, even if they are

---

[6] The exact wage ratio is not determined unless we know the international equilibrium prices for cloth and wine, which cannot be determined without specifying the demand side of the economy. For now, it suffices to know the range of the wage ratio consistent with production according to comparative advantage.

[7] This shows that wages are at least partially determined by international productivity differences. The relation between domestic productivity and wages is, however, often very tight because many countries are not as open as is often assumed. The USA, for example, exports only about 10 per cent of its GNP.

less productive than their trading partners, if they compensate lower productivity by lower wages (see box 3.1). Furthermore, in principle all countries gain from international competition and specialization.

Box 3.1 Wages and productivity

Ricardo's trade model is a strong reminder that productivity differences between countries are very important in explaining trade flows. The link between labour productivity and trade flows in the model above is, however, too strict to be observed in practice. Other elements determining comparative advantages and productivity differences are also important. One can think of many other factors than just differences in the quality of labour to explain productivity differences – such as location, climate, or available land. However, in a broad sense, the Ricardo model seems to point at important explanations for trade and holds up in empirical research (see, for instance, Irwin, 2002 and box 3.3, p. 81). In general, what we expect to see is a specific relationship between labour productivity and wages: countries with high labour productivity have high wages.

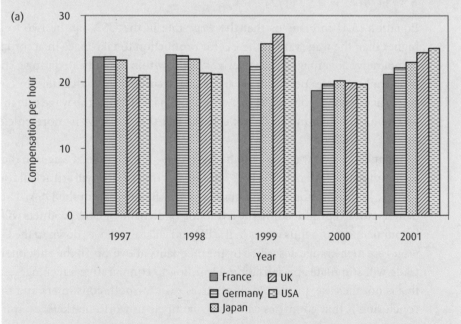

Figure 3.1 Wages per hour and GDP per hour for selected countries, 1997–2001.
a compensation per hour worked, US$.
b GDP per hour worked, US$.
Source: Groningen Growth and Development Centre (GGDC), Total Economy Database (August 2003). GDP per hour, US dollars 1999, PPP corrected.

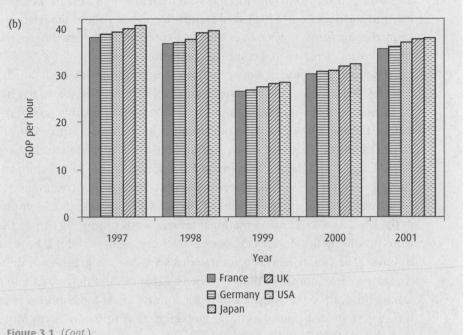

Figure 3.1 (*Cont.*)

With the Ricardo model in mind, the information given in figure 3.1 can help us to understand the world economy. Take Japan, for instance, which has had major difficulties in competing in the world markets since the 1990s. Comparing figures 3.1a on the wages paid per hour and 3.1b on per-hour labour productivity, we immediately note that wages in Japan are relatively high, but this is not backed up by relatively high labour productivity. With the Ricardo model in mind, we have at least a partial explanation for Japan's current economic troubles.

3.3 Comparative advantage versus competitiveness

Sometimes comparative advantage of countries is confused with the *competitiveness* of firms. Conventional wisdom holds that nation-states, just like firms, can benefit from competitive advantages or suffer from competitive disadvantages. Politicians, for example, like to refer to such issues. In the West, for instance, the argument that the rich countries are harmed by a competitive disadvantage as a result of (too) high wages is widespread. Following this logic, politicians and other opinion-makers then argue that wages must be reduced in order to avoid loss of jobs as a consequence of the re-location of many activities by multinationals to low-wage countries. In addition, it is often claimed that lower productivity levels at home compared to those abroad imply that the race for competitiveness has been lost. This kind of rhetoric has often led, and still does lead, to heated and confusing debates about the relations between countries and firms, which makes it useful to point out the main differences between countries and firms when it comes to competitiveness.[8]

First, if a firm is more expensive than another firm which makes a similar product, it cannot sell its product in the market, and will no longer be able to pay its workers, its owners, or its bank. The bottom line is that it will probably go out of business unless it changes its strategy. In our example in section 3.2, this means that if the wage rate in the USA is between two and six times higher than the wage rate in the EU, a cloth-producing firm in the EU will not be able to sell cloth and will go bankrupt, as will the wine producer in the USA. In each country, however, the other sector will flourish: output of wine in the EU will increase, as will output of cloth in the USA. As a result of international trade, a cloth-producing firm in the EU or a wine-producing firm in the USA is no longer competitive and will be forced out of business. The countries in which these firms are operating, however, do not face a similar problem: output of the other sector expands (and in this sense they remain 'competitive', although using this word for countries may cause more confusion than it resolves). Indeed, countries never go bankrupt as firms do. A country may face economic problems and may lose market share for particular goods in the world market. But it will never go out of business. Consider, again, what happens if the wage ratio is *not* within the limits imposed by (3.4) – e.g. because the wage rate in the USA is seven times as high as the wage rate in the EU. As stated before, all demand will shift from the USA to the EU because consumers are better off buying all products in the EU (even cloth). The subsequent reduction in the demand for cloth in the USA will diminish labour demand there, which lowers wages in the USA until the *country* has restored its 'competitiveness' – that is, until the US wages are within the limits imposed by (3.4) derived from comparative advantage. As we already noted above, market forces make the Ricardian model work: the fact that firms go bankrupt can be a sign that comparative advantage works!

Second, note that it might be bad news for the competitive position of a firm if its main (foreign) competitor gains market share, but that this does not hold for countries. For a Japanese multinational like Sony, the growth of a main competitor such as the Dutch Philips company may be a sign that Japanese production costs are too high relative to Dutch production costs. This holds, for example, if wages in the Netherlands relative to those in Japan are not consistent with maintaining electronics production in Japan, possibly reflecting the transition process towards specialization according to comparative advantage. In this case, given productivity levels and wages, Sony will eventually have to close its doors, or to move production to a country with

[8] Countries and firms are not the same. What holds for firms is therefore not necessarily relevant or important for countries, as pointed out by Krugman (1995) and many others.

a comparative advantage in the electronics industry. This type of reasoning does not hold for countries. A high growth rate in the Netherlands is in fact good news for Japanese firms as they will face a larger export market in the Netherlands, which will enable them to increase export sales. If (relative) labour productivity does not change, this will not affect relative wages between the countries.

Third, note that the process of specialization according to comparative advantage may seem unfair to individual firms. Douglas Irwin (2002), for example, recalls that in the 1980s Lee Iacocca, the CEO of the Chrysler car factory, complained that Chrysler was at least as 'competitive' as its Japanese rivals, but was still losing market share. He therefore argued that competition had to be 'unfair' in some sense. In this period, many popular books were written on the economic struggle between the USA, Japan and Europe, often with gloomy conclusions regarding the competitive position of 'old' economies such as the USA and Europe.[9] But our example regarding comparative advantage shows that it is perfectly sensible that such a firm could lose market share if another sector in the economy, such as cloth or chip production, is relatively more productive than the car industry. It is important to understand that the theory of comparative advantage demonstrates that even if a firm is *more* productive than a foreign counterpart, it might still lose market share because other domestic firms might even have a higher productivity advantage relative to foreign firms. Failing to understand this line of reasoning may unintentionally stimulate counterproductive discussions about unfair competition and the need for protectionist measures.

Fourth, the example also highlights an aspect of multinational firm behaviour. Many multinational firms in OECD countries move – or plan to move – their often low-skilled assembly activities to low-wage countries. This is often seen as an unwelcome aspect of globalization as it forces wages down in the home countries. This may happen for two reasons. Firms re-locate to low-wage countries and the workers in these companies become unemployed, or the simple threat to re-locate to low-wage countries forces wages down at home in order to prevent such re-location. Below the surface, however, comparative advantage is still at work. What often happens in these cases is that a low-wage (and relatively low-productivity) country is specializing in a sector in which it has a comparative advantage (in this case, assembly), while the high-wage country is losing a sector in which it has a comparative disadvantage. The fact that the owner(s) of the newly established assembly plant in the low-wage country might live elsewhere, such as in the high-wage country, does not change this fundamental observation that re-location may be a manifestation of comparative advantage. Low-productivity countries need low wages in order to be able to attract the low-skilled labour-intensive assembly plants which will help them and the world to raise their welfare level.

---

[9] For an example, see Thurow (1993).

Finally, a current account deficit is sometimes seen as an indication that a country is less competitive than other nations. As we explained in detail in chapter 2, as a matter of accounting principles, the sum of the current account balance and the capital account balance is always equal to zero. This indicates that a current account surplus or deficit is determined by *macroeconomic* forces, such as the relation between savings and investments and international lending. A current account surplus or deficit is determined by these macroeconomic variables, and *not* by specialization patterns caused by comparative advantage, as explained in chapter 2.[10]

3.4 Comparative advantage: the neo-classical answer

The model of comparative advantage based on technology differences discussed in section 3.2 explains that trade is welfare-enhancing for all participants as a result of benefiting from differences in labour productivity between countries. These differences, however, were given exogenously (see, for example, table 3.1), and not explained by the model. In the 1930s, economists felt uneasy with this assumption. Why should productivity differ between technologically similar countries, such as the UK and the USA? These countries had more or less the same access to equivalent technologies; furthermore, rising international trade flows and improving communication technologies implied that knowledge differences were getting smaller. Economists, therefore, increasingly became unhappy with the notion that trade was

---

[10] Some further discussion may clarify this. In the comparative advantage example, a country always has a balanced current account in equilibrium, because of Walras' Law, which states that equilibrium in one market implies equilibrium in the other market if there are just two markets. If we take the EU as an example, in autarky the value of demand for wine and cloth must be equal to the value of supply of both commodities

$$p_{EU,wine}D_{EU,wine} + p_{EU,cloth}D_{EU,cloth} = p_{EU,wine}S_{EU,wine} + p_{EU,cloth}S_{EU,cloth}$$

or equivalently

$$p_{EU,wine}(D_{EU,wine} - S_{EU,wine}) + p_{EU,cloth}(D_{EU,cloth} - S_{EU,cloth}) = 0$$

In the trading equilibrium, however, the EU is exporting wine, so it produces more than it consumes at home

$$(D_{EU,wine} - S_{EU,wine}) < 0$$

According to the equation above we, now have

$$(D_{EU,cloth} - S_{EU,cloth}) > 0$$

That is, the EU imports cloth. The same inequalities with opposite signs hold for the USA; otherwise, the global markets for cloth or wine would not be in equilibrium. Consequently, the markets for cloth and wine are in equilibrium, and the current account is balanced in both countries. However, by introducing the capital market, Walras' Law holds for *three* markets (cloth, wine and assets), implying that the sum of excess supply or demand in the three markets must be in equilibrium. Specifically, equilibrium in two markets implies equilibrium in the third market. This means, however, that the current account no longer has to be in equilibrium in both countries, because it is potentially balanced by the capital market.

explained by productivity differences alone. They started to realize that technology itself might not be too different between countries, but other factors could be responsible for productivity differences – such as differences in *factor endowments*. France exports wine to the Netherlands not because potential wine producers in the Netherlands are less productive than farmers in France, but because abundant sunshine in combination with hills that are ideal for planting grapevines are better suited for wine production than the wet climate in the Low Countries (in this example, climate is a production factor).

The so-called Heckscher–Ohlin model, also known as the Heckscher–Ohlin–Samuelson model or the factor abundance model, takes this idea to its extreme by explaining international trade only through differences in factor endowments between countries. The reasoning of the model is quite simple, although its mathematics can be complicated. We start by making the following six assumptions:

- There are two countries, 1 and 2, each producing two homogeneous goods, cloth (C) and steel (S), using two factors of production, capital (K) and labour (L). Country 1 is assumed to be relatively well endowed with labour, compared to country 2.
- Production functions for cloth and steel are identical in the two countries, but they have different factor intensities – i.e. for given factor prices the cost-minimizing input combination differs. We simply assume that steel is relatively more capital-intensive to produce than cloth at given factor prices.
- The (relative) supply of capital and labour differs between the two countries, and is perfectly mobile between sectors within a country, but perfectly immobile between countries. This implies that factor prices are the same in the two sectors within a country, with or without international trade.
- Production is perfectly competitive and characterized by constant returns to scale, for both cloth and steel.
- Consumer tastes and preferences are identical in the two countries such that, for the same price of cloth relative to steel, the ratio of cloth consumption to steel consumption is the same in the two countries.[11]
- There are no barriers to trade of any kind – that is, no transport costs and no tariffs or other policies restricting or influencing international trade flows.

Section 3.5 first analyses what these six assumptions imply for an individual country in autarky – that is, without international trade. Section 3.6 then investigates the consequences for the economy if international trade is possible.

3.5 The closed economy

Perfect competition in combination with constant returns to scale implies that the market price for a good is equal to the costs of producing that good. If profits

---

[11] These are called identical and 'homothetic' preferences.

are positive, a new firm will enter the market, which increases supply and reduces profitability. This will continue until profits are zero. The costs of production consist of the amount of labour necessary to produce a unit of good i, a_{Li}, say, multiplied by the wage rate w, and the amount of capital necessary to produce a unit of good i, a_{Ki}, say, multiplied by the rate of return on capital r. In short, we have

$$p_i = Costs = a_{Li}w + a_{Ki}r, \quad i = c, s \tag{3.5}$$

Equation (3.5) simply states that the market price of cloth or steel equals the cost of production. Evidently, we have used the assumption that capital and labour are perfectly mobile within countries as factor prices w and r are the same in both sectors. Slightly rewriting (3.5) gives

$$a_{Ki} = \frac{Costs}{r} - \frac{w}{r}a_{Li} \tag{3.5'}$$

Taking the wage rate and the rental rate as given, (3.5') provides all combinations of labour and capital inputs a_{Li} and a_{Ki} with the same costs of production. In figure 3.3, these are represented as straight (isocost) lines, such as the dashed lines c_1, c_2 and c_3. Each isocost line represents different combinations of capital and labour with the same total costs, given the wage rate and rental rate. The latter determine the slope of the isocost line, which is equal to *minus* the wage rate divided by the rental rate: $-w/r$. The total cost of production determines the intercept of the isocost lines. Obviously, the more capital and labour used, the higher the total costs: that is, total costs in figure 3.2 are highest for c_1 and lowest for c_3. Lines closer to the origin thus correspond to a lower cost of production. An isoquant (box 3.2) depicts different combinations of capital and labour yielding the same level of production for a particular good, and is indicated by the **bold** curve in figure 3.3.

   Once a firm has determined its optimal production level, say the level indicated by the isoquant in figure 3.3, it will choose the lowest possible cost of production. Graphically, this holds for the isocost line tangent to this isoquant, as indicated by point A_0 in figure 3.3. This is the minimum cost combination of capital and labour to produce the good. Figure 3.3 also illustrates what happens if the relative factor rewards change, say if labour becomes relatively less expensive such that $(w/r)_0 > (w/r)_1$. This implies that the isocost line rotates counter-clockwise, shifting the point of tangency with the isoquant to point A_1 in figure 3.3. As capital has become relatively more expensive, firms do what they can to avoid rising costs by substituting cheap labour for expensive capital in the production process. It is important to realize that this reasoning can also be applied to the two-country case if relative factor rewards differ between countries – say, if one country is relatively abundant in labour, which is therefore relatively cheap,

Box 3.2 Isoquants

In this box we present a quick reminder about isoquants. If there are two or more inputs needed and/or available to produce a final good, we call the set of all *efficient* input combinations an *isoquant* (see figure 3.2). The isoquant can be derived from a production function: for example, $Y = K^\alpha L^{(1-\alpha)}$, where output Y is produced using capital, K, and labour, L, with $0 < \alpha < 1$. The same level of output can be produced using many different combinations of capital and labour. Figure 3.2 illustrates this for the isoquant $Y = 1$, where the shaded area shows all input combinations producing at least 1 unit of good Y. The input combination at point A, therefore, enables the entrepreneur to produce 1 unit of good Y. However, to produce 1 unit of good Y the entrepreneur could use either less labour at point B than at point A, or less capital at point C than at point A, such that point A is not an efficient input combination to produce 1 unit of good Y. As such, point A is not part of the $Y = 1$ isoquant, in contrast to points B and C, which are both part of the $Y = 1$ isoquant. The curvature of the isoquant is explained by the standard assumption of diminishing returns to capital or labour.

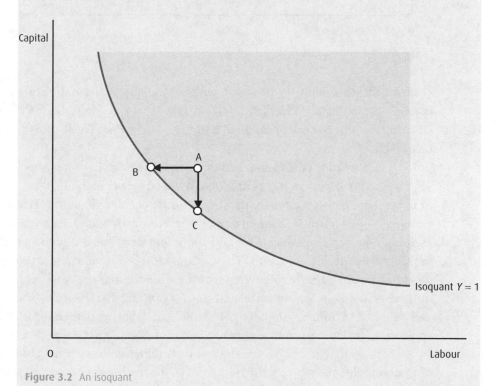

Figure 3.2 An isoquant

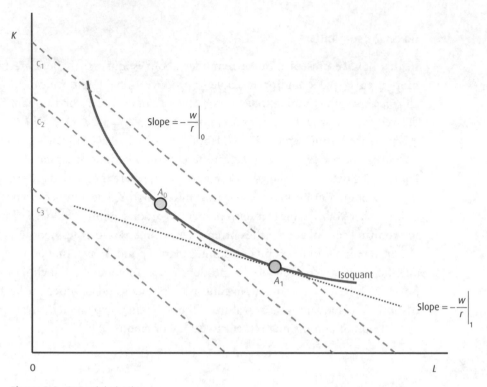

Figure 3.3 Cost minimization

ensuring that this country produces at point A_1 in figure 3.3, and the other country is relatively abundant in capital, implying that labour is relatively expensive and ensuring that this country produces at point A_0 in figure 3.3. We discuss this further below.

We now derive the relationship between goods prices and factor prices. The simplest way to do this is a method introduced by Abba Lerner in the 1930s, as depicted in figure 3.4. The isoquant in figure 3.3 gives different combinations of capital and labour, enabling the production of a certain amount of one good. Figure 3.4a, however, not only depicts isoquants for both cloth and steel, but also very special ones: the so-called *unit value* isoquants. These isoquants represent the production of each good that is worth 1 dollar of revenue when sold in the market. We have drawn the unit value isoquants for both steel and cloth, assuming that the price of steel is p_s and the price of cloth is initially p_{c0}. Obviously, if the price of steel, for example, is equal to p_s, we have to produce only $1/p_s$ units of steel to get 1 dollar of revenue, as $p_s \times (1/p_s) = 1$. The unit value isoquant is therefore *inversely related* to the price of a commodity: the more expensive a good is, the fewer units have to be produced to get 1 dollar's worth of revenue.

Now suppose that both commodities are produced. What does this imply for factor prices? Since the prices of final goods must be equal to the total costs of production,

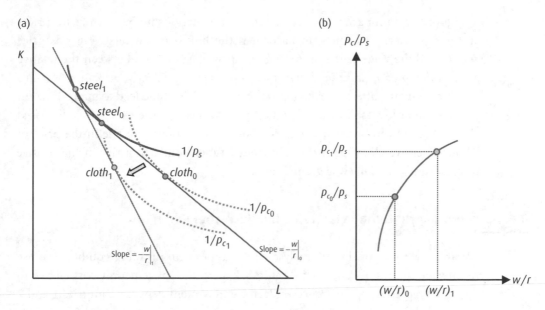

Figure 3.4 Lerner diagram, a goods prices and b factor prices

as is clear from (3.5), and both goods are produced, the minimum cost combinations of capital and labour for the unit value isoquants $1/p_s$ and $1/p_{c0}$ must be points of tangency with a unit isocost line. Because both sectors are confronted with the same wage rate and capital returns, this implies that the two optimal production points must lie on the same unit isocost line, representing combinations of capital and labour that cost 1 dollar. In figure 3.4a, these points are labelled $steel_0$ and $cloth_0$. As an aside, note that figure 3.4a also reflects the fact that, for given factor rewards, the production of steel is more capital-intensive than the production of cloth: the capital/labour ratio (equal to the slope of an imaginary line from the origin to the production points) is larger for steel than for cloth.

We can now analyse quite easily what happens if relative goods prices change. Suppose, for example, that the price of cloth increases to $p_{c1} > p_{c0}$. This implies that we have to produce fewer units of cloth to produce a dollar's worth of revenue, so the unit value isoquant for cloth shifts towards the origin from $1/p_{c0}$ to $1/p_{c1}$. As explained above, we can produce both goods only if the optimal production points are tangent to the unit isocost line. Obviously, this implies that the unit isocost line must rotate clockwise, leading to the new optimal production points $steel_1$ and $cloth_1$ in figure 3.4a. The slope of the unit isocost curve has increased, implying that the wage rate has increased relative to the rental rate. An increase in the price of cloth, therefore, leads to a higher relative wage rate. Intuitively, this makes perfect sense. Since cloth is labour intensive, labour benefits the most from this price increase.[12]

[12] In fact, this relationship has a name: it is called the Stolper–Samuelson theorem. This is an important theorem and we shall use it in chapter 13 to discuss the effects of globalization.

Figure 3.4b summarizes the discussion on the relationship between factor prices and goods prices. It depicts, in particular, the link between relative goods price p_{c0}/p_s and the wage/rental ratio $(w/r)|_0$, as well as the link between the relative goods price p_{c1}/p_s and the wage/rental ratio $(w/r)|_1$. Clearly, we can repeat this exercise for many different relative goods prices, which would lead to many different wage/rental ratios, as illustrated by the curve connecting the two points discussed above. The bottom line is that this is a positive relationship: a rise in the price of labour-intensive cloth raises the wage/rental ratio. Similarly, a rise in the relative price of steel lowers the wage/rental ratio.

3.6 Open economy international trade: the Heckscher–Ohlin result

We are now in a position to analyse what happens in a trading equilibrium. We re-interpret points A_0 and A_1 in figure 3.3, with the tangent unit cost curves in figure 3.3 representing differences in factor endowment between countries 1 and 2 (and no longer as changes of good prices or factor rewards). Country 1 is relatively labour-abundant and country 2 is relatively capital-abundant. It is now straightforward to derive the Heckscher–Ohlin theorem in conjunction with figure 3.4b. For convenience, we copy figure 3.4b in figure 3.5.

Because country 1 is relatively more labour-abundant than country 2 this implies in autarky: $(w/r)_1 < (w/r)_2$.[13] From figure 3.5 we infer that in this case the relative price of labour-intensive cloth is lower in country 1 than in country 2: $(p_c/p_s)_1 < (p_c/p_s)_2$. Intuitively, this makes perfect sense. In the labour-abundant country, labour-intensive cloth is less expensive than in the capital-abundant country because its relatively high supply of labour leads to lower relative wages, which makes cloth production less expensive. This relative price difference is the basis for international trade, as summarized in figure 3.5 by the points Autarky$_1$ and Autarky$_2$. Once costless international trade of final goods is possible, individual entrepreneurs exploiting arbitrage opportunities between the two countries will ensure that the price of cloth and the price of steel is the same in both countries, and so will the relative price of cloth compared to steel. As illustrated in figure 3.5, the trade equilibrium price – say, $(p_c/p_s)_{tr}$ – will be anywhere between the two autarky prices: $(p_c/p_s)_1 < (p_c/p_s)_{tr} < (p_c/p_s)_2$. The relative price of cloth will therefore be higher in the trade equilibrium for country 1 and lower for country 2. Consumers and producers will react differently to these price changes. In particular, consumers in

[13] In principle, there are two different versions of factor abundance – the *physical* definition, arguing that country 1 is labour-abundant if the labour/capital ratio is higher than in country 2, and the *price* definition, arguing that country 1 is relatively labour-abundant if its wage/rental ratio is lower than in country 2. The two definitions are not necessarily identical, because the price definition reflects not only supply conditions but also demand conditions. Since we have assumed that countries are identical in all aspects, except with respect to relative factor endowments, the two definitions give the same result in our case.

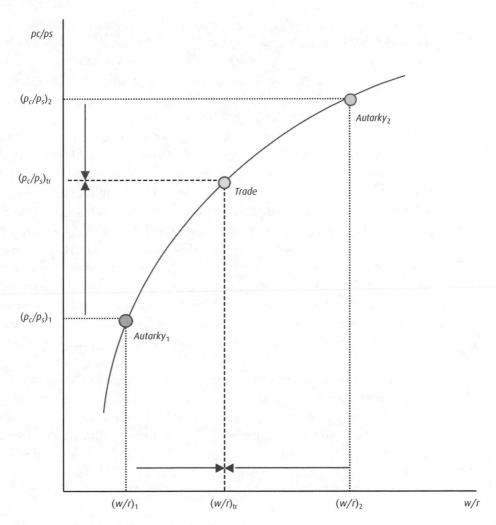

Figure 3.5 The impact of international trade

country 1, where the price of cloth has risen, will purchase less cloth, while producers will increase production. Since production was equal to consumption in autarky, the result is that production will exceed consumption in country 1 in the trade equilibrium. Consequently, labour-abundant country 1 will export cloth. The reverse reasoning holds for capital-abundant country 2, which exports steel. This is the Heckscher–Ohlin theorem: *A country will export the good that intensively uses its relatively abundant factor of production, and it will import the commodity that intensively uses its relatively scarce factor of production.*

Trade ensures that the (relative) good prices become identical in the world market. As noted above, the price of cloth increases in country 1 because of the extra demand from country 2, while the price of steel declines because it is imported from country 2. The reverse holds for country 2. As indicated in figure 3.5, the identical (relative) price of commodities in the two countries in the trade equilibrium ensures that the (relative) factor rewards, say $(w/r)_{tr}$, are also equalized anywhere between the autarky extremes: $(w/r)_1 < (w/r)_{tr} < (w/r)_2$. This is called *factor price equalization*. In country 1, the relative wage rate rises; in country 2, it falls. On average both countries gain from trade: the reward of the abundant factor increases and the reward of the scarce factor decreases. So, the net effect is positive.

We noted above that in country 1 the steel sector shrinks and the cloth sector grows, while the reverse occurs in country 2. One may wonder how this can be an equilibrium if the steel sector releases relatively more capital than labour because the growing cloth sector needs relatively more labour than capital? The answer is given in figure 3.3. Suppose that the figure describes the cloth sector. If the relative price of cloth increases, the relative wage increases in country 1. Figure 3.3 then shows that labour is substituted for capital in order to compensate for this wage increase. As a consequence, the production of cloth becomes more capital-intensive, which is exactly what is needed because the shrinking steel sector releases relatively more capital. So, although cloth is the labour-intensive commodity, its production technique becomes more capital-intensive, as indicated by a shift from point A_1 to A_0 in figure 3.3 (the remaining steel production also becomes more capital-intensive, for the same reason).

It is important to understand the main difference between the Ricardian model and the Heckscher–Ohlin model. In the Ricardian model, technology differences, resulting in wage differences between countries, cause international trade flows. In the Heckscher–Ohlin model, differences in factor endowments trigger international trade. Although in both models the prices of final goods will be equalized, factor prices will be the same in trade equilibrium only in the Heckscher–Ohlin model. Box 3.3 provides a critical evaluation of this issue.

3.7 Factor endowments and competitiveness

We discussed the difference between comparative advantage and competitive advantage for the Ricardian model in section 3.3. To a large extent, the same discussion applies to the Heckscher–Ohlin model. Firms producing the same commodity compete with each other in the international market. In equilibrium, they cannot be more expensive than their foreign competitors. If they are, they will lose market share. In the simple version of the Heckscher–Ohlin model, this will not be the case in the trade equilibrium: if both countries produce both goods, factor prices will be equal in the two countries, and so will production costs.[14] But until factor prices are equalized, cost differences will determine the competitive position of firms.

[14] See, however, section 3.8.

Box 3.3 Empirical tests of factor abundance: Ricardo revisited?

In order to understand the empirical tests used for evaluating the Heckscher–Ohlin theorem, which argues that a country tends to export those goods that use its relatively abundant factors of production relatively intensively, we must realize that these tests are based on estimating the amount of a factor of production incorporated in international trade flows in relation to a nation's *factor abundance*. Using a similar procedure as the calculations underlying table 3.1 for the Ricardian model, we can define unit labour requirements a_{Li}, where i refers either to cloth or steel, indicating the amount of labour needed to produce 1 unit of output. If we let X denote a country's production and C its consumption of a good, it can be shown (see the appendix to this chapter, p. 94) that the following relationship holds if the two countries have the same technologies

$$F_L \equiv a_{L,cloth}\left(X_{cloth} - C_{cloth}\right) + a_{L,steel}\left(X_{steel} - C_{steel}\right) = L_{country} - share_{country}L_{world}$$

$$(3.6)$$

To start with, take the right-hand side of (3.6). That is

$$L_{country} - share_{country}L_{world}$$

The first term simply refers to the labour endowment of the country, whereas the last term is the product of the country's share in world GDP and the total world endowment of labour. We say that a country is relatively labour-abundant if its labour endowment is higher than its GDP equivalent share of the world's endowment of labour. If so, the right-hand side of (3.6) is positive; and as it is an equality, the left-hand side, the term defined F_L, must then also be positive. But what does this mean? Note that it is the product of factor intensities a_{Li} and exports, and as such measures the labour content incorporated in export flows. According to the Heckscher–Ohlin theorem, a labour-abundant country will export the labour-intensive good, in this case cloth. That means that $X_{cloth} - C_{cloth}$ is positive and $X_{steel} - C_{steel}$ is negative. Equation (3.6) now indicates that, if a country is relatively labour-abundant, the term $a_{L,cloth}\left(X_{cloth} - C_{cloth}\right)$ is more positive than the term $a_{L,steel}\left(X_{steel} - C_{steel}\right)$ is negative when weighed with the factor intensities – that is, the labour incorporated in the net exports of all goods in the economy is positive.

The attractive aspect of (3.6) is that it holds quite generally if countries share the same technology, and if we allow for more countries, more goods and more factors of production, as is shown in the appendix to this chapter. Once we know the unit input requirements – that is, once we have estimated the state of the technology – we can simply calculate the factor incorporated in net exports and compare it with the country's estimated relative factor abundance. A rather weak test of the theory is a simple estimate to see if it predicts the correct sign. If the theory has sufficient explanatory power, it should do significantly better than a 50 per cent correct prediction, which is the equivalent of a flip of a coin.

Table 3.3 Sign tests of factor abundance

Country	Identical technology	Different technology
All countries	0.50	0.62
Bangladesh	0.33	0.78
Indonesia	0.22	0.67
Portugal	0.22	0.78
Greece	0.11	0.56
Ireland	0.67	0.44
Spain	0.22	0.78
Israel	0.67	0.89
Hong Kong	0.67	0.89
New Zealand	0.44	0.22
Netherlands	0.44	0.44
France	0.33	0.33
West Germany	0.56	0.67
UK	0.67	0.78
USA	0.89	0.56

Source: Feenstra (2004, p. 49), who discusses Trefler (1995).

Table 3.3 shows some results of an influential study by Daniel Trefler (1995). He uses a sample of thirty-three countries and distinguishes between nine factors of production. If there are M factors and C countries, there are MC observations, in this case therefore 297. The numbers in the second column of table 3.3 indicate the percentage of the number of cases for which the sign test was satisfied – that is, for which the sign on the left-hand side of (3.6) coincides with the sign on the right-hand side. Since a completely random pattern of signs would generate correct signs in 50 per cent of all cases in a large sample, and because this also holds for all countries taken together in the sample, the sign test fails completely. Flipping a coin is as good a prediction as the Heckscher–Ohlin model.

The third column of table 3.3 reports the result of the sign test if we drop the assumption of identical technologies but impose uniform technological differences instead: that is, if a country is x per cent more efficient in the production of some final good, it is also x per cent more efficient in the production of any other final good. Allowing for this type of technological differences between countries improves the test results to a correct prediction in 62 per cent of the cases for all countries taken together. Further empirical studies along the lines of differences in technology have further improved the performance of the sign test. Debaere (2003), for example, sub-divides all countries into two groups (northern countries and southern countries) and, by so doing, increases the validity of the Heckscher–Ohlin model according to the sign test. Moreover, taking a closer look at technology differences between countries, Davis and Weinstein (2001) show that the sign test holds up in 86 per cent of the cases, significantly improving on the uniform technology differences estimate reported in the third column of table 3.3. So, it seems that the sign test can be adequately passed after all. Paradoxically, however, allowing for technological differences between countries to improve upon the sign test brings us right back to Ricardo's world of technology differences. So, although more advanced econometric work improves the validity of the tests we describe above, it is not clear whether we are testing Heckscher–Ohlin type of models or Ricardian models. Probably, both causes of trade operate simultaneously. From a practical point of view, this may be irrelevant: comparative advantage works, no matter what causes it!

After a trade shock, the Heckscher–Ohlin model helps us to explain the direction of the adjustment process. A clear example of such a shock is the fall in 1989 of the 'Berlin Wall' that meant that East Germany and West Germany, which had been part of two largely separate trade systems, suddenly experienced the possibility of a transition towards a new trade equilibrium. Firms involved in labour-intensive production in labour-abundant countries will be able to gain a competitive edge relative to foreign firms, and similarly for firms engaged in capital-intensive production in capital-abundant countries. Again, as in the Ricardian world explained in section 3.3, discussions about unfair competition may be caused by failing to understand what drives international trade flows. More specifically, and recalling that the technology is the same in the two countries in the Heckscher–Ohlin set-up, even if firms are as efficient as their foreign competitors, they can still lose market share. This is not necessarily a sign of unfair competition, but may just reflect cost differences caused by differences in factor endowments, which out of equilibrium would result in lower wages and thus a competitive edge for labour-intensive production in labour-abundant countries.

3.8 Fragmentation[15]

In the above argument, the role of multinationals has been more or less implicit. However, such firms are the key carriers of trade (see box 3.4). How does this

---

[15] This section is a little more advanced than the other sections, but your efforts will be greatly rewarded!

observation relate to the neo-classical theory of trade, as introduced above? As explained in sections 3.2 and 3.3, in the Ricardian model with technology differences the trade equilibrium is characterized by wage differences, leading to multinational firms trying to reduce the total costs of production. The trade equilibrium in the simple Heckscher–Ohlin model (two final goods produced in two countries using two factors of production) is characterized by factor price equalization, which appears to rule out multinational behaviour. Given that countries are identical in all aspects, except with respect to their factor endowments, there is no incentive to become a multinational firm in this case.

It is important to note that factor price equalization depends on the fact that both countries produce both goods in equilibrium. Suppose that after the opening of trade one of the countries becomes completely specialized before factor price equalization is completed. The country that becomes completely specialized cannot shift more resources towards the export sector, because all factors are already employed in this sector. Another reason why factor price equalization might not occur is the presence of trade barriers, which artificially drive a wedge between home prices and prices in the world market, preventing factor price equalization from occurring. A third reason for the absence of factor price equalization is that there are more than just two final goods and factors of production in the real world. It is then quite possible for countries to exhibit differences in the rewards to factors of production, such as countries with high real wages and countries with low real wages, even in a free trade equilibrium.[16] In all these cases, the absence of factor price equalization provides an incentive for multinational firms to become active. Box 3.4 discusses some suggestive evidence.

For example, if a firm has the opportunity to use capital services and labour services at different locations or break up the production process in different steps, it could split up (capital-intensive) headquarter activities from (labour-intensive) production activities. This division of the production process in different stages or components is called the *fragmentation of production activities*. If relative wages are lower in the foreign country, the firm might consider re-locating its production activities abroad. This strategy reduces the demand for labour in the home country, and increases the demand for labour in the foreign country. A new equilibrium will be established once factor price equalization is established again, or once all headquarters of all multinational firms are in the home country and all production activities are based in the foreign country before factor price equalization occurs. Following Deardorff (2001), we can show the logic of this reasoning by using a variation on the figures we have already introduced to illustrate the Heckscher–Ohlin model.

---

[16] More specifically, countries may be divided into 'clubs', with factor price equalization holding for countries in the same group, but not for countries in different groups.

Box 3.4 Multinationals, fragmentation and investment

Data on multinational behaviour and fragmentation are notoriously difficult to obtain. However, some statistics are available. Table 3.4 presents some evidence on FDI and fragmentation in the periods 1986–90, 1991–5 and 1996–9. A fairly well-known aspect of descriptive international statistics is the fact that international trade has grown faster than income (as measured by GDP). This is also evident from the last two rows of table 3.4, indicating that exports of goods and services have risen more quickly than income levels in each of the five-year periods selected. What is less well known is the fact that FDI grows even faster than international trade flows. This is evident from the first two rows of table 3.4. Moreover, the associated affiliate activity of multinational firms has grown faster than income as well, as the third row in table 3.4 shows. Sales of foreign affiliates grow more slowly, however, than FDI inflows or FDI stocks (except in 1991–5). Table 3.4 is a reminder that studying multinational firm behaviour is as important as studying standard international trade theory.

Table 3.4 Multinationals, investment, trade and income

	Annual growth rate (per cent), all countries		
	1986–90	1991–5	1996–9
FDI inflow	24.7	20.0	31.9
FDI stocks	18.2	9.4	16.2
Sales of foreign affiliates	15.8	10.4	11.5
Exports of goods and services	15.0	9.5	1.5
GDP at factor cost	11.7	6.3	0.6

Source: UNCTAD, *World Investment Report* (various years).

Figure 3.6 illustrates fragmentation in a Heckscher–Ohlin setting. In figure 3.4, we explained unit cost lines, the slope of which depends on the wage/rental ratio. If we have two countries and factor price equalization, one unit cost line suffices to determine the wage/rental ratio. In the absence of factor price equalization, we need two unit cost lines, one for each country, to determine the two wage/rental ratios. These lines have different slopes, reflecting different relative factor rewards in each country. They are indicated by the lines *AB* and *CD* in figure 3.6.

Suppose that final good *X* is produced only in one country. The unit value isoquant for good *X* is drawn in figure 3.6, with the corresponding unit cost line *AB*. Comparing the slope of the unit cost lines between the two countries indicates that the *X*-producing country is relatively labour-abundant: labour is relatively less expensive

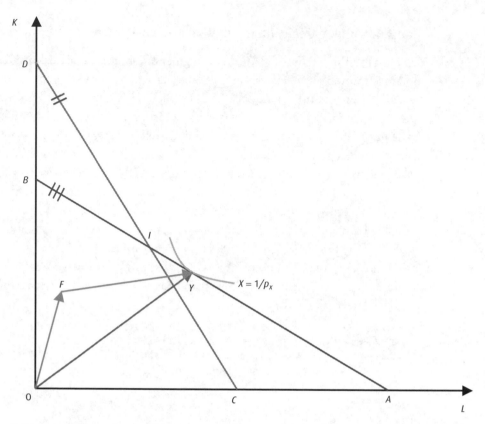

Figure 3.6 Fragmentation possibility

there than in the other country because the slope of the unit cost line is less steep. The hypothetical fragmentation possibilities are explained in figure 3.6. We assume that it is technically feasible to produce good X in two different ways:

1. Good X can be produced directly in one production step using the combination OY of capital and labour, as indicated by the straight line from O to Y in figure 3.6.

2. Good X can be produced using a mix of two technologies in two steps. The first step is relatively capital-intensive and uses a combination OF of capital and labour, while the second step is relatively labour-intensive and uses a combination FY of capital and labour. The vector sum of the two-step technology also takes OY capital and labour.

When will fragmentation be applied? For ease of exposition, we will assume that fragmentation itself is costless (see, however, the discussion below):

- *Case 1* implies a trivial application of fragmentation. If using two different techniques reduces the total amount of factors of production needed to produce a given amount of products, then these techniques will always be applied somewhere

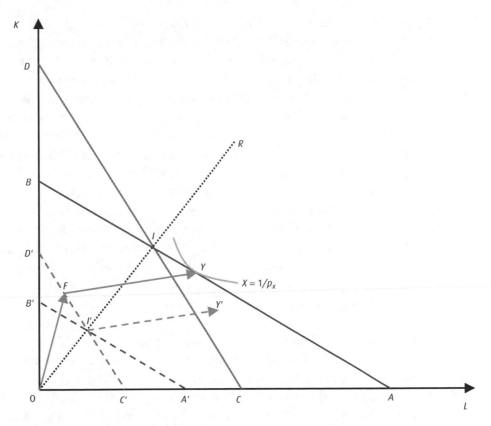

Figure 3.7 Fragmentation profitability

in a world with profit-maximizing firms. One of the central assumptions of the Heckscher–Ohlin model is that technological differences between countries do not exist. So, if using a specific combination of techniques reduces the total amount of production factors needed for production, it is profitable in at least one country to use this combination of techniques. To avoid this trivial possibility, we have already assumed that the vector sum of the two-step technology also uses *OY* capital and labour.

- *Case 2* indicates that a more interesting possibility for fragmentation arises if the combination of different techniques uses exactly the same amount of factors of production. First, suppose that the production process is split into *OF* and *FY* *within* the labour-abundant country. Given that fragmentation is costless, this is always a possibility. Note, however, that the firms in the economy have no incentive to do so: no profits can be made from fragmentation within the same country as the sum of the factors of production *OY* is as it was before. Consequently, there are no cost gains from fragmentation within the same country, and hence there is no incentive for fragmentation to take place.

Second, suppose that *international* fragmentation is possible: that is, the two steps of the fragmented production process can take place in two different countries. Intuitively, you might expect that it becomes profitable to shift the relatively capital-intensive part *OF* of the fragmented production process to the capital-abundant country and keep the labour-intensive part *FY* at home. This is indeed the case, as can be inferred from figure 3.7. This can be understood as follows. Shift the two isocost lines inwards to $A'B'$ and $C'D'$. These are parallel to *AB* and *CD*, respectively. Because the slopes do not change, the shifted curves reflect the same relative factor prices as before. They are shifted inwards in such a way that the tip of the capital-intensive part of the fragmented production process *OF* just touches $C'D'$, which reflects relative factor prices in the capital-abundant country. Now it is important to realize that all points on an isocost line cost the same – this is, of course, why it is called an isocost line in the first place. There is one point that lies on both isocost lines, point I'. So in the capital-abundant country the combination of capital and labour, *OF*, costs the same as the combination, OI'. But the combination of capital and labour, OI', is also a point on the isocost line $A'B'$ that represents the relative factor prices in the labour-abundant country. So OI' costs the same in both countries, because this point is on both lines: OI' represents the cost of producing *OF* in the labour-abundant country *and* in the capital-abundant country. If we now add *FY*, the vector which represents the labour-intensive part of the fragmented production process, to OI', we can finally calculate the total cost of shifting the capital-intensive production part to the capital-abundant country, and keeping the labour-intensive part in the labour-abundant country. The total costs are indicated by the tip of $OI'Y'$ (where $I'Y'$ is the same vector as *FY*, but shifted downwards so that *F* touches I').

What can we conclude? The construction shows that the bundle of production factors indicated by the tip of $OI'Y'$ now costs the same in the labour-abundant country as the total cost of the fragmented production technology. The tip of the vector $OI'Y'$ lies strictly *below* the isocost line *AB* and thus represents lower costs. So, outsourcing the capital-intensive part to the capital-abundant country (where capital is relatively less expensive) represents a *cost gain*. The cost gain of fragmenting the production process thus equals the difference between *Y* and Y'. In principle, we can use the same technique if fragmentation is costly. The extra investment needed to fragment the production process can be represented by magnifying the length of *FY* (and $I'Y'$). However, as long as the vector summation described above still results in a bundle of production factors below the isocost line *AB*, it is cost-reducing to fragment the production process.

- *Case 3* involves changing factor prices. So far, we have assumed that factor prices themselves do not change as a result of the fragmentation process. This implies that the isocost lines can be drawn parallel to each other in our vector summations. However, one might expect that if fragmentation takes place in large quantities, the process of fragmentation could change factor prices or even bring about factor price equalization. After all, as a result of fragmentation the relative demand for capital in the capital-abundant country increases and the relative demand for labour in the labour-abundant country decreases. Unfortunately, relative factor prices can change in quite complicated ways, since they are the result of three effects. First, after fragmentation is completed, demand for both factors of production increases in the capital-abundant country, as indicated by *OF*. The slope of *OF* reveals which factor demand increases relatively the most, in this case the demand for capital. Second, the part of production that is now produced abroad is no longer produced at home, which releases factors of production used in the production process at home. Third, a part of the fragmented production process is still produced at home, compensating the second effect mentioned above. How relative factor rewards change depends on the net effect of all three economic forces. It is therefore not certain that fragmentation increases the likelihood of factor price equalization. Fragmentation is an example of *international capital mobility*. Capital is far more mobile than labour, as we highlighted in chapter 1. It is, however, relatively straightforward to analyse the effects of migration. This is done in box 3.5

Box 3.5 The economic effects of international migration[a]

It is relatively straightforward to show the economic consequences of international migration, given the available amount of capital in each country. Suppose there is only one final good, produced under constant returns to scale using labour and capital in two countries, Home and Foreign. Given the available amount of capital, there is diminishing marginal productivity of labour and thus, given the price of the final good, of the value marginal product of labour (VMPL), which in a competitive economy is equal to the wage rate. Suppose that Home initially has L_H and Foreign has L_F labour available. Figure 3.8 gives the VMPL curves, where the length of the horizontal axis is equal to the total world labour force $L_H + L_F$ and the initial distribution of labour is given by point E_0. International migration implies that any increase (decrease) in L_H must correspond to a similar decrease (increase) in L_F. The left-hand vertical axis depicts the VMPL in Home and the right-hand vertical axis depicts the VMPL in Foreign. Both are downward-sloping curves; for Home relative to the left-bottom origin and for Foreign relative to the right-bottom origin. Given the initial distribution of labour indicated by point E_0, these curves determine the respective wage rates w_{H0} and w_{F0} as indicated in figure 3.8.

Since the initial wage rate is higher in Foreign then in Home there is an incentive for labourers to migrate from Home to Foreign. If international labour

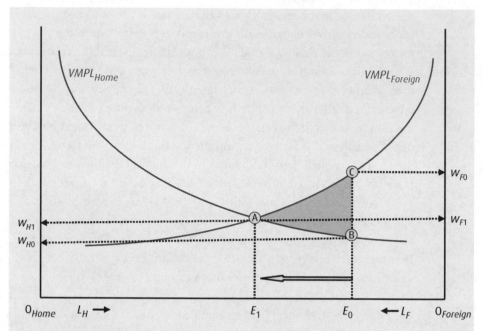

Figure 3.8 Labour re-allocation between Home and Foreign

migration is allowed this process will continue until the wage rates are equalized in the two countries. In figure 3.8 this occurs at point A, which corresponds to a migration flow equal to the distance between E_0 and E_1. The world economy is better off when migration is allowed because world output increases as a result of the migration flow. The net output gain is given by the shaded area A, B, C. To see this, note first that the area under the VMPL curve gives the level of output. The reallocation of labour and the corresponding fall (rise) of the wage rate in Foreign (Home) means that Foreign will increase its output and that Home will decrease its output. Since the output increase in Foreign more than offsets the output decrease in Home (because the migrated labour force is more productive in Foreign, which is reflected by the higher wage rate) it ensures that world output rises. In terms of figure 3.8, the output gain for Foreign is equal to the area E_0, E_1, A, C and the output loss for Home is equal to the area E_0, E_1, A, B. The net output gain is therefore given by the shaded area A, B, C. Note, most importantly, that labour migration is an alternative means for equalization of wage rates between countries. In this respect, it is frequently argued that international migration and trade flows are substitutes for each other.

---

[a] The reader will note that this analysis is very similar to the analysis of capital flows (see chapter 7).

3.9 Fragmentation: an evaluation

Trade and the MNE

Although the explanation of some of the forces underlying the fragmentation process outlined in section 3.8 is appealing, interesting and intuitively plausible, it still only partly explains the existence of multinational firms (see also chapter 12). The most important aspect we have failed to explain is why headquarter activities and production activities are part of a single entrepreneurial unit – that is, why they belong to the same firm. A more complete model should include elements that explain why these activities are not undertaken by separate firms (as would be possible, without additional costs, in a constant returns to scale world). The so-called 'Ownership, Location and Internalization' (OLI) approach, developed in the international business literature by Dunning (1977), lists the factors that are relevant to firms, in order to become multinational and to keep all activities within a single entrepreneurial unit. That is, the OLI framework brings together three lines of argument, or theories, to explain why companies engage in foreign activities in the first place.

According to Dunning, three conditions need to be satisfied in order for a firm to become a multinational, summarized in the OLI acronym:
- **O** – Ownership advantage
- **L** – Location advantage
- **I** – Internalization advantage.

Ownership advantages derive from firm-specific 'capabilities', 'competencies', or 'resources' that give foreign firms a competitive edge over domestic rivals. By and large, ownership advantages result from the fact that 'knowledge capital' in the broadest sense can be transported at low cost to foreign production facilities. These services often employ high-skilled workers in the R&D, marketing and science activities of the multinational firm. These advantages (based, for example, on a patent or trade mark) allow the firm to overcome the disadvantages of a foreign location.

Location advantage implies that foreign production is more profitable than exports. Location advantages are associated with specific host countries, which distinguish the latter positively from alternative locations. These advantages differ between horizontal and vertical multinationals. Assuming plant-level economies of scale, trade costs are important. Without trade costs, all production would be concentrated in a single location. Foreign locations are served by exports. For vertical multinationals, location advantages result from the exploitation of factor price differences. High-skilled and low-skilled production processes can be based in different countries. This is what we explained in section 3.8 on fragmentation. In contrast to the horizontal multinational case, low barriers to trade stimulate vertical multinational behaviour, because products can easily be shipped back home again.

Internalization advantages make it more profitable for a firm to undertake foreign production itself, rather than licensing it to a foreign firm. Internalization advantages imply that the above benefits can be reaped by the firm by internalizing the associated activities inside the boundaries of the organization, rather than by arm's length transactions. For instance, an MNE may reap scope economies by producing an international product portfolio under a single organizational roof. This relates to the difficult discussion as to what exactly defines a firm, and what the extent of the firm is. In box 3.6, we review this discussion in greater detail.

Box 3.6 The extent of the firm

Helpman and Krugman (1985) try to explain the extent of the firm in an extended Heckscher–Ohlin model by assuming that – besides a labour-intensive standard food sector that uses capital and labour – the manufacturing sector also uses capital-intensive headquarter services. These so-called 'headquarter services' are a label for R&D, reputation, marketing, distribution and management activities and the like, which are executed centrally. These are combined with capital and labour to form a final product. Headquarter services are adapted by each firm to make it suitable for the production of its goods or services and can be located in different countries. This assumption ensures that the production plant- and the firm that produces these headquarter services are tied together, and are not provided by separate firms. It is further assumed that there are plant- and firm-specific fixed costs that imply increasing returns to scale at the firm level and the plant level. This is used as an additional force to tie the plant and the headquarter together. Once the sunk costs have been expended, the services cannot be used elsewhere.

In principle, this set-up implies that the concentration of all production in a single location is cost-minimizing, unless restrictions to trade are present (transportation costs or tariffs) or product prices differ across countries because factor prices are not equal. This type of multinational model is particularly useful for explaining vertical multinationals – that is, multinational production by 'slicing up the value chain' in a fragmentation process. Most multinational production, however, is not of the vertical but of the horizontal type, implying that firms duplicate similar types of technologies in different countries (including marketing, management and many other 'headquarter-type' activities). This type of multinational production mostly takes place between similar countries – that is, between countries with similar relative factor endowments and similar factor prices. Different explanations for understanding horizontal multinationals are clearly needed. We return to this issue in chapter 5.

The MNE and trade

A complementary question is how the MNE may contribute to the emergence and development of comparative advantage. Here, a key concept is *path dependency*. If, for whatever reason, a country is ahead of the rest of the world in terms of successful entrepreneurial behaviour in one industry or the other, this may trigger a vicious circle of building up a greater comparative advantage in that industry. If Hewlett and Packard had not started their entrepreneurial activities in California's Silicon Valley, the USA might not have developed a comparative advantage in the semiconductor and software industries. However, they did. As a result, Silicon Valley and the USA have developed a multi-billion industry with the globe's leading MNEs in their industries, which clearly define an American comparative advantage. Similarly, historical path dependencies initiated by 'accidental' entrepreneurial successes have 'dictated' that the City of London is Europe's financial centre, or that Holland is the world's number one producer of cut flowers. Success breeds success, implying that comparative advantages may well emerge from path-dependent processes of entrepreneurial innovation and attraction.

Related to this, Neary (2004) developed an oligopoly model of cross-border mergers that supports the above logic. Assume that the Home country can benefit from a comparative advantage *vis-à-vis* a Foreign country in a particular industry x. Apart from that, the Home and Foreign countries are identical. Take the case where the costs of production are the key to success in this industry x. That is, firms from the Home country have lower production costs than their rivals from the Foreign country, for whatever reason (e.g. lower wages or access to raw material). Then, in the imperfect competition world, the low-cost Home firms face an incentive to acquire their high-cost Foreign rivals. In so doing, the Home firms increase their profits. As a result, the Home firms start to engage in FDI by acquiring their Foreign rivals. This further increases the Home country's comparative advantage by triggering international specialization. As a consequence, the countries will trade even more in accordance with comparative advantage, from which both the Home and the Foreign country will benefit, as explained above. We return to this issue of imperfect competition and trade on the one hand and the role of the MNE on the other in greater detail in chapter 5.

3.10 Conclusions

This chapter has focused on comparative advantage, perhaps the most fundamental insight of international economics. If countries either completely or partially specialize production according to their comparative advantage, they can reap the benefits of the gains from specialization in terms of achieving higher total production and welfare levels. The underlying causes of comparative advantage can be different. It can be technology-driven (Ricardo) or it can derive from the relative cost differences resulting from different relative factor endowments (Heckscher–Ohlin). As was to be expected, empirical research indicates that both elements (technology and factor abundance) are important for explaining the composition of international trade flows. Throughout the chapter, we have emphasized the fact that the comparative advantage for nations should not be confused with the competitiveness of individual firms. In conjunction with this observation, we also discussed the opportunities arising for multinational firms to benefit from the comparative advantages of different nations, be they technology-driven or factor abundance-driven, to reduce the total costs of production, particularly through the ever-more popular method of fragmentation (or 'slicing-up-the-value-chain') in which different parts of the production process are located in different countries. It remains to be explained why this is done by a single multinational firm instead of a multitude of interconnected national firms. A first step was taken by pointing out that such an explanation must be based on the joint presence of three advantages – ownership, location and internalization – as suggested in Dunning's (1977) international business theory of the MNE. The second step will be taken in chapter 12, where we discuss the important cultural factors that are important for the behaviour of MNEs.

Appendix: Heckscher–Ohlin algebra

This appendix discusses some Heckscher–Ohlin algebra that is useful when we are confronted with empirical data. Let index i denote the factor of production, index j the final good, index k the country, p_j the price of good j, V_i^k the available endowment of factor i in country k, C_j^k the consumption level of good j in country k, X_j^k the production level of good j in country k and T_j^k the export of good j for country k. We summarize the state of technology by letting a_{ij} denote the cost-minimizing input requirement of factor i for producing one unit of good j. Note that these input requirements depend, in particular, on the relative factor prices. We will assume, however, that the production technology is the same for all countries in the world. If input i is fully employed, the sum of the use of factor i for all goods, which is equal to the unit input requirement times the production level, must be equal to the endowment

$$V_i^k = \sum_j a_{ij} X_j^k, \quad \text{or} \quad \mathbf{V}^k = \mathbf{A}\mathbf{X}^k \tag{A3.1}$$

where the bold notation indicates a vector or matrix, appropriately defined. Since demand is identical and homothetic, country k's share in world consumption of each good j is proportional to its share in world income, s^k, say

$$C_j^k = s^k C_j^{world}, \quad \text{or} \quad \mathbf{C}^k = s^k \mathbf{C}^{world} \tag{A3.2}$$

On a global scale, world production is equal to world consumption: $\mathbf{C}^{world} = \mathbf{X}^{world}$. In addition, trade must be balanced for each country, such that $s^k = \mathbf{p}'\mathbf{X}^k / \mathbf{p}'\mathbf{X}^{world}$. As the exports of a country are, by definition, equal to production minus consumption, we get

$$T_j^k = X_j^k - C_j^k, \quad \text{or} \quad \mathbf{T}^k = \mathbf{X}^k - \mathbf{C}^k \tag{A3.3}$$

If we now pre-multiply (A3.3) using the technology matrix $\mathbf{A}$, label the result $\mathbf{F}^k$ and use the above, we derive

$$\mathbf{F}^k \equiv \mathbf{A}\mathbf{T}^k = \mathbf{A}\mathbf{X}^k - \mathbf{A}\mathbf{C}^k = \mathbf{V}^k - s^k \mathbf{A}\mathbf{X}^{world} = \mathbf{V}^k - s^k \mathbf{V}^{world} \tag{A3.4}$$

The components F_i^k on the left-hand side of (A3.4) are the factor content of trade and the components on the extreme right are the deviation between a country's available factor of production and its GDP equivalent share of the world total. If the latter is positive for factor i, we say that the country is relatively abundant in factor i. According to (A3.4), the factor content of its export flows must then also be positive.

Trade and competitive advantage

KEYWORDS

intra-industry trade
internal returns to scale
love-of-variety effect

Grubel–Lloyd index
gains from trade
strategic industrial policy

imperfect competition
monopolistic competition

4.1 Trade and imperfect competition

The explanations for international trade flows based on comparative advantage, driven by differences in technology or factor abundance, greatly enhance our understanding of the benefits of international (partial) specialization, the division of labour and the implications for international trade flows. These theories, however, are especially useful to explain so-called *inter*-industry trade flows – that is, trade in different types of commodities, such as wine for cloth, movies for cars, or iron ore for tuna fish. However, a large part of international trade flows is of the *intra*-industry type – that is, similar trade within one broader category, such as the exchange of television sets for television sets, cars for cars, or engineering services for engineering services. This type of trade might seem wasteful at first sight. Why would you import something you cannot only produce yourself but you are also exporting? Although first noted by Verdoorn (1960), the importance of intra-industry trade flows became clear after the influential empirical study by Grubel and Lloyd (1975), who demonstrated that a substantial part of international trade flows is of the intra-industry type. Box 4.1 provides greater detail on this. It posed a problem for trade theorists because the two models they had at their disposal – the Ricardo (technology) model and the Heckscher–Ohlin (factor-abundance) one – are ill-suited for explaining intra-industry trade. It was not until the late 1970s and the early 1980s that trade theorists were able to meet this challenge by incorporating imperfect competition into their models to explain intra-industry trade.

In recent years, imperfect competition has become as important in the international economics curriculum as the standard neo-classical Ricardo and Heckscher–Ohlin models. This chapter focuses on explanations of intra-industry trade based on models of imperfect competition. These models are characterized by the simple fact that a single firm has at least some market power, by being able to influence the market-clearing price to some extent. This chapter thus neatly relates to the international business literature, for two important reasons:

- First, the international business literature about MNEs is clearly dominated by an (often implicit) assumption of imperfect competition. In effect, in the world of multinationals, perfect competition rarely occurs at all, if ever.
- Second, the concept of competitive advantage is central to the international business literature about multinationals. After all, in that literature, a (perhaps even the) key question is why some multinationals out-perform others – or, to put it differently, why some MNEs have been able to develop competitive advantages, while others have not.

Box 4.1 Intra-industry trade

It is easy to come up with examples to show the relevance of intra-industry trade – that is, the simultaneous import and export of similar types of goods and services – by giving specific examples, such as the mutual import and export of CD players, television sets and the like. In practice, measuring intra-industry trade is a bit more difficult, because even at a very detailed level of aggregation most commodities have different characteristics: a Sony CD player performs the same basic functions as a Philips CD player, but they are not quite the same. Given the level of aggregation, economists have developed a simple measure for intra-industry trade known as the Grubel–Lloyd (GL) index. For sector i in a particular country this index is defined as follows:

$$GL_{sector\ i} = 1 - \frac{|Export_{sector\ i} - Import_{sector\ i}|}{Export_{sector\ i} + Import_{sector\ i}} \tag{4.1}$$

The symbol $|...|$ indicates that the absolute value of the difference between the exports of sector i and the imports of sector i should be taken.[a] The maximum value the index can take is equal to one. Its minimum value is zero:

- Suppose, on the one hand, that the amount of imports and exports in sector i is exactly the same. In this case,

$$Export_{sector\ i} - Import_{sector\ i} = 0 \quad and \quad GL_{sector\ i} = 1$$

which is its maximum value. As imports and export for this sector are the same, it is a clear case of *intra*-industry trade.

- Assume, on the other hand, that either exports for sector i are zero or imports for sector i are zero. In this case, the last term in (4.1) is equal to 1 (it is either exports/exports or imports/imports) and

$$GL_{sector\ i} = 1 - 1 = 0$$

which is its minimal value. As the good is either only imported or only exported, this is a clear case of *inter*-industry trade, so its measure of intra-industry trade (the Grubel–Lloyd index) is zero.

[a] It is therefore exports–imports if exports are larger than imports for sector i, and imports–exports if imports are larger than exports for sector i.

As an indication of the importance of intra-industry trade, the OECD uses the share of an individual sector in a country's total trade to calculate a weighted average of intra-industry trade for each country (the weights therefore differ as individual countries specialize in particular sectors). These weighted Grubel–Lloyd indices are reported in table 4.1 and illustrated in figure 4.1 for a selection of countries.

Table 4.1 Manufacturing intra-industry trade (per cent of total manufacturing trade), 1988–2000

Countries	1988–91	1992–5	1996–2000	Change
High and increasing intra-industry trade				
Czech Republic	n.a.	66.3	77.4	11.1
Slovak Republic	n.a.	69.8	76.0	6.2
Mexico	62.5	74.4	73.4	10.9
Hungary	54.9	64.3	72.1	17.2
Germany	67.1	72.0	72.0	5.0
USA	63.5	65.3	68.5	5.0
Poland	56.4	61.7	62.6	6.2
Portugal	52.4	56.3	61.3	8.9
High and stable intra-industry trade				
France	75.9	77.6	77.5	1.6
Canada	73.5	74.7	76.2	2.7
Austria	71.8	74.3	74.2	2.4
UK	70.1	73.1	73.7	3.6
Switzerland	69.8	71.8	72.0	2.2
Belgium/Lux.	77.6	77.7	71.4	−6.2
Spain	68.2	72.1	71.2	3.0
Netherlands	69.2	70.4	68.9	−0.3
Low and increasing intra-industry trade				
South Korea	41.4	50.6	57.5	16.1
Japan	37.6	40.8	47.6	10.0
Low and stable intra-industry trade				
New Zealand	37.2	38.4	40.6	3.4
Turkey	36.7	36.2	40.0	3.3
Norway	40.0	37.5	37.1	−2.9
Greece	42.8	39.5	36.9	−5.9
Australia	28.6	29.8	29.8	1.2
Iceland	19.0	19.1	20.1	1.1

Source: *OECD Economic Outlook*, 71, 13 June 2002, ch. 6, table VI.1, p. 161. A country is classified as 'high' if intra-industry trade is larger than 50 during the whole period, and 'increasing' if intra-industry trade increases by more than 5 percentage points between the first and last period.

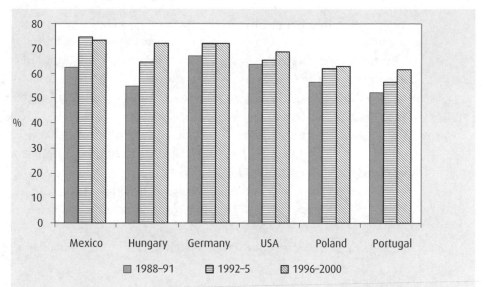

Figure 4.1 Manufacturing intra-industry trade: high and intra-industry trade increasing countries, per cent of total manufacturing trade
Source: See table 4.1.

It is worth mentioning a few basic observations regarding table 4.1 and figure 4.1. It is important to keep in mind that the factors listed here are *characteristics of* intra-industry trade, not *explanations for* intra-industry trade.

- First, it is not clear whether or not the data reflect pure horizontally differentiated trade in similar goods (that is, trade in cars of similar make and price), or whether the data reflect trade in vertically differentiated products (for example, high-quality clothing exports and low-quality clothing imports). The sector data in table 4.1 are based on two-digit Standard International Trade Classification (SITC) product classes. This is very detailed, but even more detailed analyses are possible. To a certain extent the intra-industry trade phenomenon reflects problems of aggregation: some goods are classified within a single product category, but are in fact different products. The product category 'cameras', for example, ranges from single-use cameras to the most expensive professional equipment.

- Second, intra-industry trade tends to be high in sophisticated manufactured products, such as electronics. Highly specialized manufacturers are active in these sectors, offering goods or services for special markets. This shows up in international trade statistics as high levels of intra-industry trade. For those products, opportunities for outsourcing are larger than in more standardized products, as complex goods often constitute a large number of specialized components, facilitating the involvement of specialized producers. This is known as 'slicing-up-the-value-chain' (see chapter 3).

- Third, countries that are very open – say countries where both imports and exports account for more than 50 per cent of GDP such as Austria, Belgium, the Czech Republic, Hungary and the Netherlands – often show high levels of intra-industry trade.
- Fourth, countries that receive a large inflow of FDI also tend to have large and rising levels of intra-industry trade. This holds, for example, for some transition economies – such as the Czech Republic, Hungary, Poland and Slovakia, with large FDI inflows from Europe (particularly Germany) – and for Mexico, with large FDI inflows from the USA towards the so-called *maquiladora* (see also chapter 5, box 5.5). In both cases, the strong connections between parent company and subsidiary contribute to high intra-industry trade flows.

4.2 Understanding intra-industry trade: monopoly power

The models of comparative advantage discussed in chapter 3 attempt to explain international trade flows under perfect competition – that is, under circumstances where the individual firm takes the price in the market as given and assumes that it cannot effectively influence this price. It is straightforward to list examples in which this is an implausible assumption:

- The Toyota motor company realizes that it is one of the world's largest producers of automobiles and can therefore influence the extent of competition in most of the markets where it is active.
- Microsoft realizes that it has almost a monopoly position in many parts of the software market for computers, which enables it to largely determine its price under monopolistic conditions.
- In many countries, only a few large banks determine the extent of competition in the financial sector.

Various measures have been put forward to give an indication of the degree of competition in a particular market, usually based on the number of firms active in that market.[1] Such measures are far from perfect because a market can display monopoly power even if there are many active, but colluding, firms, or a market can be quite competitive even if there are only a few active firms, but the mere threat of entry into

---

[1] Examples are concentration ratios, which measure the sum of the market shares of the top four, five, or eight firms in a market, and the Herfindahl index, which measures the sum of the squared market shares of all firms in the market.

the market by outsiders can prevent monopolistic behaviour.[2] Nonetheless, it is safe to conclude that competition in many markets is far from perfect. Unfortunately, there are many ways in which a market can behave in accordance with *im*perfect competition, even though there is only one way in which it can behave in accordance with perfect competition. This implies that the theory of international trade dealing with imperfect markets consists of many different models. In this and other chapters, a subset of these models will be introduced.

The underlying main cause for most international trade models of imperfect competition is the presence of internal increasing returns to scale. That is to say, when a firm's volume or quantity of production increases, the average costs of production fall (see figure 4.2). The presence of fixed costs at the firm level, like overhead costs, is a main reason for average costs to fall when production expands, since the fixed costs can be divided over more units of production.[3] In the constant returns world of the Ricardo and Heckscher–Ohlin models, even the smallest profit in a market is an incentive for a new firm to enter, no matter how small the scale of production. After all, under constant returns to scale conditions, the size of a firm's production has no implications for a firm's unit costs, which are identical whether the firm produces 2 units or 2 million units. In reality, this is often not the case. In the aircraft industry, for example, large initial investment costs prevent the easy entry of new aircraft manufacturers. So what is the relationship between increasing returns to scale and market competition?

From basic microeconomic theory, we know that the first-order condition for profit maximization for a firm, producing any type of good or service, is equality of marginal costs (mc) and marginal revenue (mr): $mc = mr$. Under perfect competition, where the firm takes the price of the good (p) as given such that the price of the good is equal to marginal revenue ($p = mr$), this optimality condition implies that $mc = p$, stating that marginal cost is equal to the price of the good. With firm-specific or internal increasing returns to scale, figure 4.2 shows that this pricing rule is never a possible equilibrium outcome. The average cost curve in figure 4.2 is declining as the firm's production increases due to increasing returns to scale (in this case, the presence of a fixed investment cost before production starts). Because marginal costs are constant in figure 4.2, the average cost curve lies everywhere above the marginal cost curve. The equality of price and marginal cost, the condition which should hold

---

[2] This is one of the issues that is central to another branch of economics: industrial organization (or IO). IO is, basically, the economics study of competition. In this and later chapters, we shall make extensive use of IO models and tools (see, e.g., chapter 12's introduction of the game theory of Bertrand duopolies).

[3] In contrast to internal or firm-specific increasing returns to scale, the analysis of external increasing returns to scale does not require a market structure of imperfect competition. With external increasing returns to scale, the firm's average costs fall as the volume or quantity of production of the *industry* to which the firm belongs expands. This form of scale economies is compatible with perfect competition.

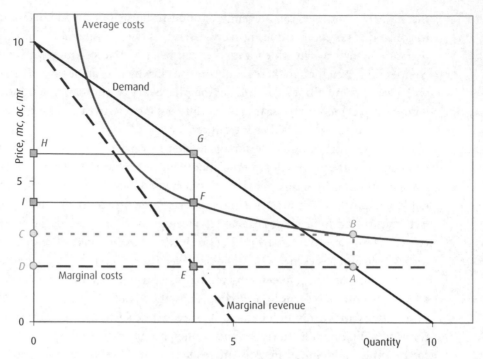

Figure 4.2   Increasing returns to scale and perfect and imperfect competition, demand and costs

under perfect competition, occurs at point *A* in figure 4.2. The associated average cost of production is determined by point *B* in the figure. As the price is lower than the average cost of production, the firm would make a total loss of *ABCD* units if it were to behave as a perfect competitor. Clearly, this cannot be a viable economic outcome. Perfect competition is thus not consistent with this type of increasing returns to scale.

Various types of imperfectly competitive behaviour are consistent with the increasing returns to scale assumption. One particular option, in which the firm behaves as a monopolist on this market, is illustrated in figure 4.2. If the firm is a monopolist, it realizes that its relevant marginal revenue curve is generated by the market demand curve itself, as illustrated in figure 4.2. The first-order condition for profit maximization in this case occurs at point *E*, where marginal revenues are equal to marginal costs. From the demand curve, we can infer the price level corresponding to this level of sales at point *G*. Similarly, the average cost curve at point *F* determines the cost of production. As the latter are lower than the price level, the firm is able to make positive profits equal to the area *FGHI* in figure 4.2. Other types of imperfect competition, such as a duopoly, oligopoly or monopolistic competition, can in principle also be consistent with increasing returns to scale (see p. 110).

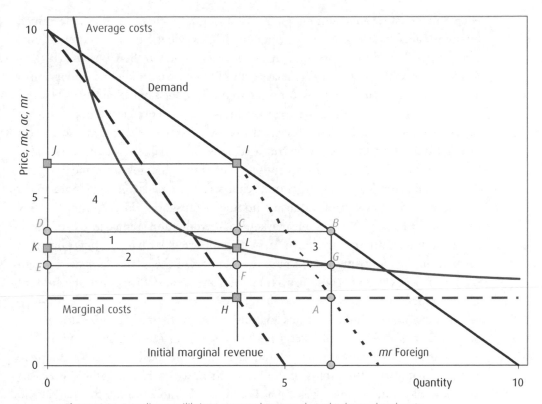

Figure 4.3   A trading equilibrium: monopoly versus duopoly, demand and costs

4.3 The trading equilibrium

How does trade enter into this picture? Assume that the Home market is characterized by a monopoly and that there exists an identical foreign firm with the same cost structure and the same demand function in the Foreign market. The analyses can potentially become complicated because we do not know beforehand how many firms will enter the market. This is crucial because a firm will like to know how other firms will behave. This problem is not important in standard trade models with perfect competition, because the market price is given and cannot be affected by the behaviour of single firm because it is too small. By assumption, knowing the behaviour of competitors is not important in a monopoly from the perspective of the Home monopolist, because there are no other firms in Home. In oligopolistic markets this issue, however, becomes very important, as we shall show below.

Figure 4.3 partially repeats information from figure 4.2. It shows, in particular, that in autarky (without international trade) the Home firm, as a monopolist, will equate marginal revenue and marginal cost at point H, charge a price determined by point I and achieve total profits equal to $IJKL$. So what happens if international trade is possible and the foreign firm can also sell goods in the Home market? To facilitate the analysis we initially make a simplifying *assumption*: the Foreign firm assumes that the Home firm will continue to produce the same quantity as before.[4]

Once the Home market is open to competition from the Foreign country, a Foreign firm may enter the market. The Foreign firm knows that the residual demand curve it faces is from point I downwards, with an associated marginal revenue curve indicated by *mr foreign* in figure 4.3. Consequently, equating marginal revenues and marginal costs at point A in figure 4.3, the entrant charges a price determined by point B. As the Home and Foreign firm produce a homogeneous good, this becomes the new market-clearing price in the Home market. Total production is equal to DB, of which DC is produced by the domestic firm and CB is imported. We have to show only what happens in the Home market, because by assumption the analysis for the Foreign market is identical. So for both firms total sales are equal, DB, of which the amount CB is exports.

What can we conclude from this analysis? First, profitability for the Home firm has decreased, because the market price has fallen from J to D. The reason for this is simple: increased competition – a new entrant to the market – results in a price decrease that affects the profits of the Home firm, which is able to hold on to its domestic sales only at a lower price. The Foreign firm is able to enter the market and make a profit in its export market. In the end, both firms expand production and profits are based on the average cost curve at point G. The reason is that total sales of both firms equal DB, because both firms export to each other's market and average cost is determined by total sales: Home sales plus exports to the Foreign market.

The *change* in total profits as a result of introducing international trade flows is the net result of four different effects, as indicated in figure 4.3:

- Area 1 K L, which is the part of the initial monopoly profits that is unaffected by the new entrant

- Area 2 E F, which is an increase in initial monopoly profits resulting from a larger sales volume reducing average costs

- Area 3 F G, which is an increase in profits resulting from sales to the export market

[4] This is a standard assumption in many game-theoretic models of competition, known as the Cournot assumption (see chapter 12).

- Area 4 D [4] c, which is a decrease in initial monopoly profits due to increased competition.

Note that Area 3 is the export profits of the Foreign firm that has entered the Home market, but because the two countries are identical we know that the profits of the Home firm in the export market are also equal to Area 3. The net effect of the increased competition must be a reduction in total profits, as the Home firm was initially a profit-maximizing monopolist. The consumers in both countries gain from this increased competition by being able to purchase more goods at a lower price. The net welfare effect for the two countries under these circumstances is positive as the consumers' gain is larger than the domestic firm's loss.

In the final equilibrium, total sales in the Home market are higher and the price is lower than in the situation of a monopoly. At this point, we have a very simple explanation for intra-industry trade (see box 4.2 for two examples of alternative explanations). Both firms have an incentive to enter each other's market. Each individual firm thinks that it can consolidate profits in the Home market and gain some extra profits in the Foreign market. However, both firms are identical and use the same kind of reasoning, and both will enter the other market. The result is not only more competition, but also trade in similar (in this case, identical) final goods. In chapter 10, we shall discuss the consequences of imperfect competition for trade policy, where we will emphasize that these consequences are in general different from those under perfect competition.

To facilitate the analysis above we have assumed that the entrant takes the sales of the incumbent firm as given. As a rule of thumb, a firm could assume this, but most firms continuously look for opportunities to increase profits. The question then becomes if the assumption of given market behaviour is correct. The answer is: no. The incumbent firm is suddenly confronted with foreign competition in its domestic market and will almost surely reconsider its market position in the face of this new competition. How this affects the final market outcome is explained in the appendix 4A (p. 120) using the concept of 'reaction curves', indicating how a firm changes its behaviour in response to a change in its opponent's behaviour. If firms repeatedly reconsider their position given the (changed) behaviour of the other firm, this will influence the final market equilibrium. We shall return to this issue, and to the consequences for trade policy, in chapter 10. Moreover, in chapter 12, we shall discuss related concepts from the game theory of competition. For now, it suffices to conclude that opening up markets to international competition reduces the monopoly power of domestic firms, lowers prices and stimulates sales. Although this is good news for consumers, it is not necessarily good news for the firms active in those markets, compared to the pre-trade situation.

Box 4.2 Alternative explanations for intra-industry trade

Most explanations of intra-industry trade involve analyses of imperfect competition. Some other straightforward explanations, of which we give two here, are also possible:

• First, climate differences can potentially explain intra-industry trade. An example might clarify this. Suppose that a northern hemisphere country and a southern hemisphere country are able to grow oranges during the summer. Since summer in the two hemispheres occurs at different points in time, this could lead to intra-industry trade in our statistics: the two countries are both exporters and importers of oranges, but at different times during a year.

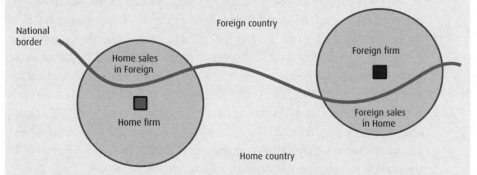

Figure 4.4 Intra-industry trade as a result of transportation costs

• Second, transportation costs may explain intra-industry trade. This is illustrated in figure 4.4. As a result of the costly transportation of their goods, the two firms in figure 4.4, the Home firm and the Foreign firm, have a limited market area within which they can sell their goods. Beyond that market area, transportation costs are simply too high. This is indicated by the circles in figure 4.4. The market areas cross the national border, indicated by the solid line. Assuming that the two firms sell identical products, it is clear that some consumers in the Foreign market can purchase the good only by buying from the Home firm as there is no domestic supplier within reach of their demand. Similarly, some consumers in the Home market can purchase the good only from the Foreign firm. In our trade statistics, this *mutual bilateral trade* is recorded as intra-industry trade.

In chapter 5, we shall analyse the role of transportation costs further.

4.4 Strategic interaction between firms: the Airbus–Boeing example

The imperfect competition model is an important tool in the analysis of a wide array of issues in international trade. In chapter 12, for example, we shall briefly discuss the example of dumping. In box 4.3, we introduce the case of Fuji and Kodak, as an example of the way in which this type of logic is used in the domain of international business to deepen our understanding of competition among multinationals. In this section we shall show how the imperfect competition model can give an insight into one of the potential roles of the government regarding market intervention, a key issue in the international economics literature.

By taking another look at figure 4.3, we can show how government support can potentially have a role to play. Suppose the Home government subsidizes the production of the commodity in such a way that the marginal costs curve shifts downwards by giving a subsidy for each unit of sales. The implications are straightforward. Production increases, the profit-maximizing market price decreases and the profits of the firm increase. In this situation, it becomes more difficult for a Foreign potential rival to enter the market and compete with the Home firm. As a result of the lower average costs (due to a larger sales volume), the Home producer can undercut its rival and drive the Foreign firm out of the market. A subsidy can thus be used, or misused, to influence the market outcome. This opens the door to lobbyists for government support for specific industries, on the basis of appealing to the general interest rather than the interests of the firm(s) the lobbyists represent. Table 4.2 drives this argument to its extreme using the Airbus–Boeing example of strategic interaction in the market for wide-body aircraft.

Table 4.2 makes the following assumptions. Each firm alone can make a profit in the market. So, for example, if Boeing produces a wide-body aircraft and Airbus does not enter the market, Boeing will make a profit and Airbus will not (but Airbus will also not make a loss). This situation is indicated in table 4.2 by (profit, 0): Boeing makes a profit and Airbus earns 0. The same holds if Airbus has the market for itself, as indicated by (0, profit) in table 4.2. If both firms enter the market, they will both incur a loss. Sales per firm are not high enough to cover the huge fixed costs that characterize the wide-body aircraft industry. This is indicated by (loss, loss) in table 4.2. Finally, both firms may decide not to enter the market in which case both earn nothing, as indicated in the table by (0, 0).

Now suppose that the EU decides to give a subsidy to Airbus large enough to cover potential losses. This has two effects: (i) the subsidy ensures positive profits for Airbus and (ii) the subsidy deters Boeing from entering the market. Table 4.3 gives the strategic pay-off matrix for the market for wide-body aircraft after Airbus has received a subsidy from the EU. It shows that, irrespective of Boeing's strategy,

Box 4.3 Imperfect competition in international business: Fuji versus Kodak[a]

As noted in the introduction to this chapter, the international business field shares the interest of international economics in imperfect competition. In chapter 12, we shall provide a number of examples. For now, it suffices to briefly discuss the case of duopolistic competition between Fuji and Kodak in Japan and the USA. Both firms are active in the global market for photography films, and both firms have been heavily involved in American–Japanese trade disputes. From 1983 to 1995, Kodak experienced a major decline in market share in Japan. This led Kodak to make accusations of a Fuji–MITI alliance or conspiracy (MITI is Japan's influential and powerful Ministry of International Trade and Industry). Kodak launched the official allegation that Fuji and MITI had conspired to exclude Kodak from Japanese distribution outlets. In late May 1995, the US Trade Representative Office (USTR) accepted Kodak's complaint. In response, MITI turned to the WTO, asking the latter to settle the dispute. Clearly, this is a nice example of how multinationals may use international trade politics in their competitive battle against foreign rivals.

The theory of imperfect competition can be used to analyse this case. In the context of the Fuji–Kodak dispute, a relevant subtheory is the mutual forbearance or multi-market collusion theory (see van Witteloostuijn and van Wegberg, 1992). This subtheory argues that a peaceful high-price–high-profit cartel is more likely to be sustainable if the firms involved meet one another in several markets, such as in different countries. Each of them then develops a small market share in their rival's home market as a disciplinary threat, called a 'hostage arrangement'. In Fuji's and Kodak's case, this would imply that Fuji should build a small market share in the USA and that Kodak should hold a similar small market share in Japan. In so doing, both duopolists could credibly threaten to punish their rival – for example if the latter launched a price war in its rival's home market – not only in its export market, but also at home. This mutual threat of retaliation in two markets disciplines both firms, helping them to keep prices and profits high. In this way, Fuji and Kodak were implicitly able to uphold a peaceful cartel type of arrangement, to their mutual benefit.

Such a multi-market collusion equilibrium may collapse if one of the oligopolists thinks that it is strong enough to win a competitive battle, at home and abroad. In the Fuji–Kodak case, Fuji did precisely that, correctly assuming that it could benefit from competitive advantages in such areas as distribution, innovation, manufacturing and marketing. Consequently, Kodak started to lose market share. If this interpretation holds true, then Kodak's market share is not so much the result of Fuji's anti-competitive behaviour (by conspiring with MITI), as claimed by Kodak, but quite the opposite: rather, Fuji destroyed the anti-competitive two-market collusion equilibrium by launching a really competitive battle. In the end, the WTO agreed with the Fuji–MITI interpretation, and declared that Fuji's behaviour was legal.

[a] Adapted from Tsurumi and Tsurumi (1999).

Table 4.2 Airbus–Boeing strategic interaction pay-off matrix[a]

(Boeing pay-off, Airbus pay-off)		Airbus strategy	
		Produce	Do not produce
Boeing strategy	Produce	(loss, loss)	(profit, 0)
	Do not produce	(0, profit)	(0, 0)

[a] In chapter 12, we shall explain the pay-off matrix tool in greater detail.

Table 4.3 Strategic interaction pay-off matrix after Airbus subsidy

(Boeing pay-off, Airbus pay-off)		Airbus strategy	
		Produce	Do not produce
Boeing strategy	Produce	(loss, profit)	(profit, 0)
	Do not produce	(0, large profit)	(0, 0)

it is optimal for Airbus to enter the market, as it will always make a profit. This, in turn, ensures that Boeing will not enter the market, thus further increasing Airbus' profits.

In fact, this example has some empirical support. In the early 1970s, Airbus started production of aircraft with significant government support. From the start, this created tension between the USA and the EU. As a result of the government subsidies, Airbus was able to offer discounts to potential buyers of its aircraft in the mid-1980s; after Air India cancelled an order for Boeing 757s, the US government threatened to raise a countervailing duty against Airbus unless government subsidies were cut. In the end, these tensions resulted in an agreement in 1992 which limited government subsidies to aircraft producers. The agreement allows for only a maximum of 33 per cent direct and indirect (military) subsidy on development costs. Production subsidies are no longer allowed. The agreement also restricts domestic aircraft producers from offering financing to airlines. The agreement explicitly states rules for revealing subsidies, interest rates and other conditions that might affect the competitive position of aircraft producers.

The most interesting question is, of course, how the agreement has affected the market. There is some empirical evidence that the agreement has not had a noticeable impact on relative prices, which implies that the relative competitive position of the two producers has not changed substantially. However, there is also some evidence that after the reduction of subsidies in 1992 overall prices went up, which is to be expected because the sales volume fell after subsidies were cut. The most recent controversy is related to the new super jumbo produced by Airbus, the A-380, which is expected to fly in 2006 and which was first shown to the public at large in January 2005. This will be the first super plane that will compete with the well-known Boeing 747, once referred to by the weekly magazine *The Economist* (1997) as 'a licence to print money.' One-third of an estimated US $12 billion developments costs are covered by the governments of France, Germany and the UK. The USA keeps an eye on European subsidies and has already warned the European governments that the financing of the new super jumbo might violate the 1992 agreement. There is some suspicion that Airbus is selling the A-380 at large discounts; in the long run, this is possible only if production subsidies are given, which is not allowed. The EU reacted promptly by asking for more information on military and NASA contracts for Boeing, to find out whether or not these contracts implied some form of local subsidy. Boeing has claimed that the total market for super jumbos is too small for both planes. This appears to bring us right into the world described in tables 4.2 and 4.3.

4.5 Monopolistic competition

In the model of section 4.4, we analysed a situation in which both firms were initially monopolists in their home markets, producing identical goods. International trade changed this situation into a duopoly, which reduced the market power of both firms in both markets. The assumption that firms produce identical goods is a very strong one, which almost never holds in practice. A different framework, that of *monopolistic competition*, does not rely on the assumption of identical goods, and thus takes us a step closer to most actual situations. The central idea is simple and illustrated in figure 4.5. Two countries, *A* and *B*, each produce many varieties of a single product, such as different types of cars or different varieties of beer. In essence, each sector produces many varieties of specific products and consumers love to have a choice between different varieties: once a new variety becomes available, there is always a market for this new product as it caters to the needs of a specific *clièntele*. This is

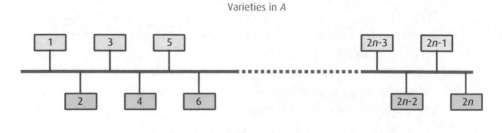

Varieties in *A*

Varieties in *B*

Figure 4.5 The varieties approach of monopolistic competition

known as the 'love-of-variety' effect. One could say a car is just a car, but most car manufacturers offer a wide choice of models and most consumers prefer to have the opportunity to choose from a wide array of varieties. On the one hand, each car manufacturer has monopoly power in its own market in the sense that it offers a unique variety. On the other hand, it faces competition from other car manufacturers who sell similar, though slightly different, products.

Each variety of a car has a unique number in figure 4.5. Both countries produce n varieties. The resources of each country are not large enough to produce the whole range of varieties, indicated by letting country A produce all odd varieties and B all even varieties. The gap between each variety indicates that product characteristics are not the same. Some consumers will find their ideal variety in this market, while others have to look for product varieties that are as close as possible to their preferences. Assume that consumers are evenly distributed over a horizontal line which indicates the market area of a specific variety. We could call this line the 'product-characteristics' line. Consumers in A who prefer variety 3 can buy their ideal variety from the producer of variety 3, but consumers between, say, varieties 1 and 5 have to choose to buy either variety 1, 3, or 5, whichever product has characteristics that serve them best, given the prices to be paid for each product. This may not be their ideal variety, but they always look for the closest alternative – that is, close to their ideal product. This set-up implies that if the gap between each pair of neighbouring varieties is the same and if they all have the same price, all producers will serve exactly the same amount of consumers. Consumers in country B face similar choices regarding the even varieties. How does a firm in such a market behave?

The situation of a typical firm in this market is illustrated in figure 4.6 for the monopolistic competition equilibrium, which is based on three assumptions:

1. The number of sellers is sufficiently large so that each firm takes the behaviour of other firms as given
2. Products are heterogeneous; buyers have preferences for all types of products
3. There is free entry and exit of firms into and out of this market.

The monopolistic elements are all those characteristics that distinguish a product from another product and give the firm some market power. The demand curve is downward-sloping, because a firm can increase its market share by reducing its price. Some consumers who were previously buying adjacent varieties now turn to this producer as a result of the price reduction. The large number of firms in the market and the possibility of free entry and exit of firms provide the competitive elements.

Figure 4.6 represents the market demand and cost conditions for a representative firm. Each firm assumes that its competitors do not react if it lowers its price. The location of the demand curve facing the producer of a variety depends on the pricing behaviour of all other producers, and in particular of the adjacent producers of close

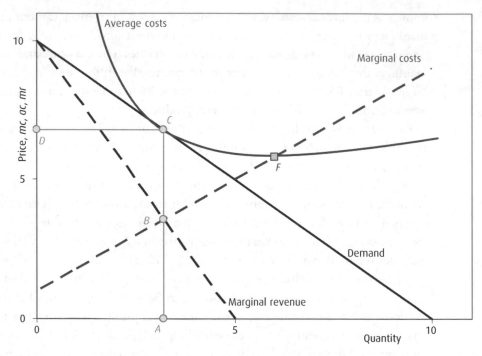

Figure 4.6 Monopolistic competition, demand and costs

substitutes. If they decide to reduce their price, the demand curve will shift down-wards. New firms entering the market will also shift the demand curve downwards because a number of customers will abandon this firm to purchase from the new firm. Similarly, the demand curve will shift upwards if other firms exit the market, thereby increasing the customer base for this firm. The differences with perfect competition and monopoly are clear. In the case of perfect competition, the demand curve will be a horizontal line and there is no need to consider the actions of other firms. In the case of a monopoly, the firm will be faced with a downward-sloping demand curve, but the firm does not have to take the actions of other firms into account, because there are no other firms.

Figure 4.6 depicts the monopolistic competition outcome of this process. The firm behaves as a monopolist in its market segment by equating marginal cost and marginal revenue at point B, leading to price D and quantity A. However, as indicated by the tangency of the average cost curve to the demand curve at point C for the production quantity A, the price the firm charges is exactly equal to the average costs of production. The firm therefore does not make (excess) profits. This aspect of the monopolistic competition equilibrium is caused by the competitive pressure of other firms in similar market segments in combination with the assumption that firms can freely enter and exit the market.[5] If the representative firm made a profit, other firms would enter the market until these profits disappeared. Similarly, if the representative firm would make a loss, some firms would leave the market, which would increase the market share for the remaining firms, which in turn would allow them to reduce their loss. This process continues until the loss disappears. In equilibrium, therefore, the representative firm makes zero profits, as illustrated in figure 4.6.

The situation illustrated in figure 4.6 is Chamberlin's (1933) famous tangency solution of monopolistic competition. In the situation depicted in figure 4.6, there is a difference between equilibrium average costs (at point C) and minimum average costs (at point F).[6] This implies that there are unexploited economies of scale, which raises the question whether this is a waste of resources.[7] The answer to this question is both yes and no: yes, in the sense that indeed there is excess capacity; and no, in the sense that product differentiation introduces variety and this expands the extent of consumer choices, and thereby welfare.

4.6 Trade with monopolistic competition

What happens in the monopolistic competition model if it becomes possible for the two countries to engage in international trade? Several changes may occur simultaneously, but the most important thing to remember is that consumers love variety – that is, they always prefer more varieties of a good to fewer. Since consumers in country A after international trade will have access to varieties produced both at home and abroad, the number of varieties to choose from, and thus their welfare level, will increase. In the simplest version of the model, the total number of varieties remains the same ($2n$). Each producer, both at home and abroad, will lose half of its domestic sales to foreign competitors, since those domestic consumers can now import a variety that serves their needs better than locally produced varieties. At the same time, each producer will gain half of its previous sales by entering the foreign market and selling to foreign consumers. In this case, therefore, figure 4.6 still represents the monopolistic competition equilibrium, but total sales now consist of domestic sales and exports in equal amounts. Obviously, this gives rise to two-way trade in similar products (intra-industry trade) and gains from trade through the increase in the number of varieties to choose from. In box 4.4, we compare this chapter's intra-industry trade models with the inter-industry ones in chapter 3.

[5] In fact, the free entry assumption (or, to be precise, the costless exit one) is sufficient, as is clear from IO's perfect contestability theory (Baumol, Panzar and Willig, 1982).

[6] Herein lies a difference with the average cost curve of figures 4.2 and 4.3, where the average costs continue to fall as production expands.

[7] In this simplified treatment, we do not distinguish between short-run and long-run (average) cost curves.

Box 4.4 Models compared

At this point, the question may arise as to how the models discussed in this chapter differ from those in chapter 3. The essence of the models discussed in this chapter is that trade arises in *similar or identical commodities*, between *similar or identical countries*. Countries are identical in this chapter, and there are no productivity or endowment differences in the production processes between firms. In the Ricardo or Heckscher–Ohlin model, the lack of these differences implies that there is no reason to trade whatsoever.

Furthermore, the assumption of increasing versus constant returns to scale is essential. Internal increasing returns to scale imply imperfect competition, which makes positive profits possible. This gives an incentive for foreign firms to enter this market, leading to intra-industry trade, as we illustrated in the main text. In case of monopolistic competition, the assumption of increasing returns to scale is responsible for the fact that each variety is produced only by a single firm because a large firm could always undercut the price of a small firm as it has lower unit costs following from its larger scale of production. With constant returns to scale and perfect competition, the assumptions of identical firms and identical countries do not give rise to an underlying reason to engage in international trade.

Under more general circumstances, the increase in the number of available varieties may attract new customers. Customers that initially found the distance between their preferred variety and what the market had to offer too large and did not enter this market, may now enter because a wider range of products is available. Simultaneously, the entry of the new (foreign) firms increases competition between suppliers, making the demand curve faced by an individual supplier more elastic[8] as each firm faces closer substitutes to the product it supplies. The change in the monopolistic competition equilibrium under these circumstances is illustrated in figure 4.7.

The pre-trade equilibrium in figure 4.7 is determined by the equality of pre-trade marginal revenue and marginal cost at point B, leading to price D, quantity supplied A and equality of price and average costs at point C. Similarly, the post-trade equilibrium is determined by the equality of post-trade marginal revenue and marginal cost at point B', leading to price D', quantity supplied A' and equality of price and average costs at point C'. Figure 4.7 illustrates the following sequence of events:

• As a result of increased competition, demand has become more elastic after trade
• Other things equal, this lowers the price the firm charges and leads to a loss

---

[8] Higher elasticity implies, in our context, that consumers will decrease (increase) demand for firm x's product more in response to a price increase (cut) by this firm x.

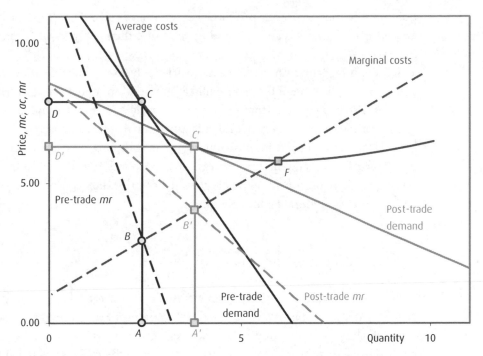

Figure 4.7 *Monopolistic competition and foreign trade pressure, demand and costs*

- The loss drives some firms out of the market and increases demand for the remaining firms, which continues until zero profits are reached.
- In the trade equilibrium, the remaining firms in the market produce a larger quantity, which allows them better to exploit economies of scale (lower average costs).
- In the trade equilibrium, consumers benefit from both lower prices (facilitated by the better exploitation of economies of scale) and from a larger range of varieties to choose from (typically, the number of firms in the trade equilibrium will be somewhere between n and $2n$).
- In the trade equilibrium, the two countries engage in two-way trade in similar products (intra-industry trade).

What did the model of monopolistic competition add to the conclusions derived in section 4.4?

- First, we have another elegant explanation for intra-industry trade flows. Firms no longer have to sell identical products, but can offer close substitutes to consumers. This adds some reality to the model.
- Second, the number of suppliers is large but limited. This is also a characteristic that can be observed in reality. A disadvantage of the model of monopolistic competition is that it assumes that varieties are different from a consumers's utility

point of view, but not from a producer's cost point of view. This allows us to draw graphs as in figures 4.6 and 4.7, and assume that they apply to all firms in the market.

- Third, consumers love variety: once new varieties become available, they will buy them. The implication of the monopolistic competition model is that consumers will now also buy varieties from foreign suppliers, leading to intra-industry trade.
- Fourth, producers will experience more competition from foreign suppliers, implying that the demand curve for individual suppliers becomes more elastic and shifts downward. In the trade equilibrium, each firm produces a larger output (now also serving foreign consumers) and charges a lower price due to more competition and better exploitation of scale economies.

4.7 Empirical support for intra-industry trade

At a basic level, it seems relatively straightforward to test models predicting intra-industry trade. In empirical work, however, some problems easily arise. Box 4.2 (p. 106) highlights, for example, the fact that trade in similar products can be explained by factors other than those that characterize the models discussed in this chapter. Grubel and Lloyd (1975) themselves pointed out that goods that are homogeneous according to basic characteristics can be differentiated by location or time – as box 4.2 highlighted. Others argue that much of what we measure as intra-industry trade is simply a matter of aggregation. As Davis and Weinstein (2002: 373) argue:

much of what we call intra-industry trade is simply a data problem that reflects the failure of our industrial classification system to capture the fact that very different goods are being lumped together.

Notwithstanding such problems, the Grubel–Lloyd (1975) study has stimulated empirical research in an attempt to explain intra-industry trade. Many studies somehow link intuitive plausible variables with some measure of intra-industry trade, such as the Grubel–Lloyd index. One expects that intra-industry trade between two countries will be high if:
- incomes *per capita* are high
- differences in level of development (as measured by differences in *per capita* GDP) are low
- the average of the countries' GDP is high.
These variables are related to the monopolistic competition model. Implicitly, it is assumed that if the incomes *per capita* of countries are high, and basic needs are fulfilled, consumers will spend a relatively large share on sophisticated manufactured

goods, such as MP3 players of various brands. If countries differ in development or income levels, it is expected that the respective consumers will have different tastes.

Similarly, intra-industry trade between two countries will also be high if:
- barriers to trade are low
- pairs of countries share a common border or language
- countries are part of some type of a preferential trade agreement (PTA).

All these variables stimulate trade flows between nations. The central idea of this type of variable is that if barriers to trade are high, in either a physical or a cultural sense, international trade will be discouraged. This, of course, holds not only for intra-industry trade, but also for trade in general.

Finally, intra-industry trade will also be relatively high if:
- the level of product differentiation within sectors is high
- scale economies are present
- transaction costs are low
- trade barriers for the industry are low.

These variables are related to *sector characteristics*, as revealed by the models discussed above.

On the basis of the above associations there have been many empirical studies relating some proxy of the variables mentioned above to a measure of intra-industry trade. Although these studies produce interesting results, generally in broad support of the *a priori* expectations, there are also some important problems. Leamer and Levinsohn (1995) focus on the following two:
- First, it is often not clear which variables to include and which variables to exclude. This raises the possibility that the study will reduce to a 'data-mining' exercise until some plausible specification has been found. Ideally, however, one would like to be guided by theory on which variables to include. Even allowing for the data-mining procedure, the share of the variance explained by these empirical studies is typically quite low.
- Second, it is often difficult to find proxies for variables that are important in theory. Take, for example, economies of scale. Ideally, based on the models described here, one would like to have information on the fixed costs of investments. As these are generally not available, researchers have to use other variables, such as industry concentration indices, to gain some indication as to whether or not imperfect competition prevails.

These issues and some other standard econometric problems stimulated the demand for more formal tests of the theories discussed in this chapter. Helpman (1987) was the first explicitly to derive a testable equation to link intra-industry trade to the model of monopolistic competition. It can be shown that for any pair of countries intra-industry trade can be explained by the following testable equation

Table 4.4 Country similarity and intra-industry trade

Measure of GDP	OECD countries		Non-OECD countries	
	GDP (PWT)[a]	GDP (IFS)[b]	GDP (PWT)	GDP (IFS)
Ln (dispersion)	1.57	0.89	−0.96	0.40
(standard error)	(0.11)	(0.06)	(0.99)	(0.24)
Ln($s^i + s^j$)	1.30	0.47	1.98	0.99
(standard error)	(0.13)	(0.06)	(0.95)	(0.10)
R^2	0.61	0.45	0.02	0.14
No. of observations	1820	1820	1320	1320

[a] PWT = Penn World Tables.
[b] IFS = *International Financial Statistics.*
  Source: Feenstra (2004).

(see appendix 4B, p. 124)

$$\ln \left(\frac{X^{ij} + X^{ji}}{Y^i + Y^j} \right)_t = \alpha_{ij} + \gamma \ln \left(s_t^i + s_t^j \right) + \beta \ln \left(\text{dispersion}_t^{ij} \right)$$

$$\text{dispersion}^{ij} \equiv 1 - [Y^i / (Y^i + Y^j)]^2 - [Y^j / (Y^i + Y^j)]^2$$

(4.2)

where X^{ij} is exports from country i to country j, Y^i is income in country i, s^i is country i's share in world GDP and a subindex t denotes time. In theory, the coefficients γ and β to be estimated should be equal to unity. The second term on the right-hand side of (4.2) indicates that intra-industry trade is larger among relatively large countries. The third term on the right-hand side of (4.2) shows the extent to which countries are similar in size. In fact, 'dispersion' reaches its maximum (of 0.5) if the countries have exactly the same size. In all other cases, it is smaller. So the more equal countries are, the higher the level of intra-industry trade.

Table 4.4 summarizes results from testing (4.2). A few remarks are in order. Income as measured by GDP should be converted into a single currency, usually the American dollar. One can convert all GDPs using PPP exchange rates as is done in the Penn World Tables (PWT), which is a very popular source for data, or one can use nominal exchange rates as is done in the International Financial Statistics (IFS) of the International Monetary Fund (IMF). Using PPP exchange rates is expected to give more structural results, because they are less susceptible to short-run exchange rate fluctuations. Table 4.4 gives estimates for both concepts of GDP. We conclude from table 4.4 that for OECD countries the signs of the variables are positive and significantly different from zero. Note, however, that the coefficients are different from unity, contrary to what theory would imply. For the non-OECD countries, the results are quite different. The coefficient with respect to dispersion is negative, which is in contrast with the model as formulated by Helpman (1987). This is to be expected because the model assumes that *all* trade is intra-industry trade, which is not an accurate description of trade between countries, particularly regarding basic agricultural goods or low-skilled labour-intensive products, where Ricardian or Heckscher–Ohlin explanations are likely to be more relevant. Nonetheless, an empirical formulation derived from a model consistent with monopolistic competition can give a reasonably accurate description of trade between OECD countries. This seems to indicate that the monopolistic competition model has some relevance in describing actual trade flows.

4.8 Conclusions

The models based on perfect competition and constant returns to scale described in chapter 3, where labour productivity differences (Ricardo) or factor endowment differences (Heckscher–Ohlin) are the driving force of international inter-industry trade flows, are not able to explain the phenomenon of intra-industry trade – that is, the simultaneous import and export of similar types of goods and services between countries. Instead, these models ensure that international competition results in (partial) specialization of countries in the production of those goods and services for which the country has a comparative advantage. The resulting trade is inter-industry trade. This contrasts sharply with ongoing empirical research, which suggests that a substantial part of international trade flows, especially of trade flows between rich countries, is of an intra-industry trade nature. This chapter has discussed several models based on imperfect competition and increasing returns that can help to explain intra-industry trade. Competitive pressure by foreign firms and strategic interaction may entice companies to engage in mutual trade flows of identical homogeneous products. Usually, increased competition leads to lower mark-ups over marginal costs, lower prices, larger volumes and welfare gains for consumers, even if two countries are identical in all aspects. Moreover, firms can engage in international trade of similar, but not identical, products, where international trade permits better use of economies of scale, lower prices and access to a larger number of varieties.

This chapter's focus on intra-industry trade and competitive advantage is highly complementary with the literature in international business. The core of the international business literature focuses on MNEs, particularly in the context of imperfect intra-industry competition, investigating why some multinationals are able to outperform others. In this context, competitive advantage is a key concept indeed. In a setting of intra-industry trade, therefore, international business (dealing with firm-level competition) and international economics (focusing on country-level trade) share a common interest. In the area of intra-industry trade, it is the firms that compete, not the countries (see chapter 3's discussion of the notions of comparative versus competitive advantage). Of course, the natural follow-up question is where firm-level competitive advantages come from. It is here where international business has much to offer. By way of illustration, box 4.5 provides some examples, which also relate to the question posed in chapter 3 as to why multinationals exist in the first place.

Box 4.5 Competitive advantage and MNEs

The sources of competitive advantage are manifold. It may be that a firm has better access to an essential raw material, is better able to come up with innovations, has developed superior marketing skills, has fine-tuned cost-reduction processes, etc. In many cases, it is a combination of different sources that produces a competitive advantage, also helping it to be sustainable. The central theory dealing with this issue is the so-called resource-based view of the firm (Wernerfelt, 1984), arguing that sustainable competitive advantages must be built on resources that are valuable, rare, difficult to imitate and costly to circumvent (Maijoor and van Witteloostuijn, 1996). In addressing the question 'why do multinationals exist in the first place?', international business studies offer a series of arguments as to why multinationals can benefit from the competitive advantages that explain their *raison d'être*.

Without any pretence of completeness, the following example may illustrate this line of argument. Multinationals may be able to be more innovative than their national counterparts by sourcing different areas of knowledge in different countries (e.g. Frost, 2001). That is, *knowledge spillovers* across a multinational's foreign subsidiaries are instrumental in technological innovation. As a result of, for example, the multinational's formal organization structure, internal informal relations and direct access to the richness of cultural diversity, it is better able to transfer knowledge across national borders than a set of independent domestic firms that engage in market transactions. More broadly, this is referred to in the international business literature as *competence building* within the multinational enterprise (e.g. Rugman and Verbeke, 2001), producing subsidiary-specific advantages that are combined at the level of the multinational into something that is valuable, rare, difficult to imitate and costly to circumvent – that is, into a sustainable competitive advantage *vis-à-vis* national companies.

Appendix 4A: strategic interaction – reaction curves

Assume that the home market is served by two firms: the former monopolist and the new foreign firm. The market form changes to a so-called oligopoly. If there are just two firms, say a firm A (subindex A) and a firm B (subindex B), the market is called a *duopoly.* This was analysed by Augustin Cournot in the nineteenth century (in 1838). Cournot takes the analysis of the main text as a starting point and investigates whether or not a final market equilibrium exists in which neither firm has an incentive to change its behaviour, given the behaviour of its competitor. He assumed that the two firms produced identical goods, such that there was only one market demand curve, and that both firms maximized their profits, *given* the demand curve and the output level of their opponent. Determining the equilibrium production levels, and associated price level, is more involved than in the case of a monopoly. We shall derive the equilibrium using some algebra, but one can understand the logic of the argument without going through all of the equations.

Let p be the market price and $q = q_A + q_B$ be the total output in the market. We focus on the problem for firm A. (Similar observations hold for firm B). The basic problem for firm A is quite similar to the problem facing a monopolist. Suppose that c is the marginal cost of production. Given the linear market demand $p = a - bq$ and the fact that total output is the sum of the outputs of firms A and B, it follows that firm A's profits π_A depend on the output level of both firms as follows[9]

$$\pi_A = (p - c)q_A = [(a - c) - b(q_A + q_B)]\, q_A \tag{4A.1}$$

Observe that (as illustrated in figure 4A.1):

- Given the output level q_{B0} of firm B, firm A maximizes profits π_A through a suitable choice of its output level – say, at q_{A0}
- If firm B changes its production level from q_{B0} to q_{B1}, then firm A's profit-maximization problem is affected, which leads to a *different* optimal choice of its output level – say, q_{A1}
- In general, therefore, each different output level of firm B leads to a different optimal output level for firm A.

The collection of all optimal output responses by firm A to firm B's output level is called firm A's *reaction curve.* In fact, we have now entered into the domain of game theory, which has figured prominently in modern industrial organization since the 1970s (see chapter 12). The reaction curve can simply be derived by maximizing the profits given in (4A.1) through a suitable choice of output of firm A

$$\frac{\partial \pi_A}{\partial q_A} = 0 \Rightarrow q_A = \frac{a - c}{2b} - \frac{1}{2}q_B \tag{4A.2}$$

- First, given that firm B produces q_{B0} units of goods, firm A's optimal output choice must determine the optimal output combination on the dashed horizontal line generated by point q_{B0} in figure 4A.1. Since firm A maximizes its profits, this

---

[9] Note that we abstract from fixed costs. Including fixed costs would unnecessarily complicate the analysis without affecting the main results.

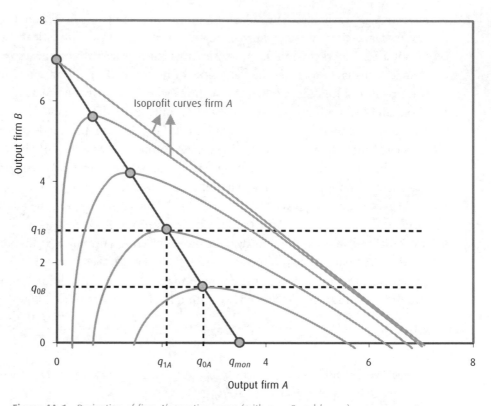

Figure 4A.1   Derivation of firm *A*'s reaction curve (with $a = 8$ and $b = c$)

dashed line must be tangent to one of its isoprofit curves, some of which are also drawn in figure 4A.1. The optimal production level for firm *A*, given that firm *B* produces q_{B0}, is therefore equal to q_{A0}.

- Second, if firm *B* increases its output level from q_{B0} to q_{B1}, this reduces the price level in the market and hence firm *A*'s profitability. Consequently, firm *A*'s best (i.e. profit-maximizing) reply is then a reduction in output, from q_{A0} to q_{A1}.
- Third, similar reactions by firm *A* to changes in the output level of firm *B* are given by the dots in figure 4A.1. Connecting all such dots gives the reaction curve of the firm.
- Fourth, note that if the output level of firm *B* is equal to zero, firm *A*'s problem reduces to that of a monopolist. Clearly, this leads to the maximum attainable profit level for firm *A*, at point q_{mon} in figure 4A.1. This is the monopoly situation that was the starting point in the analysis of the main text.

Firm *B* faces a similar problem to firm *A*. This means that, taking the output level q_A as given, firm *B* will derive its optimal (profit-maximizing) output level q_B. This was the situation described in the main text: given the behaviour of *A*, firm *B* enters the market. In the same fashion as with *A*'s reaction curve, we can derive *B*'s reaction

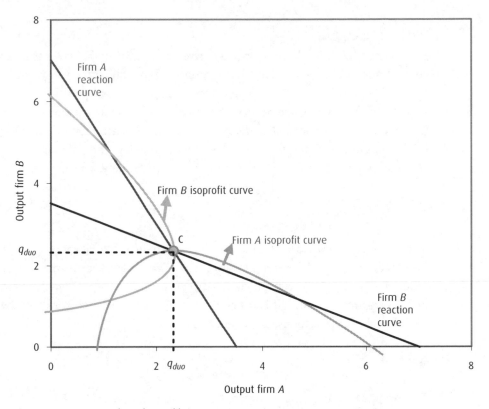

Figure 4A.2   Cournot duopoly equilibrium

curve. This is illustrated in figure 4A.2, which also includes A's reaction curve and an isoprofit curve for each firm. Note that the isoprofit curve for firm B is vertical at the point of intersection with its reaction curve because firm B maximizes its profits at that point. The market equilibrium is reached at the point of intersection of the two reaction curves, as indicated by point C in figure 4A.2, because this is the only point at which firm A maximizes its profits given the output level of firm B, while simultaneously firm B maximizes its profits given the output level of firm A. The equilibrium is at the intersection of the two reaction curves (assuming $a > c$)

$$q_A = q_B = \frac{a - c}{3b}; \quad p_{duo} = \frac{a + 2c}{3} < \frac{a + c}{2} = p_{mon} \tag{4A.3}$$

Note that the duopoly price is *lower* than the monopoly price, and that the duopoly output level, $2q_{duo}$, is higher than the monopoly output level. Apparently, more competition, as measured by an increase in the number of firms, leads to a lower price level.

Appendix 4B: Derivation of the Helpman equation[10]

It turns out that it is relatively easy to derive (4.2) in the main text. Assume that all countries are identical and that (due to economies of scale) each variety of a good is produced by a single country. The production processes of all goods are identical, so that in the absence of trade barriers the prices of all varieties are the same. To make notation simple, we normalize these to unity. As all consumers buy this variety, it is exported in identical quantities to all other countries. The GDP of a country i is equal to the sum the value of production y_k^i of each variety, k, as in (4B.1)

$$Y^i = \sum_{k=1}^N y_k^i \tag{4B.1}$$

The export X_k^{ij} from country i to j of product k is equal to $s^j y_k^i$, where $s^j = Y^j / Y^w$, as exports to a country are determined by the size of a country, because there are no price differences and because consumers have the same preferences. The only remaining differences are therefore different country sizes. Total exports from country i to j (which is the same as total exports of country j to i) is

$$X^{ij} = \sum_k X_k^{ij} = s^j \sum_k y_k^i = s^j Y^i = \frac{Y^j Y^i}{Y^w} = s^i Y^j = s^i s^j Y^w = X^{ji} \tag{4B.2}$$

This implies that total trade between the two countries equals $X^{ij} + X^{ji} = 2s^i s^j Y^w$, which can be written as the value of trade in total GDP of both countries

$$\frac{X^{ij} + X^{ji}}{Y^i + Y^j} = 2 \left(\frac{Y^i}{Y^i + Y^j} \right) \left(\frac{Y^j}{Y^i + Y^j} \right) \left[\frac{Y^i + Y^j}{Y^w} \right] \tag{4B.3}$$

Since the first two terms in parentheses on the right-hand side of (4B.3) sum to 1, squaring this equation gives (4B.4), which can be written as the testable equation (4.2) in the main text

$$\ln \left(\frac{X^{ij} + X^{ji}}{Y^i + Y^j} \right) = \ln \left(s^i + s^j \right) + \ln \left[1 - \left(\frac{Y^i}{Y^i + Y^j} \right)^2 - \left(\frac{Y^j}{Y^i + Y^j} \right)^2 \right] \tag{4B.4}$$

---

[10] See Feenstra (2004).

Firms, location and agglomeration

KEYWORDS

location of firms	structure of trade	agglomeration
transportation costs	geographical economics	multinational firms
trade and distance	multiple equilibria	fragmentation

5.1 Introduction

It is an important stylized fact in economic geography that economic activity is not evenly spread across space. This holds for all levels of aggregation – that is, at the global, national and regional level (see Hinloopen and van Marrewijk, 2005). On a global scale, for example, roughly 20 per cent of world GDP in 1998 was produced in the USA and about 20 per cent in Western Europe, whereas these regions combined contain only some 12 per cent of world population – very uneven indeed. It is well known that these distributions are characterized by *persistence* – that is, uneven distributions do not change rapidly. This does not mean that the distribution of economic activity does not change at all. In 1870, for example, Western Europe's share in world GDP was 34 per cent, while the share for the USA was only 9 per cent. Since then, the American economy has grown more rapidly than the European economy, partially in response to the increased mobility of capital and labour.

As explained in chapter 1, capital and labour mobility were facilitated by revolutionary developments in transport technology and by reductions in political barriers to trade. But why should reductions in barriers to trade result in agglomeration of economic activity in certain parts of the world? Why is economic activity not more evenly spread across the globe? This chapter studies the problem of the uneven geographical distribution of economic activity more closely. First, we illustrate the importance of *distance.* Even in today's increasingly globalized world, geographical distance is still very important, as are the economic consequences of transportation costs and other distance-related barriers to trade. We develop a simple model that incorporates familiar demand and supply relations, as well as transportation costs. This enables us to determine the location of economic activity in the presence of transportation costs. The main actor in this decision-making process is the MNE. We shall therefore focus on the location decision of multinational firms and the underlying forces for this location decision. Not surprisingly, transportation costs turn out to be an important factor in the decision to become a multinational firm. So, the analysis below takes chapters 3 and 4's observations on multinational behaviour one step further. In the current chapter, the primary perspective is international economics, with the exception of boxes 5.1–5.3, that illustrate complementary arguments from international business. More on the international business insights into the location decision of MNEs can be found in chapter 12.

5.2 Distance in economics

In chapter 1, we highlighted some aspects of the importance of distance for the world economy. In the post-Second World War period, the gradual reduction in trade barriers clearly stimulated the globalization process. It is tempting to conclude from the enormous progress in this respect achieved thus far that barriers to trade, and hence distance, are no longer important. Particularly in the light of the Internet revolution, in combination with the worldwide effort to reduce non-physical barriers to trade, one might argue that the importance of location deteriorated substantially in the late twentieth and early twenty-first centuries. This conclusion is wrong, though, as argued in box 5.1.

Box 5.1 The relevance of transportation costs

Many measures have been constructed over the years to quantify transportation costs, ranging from direct measures in terms of money to actual travel time. The most straightforward measure in international trade is the difference between the so-called CIF (cost, insurance, freight) and FOB (free on board) quotations of trade. *CIF* measures the value of imports at the point of entry in a country and covers the costs of carriage, insurance and freight. *FOB* measures value of the same commodities "free on board" – that is, the value, inclusive of all costs, of the merchandise in the exporting "port". The difference between these two values is a measure of the cost of getting an item from the exporting country to the importing country. However, this measure clearly under-estimates the actual transport costs associated with international trade, as commodities need to be transported to the exporting port, and subsequently from the importing port to the final destination.

The ratio $[(CIF/FOB)-1] \times 100$ represents the unit transport cost as a percentage of the FOB price and thus provides a measure of the transport cost *rate* on imports. Different goods have different transport costs. One expects, for example, that goods with high value added will have relatively low CIF/FOB ratios, whilst perishable and heavy goods (relative to value added) probably have higher ratios. This presumption is confirmed by Hummels (1999), who finds for the USA that the *ad valorem* freight rate is 7.6 per cent for food and live animals, but only 2.25 per cent for machinery and transport equipment. Table 5.1 gives some indication of this transport cost measure for various countries.

Table 5.1 CIF/FOB ratios, 1965–1990, per cent

Country	CIF/FOB ratio	Country	CIF/FOB ratio
Australia	10.3	New Zealand	11.5
Austria	4.1	Norway	2.7
Canada	2.7	Philippines	7.6
Denmark	4.5	Portugal	10.3
France	4.2	Singapore	6.1
West Germany	3.0	Spain	6.4
Greece	13.0	Sweden	3.5
Ireland	5.0	Switzerland	1.8
Italy	7.1	Thailand	11.0
Japan	9.0	UK	6.0
Netherlands	5.6	USA	4.9

Source: Radelet and Sachs (1998).

The differences in shipping costs can be explained by simply noting that countries located further away from major markets (such as New Zealand) face higher shipping costs, and whether or not countries are landlocked. For example, the landlocked developing countries (not shown in table 5.1) have on average 50 per cent higher transport costs than the coastal developing economies. Note also that products with very high transport costs are not even traded at all, and therefore do not show up in table 5.1. Contrary to popular opinion, Hummels shows that transport costs have *not* declined uniformly over time. He argues, in particular, that in the post-Second World War period the costs of ocean travel have increased whilst the costs of air transport have fallen. In addition, the costs of a distant travel have fallen relative to proximate transport.

For a final indication of the importance of transport costs, we can compare freight costs with other trade costs, such as tariffs. Davis (1998) finds that in the USA industry-level transport costs as a percentage of imports range from 1.9 per cent to 8.5 per cent of import values, with a mean of 4.8 per cent. Industry-level tariffs range from 0.5 per cent to 15.4 per cent, with a mean of 4.1 per cent. Transport costs as such, therefore, seem to be at least as important as policy-induced trade barriers.

Table 5.2 Regional trade pattern of Europe, 1860–1996, percentage of total export, import

	Europe	USA	South America	Asia	Africa	ROW
Export						
1860	67.5	9.1	7.7	10	3.2	2.5
1910	67.9	7.6	4.2	9.8	4.8	2.4
1996	76.2	7.2	2.1	10.7	2.5	1.3
Import						
1860	61	14.3	7.8	12.1	3.2	1.7
1910	60	14	8.2	10	4.5	3.4
1996	70.7	8.5	2.9	10.5	2.7	4.7

Note: ROW = Rest of the World.
Source: Baldwin and Martin (1999).

What does the presence of transport costs and other trade barriers mean for international trade flows? A simple back-of-the-envelope calculation is illuminating. Suppose the share of a country or region in world GDP is 10 per cent. If the world economy is completely integrated and firms of that country or region are indifferent as to whom they sell, they would earn an average of 10 per cent of their income from domestic sales and 90 per cent from foreign sales.[1] This reasoning implies, for example, that Western Europe or the USA would sell approximately 20 per cent to domestic buyers and 80 per cent to foreign customers. Exports as a percentage of GDP should be 'at least' 80 per cent.[2] In reality, the share of exports to GDP is around 10 per cent in the USA and about 40 per cent in the EU (the latter figure includes exports between European countries), much lower than a completely integrated world economy without any barriers to trade flows whatsoever would predict.

Table 5.2, which represents the country composition of trade flows for the EU between 1860 and 1996, reflects this observation in a different way. It allows us to draw two broad conclusions:

- First, the shares of destination countries for the EU exports and of origin countries for EU imports are very stable over long periods of time. Since the 1860s, Europe has exported primarily to itself; the share of other export regions is rather small. In contrast, the completely integrated world reasoning above suggests that the export

---

[1] There are many possible objections against this back-of-the-envelope line of reasoning. For example, many commodities are not traded at all, since they are non-tradable or firms have special preferences that could bias them against particular destinations, because they are not familiar with other cultures. But as a back-of-the-envelope calculation this reasoning is valuable.

[2] The term 'at least' signals the difference in the value measure (trade flows) and the value added measure (production).

shares for Europe and the USA would be more or less the same, as they have a similar share in world GDP (and similarly for European imports).

• Second, based on the large intra-European trade flows, it is tempting to conclude that distance is quite important for explaining trade flows, since most trade occurs between countries that are geographically close together. The world is thus far from completely integrated, and home markets are still very important in the world of commerce.

The so-called 'gravity' model of international trade flows looks more closely at the link between distance and trade. The main idea of this model is simple: bilateral trade between two countries is large if the two economies are large and if they are close to each other. The smaller the countries are or the further apart they are from each other, the smaller is the bilateral trade flow. The gravity model is one of the most successful empirical models in international trade, with typically about 70 per cent of the variance in trade flows explained by it ($R^2 = 0.7$). Most researchers, however, feel uncomfortable using the gravity model, because the basic formulation lacks a sound theoretical foundation.[3] The standard practice is to include variables that are plausible when it comes to explaining bilateral trade flows, but which are hard to incorporate into a theoretical formulation of the gravity model – such as a common language (positive contribution), being landlocked (negative contribution), cultural differences (negative contribution), sharing a common border (positive contribution) and the size of the population (positive contribution).

In general, studies using the gravity model find that distance is very important, which introduces a spatial or geographical element into the modelling of trade flows. In most standard trade theory, countries are dimensionless points; the exact relative location of these points in space is of no importance. This is no longer the case in the gravity model, where geography becomes important and the position of a country relative to other countries determines its market potential. The role of geography is probably even larger than the role of distance in the gravity model suggests. Gallup, Sachs and Mellinger (1998) find a clear relationship between physical geography and economic development. They point to the relationship between climate and health – for example, the prevalence of malaria or premature deaths caused by infectious diseases in certain parts of the world, or the relation between climate and agricultural productivity. In general, they find a close relationship between climate and economic growth. They also find that being landlocked is particularly bad for economic development.

---

[3] The standard formulation to explain bilateral trade flows T_{ij} between countries is a log-linear relation

$$\ln T_{ij} = \alpha \ln Y_i + \beta \ln Y_j + \gamma \ln dis_{ij} + \delta \ln Z$$

where i and j are country indices, Y is income, dis_{ij} is the distance between countries i and j and Z represents possible other variables. Harrigan (2003) reviews the existing literature on the gravity model.

Based on findings like these, one may be inclined to think that 'geography is destiny'. However, the following qualifications are in order:

- First, if geography is important in the sense of (economic) distance, this implies that investments in infrastructures or technologies that reduce distance could change destiny.
- Second, history shows that no centre of economic production remains a centre forever. After the seventeenth century, the Netherlands was overtaken by the UK as the leading economic power. The UK was subsequently leapfrogged by the USA in the twentieth century. Many Asian countries were 'peripheral' in the world economy in the 1950s and 1960s, but are no longer so today. China is the most recent and prominent example of this change in economic–geographic circumstances. Some commentators argue that China is becoming a new global centre of production, likely to catch-up with the USA within a couple of decades. In chapter 11 we shall discuss the likelihood of China catching-up with the USA, but it is obvious that, as new centres of economic activity develop, this will affect the relative geographical position of other countries.

The study of the rise and fall of economic centres has recently become one of the most active new fields of research in international trade and growth theory: it is called geographical economics.

5.3 Geographical economics

Living in a centre of economic activity can be very attractive. Meeting a business associate is easy and cost-efficient if she works at the same location. For consumers, the clustering of amenities such as bookshops, cinemas and restaurants in cities makes it attractive to live in such an agglomeration. On the downside, housing rents will be high in large agglomerations, and congestion, crime or pollution will most likely be a problem. Modern theories of location show how the balance between agglomerating and spreading forces determine the fate of a location. If agglomerating forces are particularly strong in a location, it could become a centre of economic activity. If spreading forces dominate, however, it could turn this location into a peripheral one. In trade theory, two separate strands of thinking about the location of economic activity dominate the literature. One strand has a strong footing in neo-classical theory and looks at the consequences of international factor mobility. The other strand was developed by Paul Krugman and others in the 1990s, and is known as the 'new economic geography' or 'geographical economics'. It looks at the effects of factor mobility on modern variants of trade theory.[4]

---

[4] We prefer the latter name because the main aim of the new theories was to put more geography into economics, rather than the other way around.

In the neo-classical tradition of trade modelling, the location of production is determined by the availability of technologies (the Ricardian model) or by the location of factor endowments (the Heckscher-Ohlin model). Once international trade is permitted, these characteristics determine which country specializes in which product, according to the logic of comparative advantage. As we saw in chapter 3, countries either specialize in the products for which they have a technological advantage (the Ricardian model) or in the products that use the relatively abundant production factor relatively intensively (the Heckscher-Ohlin model). This implies, for example, that land-abundant countries specialize in agricultural products. The factor price equalization theorem in the Heckscher-Ohlin model adds to this conclusion that commodity trade and factor mobility are substitutes. With complete factor price equalization, the economic incentive for migration of production factors is absent. However, it is well known that factor price equalization does not hold in reality:[5] it is easy to find examples where wages between developed and developing countries vary by a factor of 30 or more. If (some) factors of production become internationally mobile, factor price differences between countries will stimulate factors of production to move to those countries where they were initially scarce. In the Heckscher-Ohlin model, this reduces trade. Industrial sectors using a particular production factor intensively will re-locate to those places where factor rewards are initially high, thereby reducing the differences in endowments between countries. As countries become more similar, the empirically observed core–periphery patterns become more difficult to explain. In the simple Ricardian model, international labour mobility implies that all production will take place in the country with the highest *absolute* advantage. As labour is the only factor of production, wages are higher in the country with the highest absolute advantage. Unlike the Heckscher-Ohlin model, countries become more dissimilar, and centres of production are a more likely outcome.

The role of geography, however, is rather limited in both of these archetypical neo-classical trade models. The spatial distribution of the factors of production is given beforehand and transportation costs are absent. There is no role for 'market potential', as highlighted by the gravity model. The geographical position of a country or region relative to other countries plays no role at all. The geographical economics approach changes all this by incorporating the role of geography explicitly into its models. In this approach, the location decision of individual firms or workers is at the heart of the analysis. The production of manufactured goods is characterized by increasing returns to scale at the firm level, implying an associated market structure of imperfect competition (see chapter 4). Due to increasing returns to scale, the firm with the largest market, and thus the lowest cost per unit of sales, will gain a

---

[5] See Leamer and Levinsohn (1995).

competitive edge over other producers, capturing the whole market for its product.[6] Subsequently, each of these firms has to find the best location.

The fundamental question is: what is the preferred location? One possible answer is: where the market is large. In turn, the market is large where other firms and workers are located. This circular reasoning is crucial in the geographical economics approach. It hinges upon the existence of transportation costs – that is, the costs associated with the transfer of goods from one location to another. In the absence of transportation costs, location is not important, as each market can be served from all possible locations with no extra costs involved. With transportation costs, location becomes important, because the decision to set up production in the periphery will make a product relatively expensive for the consumer in the centre due to transportation costs, whereas locating in the centre will avoid these transportation costs. This implies that the interaction between various countries or regions becomes important. Some countries have a high market potential, whereas others do not. Countries with a high market potential will be able to attract new firms, which further increases their market potential, again attracting new firms, etc.

To see how important transportation costs are, it is instructive to investigate what happens if transportation costs decline, starting from autarky. In autarky, local production necessarily equals local consumption for all commodities because trade is not possible. Production will be spread over many regions and countries. What happens if transportation costs decline and the migration of factors of production becomes possible? Production factors will migrate to those locations where (real) factor rewards are the highest. In geographical economics models, however, relative factor prices are not determined by differences in technology, as in the Ricardian model, or by relative factor endowments, as in the Heckscher-Ohlin model, but by location. In large centres of production, factors of production are abundantly present. Simultaneously, local demand for production factors is also large, such that real factor rewards can still be relatively high compared to the periphery where production factors are relatively scarce. In the periphery, local demand is small and most commodities have to be imported. These commodities are more expensive than in the centres of production because they have to be imported at relatively high costs due to the need for transportation.

---

[6] Typically, such a production function could have the form $L = f + mx$, where L is the total labour requirement, f is the fixed labour requirement and m is the marginal labour requirement for the production of x units of a product. Increasing the total amount of sales reduces the average labour requirement because the fixed costs can be divided over a larger amount of sales, and mill prices can be lower than of those of smaller competitors (see also figure 4.3). In the neo-classical trade models, studying individual firm behaviour is not relevant due to the assumption of constant returns to scale: firm sales have no effect on unit costs.

Agglomerations or centres of production are able to attract factors of production from the periphery. An inflow of, for example, labour further increases market size, stimulates demand, raises profits and, finally, also pushes up wages. Factor abundance thus leads to higher factor rewards instead of lower factor rewards, as is the case in the Heckscher-Ohlin model. Hence, the geographical economics approach gives a more explicit role to geography, but the interaction of increasing returns to scale, market size and transport costs also makes the analysis more complex. Typically, these models are characterized by multiple equilibria: the outcome of the dynamic process could *a priori* end up in one of several potential long-run equilibria. This immediately raises a number of questions:

- How does an equilibrium get established?
- Are all equilibria similar from a welfare perspective?
- What is the relationship between each equilibrium and trade?
- Can policy be used to move an economy from one equilibrium to another?

The answers to these questions are intrinsically difficult, but fortunately the main issues at hand can be illustrated by means of a simple example.

5.4 The geographical economics approach: an example

This section discusses an illuminating example that illustrates the main elements of the geographical economics approach.[7] Suppose there are two regions (or countries), North and South, and two sectors of production, manufacturing and agriculture. The manufacturing industry produces differentiated products. Each firm produces a single variety of the product. Production is characterized by internal economies of scale. The costs per unit of output therefore fall as a firm expands its production level. As a result, each firm produces only one variety.[8] A firm can reside either in North or in South – that is, a firm has to decide where to produce. It is this location decision that drives the example.

Total demand for each variety of manufactures in this example is exogenous. We assume that each firm sells 4 units to workers in the manufacturing industry and 6 units to the farmers. Total demand for each variety is therefore 10 units (6 + 4). The production of agriculture, and hence the demand it generates, is location-specific. Its spatial distribution is exogenously given: we assume that 4 units are sold in the North and 2 units in the South. The location of the workers in the manufacturing sector, and hence the 4 units they demand at that location, is not exogenous. Workers

---

[7] A simpler version of this example can be found in Krugman and Obstfeld (1994, p. 185).
[8] That is, economies of scope are taken to be absent.

Table 5.3 Geography of sales

	Sales in North	Sales in South	Total sales
All firms in North	$4 + 4 = 8$	$0 + 2 = 2$	10
All firms in South	$0 + 4 = 4$	$4 + 2 = 6$	10
25% firms in North, 75% firms in South	$1 + 4 = 5$	$3 + 2 = 5$	10

can move, but farmers cannot. The role of the immobile farmer is important as it ensures that there is always positive demand in *both* regions. Finally, transport costs between North and South are €1 per unit. The firms choose location to minimize transport costs.

We are now able to determine the location decision of each firm. First, we can calculate the regional sales of each firm, given the location of the other firms. In table 5.3, three (non-exhaustive) possibilities are given: all firms in North, all firms in South, or 25 per cent of all firms in North and 75 per cent of all firms in South. Sales in each region are equal to the sales to the workers in manufacturing plus the sales to the farmers. Take, for example, the last row in table 5.3. The firm sells 5 units in North, namely 4 to the farmers located in North + 1 (= 25% × 4) unit to the manufacturing workers located in North. Similarly, the firm sells 5 units in South, namely 2 units to the farmers located in South + 3 (= 75% ×4) units to the manufacturing workers located in South.

Second, using Table 5.3, we can construct a *decision table* by calculating transport costs as a function of the firm's location decision, given the location of the other firms. Suppose, for example, that all firms are located in North. Table 5.4 indicates that transport costs for a firm locating in South will then be €8, namely €4 for sales to the farmers in North and €4 for sales to all workers in manufacturing located in North (abstracting from sales to its own workers). Similarly, if the firm located in North, transport costs would be only €2 for the sales to the farmers in South. Since transport costs are minimized by locating in North if all other firms are located in North, the firm decides to also locate production in North. As table 5.4 shows (second row), a firm will locate in South if all other firms are also located there, whereas (last row) the firm is indifferent between locating in North or South (since transport costs are the same if the firm locates in either region) if 25 per cent of the firms are located in North and 75 per cent in South.

On the basis of this example, we can illustrate five distinctive characteristics of the geographical economics approach:

- First, the concept of *cumulative causation* is essential. If, for some reason, a location has attracted more firms than another location, a new firm has an incentive to locate where the other firms are. Take the first row in table 5.4. If all firms are located in

Table 5.4 Transport costs, €

	If location in North	If location in South
All firms in North	0 + 2 = 2 (to farmers in South)	4 + 4 = 8 (to workers and farmers in North)
All firms in South	4 + 2 = 6 (to workers and farmers in South)	0 + 4 = 4 (to farmers in North)
25% firms in North, 75% firms in South	3 + 2 = 5 (to workers and farmers in South	1 + 4 = 5 (to workers and farmers in North)

North, a new firm should also locate there to minimize transport costs. Similarly, for the second row in table 5.4, the firm will locate in South.

- Second, table 5.4 illustrates the existence of *multiple equilibria*. Agglomeration of all firms in either North or South is an equilibrium. However, we cannot determine beforehand where agglomeration will occur. This depends critically on initial conditions – that is, on the previous location decisions of other firms.
- Third, an equilibrium may be *stable* or *unstable*. The blue entries in table 5.4 are both stable equilibria: if a single firm decided to relocate, this decision would not influence the location decisions of the other firms. The last row in table 5.4 describes an unstable equilibrium. If a single firm decided to relocate, the new location would immediately become more attractive for all other firms. This would trigger a snowball effect: all firms would follow the pioneer. In this example, only agglomeration is a stable equilibrium.
- Fourth, we note that a stable equilibrium can be *non-optimal*. If all firms are located in North, transport costs are only €2. If all firms are located in South, transport costs are €4 (see the bold entries in table 5.4). Thus, transport costs for the economy as a whole are minimized if all firms agglomerate in North. Nevertheless, agglomeration in South is a stable equilibrium.
- Fifth, table 5.4 illustrates the *interaction of agglomeration and trade flows*. With complete agglomeration – that is, all manufactures are produced in a single region – trade between regions will be of the inter-industry type (food for manufactures). In fact, this equilibrium also reflects the home-market effect: the combination of economies of scale and transport costs is responsible for the clustering of all 'footloose' activities in a single location. Due to this combination, transport costs can be minimized. The large region ends up with a large market for manufacturing goods, which can be sold without incurring transport costs. The consequence is that this region becomes the exporter of manufactured goods. Large regions tend to become exporters of those goods for which they have a large local market – hence the term 'home-market effect'. If the manufacturing industry is located in both regions, as described by the last rows in table 5.4, trade will also

be of the intra-industry type. Besides trading manufactured goods for agricultural products, different varieties of the differentiated manufactured products will be traded between both regions.

5.5 Geographical economics: a further discussion

The example discussed in section 5.4 is useful as it illustrates important aspects of geographical economics. But an example is just an example; it is not a substitute for a well-specified model. What is missing in the example? First of all, the interaction of transport costs, price-setting behaviour and location choice is missing. We simply assumed that the demand each firm faces is given, and independent of price-setting behaviour and transport costs. In fact, prices are completely lacking in the example. There is no analysis of the market structure. In the real world, prices, wages and transport costs will determine the purchasing power of consumers. One might guess that this interaction drives the location decisions of consumers and producers. Furthermore, it is a partial equilibrium model in the sense that firms do not worry about the necessary labour: wherever they decide to locate, labour is not the problem. One might notice the similarity of the above example and the new trade model discussed in chapter 4. In both models, scale economies and transport costs are important forces. The key difference is that in the above example firms can locate in either region. Consequently, the example gives rise to agglomeration and multiple equilibria.

In fact, we can use chapter 4's monopolistic competition analysis to illustrate what might happen if firms relocated to another region. This is done in figure 5.1. Figure 5.1 illustrates profit maximization for a single firm. It is instructive to take a closer look at figure 5.1 because it can be used to illustrate the economic forces at work in a model that describes the equilibrium explicitly (the discussion is based on Neary, 2001). Note that we use a different average cost (*AC*) curve than earlier, namely one with a negative slope throughout its whole domain. The latter is a result of the assumption of constant marginal costs. Also, in comparison to chapter 4, we use a non-linear demand (*D*) curve.[9]

The volume of sales is depicted along the horizontal axis and the price along the vertical axis. The *D, AC, MC* and *MR* lines are the demand curve, the average cost curve, the marginal cost curve, and the marginal revenue curves, respectively. As always, the intersection of the *MR* and *MC* lines determines the profit-maximizing volume of sales (point *A*), and the corresponding price *P* (point *B*). At point *B*, the

---

[9] The reason for the change in the *AC* and *D* curvature is the standard application in the geographical economics literature of the curves shown in figure 5.1

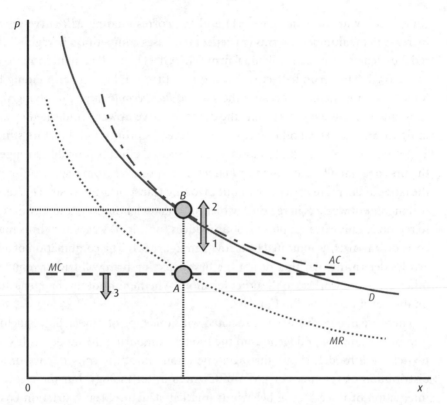

Figure 5.1   Monopolistic competition and the re-location of a firm

AC and *D* curves are at a tangent. This is the result of the assumption that firms will enter the market (in case of profits) or leave the market (in case of losses) until profits are zero. The picture thus not only describes the equilibrium condition of a single firm, but indirectly also that of the market for all products, as all firms face the same demand and supply conditions, and because in equilibrium each firm has zero profits. The main difference with the example discussed in section 5.4 is that in this setting we explicitly look at pricing behaviour (profit maximization), demand conditions (elasticities of demand and income, which determine the slope and location of the demand curve, respectively) and wages (which determine the purchasing power of consumers and the level of the marginal costs).

If we perform a thought experiment, it is simple to see which forces are present in the model. When we assume that initially all firms are divided equally over the two regions, we can ask ourselves what happens if one firm decides to move from region 1 to region 2. If this raises profits in region 1, the initial equilibrium was unstable and more firms will follow; if it lowers profits, the initial equilibrium was stable and the firm has an incentive to return to its original location. We can distinguish two immediate effects. The first is a *competition effect*, which shifts the demand curve (indicated by arrow 1 in figure 5.1) and the corresponding *MR* curve down. An increase in the number of firms (varieties) increases competition in region 2, which reduces demand for each individual firm. This effect by itself is an incentive to return to region 1. The second effect is that the new firm (and the corresponding labour force) increases demand because the *market has become larger,* implying that the subsequent income increase shifts the demand curve upward (indicated by arrow 2 in figure 5.1). Given all other factors, this increases profits and therefore stimulates agglomeration. Neary (2001) shows that the second effect is probably stronger than the first one. Finally, there is a third effect. If firms move from region 1 to region 2, the latter offers more varieties without invoking transportation costs. This raises the real income of workers in region 2, which stimulates labour migration from region 1 to region 2. This extra supply of labour reduces (nominal) wages and shifts marginal costs downwards, as indicated by arrow 3 in figure 5.1. The combination of all three arrows determines whether or not the first defecting firm will trigger migration of other firms and workers to the other location. Whether or not this happens depends on the net effect of the three arrows.

There are many advantages associated with this type of model. Since agglomeration or spreading is endogenous to the model, comparing the model with standard neo-classical models shows that agglomeration is not the consequence of a given distribution of resources or given differences in technology, but the result of the interaction of price-setting behaviour, market structure, transportation costs and increasing returns to scale. Starting from complete symmetry, and without invoking exogenous assumptions on the nature of physical geography, agglomeration and spreading of economic activity are both possible outcomes. This approach explicitly incorporates the *interaction forces* between different regions; the spatial structure is an outcome of the migration processes induced within the model itself. Although many objections can be raised with respect to a specific formulation of a geographical economics model, it remains the first type of general equilibrium model that incorporates all these features.

For our purposes, however, one possible objection to this approach is particularly serious. The migration behaviour of firms and workers is very simple: labour migration is assumed to be sensitive only to real wage differentials, and firm migration is sensitive only to differences in profits. This is a rather limited way of looking at migration. In the introduction to this chapter, we noted that the main actor in the process of international location was the MNE. Empirical research shows that firms are indeed relatively more mobile than labour. Although geographical economics is a step forward, we are still lacking a model that explains why firms become *multi-national,* and how location or geography may determine the outcome of a firm's location decision. In box 5.2, we briefly illustrate how international business insights may inform this issue, before we turn to the whole question in greater detail.

Box 5.2 The location decision of MNEs in international business

The issue of where to locate internationally – above all, in which countries (or regions) to invest – is a key theme in international business studies: what are the determinants triggering MNEs from country z investing in country x rather than y? We discuss this literature in greater detail in chapter 2. Here, an example may illustrate how insights from international business may complement those from international economics, as already discussed, by briefly summarizing the results from the exemplary study of Driffield and Munday (2000). This study investigates the relationship between the comparative advantage of UK industries, on the one hand, and entry by foreign enterprises into these industries through inward investment, on the other hand.

The data set explored is from the UK Census of Production for the 1984–92 period. The bottom line is that the relationship goes both ways: a country's (here, the UK) comparative advantage in an industry is a key attractor of inward FDI, *and* investment by foreign enterprises in an industry is an important determinant of a country's comparative advantage in this industry. Moreover, spatial agglomeration does matter. That is, an industry's comparative advantage is positively associated with the level of both inward FDI and spatial agglomeration. This nicely illustrates geographical economics' concept of cumulative causation.

5.6 Multinational behaviour

In chapter 3, we took a first look at multinational behaviour in the context of neo-classical trade theory. There, we simply assumed the presence of multinationals and studied how multinational behaviour could be made consistent with the Ricardian and the Heckscher-Ohlin trade models. Geography has traditionally been a very important factor in describing and explaining the behaviour of multinationals, and for describing the flows of FDI across countries and regions. Obviously, the location choice of headquarters and production facilities (or both) is critical in describing multinational behaviour. In box 5.3, we provide some empirical evidence on this.

Not all firms "go" multinational. Markusen (2002) identifies four main stylized facts: multinationals (i) appear to be concentrated in industries characterized by a high ratio of R&D relative to sales, (ii) tend to have high values of intangible assets, (iii) are often associated with new or technologically advanced and differentiated products and (iv) are often relatively old, large and more established firms within their sector. One of the difficulties associated with analyzing multinational firm behaviour is the difference in the driving force for becoming either a horizontal or a vertical multinational (or, of course, a hybrid combination – a case ignored here).

Box 5.3 Another look at multinationals

Detailed information on multinational firms beyond the consolidated data in their annual reports are notoriously difficult to obtain, not only because of lack of available data at the level of subsidiaries (see chapter 2 on this), but also as a result of conceptual difficulties. Take the ownership issue, as an example. A multinational is a firm that controls, by means of ownership, productive assets in more than one country. But ownership and control may vary between 0 per cent and 100 per cent. It is therefore a matter of definition when one speaks of a multinational firm.[10] Data on FDI are systematically collected by UNCTAD and the World Bank. The data show that since the 1980s FDI has grown astonishingly fast, even faster than international trade, as illustrated in figure 5.2.

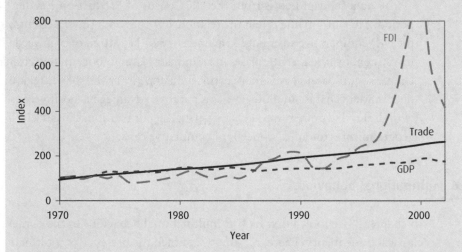

Figure 5.2 Development of world GDP, FDI and trade, 1970–2000, 1970 = 100
Data source: World Bank (2004).
Notes: GDP in constant 1995 US dollars; FDI, net inflows and trade as a percentage of GDP.

On average, worldwide nominal GDP grew more than 7 per cent per year between 1970 and 1997. During this period, international trade, measured by worldwide nominal imports, grew more than 12 per cent, whereas nominal FDI grew by almost 31 per cent. Not only did the overall level of FDI increase, it also changed from investments in manufacturing to investment in services. FDI also increasingly took place in the form of mergers (see Evenett, 2003).

Table 5.5 gives information on the sources and destinations of FDI flows, as a share of total flows. It is obvious from the data that the advanced nations are the main destinations for FDI. Although the developing countries are relatively unimportant for FDI, it is interesting to note that only ten developing countries

Table 5.5 FDI inflows and outflows, share in total flows

| Period | Country group | | | | | |
| | Developed | | Developing | | CEE | |
	In	Out	In	Out	In	Out
1983–92	77	94	23	6	0	0
1993–99	64	87	33	13	3	0

Note: CEE = Central and Eastern European.
Source: UNCTAD, *World Investment Report* (various years).

accounted for two-thirds of inward FDI into all developing countries (see Shatz and Venables, 2000).[11] China received 30.6 per cent of this FDI. China witnessed a fourfold increase of FDI in relative terms: in the period 1988–92, it received 2.9 per cent of total world FDI, compared to more than 12 per cent in the period 1993–9.

[10] The US Bureau of Economic Analysis distinguishes majority-owned foreign subsidiaries of US parents from affiliates, which are at least 10 per cent non-US-owned. The criteria are, of course, subject to discussion.
[11] Argentina, Brazil, Chile, China, Hungary, Indonesia, Malaysia, Mexico, Poland and Singapore.

In order to highlight some of the important elements, we analyse multinational behaviour by making eight simplifying assumptions:

- Firms can choose to locate production in two – identical – countries.
- Production uses only one input factor, labour.
- Marginal costs in terms of labour, C, are constant (which is assumed to be identical in both countries).
- In labour terms, there are firm-specific fixed costs, F. These costs relate to knowledge capital – for example, investment in R&D, marketing expenditures, management services, etc. They are associated with the ownership advantages of the OLI approach, as discussed in chapter 3 (see also box 4.5). These costs are only imposed once, irrespective of the firm's number of plants.
- Setting up a plant is costly, and gives plant-specific fixed costs, P. Finding a suitable location, hiring the right people, buying machines, leasing office equipment and the like, all add to the costs of setting up a production plant. For each plant, these costs are incurred once. Total plant costs equal the number of plants multiplied by P.
- Transportation costs, in terms of labour, are t. Exporting a unit of good x involves t transportation costs in terms of labour. This amount of labour can no longer be used for other purposes.

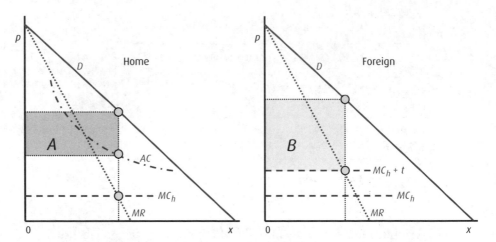

Figure 5.3 Profits in the Home and Foreign market: national exporting firm

- Headquarters also use resources, but they are assumed to be covered by the firm-specific costs F, as noted above.
- Markets are segmented. So a firm can set its price independently in both markets, without the risk of arbitrage.

With the help of the figures 5.3–5.5, we will illustrate the various options available to the firm. The left-hand side panel in each of figures 5.3–5.5 depicts the situation in the Home market, whereas the right-hand side panel depicts the situation in the Foreign market.

Suppose the firm decides to export from its home base instead of going multinational. In this case, figure 5.3 applies. The profits for Home sales are derived in the usual way. Because we have assumed fixed costs at both the plant and the firm level, production is characterized by increasing returns to scale. Equating marginal revenues, MR, with marginal costs, MC_h, gives the profit-maximizing level of sales. The associated price is given by the downward-sloping demand curve. Given the location of the average cost curve, profits from Home sales are indicated by the area A. If the firm exports to the Foreign country, the profits for exports are derived in the same manner. This is done in the right-hand side panel of figure 5.3. Equating MR to $mc_h + t$ gives the profit-maximizing level of export sales, leading to the profit level indicated by the area B.

Two remarks are in order. First, exporting incurs transportation costs, t per unit of exports, which are paid by the producer. This shifts the marginal cost curve upward by the amount t. Furthermore, we arbitrarily assign all of the fixed costs for the firm to Home profits.[12] We could have divided the fixed costs over export

---

[12] Fixed costs have to be assigned to either the Home or Foreign market, or to some sort of combination of the two. For total profits, it is immaterial what choice one makes. If corporate taxes between countries differ, the choice might become important, though (see chapter 2).

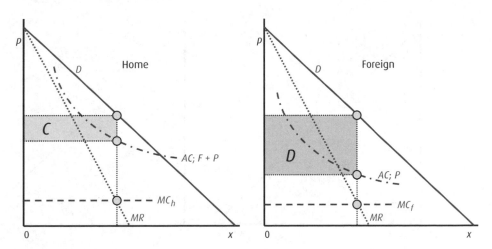

Figure 5.4 Going multinational: the horizontal case

and domestic sales, but this is a matter of accounting principles (see chapter 2). To summarize:

If a firm decides to export instead of becoming a multinational, total profits are equal to the area A + B *in figure* 5.3.

If, instead of becoming a national exporting firm, the firm decides go multinational, it has two options. It can open a single firm abroad, which implies that sales in the Foreign market are produced locally, but goods for Home consumption must now be imported. This is an example of a vertical multinational. Alternatively, it can set up two production plants, one in Home and one in Foreign. In this case, the firm avoids transportation costs, because each market is served from a local production plant, but plant-related fixed costs P have to be paid twice. This is an example of a horizontal multinational.

First, suppose the firm sets up two production plants, one in each country. This situation, in which the firm becomes a horizontal multinational, is depicted in figure 5.4. We are, again, interested in total profits. The fixed costs are assigned to the Home market. Marginal costs can differ between the two countries. We assume that marginal costs are lower in the Foreign than they are in the Home country. The reason could be that the Foreign country is more developed and has implemented social institutions with lower costs, such as a better legal system or a more efficient labour market. Local consumers are served by local production and no transportation costs have to be incurred – that is, transportation costs are zero. The average cost curve not only consists of firm-specific fixed costs F, but also of the plant-specific fixed costs P. In Home, total fixed costs are the sum of the firm-specific and the plant-specific fixed costs $F + P$. In Foreign, fixed costs consist only of the plant-specific fixed costs P. Total profits are therefore given by the shaded area $C + D$. To summarize:

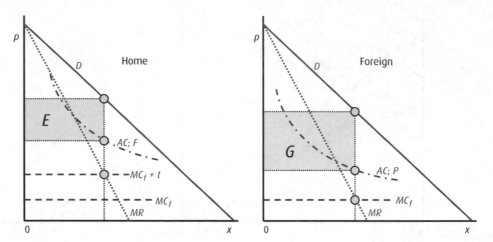

Figure 5.5 Going multinational: the vertical case

If a firm decides to become a horizontal multinational, total profits are equal to the area C + D *in figure* 5.4.

Second, suppose the firm sets up one production plant in Foreign only. This situation, in which the firm becomes a vertical multinational, is depicted in figure 5.5. Profits from local sales in the Foreign market are given by G.[13] We (arbitrarily) assign fixed costs to the Home market of this multinational, where the headquarters are located. The Home market of the firm now has to be served from abroad, which incurs transportation costs *t*. Profits in Home are equal to the area E. To summarize:

If a firm decides to become a vertical multinational, total profits are equal to the area E + G *in figure* 5.5.

The firm can now decide upon the optimal firm structure with the assistance of the decision tree depicted in figure 5.6. Comparing profits at the end for each possible decision, first on whether or not to become an MNE and second on whether or not to become a vertical multinational firm, leads to a simple optimal choice: to choose the profit-maximizing firm structure.

With the help of the model above, it is relatively easy to consider a few extensions. Until now, we have assumed that the markets in Home and Foreign are identical. In the real world, of course, markets are seldom of equal size. Suppose we drop the assumption that both countries are identical, and instead allow for differences in market size. Assume for the moment that marginal costs are the same in both countries. Note that the fixed costs can be assigned to any market: for *total* profits, it does not matter where. For the export decision and the decision to become a

---

[13] Note that we use '*G*' because '*F*' is already reserved to denote the firm-specific fixed costs.

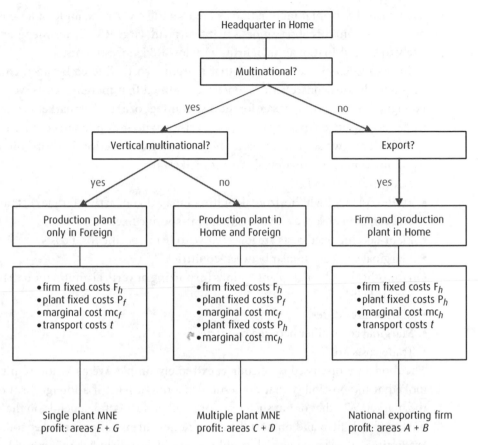

Figure 5.6 Summary of the firm's main decisions

vertical multinational, differences in market size can be very important. Suppose the Foreign market is smaller than the Home market. The decision to export and not become a vertical multinational might be more profitable, because of transportation cost differences. In the case of a vertical multinational, with only a single plant in the Foreign market, the firm has to export to the larger Home market, and thus transportation costs are higher compared to the situation of identical market size. If, instead, the firm is a horizontal multinational, it will also be affected by the difference in market size. As the Home market becomes larger, the Home-based plant sells more than the Foreign-based plant. The firm, however, still has to pay twice the amount of plant-specific fixed cost P. We conclude that the choice to become a horizontal multinational is more likely in the case of similarly-sized countries. This decision becomes more likely if t becomes higher, making transportation costs more important, or if P, the plant-specific fixed cost, is smaller. When one market is relatively small, it does not pay to invest in setting up an additional plant in the smaller market. Also, if firm-specific fixed costs increase relative to plant-specific fixed costs, horizontal multinationals are more likely. An example of an empirical hypothesis from this observation is that firms with large R&D investments are more likely to be multinationals than firms with low R&D investments.

In figures 5.3–5.5, we assumed that marginal costs differed between countries. This has obvious consequences. Since we assumed that marginal costs were low in Foreign, this could compensate for the disadvantage of a smaller market size or higher trade cost. Again, comparing the export decision with the option to become a vertical multinational, we see that the latter becomes more attractive. In short, on the one hand, horizontal multinationals are more likely if:

- Countries are similar in size
- Trade costs are high (horizontal multinationals do not arrive if trade costs are zero: one can then always avoid the extra plant-specific fixed cost)
- Plant-specific fixed costs are low relative to firm-specific fixed costs
- Marginal costs are similar between countries.

On the other hand, single plant options (exporting or vertical multinational) become more likely if:

- Market sizes differ
- Marginal costs differ between countries
- Trade costs are low.

The model we discussed is, of course, extremely simple. We have, for example, not looked at the possibility that domestic firms might react if a foreign firm entered the market. Whether or not such reactions will be successful depends on the market power of each firm and on how the entry of new firms changes market conditions. We limited ourselves to partial equilibrium models of firm behaviour and have not studied the consequences on the markets for production factors if new firms enter a market. These issues rapidly become cumbersome to analyse. The appendix to this chapter (p. 152), however, shows that models dealing with these types of problems in a general equilibrium setting still lead to similar conclusions on multinational behaviour as discussed above. Another issue abstracted from the discussion above is *where* multinationals go to – that is, in which countries or regions they decide to invest – a theme that is central in the international business domain. This issue is discussed in greater detail in chapter 12 (see also box 5.2, p. 139). Box 5.4 in the meantime provides an example from the international business literature relevant in the context of this chapter.

5.7 The boundary of the firm: outsourcing

Up to now, we have not really discussed the organizational setting of the firm. We have simply discussed multinational activities as a problem of geography: can a firm

Box 5.4 The regional bias of FDI

One way to look at the "where do multinationals invest?" question is to take a national perspective (see box 5.2): in which regions *within* a country do MNEs decide to invest? And, related to this: are multinational firms investing in *different* regions, compared to their domestic counterparts? There are arguments pointing in either direction: it may be that foreign and domestic firms reveal similar location patterns, and it may be that multinationals go elsewhere. On the one hand, examples of reasons for similarity of location pattern are explored in the main text, relating to the benefits of agglomeration. If such benefits dominate within a specific industry or set of industries, one may expect foreign firms to cluster together with their domestic counterparts. For example, if knowledge spillovers and shared supplier networks are important in the automobile industry, it is likely that BMW and Toyota will locate their US headquarters in the Detroit area, close to (Daimler)Chrysler, Ford and GM. On the other hand, domestic versus foreign location patterns might be different if, in line with the monopolistic competition theory of intra-industry trade (see chapter 4), both groups of firms specialize in product varieties that are so different that clustering together does not bring any advantages. Rather, to avoid competition for similar resources (such as high-quality labour), foreign enterprises may face an incentive to invest far away from domestic firms. For example, the German software company SAP might decide not to invest in Seattle or Washington State, Microsoft's home city and state, because both firms compete for the same type of human capital.

An example of a study dealing with this issue is Shaver (1998), focusing on the case of US manufacturing in 1987. In his study, Shaver reports evidence that the location patterns of foreign-owned establishments are *different* from those of their US-owned counterparts. In effect, foreign versus domestic ownership is the most influential explanation of differences in location pattern. Specifically, the location of foreign-owned establishments is significantly biased toward coastal states while US-owned establishments are more spread across landlocked states. Moreover, foreign firms – more than their US counterparts – tend to prefer states with low unionization rates, low wage levels and right to work legislation.

become more profitable by taking advantage of geographical differences between countries? However, if a firm decides to become a multinational, it has an additional choice. Does it keep all activities within the firm, or should it rely on market forces? In the latter case, it might simply decide that certain stages in the production process can take place better in a foreign country, but instead of organizing this stage itself it decides to buy the components from a foreign supplier not owned by the home firm. In this section, we will briefly look at the economic consequences of this type of *outsourcing*, in order to give an example of the costs and benefits of using a foreign supplier. Why a firm decides to participate in outsourcing instead of setting up an affiliate of its own abroad is discussed in somewhat more detail in chapter 12.

Outsourcing (or off-shoring) occurs when certain stages of the production process are subcontracted by a firm to foreign producers. This is why outsourcing is also known as slicing-up-the-value-chain. Vertical multinational production and fragmentation are closely related to this type of activity. The main difference is ownership. Transactions are made through local independent producers, instead of through subsidiaries.[14] But the geographical motives of outsourcing are comparable to those of becoming a vertical multinational: low local costs of production that is not counterbalanced by high transport costs or high plant-specific fixed costs. That is, this line of argument focuses on *efficiency-seeking* motives (see chapter 12 on this, as well as the OLI framework discussed in chapter 3).

A common form of subcontracting is an agreement to buy final products. Sometimes, however, the firm delivers the intermediate products (purchased from local producers or delivered by the firm itself), which are necessary for the assembly of final products. These are then sold back to the firm. Subcontracting is not a new phenomenon, but the recent international nature of these types of arrangements is. The three main advantages of sub-contracting are:

- If a firm delivers (final) products to another (foreign-based) firm, it can secure a market, and use the brand name of foreign firms. The electronics industry is a good example: television tubes often end up in television sets for different brands. The final goods producer can get access to low-cost countries without setting up a new plant, so forgoing the plant-specific fixed costs.
- The buyer of outsourced (intermediate) products can cut storage costs and can re-direct the costs of 'just-in-time (JIT) delivery to the supplier of intermediate products. More generally, by supplying to a number of customers, intermediate product producers can reap scale economies.
- A firm that outsources gains indirect access to the experience and knowledge of the foreign partner.

On the negative side of the "balance sheet" of outsourcing are the increased dependence of a firm on the foreign partner's a decisions, and of the economic circumstances in the partner countries. This increases economic uncertainty.[15] In box 5.5, we discuss the example of US outsourcing to Mexico.

[14] Here, we ignore hybrid ownership forms such as joint ventures (JVs).

[15] In the international business domain, this type of firm boundary issues are analyzed by applying transaction cost theory. In chapter 12, we briefly discuss this literature, which also deals with hybrid forms of ownership.

Box 5.5 *Maquiladoras*[16]

In 1980, Mexico started a period of rapid liberalization of international trade. In 1994, Mexico, together with Canada and the USA, entered into the North American Free Trade Agreement (NAFTA). Mexico converted itself from an inward oriented economy to an economy in which export-led growth had become important. It has been estimated that in 2000 the trading share in Mexico was about 32 per cent of GDP, almost three times as large as the share in 1980. The most internationally active firms in Mexico are the so-called *maquiladoras* – specialized assembly plants. These plants are examples of outsourcing. They import intermediate products from abroad, which are subsequently assembled in Mexico. The final products are then re-exported, mostly to the USA. Many firms are not owned by multinationals, but by Mexicans.

The *maquiladoras* are most active in the electronics, auto parts and apparel industries. These firms benefit from relatively low labour costs in Mexico compared to the USA. The importance of the *maquiladoras* for Mexico's exports cannot easily be over-stated. Value added by the *maquiladoras* sector grew at an impressive rate of 10 per cent per year, and employment grew from 460,000 workers in 1990 to 1.1 million in 2002. By 2000, the *maquiladoras* sector was responsible for 48 per cent of Mexico's exports and 35 per cent of Mexico's imports. Most of the trade of these firms is with the USA. It comes therefore as no surprise that most plants are concentrated around the US–Mexican border. For the US-based firms, this form of outsourcing is obviously motivated by low labour and transportation costs, which is consistent with the discussion in section 5.6. But this is not only good news for Mexico. The *maquiladoras* specialize in a rather small number of industries and are thus sensitive to foreign (US) business cycles and decisions of US firms to buy their products elsewhere (for example, in China). The sector does not only have an enormous growth potential, but it also faces an enormous hazard of shrinking.

[16] Box 5.5 is based on Hanson (2002).

Many heated discussions are associated with the phenomenon of slicing-up-the-value-chain, as part of the ongoing debate among the advocates and opponents of globalization (see chapter 13). As a standard part of anti-globalization rhetoric, some commentators stress the negative effects of outsourcing parts of the production process to low-wage countries: people working in sectors vulnerable to outsourcing lose their jobs in the home country. It is not always easy to find a new job, as the need for certain skills is also vulnerable to outsourcing. Workers may find that their

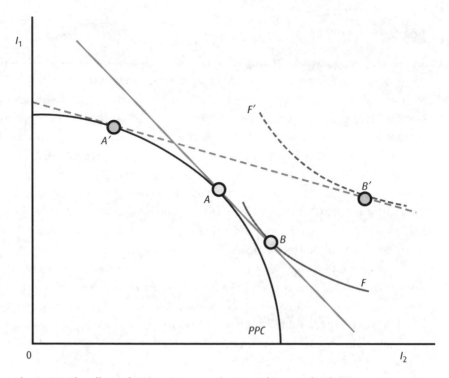

Figure 5.7 The effects of outsourcing on production and income distribution

specific expertise is no longer wanted on the labour market. For society as a whole, the process is welfare-increasing, however, as figure 5.7 shows.

Suppose that for the production of a good *F* two types of intermediate products are necessary, I_1 and I_2. To produce these intermediate products, we need capital and two types of labour, high-skilled and low-skilled. The production possibility curve (PPC) for the two types of intermediate products is drawn in figure 5.7. Points *A* and *B* give the initial situation for this economy. Note that, as drawn, I_1 is exported and I_2 is imported. It is important to observe that with international trade the economy is able to produce more of good *F* than in autarky. Suppose that the production of I_2 is low-skilled labour-intensive, and the production of I_1 is high-skilled labour-intensive. What happens if wages in Foreign decline? In a stylized way, we analyse the situation when a low-skilled labour-abundant country such as China enters the world market. The Home economy will move to *A'* – that is, it will specialize in intermediate products that are high-skilled labour-intensive, while the imports of the low-skilled labour-intensive intermediate product increases. This specialization process moves the production point from *B* to *B'*. This clearly shows that total production increases. But this is not the only consequence of outsourcing. From the Stolper–Samuelson theorem (see chapter 3), we can also conclude that the wage of low-skilled labour declines, whereas the wage of high-skilled labour increases. The economy as a whole benefits from more outsourcing, although individual groups (in this case, low-skilled workers) will tell a different story. This is why anti-globalists, politicians and unionists, for example, tend to ask for measures against outsourcing.

5.8 Conclusions

This chapter has focused on geography, location and the international location decisions made by firms. Transportation costs and other barriers to trade are still very important in shaping the world economy, particularly regarding the location decision of workers and firms. Producing far away from the centre of economic activity implies that economic agents have to pay more for transportation than if they had been located in the centre itself. Models incorporating transportation costs and mobile workers and firms show how centre–periphery structures can come about as a result of the interplay between agglomerating and spreading forces. The main actor in this location process in today's global economy is the multinational firm. We discussed some simple models of multinational behaviour to explain these processes.

So, extending trade models by introducing geography – specifically, the location decision of enterprises – helps to understand the centre–periphery structures, or patterns of agglomeration, we see in real-world economies. Moreover, by linking the geographical economics tradition to the insights of international business, we can bridge issues of comparative and competitive advantage. Box 5.6 briefly explores this bridge-building exercise.

Box 5.6 Competitive advantage and the location decision

In box 5.4, we saw that foreign-owned establishments in the USA tend *not* to cluster together with their US-owned counterparts. One might then more broadly explore the conditions under which agglomeration will not occur. In this context, Shaver and Flyer (2000) explore the following logic. On the one hand, firms are clustered together because they can then exploit external economies of agglomeration, which helps them to develop and sustain a competitive advantage. On the other hand, firms located in an agglomeration may contribute to the external economies in that centre of activity as well, implying that their competitive advantages spill over to other firms in that agglomeration. The R&D labs of a large MNE, for instance may operate as a *knowledge transfer hub* from which smaller competitors can benefit – for example, by attracting former employees from this lab or by forming alliances with the large multinational's technology partners.

It may well be that for our example of a large multinational the latter effect – the spillover of competitive advantages to smaller rivals – dominates over the 'traditional' external agglomeration effects. If so, the multinational's smaller rivals benefit more from being located in this agglomeration than the multinational itself, implying an erosion of the multinational's *relative* competitive position. Taking account of such firm heterogeneity in terms of the net benefit or cost derived from agglomeration implies the hypotheses that some firms like to cluster together, whilst others prefer not to do so, depending upon specific firm-level characteristics. Firms which can benefit from superior competitive advantages (see box 4.5) are more likely *not* to locate in their industries' dominant agglomeration, whereas their counterparts with less developed competitive positions do tend to cluster together. Indeed, for a sample of FDI ventures in the USA in 1987, Shaver and Flyer (2000) find empirical support for their argument. For example, a foreign multinational with a superior technology will invest in a US location (i.e. state) far away from the country's agglomeration (i.e. state) in the multinational's industry.

Appendix: A more general model of multinational behaviour

The main advantage of the model discussed in the main text is that it is simple. Models like these, however, rapidly become very complicated when one or more of the underlying assumptions is relaxed. Suppose, for instance, that we consider a firm in a two-country world that faces the following options: it can be a national firm in two countries, a multinational firm with headquarters in either country, or it can be a horizontal or a vertical multinational firm. The same options hold for a firm in the other country. In this case, we already have $2^6 - 1 = 63$ options to consider (we ignore the possibility of no firms at all: there always has to be at least one firm). If the number of countries is larger than two, the number of possible distributions of various types of firms rapidly becomes truly staggering. Markusen (2002) has come up with a way to analyse and visualize cases with a large number of options in a general equilibrium setting. His way of visualizing all options is by looking at *aggregate regimes*: regimes in which there are only national firms (no matter which nationality), regimes with only multinational firms (no matter which nationality) and mixed regimes with combinations of national and multinational firms.

To show how the Markusen strategy works, we use the following example. Suppose that there are two countries, Home and Foreign, and two types of industries, manufactures and food. The food sector produces a homogenous good under constant returns to scale in a perfectly competitive market, using skilled and unskilled labour as inputs. Multinational firms may arise in the imperfectly competitive manufactures market, which uses only skilled labour in the production process. The manufactures industry is characterized (in terms of skilled labour) by:

- constant marginal production costs MC
- transport costs t to ship a unit between Home and Foreign
- firm-level fixed costs F
- plant-level fixed costs P.

Note that this production structure ensures that the production of food is unskilled- and labour-intensive compared to the production of manufactures, as the latter is assumed to use only skilled labour in the production process. The difference from the model in the main text is that we now explicitly deal with demand for factors of production, which makes it a general equilibrium model, distinguishing between different types of labour.

For simplicity, we assume that there is always a production plant at the headquarter location of the firm: if a firm goes multinational, it will be a horizontal MNE. The firm now faces two basic choices, as illustrated in figure 5A.1. First, it has to decide in which country it will set up its headquarters: Home or Foreign. Second, it has to decide whether or not it becomes a multi-plant firm. If the answer to the second question is affirmative, the firm becomes a multinational. If not, we are dealing with a national firm exporting to the other market. The advantage of becoming a multinational firm is the ability to avoid the transport costs t. The disadvantage is the extra plant-level fixed cost P. Naturally, the firm sets up multi-plant production only if it is profitable to do so. Whether or not this will be the case, however, depends on the decisions made by other firms. Assume that competition in the manufactures industry is ruled by Cournot quantity rivalry among the four different types of firms, entering or exiting the market for manufactures in both countries until (excess) profits are equal to zero.

Firms may or may not decide to establish their headquarters in a country. Similarly, they may or may not decide to establish another production plant in the other country. Whether or not they make these decisions is analyzed within the model, thus determining the nature of market competition endogenously. A possible outcome, for example, is a case in which three national firms in Home and two multinationals with headquarters in Home compete in the market for manufactures in both countries with six national firms from Foreign, or with four national firms from Foreign and one multinational firm with headquarters in Foreign, etc. How many firms of each type there are in each country in the market equilibrium depends, of course, on the production structure (the parameters for fixed, marginal and transportation costs), the demand structure and the size and international distribution of the labour force.

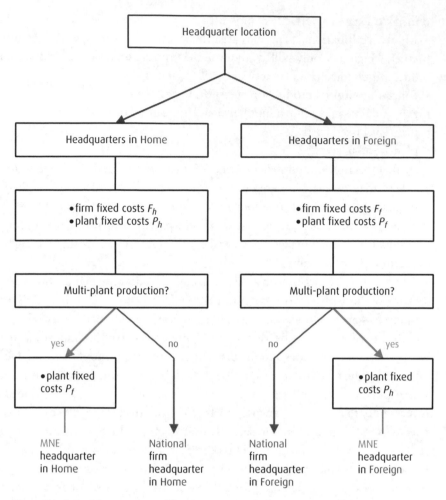

Figure 5A.1 Decision process and firm types

Figure 5A.2 summarizes the impact of different distributions of the world endowment of skilled and unskilled labour between the two countries in a so-called Edgeworth Box. At point *C*, in the centre of the Edgeworth Box, the skilled/unskilled labour ratio is the same in the two countries, being exactly equal in size. Moving from point *C* to the Northeast corner does not affect the skilled/unskilled labour ratio in either country, but it does imply that Home becomes larger than Foreign. The reverse holds if we move in the opposite direction, to the Southwest corner. Similarly, going from point *C* to the Northwest corner implies that unskilled labour becomes more abundant in Home and skilled labour more abundant in Foreign. Again, the reverse effect holds if we consider the opposite direction.

To present the main results more clearly, we identify three main types of regimes in figure 5A.3, namely (i) a regime with only *national* firms, (ii) a regime with only

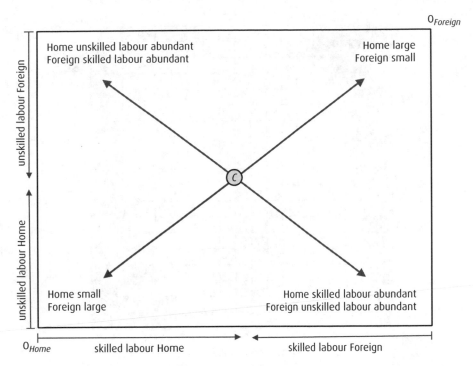

Figure 5A.2 Endowment distributions in the Edgeworth Box

MNEs, and (iii) a *mixed* regime with national firms and multinational corporations.[17] Figure 5A.3 shows the impact of all possible distributions of the world endowment of skilled and unskilled labour between the two countries for these three main types of regimes. The following observations are important:

1. If the two countries are *similar* in size and skilled/unskilled labour ratio (in the neighbourhood of the centre of the Edgeworth Box), the equilibrium is dominated by *multinational* firms.
2. If the two countries are *different* in size and/or skilled/unskilled labour ratio (in the corners of the Edgeworth Box), the equilibrium is dominated by *national* firms.
3. For *intermediate* endowment distributions, the production equilibrium is *mixed*, with both national firms and multinational firms.

All three observations correspond with stylized facts about FDI:

• Large FDI flows between similar developed nations
• Virtually no FDI flows to the small least-developed nations
• Moderate FDI flows to the Asian newly industrializing countries (NICs) and Latin America.

[17] For details, see van Marrewijk (2002, chapter 15).

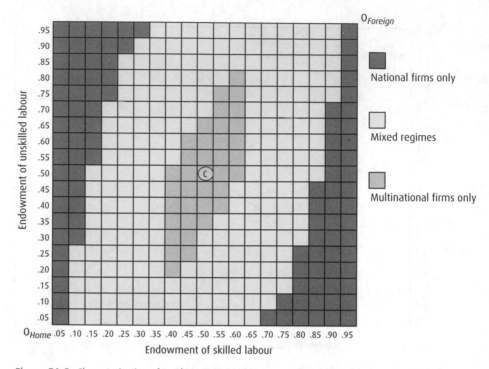

Figure 5A.3 Characterization of market structure
Source: Variation based on Markusen (2002), as used in van Marrewijk (2002, p. 311).

How can we explain these results? From the description of the structure of the model, we know that the decision to become a multinational – that is, to set up a second production plant in the other country – depends on the size of the *additional fixed plant costs* relative to the size of the *transport costs*. Now suppose that we are close to one of the corners of the Edgeworth Box – that is, either (a) the endowment ratio is very different between the two countries or (b) one country is very small and the other country is very large:

(a) If the endowment ratio is very different, there is a strong incentive for factor-abundance-type inter-industry trade. The skilled labour-rich country will specialize in the production of skilled labour-intensive manufactures. Since skilled labour is expensive in the unskilled labour-abundant country, it will be too expensive to incur the additional fixed costs of setting up an extra production plant, so that the production equilibrium is characterized by national firms producing manufactures in the skilled labour-abundant country only.

(b) If one of the countries is very small, it is important to realize that there are economies of scale associated with the production of manufactures. This makes

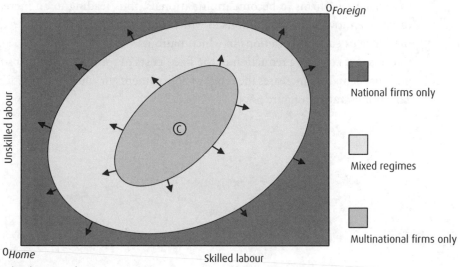

Figure 5A.4 Stylised impact of parameter changes for market structure

the small country unattractive as a home base for production (as it will be impossible to recuperate the fixed costs domestically) and as the basis for a foreign affiliate (the small market implies that the transport costs are fairly low if this market is serviced from abroad). The production equilibrium is therefore characterized by national firms producing manufactures in the large country only.

In both cases (a) and (b), the production equilibrium is characterized by national firms, which explains point 2 above. At the same time, the above reasoning also explains why multinationals arise if countries are similar, as in point 1 above, because similar countries imply similar wage rates (no specialization incentive) and similar market size (large transport costs to the other market, which can be avoided by setting up a subsidiary abroad). The intermediate cases with the mixed results (point 3 above) represent the transition from one extreme to the other.

The economic reasoning in cases (a) and (b) above also helps us to understand the main impact of changes in the key parameters in the model. Since economies of scale are important for the production of manufactures, an increase in the size of the global economy, as we have witnessed over the nineteenth and twentieth centuries, makes it easier to recover fixed investment costs. This also makes it easier for manufacturing firms to become multinationals, thus leading to an increase in the range of endowment distributions in which multinationals arise and a reduction in the range of such distributions in which national firms arise. Similarly, an increase in transport costs or a reduction in the fixed costs of multinational firms relative to national firms also increases the range of endowments in which multinationals arise. This is illustrated in figure 5A.4.

Capital, currency and crises

International capital mobility

KEYWORDS

history of capital mobility	interest parity condition	competing for capital
capital mobility	exchange rate risk	stocks and flows
capital market integration	costs and benefits	policy trilemma

6.1 Introduction

Capital, currency and crises, part III of this book, deals with an important and much-debated aspect of the global economy: *international capital mobility*. Much of the debate on the alleged pros and cons of globalization centres on this topic. Before we can analyse the possible costs and benefits of international capital mobility, we first need to learn more about international capital mobility itself, which is therefore the main objective of this chapter. We discuss various indicators of the degree of international capital mobility and we put the recent rise in international capital mobility into an historical perspective. More specifically, using quantity and price data on international capital mobility, we illustrate that the recent increase in international capital mobility is to a large extent not new at all – at the turn of the nineteenth century international capital mobility was already very pronounced. We also discuss important conceptual issues such as the difference between net and gross capital flows, as well as between stocks and flows.

After a discussion of the main trends and measurement issues with respect to international capital mobility and a brief introduction to the costs and benefits of international capital mobility in the first part of this chapter, the second part discusses the first alleged cost of international capital mobility: the loss of policy autonomy for individual countries. Much of the material used in this chapter will re-appear in chapters 7–9, indicating that this chapter sets the stage for the analysis of the implications of international capital mobility for both nations and firms.

6.2 Measuring international capital mobility

There are many possible indicators to measure the degree of international capital mobility. In this section we shall present and discuss the most important indicators, not only to show that there are large swings in the degree of international capital mobility over time, but also to demonstrate that there is a distinctive U-shaped pattern in the extent of international capital market integration.

Measuring international capital flows over time

From chapter 2, we know that the international balance of payments is constructed in such a way that a country's current account balance equals the capital account balance, and as such is a measure of *net* capital flows. The current account balance is widely used as an indicator for the degree of international capital mobility. A current account surplus (deficit) goes along with a net capital outflow (inflow). We also know from chapter 2 that the current account balance measures the difference between national savings and investment, where 'national' includes both the private and the government sector. This implies that in discussing capital mobility we must distinguish between *private* and *public capital flows*. Without international capital mobility, the current account is balanced by definition and national savings equal national investments. This puts a constraint on the economy in that domestic investment opportunities may not be realized because of a lack of domestic savings, or vice versa. We shall see that the loosening of this constraint is one of the two major potential gains of international capital mobility. A current account imbalance, be it a deficit or surplus, therefore means that a country can disentangle its national savings from its national investments.

Table 6.1 shows the development of the current account balance (*absolute* values, as a percentage of GDP) for twelve countries in the period 1870–2000. Based in part on these data, figure 6.1 illustrates the size of global net capital flows for an average of fifteen countries. A few findings stand out.

- During the period 1870–1914, the degree of international capital mobility was already quite high. In fact, after a slump in international capital flows in the interwar and the post-Second World War years until 1973, it is only fairly recently that international capital flows have again been on the increase. Based on this indicator of capital mobility, however, the size of *net* international capital flows is, on average, today still lower than it was during the period 1870–1914 (see figure 6.1).
- For some countries, the First World War and the Second World War were periods with very large capital flows. This effect is largely due to war-related government borrowing. The main point to emphasize is that there seems to be a considerable change in the degree of international capital mobility over time. This finding is backed up by the literature on the historical developments of international capital

Table 6.1 Size of net capital flows since 1870,[a] selected countries

Period	Arg	Aus	Can	Fr	Ger	It	Jap	UK	USA
1870–89	18.7	9.7	7.2	2.9	1.9	1.8	0.5	4.5	1.5
1890–1913	6.2	6.3	7.6	2.3	1.4	1.9	2.2	4.5	0.8
1914–18	2.7	7.6	3.5	3.1	–	11.7	6.6	2.9	3.5
1919–26	4.9	8.8	2.3	1.1	2.2	4.2	2.1	2.9	1.7
1927–31	3.7	12.8	3.6	1.8	1.8	1.5	0.6	2.0	0.8
1932–9	1.6	3.7	1.6	3.7	0.4	0.7	1.1	1.1	0.6
1940–6	4.8	7.1	6.5	1.8	–	3.4	1.0	7.3	1.0
1947–59	3.1	3.4	2.3	2.0	2.0	1.4	1.3	1.2	0.6
1960–73	1.0	2.3	1.2	1.5	1.0	2.1	1.0	0.8	0.5
1974–89	1.7	3.7	2.6	0.8	1.9	1.4	2.0	1.4	1.3
1990–2000	2.9	4.5	2.3	1.1	1.3	1.9	2.3	1.9	1.8

Sources: Obstfeld (1998), updated in Obstfeld and Taylor (2004, table 2.2).
Notes: [a] Size of net capital flows measured as mean absolute value of current account as a percentage of GDP, annual data.
– = Data not available.
Arg = Argentina, Aus = Australia, Can = Canada, Fr = France, Ger = Germany, It = Italy, Jap = Japan, UK = United Kingdom and USA = United States.

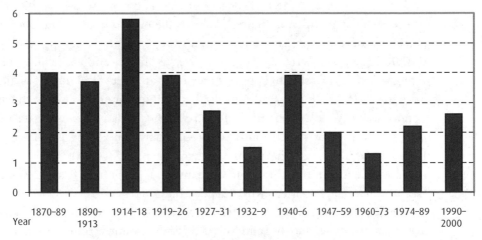

Figure 6.1 Global net capital flows, average for fifteen countries
Source: see table 6.1.
Note: Average includes countries listed in table 8.1, Denmark, Finland, the Netherlands, Norway, Spain and Sweden.

mobility. It is often argued that one of the key features of our 'global economy' is a high (and increasing) degree of international capital mobility. Table 6.1 and figure 6.1 undermine this argument, by showing that it holds only if we compare the most recent period with the first decades after the Second World War. It does

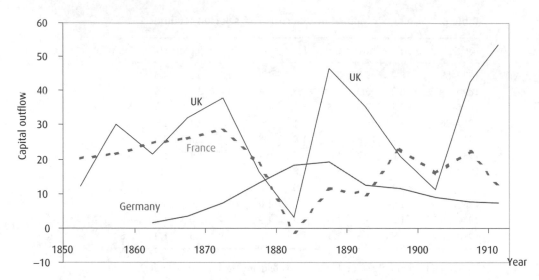

Figure 6.2 Capital outflows, 1860–1910, selected countries, per cent of national savings
Source: O'Rourke and Williamson (1999).

not hold when we compare the 1990s with the late nineteenth and early twentieth century.

To further illustrate the high degree of international capital mobility attained before the First World War, figure 6.2 shows the evolution of capital outflows as a percentage of respective national savings for the three largest European economies: the UK, France and Germany. This ratio gives us an indication as to how important foreign portfolio investment opportunities are as an outlet for domestic savings. The large share for the UK reflects its position as a colonial empire as well as the status of London as the world's main financial centre. Still, the relative size of capital outflows is high, not only for the UK but also for Germany and France. The large drop in France and the more gradual rise in Germany after 1871 is related to the substantial indemnity payments from France to Germany after the Franco-Prussian war of 1870 (see Brakman and Van Marrewijk, 1998, ch. 1).

The UK, France and Germany were net capital exporters in this period; they had on average a *net capital outflow* (and thus a current account surplus). Similar findings about the relative importance of international capital flows in this period can be found for a number of countries that were on the receiving end: countries with a *net capital inflow* (and thus a current account deficit). Argentina, Sweden and the USA, for example, all depended strongly on the influx of foreign capital. By today's standards, net capital inflows or outflows that exceed 20 per cent or more of national savings are still quite high. In 2002, for instance, the net lending as a share of national savings for the USA, Japan, the Euro area and the total of developing countries was about −20 per cent, + 9 per cent, +10 per cent and −8 per cent, respectively, where + denotes net capital outflow and − denotes a net capital inflow (see IMF, 2003, table 44). Before we can turn to an explanation of what accounts for these changes in international capital mobility, we first have to discuss some conceptual issues about measures of capital mobility, in order to understand what they do, and what they do not, measure.

Conceptual issues about measuring capital mobility

Table 6.1 is informative but it is far from the whole story about international capital mobility. For one thing, the table is based on data for a few countries only and, with the exception of Argentina, consists exclusively of currently developed countries. What about the direction and size of capital flows to developing countries? Even though the evidence is less clear-cut, and there are large differences between developing countries, for the group of developing countries as a whole there is in general a net private capital inflow, which increased in the period 1970–2003. Given the lack of national savings and the potentially large return on investment, one would also expect the developing countries to have a current account deficit and a net capital inflow. The fact that over a longer period of time the size of net private capital inflow is increasing coincides with a gradual decrease in the restrictions these countries impose on ingoing and outgoing capital flows. The size of the *net* capital inflows is, however, still quite small compared to the flows to developing countries at the start of the twentieth century. Moreover, for individual countries the flows are subject to large fluctuations.

The net private capital flows to developing countries were on average a mere 1.25 per cent of their GDP in the 1970s and 1980s, increasing to 3 per cent in the 1990s before dropping to approximately 2.5 per cent at the beginning of the twenty-first century. These private capital flows are unevenly distributed, with a few developing countries receiving the bulk of them. Table 6.2 shows the net capital flows (both private and official flows) to emerging market economies in the period 1992–2000. This recent period was chosen in part because, as we will learn in more detail in chapters 8 and 9, the 1990s were a period of financial fragility in many emerging market economies. One key feature of this fragility was the *volatility of international capital flows* to the developing countries. The data show that the capital flows can be subject to sharp reversals (in absolute terms), as vividly illustrated in figure 6.3 for Asia (witness the decline from 1996 to 1998). Even though on average and over longer periods of time emerging market economies have witnessed (increasing) capital inflows, this is not always the case for the net *private* capital inflows. Table 6.2 and figure 6.3 bring out the uneven distribution of capital flows (compare, for instance, Africa with Asia), as well as the difference between FDI and portfolio investment, with

Table 6.2 Net capital flows to emerging market economies, 1992–2000, billion US $

Year	Net private capital flows	Direct investment	Of which: portfolio investment	other private flows	Net official flows
1992	106.9	35.7	62.7	8.5	25
1993	128.6	57.9	76.8	−6.1	48.7
1994	142.3	81	105	−43.7	4.8
1995	211.4	95.8	41.4	74.2	15.7
1996	224.7	119.5	79.6	25.6	2
1997	115.2	141.3	39.4	−65.6	52.7
1998	66.2	151.6	0.3	−85.6	55.3
1999	67.4	154.6	4.8	−91.9	13
2000	36.4	141.9	17.3	−122	19.9

Source: IMF (2000).

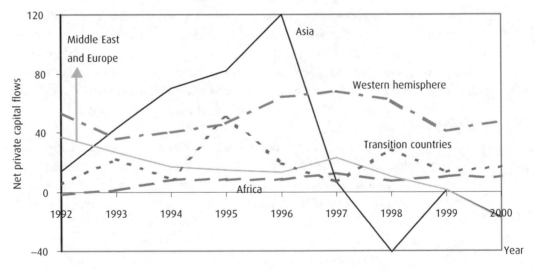

Figure 6.3 Net private capital flows to emerging markets, 1992–2000, billion $ US
Source: IMF (2000).

the latter being far more volatile than the former. With the onset of the financial crisis in Southeast Asia in the summer of 1997, the empirical evidence shows that portfolio investment and other private capital flows (mainly bank lending) decreased strongly from 1997 onwards compared to the first half of the 1990s. FDI flows were far more stable.

6.3 Issues about capital mobility

Apart from the coverage in terms of the number of countries included in table 6.1, there are some conceptual issues about the use of net capital flows as an indicator that also need to be addressed. In particular, the following issues are important when one tries to measure international capital mobility:
- International capital mobility versus international capital market integration
- Capital stocks versus capital flows
- Gross capital mobility versus net capital mobility
- The composition of capital flows
- Prices versus quantities

We will discuss and illustrate each of these issues in turn.

International capital mobility versus international capital market integration

Net capital flows are used to measure international capital mobility, but they may not tell us much about the degree of international integration of the capital markets of the countries under consideration. Suppose a small country decides to abolish all of its remaining restrictions on ingoing and outgoing capital flows to the extent that the capital market of this country becomes part of the global capital market. There is thus full capital market integration. The size of net capital flows before and after the introduction of capital mobility might nevertheless be rather small. If the return on investment in the country happens to be the same as the return on the 'worldwide' capital market, the introduction of capital mobility will not lead to capital flows at all, because there is no incentive to invest in foreign countries. We shall look at this issue in more detail below when we discuss 'prices versus quantities'. So, one can have an increase in international capital market integration without an accompanying increase in capital flows. Similarly, a country that still has restrictions left on its ingoing or outgoing capital flows can nevertheless experience substantial net capital flows if the difference between the national and the foreign rate of return on investment is large enough. In this case, we have large net capital flows coupled with a limited degree of international capital market integration.

Capital stocks versus capital flows

Capital *flows* cover only the financial transactions between residents and non-residents that take place within a certain period of time. As such, they provide no information about the *stock* of international financial assets and liabilities of a

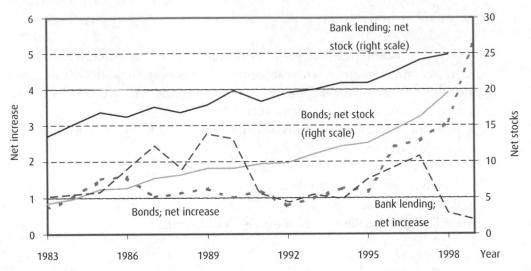

Figure 6.4 Evolution of net financing through international financial markets, 1983–1998, per cent of GDP

Source: See table 6.3.

country. Information about the latter requires a country's balance sheet containing all the relevant assets and liabilities. This year's net capital flows, as reported on the balance of payments, gives only the *change* in a country's financial assets and liabilities. Using the analogy with a firm's financial accounting system, the net capital flows are the net income of a country and the net capital stock of a country is equivalent to a firm's net worth. The difference between the various components of the net capital stock and the net capital flows is considerable. To illustrate this, table 6.3 gives the aggregate *stock* of net international financing by non-banks as a percentage of total GDP for a group of seventeen developed countries in the period 1983–99. The developments over time are illustrated in figure 6.4. International lending refers to bank lending as well as lending on the international capital market (mainly the bonds market). For the sake of comparison, the change or flow in net international financing is also reported. Table 6.3 shows a clear increase in the stock of net international financing for these countries, meaning that the degree of international capital mobility has increased. In contrast, the net increase (the flow measure) for bank lending displays no clear trend. It is only for the net increase in bond financing that we see a (relatively strong) increase. But for both flow categories, the annual net increase is always positive, which helps to explain the gradual increase over time of the total net stock of international bank lending and bond financing.

Table 6.1, our benchmark table, provided information only on the difference between capital inflows and outflows – that is, on *net* capital flows. This focus on *net* flows considerably under-states the size of the actual capital flows. Capital mobility

Table 6.3 Net financing at international financial markets, 1983–1999, per cent of GDP, seventeen countries

	Net increase			Net stocks		
	Bank lending[a]	Bond financing[b]	Total[c]	Bank lending	Bond financing	Total[c]
1983	1.06	0.72	1.62	13.54	4.31	16.97
1984	1.07	1.03	1.73	15.09	4.89	18.96
1985	1.19	1.51	2.04	16.81	6.25	21.58
1986	1.79	1.59	2.66	16.21	6.41	20.88
1987	2.53	1.04	3.16	17.56	7.79	23.10
1988	1.83	1.12	2.47	16.85	8.16	22.57
1989	2.79	1.24	3.50	17.95	9.05	24.00
1990	2.61	1.00	3.13	19.78	9.09	25.70
1991	1.06	1.17	2.02	18.29	9.70	24.82
1992	0.88	0.79	1.31	19.48	9.92	26.30
1993	1.06	1.00	1.45	19.96	11.12	27.35
1994	0.94	1.24	1.99	20.93	12.11	28.78
1995	1.48	1.17	2.44	20.89	12.61	28.96
1996	1.88	2.38	3.38	22.47	14.45	31.04
1997	2.13	2.58	3.95	24.16	16.19	34.67
1998	0.52	3.08	2.57	24.81	19.52	37.74
1999	0.40	5.30	4.05			

Source, BIS, *Annual Report*; Ostrup (2002).
[a] Bank lending: net international bank lending as measured by total cross-border claims of banks corrected for double-counting.
[b] Bond financing: international issues of bonds, notes and money market instruments minus redemptions and repurchases.
[c] Total: the sum of net bank lending and bond financing with the deduction of corresponding assets held by reporting banks.

may increase strongly, without this showing up in net capital flows. If in year 1 the capital inflow (non-residents buying domestic financial assets) is $100 billion and the capital outflow (residents buying foreign financial assets) is $90 billion, the net capital inflow is $10 billion. If subsequently, in year 2, assuming unchanged prices of assets, these numbers are $150, $140 and hence $10 billion, respectively. The net capital flow is then unchanged, suggesting no change in capital mobility. The gross capital flows, however, have increased substantially, indicating an increase in the volume of international financial transactions. Recall from table 6.1 that on average the net capital flows, as measured by our indicator current account/GDP, were 2.2 per cent and 2.6 per cent for the periods 1973–89 and 1990–2000, respectively, for the group of selected countries. If we use the *gross* financial flows (the summation of ingoing as well as outgoing financial flows over the various countries as a percentage of total GDP) for (almost) the same set of countries in the same time period, we end up with higher numbers and a clear increase of gross financial flows to GDP over time: in the mid-1970s the gross financial flows to GDP averaged 6 per cent, compared to 16 (!) per cent in the second half of the 1990s.

Gross capital mobility versus net capital mobility

With respect to the distinction between net and gross capital flows, there is another issue that needs to be emphasized. In our hypothetical example, we assumed that the relevant time period was one year. Many international financial transactions, however, have a considerably shorter time horizon. Take, for instance, transactions on the currency exchange market, where more than 90 per cent of the transactions across the world are intra-day transactions – that is, they are carried out within a single day. By taking a longer time horizon and by 'netting', we therefore exclude a very large part of the international currency transactions.

The next issue is the importance of *gross* financial *stocks*. Following Obstfeld and Taylor (2004), we again take an historical perspective, just as we did in table 6.1. Obstfeld and Taylor (2004) computed the stock of foreign-owned capital for each country for a large number of countries from 1825 onwards. They consider the asset and liability side separately – that is, they compute the value of foreign assets owned by a country as well as the value of that country's capital owned by foreigners. With country data on foreign investment, and scaled by a country's GDP, they derive the foreign assets/GDP ratio and the foreign liabilities/GDP ratio for a range of years. These two ratios provide evidence of the gross stocks of international capital over time, both owned by the country and owned by foreigners.

Summing over all countries for which data were available, table 6.4 illustrates the development of the foreign capital stock/GDP ratios. Both the foreign assets/world GDP ratio and the foreign liabilities/world GDP ratio display a similar pattern. After an increase in gross financial stocks in the period leading up to the First World War, there was a sharp decline in subsequent years. It is only from 1980 onwards that gross financial stocks again reached and surpassed the levels reached before the First World War. The unprecedented rise of the relative importance of foreign investment since 1980 indicates that the growth of international capital mobility outstripped the growth rate of GDP. The final two rows of table 6.4 show how much of the foreign-owned capital stock is owned by the UK and the USA, respectively. This is illustrated in figure 6.5. The UK's dominant position in the world economy and its position as the main financial centre until the First World War are clearly borne out by the data, as is its declining importance since 1850. The declining importance of the UK is only partially compensated for by the USA, which owned the largest share of the foreign owned capital stock in the 1950s but never reached the levels previously achieved by the UK. During the second part of the twentieth century, as countries increasingly

Table 6.4 Gross financial stocks, 1825–1938

	1825	1855	1870	1900	1914	1930	1938
Assets/GDP	–	–	0.07	0.19	0.18	0.08	0.11
Liabilities/GDP	–	–	–	0.14	0.21	–	0.11
Foreign assets: UK share	0.56	0.78	0.64	0.51	0.50	0.44	0.43
Foreign assets: US share	0.00	0.00	0.00	0.02	0.06	0.36	0.22

	1945	1960	1980	1985	1990	1995	2000
Assets/GDP	0.05	0.06	0.25	0.36	0.49	0.62	0.92
Liabilities/GDP	–	0.02	0.30	–	0.60	0.79	0.95
Foreign assets: UK share	0.40	0.21	0.20	0.19	0.17	0.16	0.15
Foreign assets: US share	0.43	0.51	0.28	0.29	0.21	0.22	0.25

Source: Obstfeld and Taylor (2004, pp. 52–3).

Notes: – = Data not available.

Sample size increases from seven in 1900 to sixty-three countries in 2000.

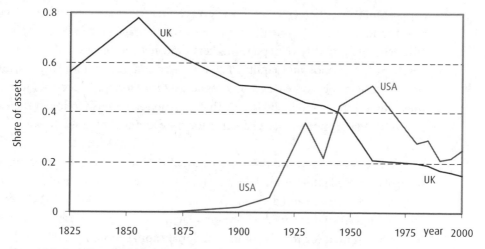

Figure 6.5 Evolution of British and American share in foreign assets, 1825–2000, share of total
Source: See table 6.3.

got rid of their restrictions on international capital flows, the share of foreign assets owned by US residents began to fall.

Table 6.1 (net capital flows) and table 6.4 (gross capital stocks) essentially present the same message. By taking an historical perspective, it becomes clear that international capital mobility was already quite substantial in 1900. It is only when one compares the pre-1980 episode of international capital mobility with the first decades after the Second World War that a strong increase in international capital mobility becomes apparent. This 'rise–fall–rise' or U-shaped pattern of international capital mobility in the twentieth century is a reminder that the current wave of globalization is not necessarily here to stay indefinitely.

The composition of capital flows

The above discussion does not imply that the current phase of international capital mobility is nothing but a return to 'pre-1914' days. To see this, note that the catch-all feature of total net capital flows or gross capital stocks hides information about the *composition* of capital mobility. This issue first of all relates to the time horizon of the financial assets: are the capital flows predominantly short-term or long-term? Short-term capital flows cover those assets with a horizon of a year or less, such as a three-month loan to a foreign firm or a five-month savings deposit held at a foreign bank. Long-term capital flows have a longer time horizon, like the purchase of ten-year foreign government bonds or FDI. The composition has changed over time. In the first era of international capital mobility (1870–1914), capital flows were mainly long-term, whereas an important feature of the second era of international capital mobility (1980–?) is that short-term capital flows have become relatively more important. This development, combined with the fact that in many (developing) countries the liquidity of capital markets (and hence the tradability of long-term assets such as bonds and equity) has increased, has important implications. For one thing, it has become easier and less costly for (foreign) investors to pull back their funds if they (suddenly) decide that they no longer wish to invest their savings in a particular country. (See chapter 8 for data and a related analysis on currency crises.)

The different composition of international capital flows in the first and second wave of increased international capital mobility is also important when one considers the *direction* of the capital flows. During the first wave (1870–1914), long-term capital flows from developed to developing countries were far more important and mainly accounted for the rise of international capital mobility. FDI and long-term (bond) financing were far more important than short-term flows. This has now changed. The recent increase in international capital mobility is much more due to the increase of short-term flows between developed countries. This explains why, notwithstanding the overall increase of international capital mobility, the increase (if at all) in capital flows from the capital-rich/developed countries to the capital-poor/developing countries is rather limited (we return to this issue in chapter 7, when we discuss the potential benefits of international capital mobility). To bring home this last important point it is worth quoting the seminal study by Obstfeld and Taylor (2004, p. 249) at some length:

To summarize: for all the suggestion that we have returned to the pre-1914 type of global capital market, there is at least one major qualitative difference between then and now. Today's foreign asset distribution is much more about asset 'swapping' by rich countries – mutual diversification – than it is about the accumulation of large one-way positions, which is the key component of the development process according to standard textbook treatments. Modern capital flows therefore are more about hedging and risk sharing than about long-term finance and the mediation of saving supply and investment demand between countries.

Prices versus quantities

A final issue with respect to the limitations of using the current account balance, and thus net capital flows, as an indicator for international capital mobility is that these data (and in fact all the data so far on international capital mobility) provide no information on prices. Tables 6.1–6.4, used to illustrate international capital mobility, are incomplete without information on the prices of financial assets. They may also be misleading because, with a high degree of international market integration, the prices of a particular financial asset may no longer differ between countries, eliminating the incentive for cross-border capital flows. A supplementary cross-country comparison of the prices of financial assets is useful. The most important prices are the interest rates. At the country level, a price comparison typically entails a comparison between the interest rate on a domestic financial asset and the foreign interest rate on a similar asset. The integration of international capital markets – and thereby the degree of international capital mobility – are said to have increased if the interest differential narrows. To see this, assume that we have perfect international capital mobility – that is, there are no capital restrictions whatsoever for financial assets. Assume also that other potential transaction costs are the same across countries: broker fees, political risks or exchange rate risk do not differ between countries. If the interest rate on a ten-year government bonds, r_{home}, were 7 per cent in Home whereas the given interest rate on the corresponding asset in the rest of the world (Foreign), $r_{foreign}$, was 5 per cent, the arbitrage profit opportunity would ensure a capital inflow from Foreign to Home until the interest rate in Home was also 5 per cent. Under these assumptions, any deviation of r_{home} from $r_{foreign}$, however small, would lead to continuous capital inflows or outflows. Capital flows would cease to exist only when $r_{home} = r_{foreign}$ – that is, when the capital account was in equilibrium. In reality, capital mobility is not perfect and the transaction costs are usually not the same across countries. Taking transaction costs (TC) and risk differences into account, one would expect that

$$r_{home} = r_{foreign} + risk + TC \tag{6.1}$$

In (6.1), the TC cover all kinds of transaction costs that, besides the actual interest rates, have a bearing on the rate of return for portfolio investors. So, TC includes capital controls such as tax on capital inflows or outflows and market transaction costs. For the sake of simplicity, we assume that all these transaction costs concern Home only, so that $TC > 0$. The risk difference may relate to political and expected exchange rate risks. The latter are particularly important for international investors: if the currency of Home is expected to depreciate against the Foreign currency, portfolio investors will ask for a higher interest rate in order to be compensated for this exchange rate risk. Suppose, for simplicity, that apart from the exchange rate risk there are no other risks and that transaction costs are zero. Equation (6.1) then becomes

$$r_{home} = r_{foreign} + dE; \quad TC = 0, \quad risk = dE \tag{6.1'}$$

where E is the exchange rate between Home and Foreign: the price of 1 unit of foreign currency in units of home currency, so that a rise in E implies a depreciation of the Home currency. The term dE denotes the change in the exchange rate (see chapter 8). Equation (6.1') is a simple version of the so-called uncovered interest parity (UIP) condition, which is important from a policy perspective. Taking the foreign interest rate $r_{foreign}$ as given, it indicates that in a world with a high degree of international capital mobility the domestic interest rate r_{home} can differ from the foreign interest rate $r_{foreign}$ only if the exchange rate between Home and Foreign is *not* fixed! In section 6.4 and in chapter 7, we shall explain this in more detail and discuss the empirical tests of this condition.

To get an indication of the degree of capital market integration in the period 1880–1994 (roughly the same period as covered in tables 6.1 and 6.4) based on (6.1), we focus on the evolution of *interest rate differentials*. To avoid as many transaction costs as possible and to eliminate exchange rate changes, we again follow Obstfeld and Taylor (2004) and compare the mean and standard deviation of the interest rate differential between sterling-denominated assets sold in New York and in London over a long period of time. Since we are concerned only with assets denominated in the same currency (in this case, the British pound sterling), we do not have to worry about exchange rate risk. A low mean and standard deviation indicates a high degree of capital market integration for these assets and a high degree of international capital mobility for this segment of the capital market. Figure 6.6 shows that the standard deviation was at its lowest in the period 1870–1916, then increased sharply before coming down over a long period of time after 1980. Just like table 6.1, figure 6.6 therefore suggests that capital mobility (between the USA and the UK) was very high before the First World War, decreased strongly in the interbellum and in the Second World War, before increasing again from 1970 onwards. Similar evidence for different episodes and countries about the difference between (implied) interest differentials support this conclusion.

The question how to explain these swings in international capital mobility is discussed in section 6.4. Before we continue, however, we consider one more piece of

Figure 6.6 Interest rate differential, 1880–1999, London–New York, standard deviation of the difference
Source: Obstfeld (1998).

price evidence on the degree of international capital mobility. Figure 6.6 and our UIP condition (6.1′) deal with nominal interest rates. What about the convergence of *real* interest rates? The real interest rate in period t is equal to the nominal interest rate in period t minus the expected inflation rate, π, where expectations are formed in period t regarding the inflation in period $t + 1$. Portfolio investors are interested in their real rate of return, so that the various expected national inflation rates are relevant for determining their optimal allocation. Capital will flow from countries with a low real interest rate to countries with a high real interest rate. From the standard theory of economic growth and development (to be discussed in chapter 11), we know that this implies that capital flows from capital-rich to capital-poor countries. These flows will not only narrow the gap between the capital stock of the rich and poor countries, they are also expected to lead to real interest rate convergence between the countries. Since the real interest rate for Home (i_{home}) is defined as the nominal interest rate minus the inflation rate in Home ($r_{home} - \pi_{home}$) and similarly for Foreign, we can rewrite (6.1′) as $i_{home} - i_{foreign} = dE + (\pi_{home} - \pi_{foreign})$.[1] The empirical question focuses on how large the real interest rate differential $i_{home} - i_{foreign}$

---

[1] We assume that the expected inflation rate is equal to the current inflation rate, which holds for simple extrapolative expectations.

is, and how it develops over time. The answer depends on the *time horizon*. If, as before, we take an historical perspective and consider only studies based on very long time series, the available evidence indicates that the mean real interest rate differential is typically very close to zero, suggesting a high degree of international capital mobility.[2]

6.4 Determinants, benefits and costs of capital mobility

O'Rourke and Williamson (1999) distinguish between three explanations for the rise of international capital mobility in the late nineteenth and early twentieth century and the demise of international capital mobility in the period that followed. The first explanation is *technology*. As with the trade in goods (see chapter 1), the lowering of transportation and communication costs provided a strong stimulus for cross-border financial transactions. The introduction of the telegraph, and its widespread use from 1860 onwards, above all made it possible for price differentials between geographically distinct financial markets to fall substantially. As (6.1) predicts, a lowering of transaction costs (in this case, transportation and especially communication costs), will narrow price differentials. The technology factor can help to explain why international capital mobility rose initially, but not why it decreased from the 1920s onwards.

The second explanation is the role of *financial institutions*. The development of new financial products stimulated international capital mobility. Leading economists in the research of the historical development of the international financial system, such as Michael Bordo, Barry Eichengreen, Maurice Obstfeld and Alan Taylor, stress a particular institution: the system of *fixed exchange rates* that most developed countries came to adopt in the second half of the nineteenth century, the so-called 'gold standard'. The details of the system need not concern us here, but two points are worth mentioning.

- First, under the gold standard countries could maintain the fixed exchange rate (all currencies traded against a fixed gold price) only if they geared their domestic monetary and fiscal policies towards the fixed exchange rate objective. This boosted capital mobility, see (6.1), because it reduced the exchange rate risk.
- Second, until the 1920s countries using the gold standard were willing to subordinate their domestic policies for the fixed exchange rate objective. In terms of (6.1'),

---

[2] Countries for which data are available for a very long period and at a high frequency are usually developed countries. This results in a bias because we expect capital market integration to be stronger for these countries compared to a sample in developing countries which are also included.

they were willing to give up the use of their domestic interest rate r_{home} to steer the domestic economy. For the exchange rate to be fixed ($dE = 0$) in a regime of international capital mobility, Home's policy-makers cannot allow the national interest rate to deviate from that in the rest of the world. This willingness was enhanced by the notion that policy-makers could not and should not try to steer the economy using interest rate policies. From this perspective, subordination did not seem a very large price to pay.

The third (and most important) explanation for the changes in international capital mobility during the twentieth century is the role of *politics*. The subordination of domestic policies to the exchange rate objective became increasingly open to debate from the 1920s onwards. Policy-makers increasingly wanted to be able to steer the domestic economy through the use of domestic stabilization policies. In some countries (notably the UK) the gold standard also became to be seen as a straitjacket because the fixed parity between the national currency and gold was thought to hurt the export sector and economic growth. Moreover, the economic depression of the 1930s stimulated the change in policy preferences towards domestic policies and against the fixed exchange rate. The collapse of the gold standard and the switch to flexible exchange rates meant that countries actively tried to boost their economies by a devaluation of their currency. These *competitive devaluations* were looked upon as harmful for the economy (see box 6.1). The collapse of the gold standard meant a decrease of international capital mobility (because of the increased exchange rate risk), which was further enhanced by the introduction of capital controls. International capital mobility was deemed to be *destabilizing*.

Box 6.1 The spider web spiral

The basis of the present international economic order was laid during and immediately after the Second World War. The primary concern in the consultations was not to repeat the disastrous experience of the international economic relations of the inter-war period. During the Great Depression in the 1930s, the 'beggar-your-neighbour' policies, in which each country tried to transfer its economic problems to other countries by depreciating its own currency and imposing high tariffs (such as the US Smoot–Hawley Act in 1930), led to an almost complete collapse of the international trade system, further exacerbating and prolonging the economic crisis. The impact of the 'beggar-your-neighbour' policies on international trade is aptly illustrated by the 'spider web spiral', measuring the size of world imports in each month by the distance to the origin (see figure 6.7). In a period of only four years, world trade flows dropped to one-third of their previous level (from January 1929 to January 1933, world imports fell from $2,998 to $992 million US gold dollars per month).

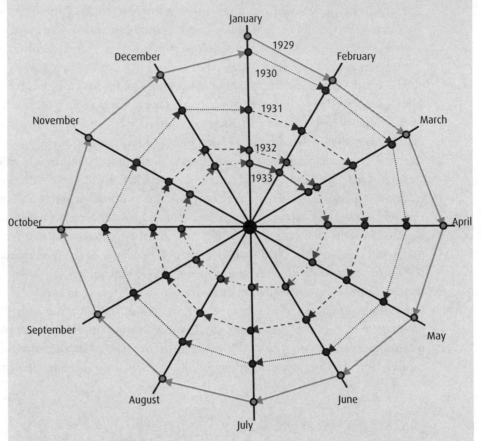

Figure 6.7 Spider web spiral: world imports, January–December 1929–1933, million $ US gold[a]
Source: Van Marrewijk (2002).
Note: [a] Values in January (1929–1933): 2,998, 2,739, 1,839, 1,206, 992.

The signing of the Charter in 1945 in San Francisco laid the foundations of the United Nations as an international organization. The system of international bodies developed afterwards is known as the 'United Nations family'. Although consultations took place within the United Nations, arguably the most important international organizations – the IMF and the World Bank (WB) on financial issues and the GATT, later to become the WTO, on international trade issues – were eventually located outside the United Nations. The post-war international economic order is therefore sometimes called the GATT/WTO–IMF/WB order.

After the Second World War there was a general agreement that competitive devaluations had to be prevented and that a system of fixed exchange rates was to be preferred over a system of flexible exchange rates. At the same time, national governments thought it important to be able to pursue domestic economic policy objectives, which implied the need for some degree of policy independence. Under the so-called 'Bretton Woods system' of fixed exchange rates (1945–73), the participating countries tried to combine these two objectives: fixed exchange rates and a certain degree of policy independence. How was this achieved? Countries limited the degree of international capital mobility through exchange rate and other capital controls. In terms of (6.1), this amounts to increasing the transaction costs, so that even with limited (exchange rate) risks (from the fixed exchange rate regime: $dE = 0$) domestic and foreign interest rates need not be the same, $r_{home} \neq r_{foreign}$, as long as there is only a limited degree of capital mobility. Of course, there was some international movement of capital, but this mainly came about through public and not private capital flows. The role of the IMF was crucial in this respect, as it assisted countries with current account imbalances. More specifically, countries with a current account deficit, so that national savings fell short of national investments, could draw upon the IMF to finance the difference. We return to the relationship between fixed exchange rates, international capital mobility, and policy independence on p. 182.

After the collapse of the Bretton Woods system in the early 1970s, there was a return to flexible exchange rates – that is to say, no international system of fixed exchange rates came to replace the Bretton Woods system. On a regional (European) and bilateral level exchange rates remained fixed, but after 1973 the major currencies (US dollar, British pound sterling, German mark and Japanese yen) floated relative to each other. With flexible exchange rates, the case for international capital mobility became stronger. There is clear evidence that fixed exchange rates gradually went out of fashion after 1973. About 75 per cent of all countries had *de jure* or *de facto* fixed exchange rates in 1973, decreasing to fewer than 50 per cent in 2000. Most capital controls in developed countries were gradually abolished in the period 1973–90. Similarly, emerging market economies in Latin America, Asia and the CEE countries were urged by institutions such as the IMF and the WB to engage in capital account liberalization – that is, they were stimulated to lift their restrictions on capital flows. IMF indices of capital account restrictions reveal that this process really took off (on average) for developing countries after 1990, which is about a decade after the corresponding policy change in the developed countries really began (IMF 2002; Kaminsky and Schmukler, 2003). The favourable initial experience of the developed countries with the lifting of capital restrictions and the subsequent increase of international capital mobility probably helped to convince the developing countries to do the same in the first half of the 1990s. In essence, politics was the decisive factor in the comeback of international capital mobility. Technological changes (the rise of information and computer technology (ICT), as well as the introduction of new financial instruments) also facilitated the increase of international capital mobility, but the political factor was of over-riding importance as countries took the decision to abolish most restrictions on international capital flows. In the 1990s, the initial optimism about the benefits of this second wave of widespread international capital mobility received a serious blow because of the financial crises that occurred in many emerging markets. Many policy-makers and economists believed that international capital mobility was a main cause for these crises. This prompted pleas for the (re)-introduction of limits on capital mobility. It also became clear that financial account liberalization could be destabilizing when the supervision and regulation of the domestic financial sector was weak. In chapters 9 and 10 we shall deal with the impact of international capital flows on financial crises, the possible policy responses to prevent a crisis and policies to limit the fall-out if a crisis happens.

To understand the come-back of international capital mobility, it also helps, as emphasized by the IMF (2002), to realize that international trade and financial integration are complementary. The rise of international trade flows analysed in part II of this book increased the 'demand' for international capital mobility – that is, trade flows call for international financial services to accompany them. Cross-border credit will be stimulated as exporting firms may want to rely on financial services in the importing country, or exporting firms may want to use financial markets to insure themselves against the exchange rate risks that go along with international trade (see chapter 8). Conversely, an increase in international capital flows may trigger higher international trade flows. FDI, such as setting-up of a new production plant abroad, may go along with more trade if, for instance, the firm undertaking the FDI imports capital goods from its home country for its construction. For the period 1975–99, the IMF (2002, figure 3.2) concludes that trade openness (exports + imports relative to GDP) and financial openness (stocks of FDI + portfolio investment flows relative to GDP) are positively correlated, with a correlation coefficient for the developing countries (where the trade and financial integration is heavily criticized) of 0.66.

6.5 Summing up and looking ahead

We have shown that international capital mobility is not constant over time. Even though the degree of international capital mobility has increased in recent years, it is by some standards today still lower than it was a hundred years ago. It is also clear that the composition and direction of international capital flows has changed over time. The merits of international capital mobility are not undisputed, so it is safe to conclude that the case for free capital mobility is less clear-cut than the case for free international trade. But why? In the remainder of this chapter and in chapters 7 and 8 we shall argue that the ambiguity with respect to the benefits of international capital mobility arises from the fact that financial transactions are special because of the associated risks involved.

We distinguish between two main benefits and two main costs of international capital mobility. To some extent these benefits and costs have already been introduced. Here we simply state the principal benefits and costs, as they provide a roadmap for the remainder of this chapter and for chapters 7–9 that follow.

Benefits

- The disentangling of national savings and investment, which allows more efficient (geographically unconstrained) channelling of funds (chapter 7).
- The reduction of risk involved in financial transactions (chapter 7).

Costs

- The limitation of national policy independence (section 6.6)
- The increase of financial fragility (chapter 9) and the role of currency instability (chapter 8) in bringing about more financial fragility.

Before we continue, two observations can already be made:
- First, it is difficult to *quantify the balance of the benefits and costs*, not only because the benefits and costs are hard to measure, compare and quantify, but also because of the lack of a counter-factual. In assessing the net gains of international capital mobility one would like to have a benchmark as to what would have happened to the economy if there had been no capital mobility. This counter-factual world does not exist.
- Second, despite these caveats, there are attempts to quantify the impact of capital mobility on, for instance, GDP growth. There is no consensus in the empirical literature that the net gains are positive – that is, that capital market integration stimulates GDP growth. There are, however, many individual historical and recent cases of countries for which the net benefits are positive. This raises the question why some countries benefit from more financial openness, while other countries do not. This question will be addressed in chapter 7.

To conclude, if international capital mobility is a mixed blessing in the sense that (at times) financial fragility may increase, this raises the question of the proper response to, or prevention of, financial fragility. This question revolves around the role of policy, a topic discussed in the second part of chapter 10.

6.6 Policy autonomy

Before concluding this chapter, we shall discuss the first main cost of international capital mobility: the *loss of policy autonomy or policy independence*. Our discussion above on the changes in capital mobility over time relates to three policy objectives: (1) a fixed exchange rate, (2) monetary policy independence and (3) capital mobility. It turns out that only two of these three policy objectives can be achieved at any one point in time, at the expense of the third. This can be illustrated most effectively if we interpret 'risk' in (6.1) as consisting of exchange rate risk dE only, that is

$$r_{home} = r_{foreign} + dE + TC \tag{6.1''}$$

Assume that we are dealing with a small country that takes the Foreign interest rate $r_{foreign}$ as given. If there is capital mobility (objective (3)), the transaction costs are very low, such that (6.1'') reduces to $r_{home} = r_{foreign} + dE$. This implies that expected changes in the exchange rate are the only reason for an interest rate differential between Home and Foreign. With full international capital mobility, policy-makers must therefore choose between monetary policy independence (objective (1) – that is, a possible deviation between Home and Foreign interest rates) and a fixed exchange rate (objective (2)). If, for example, they decide to fix the exchange rate ($dE = 0$), this automatically implies $r_{home} = r_{foreign}$, making monetary policy independence impossible. Similarly, if they decide to strive for monetary policy independence, this automatically makes a fixed exchange rate impossible ($dE \neq 0$). The only way in which objectives (1) and (2) can be achieved simultaneously is by giving up objective (3), in which case (6.1'') reduces to $r_{home} = r_{foreign} + TC$, since $dE = 0$. A country can then steer its own interest rate (retain policy autonomy) and have a fixed exchange rate at the cost of immobile capital, which prevents portfolio investors directing capital flows to or from Home so as to benefit from the interest rate differential. In addition, Home could use exchange rate controls that limit or even foreclose the convertibility of the currency.

The incompatibility between objectives (1)–(3) was pointed out by Nobel laureate Robert Mundell in the early 1960s. It is called the *incompatible trinity, incompatible triangle*, or *policy trilemma* and provides a categorization scheme that helps us to understand the changes in capital mobility over time. Figure 6.8 illustrates the trilemma. In each triangle of the figure the two squares indicate the objectives pursued by the government, whereas the circle at the top of the triangle indicates the policy objective that cannot be met. The trilemma indicates that there is a price to pay for policy-makers when they want to achieve full capital mobility. Until recently, the majority of policy-makers in small, open economies and in most emerging markets opted for the fixed exchange rate objective alongside capital mobility. This makes sense because with a large export sector a country puts great weight on a stable exchange rate, which

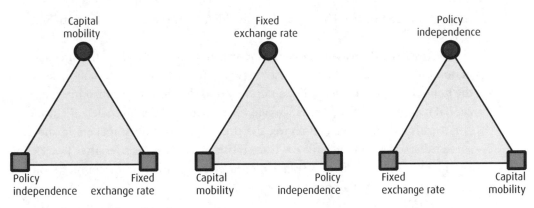

Figure 6.8 The policy trilemma.

is also a means to bring down inflation for emerging markets. As a consequence, the policy autonomy of these countries was considerably reduced. Three questions come to mind:

- Is the loss of policy autonomy really a cost from the perspective of a country's social welfare?
- Is the policy trilemma vindicated empirically?
- What made countries in the late 1990s re-consider their position with respect to the policy trilemma?

Is the trilemma for real?

Some economists would argue that the loss of policy autonomy is not a 'loss' at all. A decrease in policy autonomy means that policy-makers have less leverage on the domestic economy. From a social welfare point of view, this constitutes a cost only if the policy-makers use their autonomy to increase social welfare. If policy-makers use the domestic interest rate as an instrument and the economy ends up as a result with a higher inflation rate and lower production, social welfare is probably best served by restricting policy autonomy.

Suppose, for instance, that the credibility of domestic monetary policy is low. With international capital mobility the domestic interest rate r_{home} exceeds the world interest rate $r_{foreign}$ because of the risk premium attached to investing in Home (see (6.1)). As argued above, without a fixed exchange rate this country has policy autonomy. Because of the low credibility of its monetary policy, however, this autonomy is rather expensive because it results in a higher interest rate for Home, which hurts the economy. From a long-run perspective, the switch to a fixed exchange rate may reduce the policy autonomy and simultaneously be good news for the economy as it signals to international capital markets that the domestic policy can no longer be discretionary. The risk premium will fall, and so will the domestic interest rate.

The costs of a decrease in policy autonomy not only depend on the effectiveness of domestic monetary policy, but also on preferences. If domestic policy-makers and the public at large consider policy autonomy to be less important than international capital mobility or a fixed exchange rate, there is no real loss to society if autonomy is not pursued. As explained above, the preferences of policy-makers in the gold standard era were rather different from those in the first decades after the Second World War, which helps to explain the different positioning of countries on the incompatible triangle in these two periods.

Does the trilemma really exist?

Is there empirical evidence to confirm the hypothesis that policy autonomy decreases when international capital mobility is high? Obstfeld, Shambaugh and Taylor (2003) confirm this hypothesis using data for the three periods (gold standard, Bretton Woods, and post-Bretton Woods) and estimate a variation of (6.1)

$$dr_{i,t} = \alpha + \beta dr_t^b + \mu_{i,t} \tag{6.2}$$

where i denotes the country, t denotes the year of observation, r^b is the benchmark interest rate and μ is the error term. The operator d indicates that this equation is estimated in first differences so as to ensure stationarity of the interest rates. The benchmark interest rate is the US short-term interest rate for the Bretton Woods period. For the post-Bretton Woods period, the benchmark varies (see Shambaugh, 2004, for details). The benchmark interest rate fulfils the role of our theoretical interest rate $r_{foreign}$ in (6.1).

If there is perfect capital mobility and exchange rates are irrevocably fixed, we expect that $\beta = 1$: there is a one-to-one correspondence between the two interest rates and policy autonomy would be reduced to zero. If capital mobility is less than perfect and/or exchange rates are not fixed, we expect that $\beta < 1$. So, for the three periods under consideration, the β-coefficient should be the lowest for the Bretton Woods period and the highest for the gold standard period. Table 6.5 confirms that the main hypothesis holds.

The β-coefficient reported in table 6.5 is insignificant for the Bretton Woods period in which international capital mobility was limited. An insignificant β-coefficient means that changes in the benchmark interest rate have no impact on the domestic interest rate, an indication of policy autonomy. For the other two periods under consideration, there is a significant impact, indicating a limited degree of policy autonomy. The fact that $\beta < 1$ in all cases shows that even with a high degree of capital mobility and fixed exchange rates, there is still room for some policy independence.

Table 6.5 Looking for the trilemma: estimates of β

Policy regime	All observations	Fixed exchange rate regimes only
Gold standard	$0.42\ (0.03)^{a}$	$0.52\ (0.04)$
Bretton Woods	$-0.11\ (0.14)$	$-.05\ (0.12)$
Post-Bretton Woods	$0.36\ (0.05)$	$0.46\ (0.04)$

Source: Obstfeld, Shambaugh and Taylor (2003).
Notes: ^{a} Standard errors in brackets.

From a trilemma to a dilemma?

After the collapse of the Bretton Woods regime in 1973, international capital mobility increased gradually up to a point in the early 1990s when most developed countries and many emerging market economies were characterized by (almost) full international capital mobility. At the same time, many countries still had a fixed exchange rate. Even though there was no longer an international *system* of fixed exchange rates, there were relatively few countries with a floating exchange rate. Most countries pegged their currency to the US dollar or, in the case of the European countries, to the German Mark. At the beginning of the twenty-first century, fixed exchange rates had become less popular and the group of countries with a fixed but adjustable exchange rate had significantly decreased relative to the 1970s. Based on the research by Levi-Yeyati and Sturzenegger (2002, 2003), it is clear that exchange rate pegging is still the dominant exchange regime, while simultaneously this dominant position diminished between 1974 and 1999. In 1974, 70 per cent of the countries opted for a peg and less than 20 per cent opted for a pure floating exchange rate (the share of intermediate regimes, such as a crawling peg or a dirty float, slightly increased in the period 1973–99). The most important change between 1974 and 1999 is that the floating exchange rate has become far more popular at the expense of the pegged exchange rate. In 1999, the share of countries with a floating or flexible exchange rate had increased to 30 per cent and the share of countries with a pegged or fixed exchange rate had dropped to 50 per cent. The increased popularity of floating exchange rates is quite recent, dating back to the second half of the 1990s. We will see in chapter 8 that this is precisely the period of exchange rate turmoil, when a considerable number of (developing) countries experienced a currency crisis.

What happened? In a nutshell, with increased international capital mobility, fixed exchange rates became vulnerable to speculative attacks by portfolio investors. These attacks led to currency crises that forced countries to effectively give up their fixed exchange rate. Starting with the currency crises in the European Monetary System (EMS) (1992–3), which effectively destroyed this forerunner of the European Monetary Union (EMU), a host of currency crises followed. From the Mexican peso crisis (1994–5), to the currency crises in Southeast Asia (1997), Russia (1998), Brazil (1999), Turkey (2001) and Argentina (2002), to mention only the most important ones, the outcome was invariably the same: the countries involved were forced to give up their fixed exchange rate. In chapter 8 we shall analyse the causes and consequences of currency crises. Here, we are concerned only with the relationship between these crises and policy autonomy. According to some policy-makers and economists, the currency crises of the 1990s showed that the rise of international capital mobility reduced the trilemma to a *dilemma*. To see this, assume that the Home country has perfect international capital mobility and a fixed exchange rate. If for some reason investors start to doubt the credibility of the fixed exchange rate, there will be a capital outflow. Unless the domestic interest rate is increased to compensate investors for the perceived exchange rate depreciation, the fixed exchange rate cannot be maintained. The interest rate hike depresses the domestic economy, but may still not be sufficient to calm down the investors. The conclusion is that any fixed exchange rate is vulnerable to speculative attacks. In this case, we have a simple policy dilemma: a country should opt for either full capital mobility or a fixed exchange rate, but not for both. If one chooses capital mobility there are only two options left for the exchange rate: to fix the exchange rate once and for all or to have a floating exchange rate. The first option implies giving up your own currency. This route has been taken by the countries that opted for monetary union (EMU) or dollarization. The majority of the former 'fixers' opted, however, for a more flexible exchange rate.[3]

Locational competition and capital mobility

The cost of international capital mobility in terms of a loss of policy independence is not confined to monetary policy but is also an issue for *fiscal policy*. This becomes clear when we think of international capital mobility as a case of FDI where firms have to decide where to locate production. What does the cross-border mobility of 'footloose' firms imply for the tax and spending decisions of national governments? If taxation is looked upon by internationally mobile capital only as a burden and not also as a means to finance expenditures (infrastructure, education, etc.) that are of direct or indirect use for 'footloose capital', international mobile capital will locate in the country with the lowest tax rate. Individual countries might therefore see their

---

[3] In our discussion of policy autonomy and international capital mobility, we assumed that we were dealing with a small Home country taking the foreign interest rate $r_{foreign}$ as given. Suppose, instead, that Home and Foreign are two large countries coordinating their monetary policy actions. If Home and Foreign decide to have full international capital mobility and a fixed exchange rate, policy coordination can rescue their policy autonomy as long as they find that this is in their mutual interest. In that case, they can collectively decide upon the level of interest rates and as long as they keep $r_{home} = r_{foreign}$ the requirement for the fixed exchange rate $(dE = 0)$ can be met even with complete international capital mobility.

Box 6.2 EU countries and the effective income tax rate

For the EU countries, table 6.6 shows the development of corporate income taxes for the period 1990–9, an era of increasing economic integration. These tax rates differ from the 'nominal' tax rates as they take into account the implications of differences in the tax base, allowances for depreciation and the like that exist between the EU countries. The reported data are based on the financial accounts of individual firms. Although table 6.6 offers no conclusive evidence, a number of things are worth pointing out:

- The large countries of the EU (Germany, France, Italy and the UK) clearly have an above-average tax rate.[a]
- The smaller and 'peripheral' countries (Greece, Portugal and Spain) started out with a below-average tax rate, but their corporate income tax rates clearly *in*creased during the 1990s. Ireland has been a notable exception.
- The average EU corporate income tax rate has been fairly constant through time – in any case, shows no discernible downward trend.
- The standard deviation has strongly decreased from 1990 to 1999; so there is some tax rate convergence, but not towards the lowest rate.

Table 6.6 Effective corporate income tax rates across the EU, 1990–1999, per cent[a]

	1990	1991	1992	1993	1994	1995	1996	1997	1998	1999
Austria	18	22	14	16	20	17	24	25	21	24
Belgium	17	16	22	23	23	24	23	22	21	17
Denmark	33	32	30	30	32	32	31	31	32	31
Finland	45	37	34	24	26	27	28	28	28	28
France	33	33	33	33	33	36	35	38	38	38
Germany	48	49	49	44	41	41	41	40	40	41
Greece	11	11	24	29	29	31	33	35	35	35
Ireland	20	22	19	20	17	22	21	21	24	22
Italy	38	41	47	50	44	46	45	43	44	40
Netherlands	31	32	32	31	31	31	32	31	31	30
Portugal	17	20	27	25	20	23	22	21	24	25
Spain	27	28	29	27	25	24	26	26	26	29
Sweden	31	32	30	19	28	27	28	28	28	28
UK	33	31	31	30	30	30	30	29	29	29
Average	28.7	29	30.2	27.7	28.4	29.3	29.9	29.8	30	29.8
Weight. av.[b]	35.5	36.1	37.3	35.3	34.1	35	35.1	34.8	34.9	34.6
St dev.	10.6	9.8	9.1	9.0	7.4	7.5	6.8	6.7	6.8	6.5

Source: CPB (2001, p. 27).
Notes: [a] Data for Luxembourg not available.
[b] Weighted average; weights are country GDPs.

These four observations offer some (preliminary) support for the lack of a race-to-the-bottom in the EU. Large countries persistently have higher tax rates and smaller countries even display some 'catching-up' in terms of their tax rates.[b]

a These four countries are also the 'core' countries in the sense that their share in total EU manufacturing production is about 75 per cent. This share remained fairly constant through the 1990s.
b Note that we do not claim that there is no tax competition at all in the EU. Sinn (2002, p. 8), for instance, shows that the average tax burden for subsidiaries of US companies in the EU decreased strongly in the various EU countries between 1986 and 1992.

autonomy to set tax rates at a level that they see fit reduced in the case of international capital mobility. Stronger still, in an attempt to attract mobile capital, countries might engage in *tax competition*, an example of locational competition in which national governments use their tax and spending policies so as to lure mobile capital to their 'location'. Tax competition is argued to be welfare-reducing because it results in suboptimal (that is, too low) levels of taxation and tax-financed government expenditure. To prevent such a 'race-to-the-bottom' the coordination of tax policies is called for. The empirical evidence on tax competition is mixed, but as yet there is no discernible trend towards fierce tax competition. On the contrary, there are even cases where international capital mobility is very high and a race-to-the-(tax)-bottom has not (yet) occurred. Box 6.2 illustrates this for the EU and the corporate income tax rate.

Taxes are, however, part of a two-sided coin. Locational competition is not only about taxes, but also about location-specific government expenditures, which affect the quality of a country's social and economic infrastructure, and hence their attractiveness. Tax and spending policies represent two opposing forces. All other things remaining the same, higher taxes stimulate mobile capital to leave the country. Similarly, an increase in public spending stimulates mobile factors to stay, as this spending enhances the attractiveness of the location for the mobile factors of production. All things do not remain the same in the sense that higher taxes typically also imply higher public spending levels, and vice versa. This may explain the absence of a race-to-the-bottom in (for instance) the EU countries (see box 6.1). One thing is clear, though: international capital mobility potentially reduces the degrees of freedom for national fiscal policy. In this sense, it represents a *cost*.

6.7 Conclusions

From our discussion of the data on international capital mobility we conclude that there is a particular pattern in the development of international capital mobility, which was already high and on the increase in the first years of the twentieth century.

This process came to a halt after the First World War. In the inter-war years, the degree of international capital mobility gradually fell, going into a freefall in the first decades after the Second World War. It is only quite recently, from approximately 1980 onwards, that we (again) see a clear and strong increase in the degree of international capital mobility. The second part of this chapter focused on the question as to what caused this U-shaped pattern in the development of international capital mobility after 1900. After a brief introduction to the main costs and benefits of international capital mobility, we dealt with the first cost: the loss of policy autonomy. Whether increased capital mobility really decreases the policy freedom for national policy-makers is less clear-cut than our analysis of the incompatible triangle may suggest. The discussion of the other main cost of international capital mobility, increased financial fragility, is such an important issue that it will occupy a chapter of its own (chapter 9). We now turn, in Chapter 7, to the potential benefits of increased capital mobility.

Gains from capital market integration

7.1 Introduction

In chapter 6, we discussed some stylized facts about international capital mobility. In this chapter, we take the discussion a step further and analyse the potential benefits of international capital market integration. We will restrict ourselves to the two main benefits of capital market integration:

- The first concerns the possibility that international capital flows channel national savings to its most productive investment opportunities, irrespective of the location of these opportunities.
- The second is that international capital mobility permits a spreading of investment risk.

What does it mean if we say that capital market integration and the resulting international capital flows allow for an improved allocation of savings and investments? Similar to international commodity trade, capital market integration implies that markets are inter-related and that international arbitrage is important. By looking at the behaviour of national savings and investments, the degree of international capital market integration and its welfare consequences can be analyzed. Analyses such as these, however, often show unexpected results. One of the predictions, for example, that follows from a simple macroeconomic savings–investment (S–I) model is that capital should flow from capital-rich to capital-poor countries. This prediction is, however, (often) at odds with the facts. Attempting to understand findings such as these is one of the themes of this chapter. What, then, is the bottom line of international capital market integration: does it increase or decrease economic growth? The answer is positive, but not without qualifications.

The second potential benefit of international capital mobility is risk diversification. This is beneficial for the individual (risk-averse) investor, who is no longer dependent on the proceeds of a single or limited set of domestic investments. By taking the perspective of an individual portfolio investor we are reminded of the fact that financial transactions are characterized by incomplete, asymmetric information. This offers a useful starting point for the analysis of the financing of firm investment that closes this chapter. In chapter 9 we shall intensively use the asymmetric information framework introduced in this chapter for analyzing financial crises.

Two observations on what this chapter is *not* about are also important. It does not deal with FDI, because we covered this in chapter 5 and it does not deal with the policy implications of international capital mobility, which has to wait until chapter 10.

7.2 International allocation of savings and investment

From the balance of payments accounting we know that a current account surplus (deficit) has to be matched by a capital outflow (inflow). This is why the current account is a useful indicator for (net) international capital flows between a country and the rest of the world (see table 6.1, p. 163) for an illustration. From the national income accounting in chapter 2 we also know that the current account balance *(CA)* by definition equals the difference between national savings S and investments I: $S - I \equiv CA$. The term 'national' indicates that both the private and the government sector are included.

From this accounting identity it becomes clear that a national savings surplus, $S - I > 0$, has to be invested abroad. This is reflected in a corresponding capital outflow.[1] Similarly, if national savings fall short of national investment, there has to be a capital inflow to match this difference. But what causes these capital inflows or outflows? We need a model to understand the *determinants* and *direction* of international capital flows. A simple macroeconomic model will do the job.

A macroeconomic model

Financial transactions are different from goods transactions. The main difference is the *degree of risk* that is involved. Savings are channelled directly through capital markets or indirectly through financial intermediaries (e.g. banks) towards investment opportunities in the expectation that the investments will yield a positive return or

---

[1] Recall from chapter 2 that this corresponds to a *negative* capital account on the balance of payments, which is caused by the accounting methodology. A national savings deficit thus corresponds with a *positive* capital account of the balance of payments.

(a)

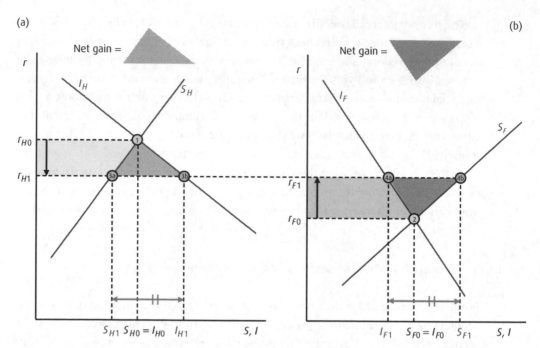

(b)

Figure 7.1 Capital mobility is welfare-enhancing

future income stream. To induce agents to save more and reduce current consumption, the interest rate, r, has to increase. Also, when the risk of financial transactions increases, the interest rate has to increase to compensate savers for the higher risk involved. These considerations suggest the following set-up for the savings function, S, for the Home country (subindex H) and the Foreign country (subindex F)

$$S_H = S_H(r_H); \quad S_F = S_F(r_F) \tag{7.1}$$

Turning to investment I, here the interest rate is important, too. Each investment project increases the existing capital stock. This raises the productivity of capital, but each new addition to the capital stock makes a smaller contribution to the productivity of capital due to the law of diminishing marginal returns (see also chapter 11). What is the optimal or equilibrium level of investment in this case? Investment takes place until the contribution of the latest, or marginal, investment project to productivity equals the cost of capital. The cost of capital, or the cost of financing an investment project, is equal to the interest rate r. Investment will thus take place until the marginal productivity of capital (MPC) equals the cost of capital r. These considerations suggest the following investment function, I, for the Home country and the Foreign country

$$I_H = I_H(r_H); \quad I_F = I_F(r_F) \tag{7.2}$$

Figure 7.1 illustrates the first major potential advantage of international capital mobility. For Home and Foreign, the respective national savings and investment schedules are drawn. The savings curves are upward-sloping, and the investment curves are downward-sloping. In the absence of international capital mobility the equilibrium interest rates at which national savings equals national investment are r_{H0} (at point 1 in figure 7.1) and r_{F0} (at point 2 in figure 7.1) for Home and Foreign, respectively. Note that, without international capital mobility, the Home interest rate is higher than the Foreign interest rate. Because at these equilibrium interest rates national savings equals national investment, we also have a current account balance. There is no net capital inflow or outflow, which is consistent with the assumption of no international capital mobility.

It is now straightforward to illustrate that the introduction of international capital mobility makes both countries better off. This follows from the fact that international capital mobility implies that there will be one worldwide interest rate somewhere in between r_{H0} and r_{F0} for both countries. If this were not the case, profits could be made by redirecting savings towards (or away from) the country with the higher (lower) interest rate. Both countries gain *despite* the fact that the interest rate increases in one country and decreases in the other. In the Home country, welfare improves because the increase in investor surplus (the area in between the Home investment schedule and the change in interest rates; see below) is larger than the decrease in savings surplus (the area in between the Home savings schedule and the change in interest rates). Similarly, in Foreign welfare improves because the increase in savings surplus (the area in between the Foreign savings schedule and the change in interest rates) is larger than the decrease in investor surplus (the area in between the Foreign investment schedule and the change in interest rates).

Equality of interest rates holds only in the absence of country-specific risks. If these are present – for example, in the form of a country-specific risk premium for Home or the expectation of an exchange rate depreciation for Home, then Home's interest rate will be higher than the world interest rate even with perfect capital market integration. In fact, in the case of flexible exchange rates, arbitrage ensures that the UIP condition holds, in which exchange rate expectations are exactly matched by an interest rate differential between Home and Foreign (box 7.1).

In autarky, Home finds itself in point 1 and Foreign in point 2 in figure 7.1. Once capital mobility is permitted, capital will start to flow from Foreign to Home because Home has higher interest rates than Foreign. As a result, the interest rate in Home will start to fall because of the additional (foreign) savings that now become available. The drop in the Home interest rate will increase national investment and discourage national savings (compared to the case without international capital mobility). In Foreign, the opposite will happen, and as a result national savings will increase and national investment will decrease. The incentive for further re-allocation of

Box 7.1 How to test for UIP

In chapter 6 we used the following version of the UIP condition

$$r_{home} = r_{foreign} + dE$$

where we assumed no transaction costs and $risk = dE$ (see (6.1′)). This simple condition has been the subject of a vast amount of empirical research into the validity of the UIP condition. If we restrict ourselves to two countries, Home and Foreign, the UIP condition can be empirically tested as follows

$$dE = \frac{E_{t+1} - E_t}{E_t} = \alpha + \beta(r_{H,t} - r_{F,t}) + \mu_t \tag{7.3}$$

where t is the time index, α and β are coefficients to be estimated and μ is the error term. Regression analysis can first provide an estimate of the coefficients α and β and their error bounds, which then, secondly, can be used test the UIP hypothesis. If UIP holds (perfectly) the estimated parameters should be: $\alpha = 0$ and $\beta = 1$. However, most of the corresponding research finds that:
- α is not zero; mostly this coefficient is significantly differently from zero
- β is not 1; often β is significantly negative.

What do these findings imply? The fact that β is different from 1 and negative indicates that when at time t the interest rate at Home is larger than Foreign ($r_{H,t} > r_{F,t}$), this goes along with a decrease in the exchange rate E from t to $t + 1$. That is to say, it goes along with an appreciation of Home's currency. This is in contradiction with the UIP condition, which states that such a positive interest rate differential should be accompanied by an equiproportional currency depreciation from period t to $t + 1$. The fact that the α-coefficient is statistically different from zero is evidence against the notion that perfect capital market integration implies equal interest rates between countries. One explanation for this finding is the presence of transaction costs between countries (see chapter 6). Costs such as these result in interest rate differentials even if there are formally no limits to international capital mobility.

international capital flows (from Foreign to Home) will stop if the two interest rates are equal, $r_{H1} = r_{F1}$. This situation is represented by the points labelled 3 and 4 in figure 7.1: Foreign has a net capital outflow that corresponds to a savings surplus of $S_{F1} - I_{F1}$, whereas Home has an equally sized net capital inflow that corresponds to an investment surplus of $I_{H1}-S_{H1}$. Thanks to international capital mobility, Home is able to increase its level of investment (at a lower interest rate than in the case of capital market segmentation), and Foreign enjoys a higher rate of return on its savings compared to autarky. The net gain for both countries is indicated by the two triangles in figure 7.1. The net gain for Home is positive because the gain for the demanders of funds (as represented by the investment schedule) outweighs the loss for the suppliers of funds (as represented by the savings schedule). The introduction of international capital mobility leads to a lower interest rate in figure 7.1a. This amounts to a loss for the suppliers of funds equal to the area r_{H0}, 1, $3a$, r_{H1} in figure 7.1a. The gain for the demanders of funds is given by the larger area r_{H0}, 1, $3b$, r_{H1}. The net gain for Home is therefore equal to the area 1, $3a$, $3b$, as indicated above in figure 7.1a. Similarly, the net gain for Foreign is also positive because here the gain for the suppliers of funds, equal to the area r_{F0}, 2, $4b$, r_{F1}, outweighs the loss for the demanders of funds, equal to the area r_{F0}, 2, $4a$, r_{F1}, which results from the rise in the interest rate in Foreign after the introduction of international capital mobility. The net gain for Foreign is therefore equal to the area 2, $4a$, $4b$, as indicated above in figure 7.1b.

The analysis above hinges on the fact that the position of the savings and investment schedules in figure 7.1 differs between Home and Foreign. There could be numerous underlying reasons for this difference, such as differences in country size, technology, preferences and the like, but we restrict ourselves to the case where Home and Foreign differ only in terms of the savings schedule (the investment schedules are identical). Assume that, for any interest rate level, Home will save less out of its national income than Foreign. Saving by definition means that present consumption will decrease, but that future consumption will increase. For any given interest rate, the amount of savings therefore expresses a country's *time preference* with respect to consumption now or in the future. If the inhabitants of Home save less than those of Foreign for a given interest level, this implies that Home attaches a relatively low weight to future consumption. Similarly, Foreign's preferences are biased towards future consumption. We can consider current consumption and future consumption as just two commodities. Differences in preferences for two commodities are reflected in relative prices of these commodities. This also holds in this case. The relative price of present consumption in terms of future consumption is just $(1 + r)$, and is therefore reflected by the interest rate: to give up 1 unit of present consumption your return is $(1 + r)$ units of future consumption. The quantity $(1 + r)$ is also called the time preference with respect to consumption now or in the future. It is the price of having consumption now rather than in the future. So, the higher the degree of time preference, the higher will be the interest rate. Given that Home and Foreign differ in terms of their time preference for consumption, international capital mobility will leave both countries better off. The difference between Home and Foreign in terms of their time preference is an incentive for international capital flows to emerge.

In fact, the mechanism is exactly the same as with the exchange of goods for goods in international trade flows, as explained in detail in chapter 3. The only difference is that we are now dealing with *inter-temporal trade* – that is, trade in goods over time. By lending to Home, Foreign can increase its future consumption of goods. In this manner, the capital flow from Foreign to Home enables Foreign to consume more in the future. What's in it for Home? It is able to increase its present consumption of goods. So given the difference in their time preference for consumption, international capital mobility can make both countries better off. The incentive for 'trade' – here, for international capital flows from Foreign to Home – is that in autarky the relative price of present consumption in terms of future consumption is lower in Foreign than in Home. That is to say, without international capital mobility the interest rate in Home will be higher than in Foreign, and this induces capital flows. Without exchange rate risks or transaction costs, this will lead to interest rate convergence between countries.

7.3 The degree of international capital market integration and a puzzle

A major implication of figure 7.1 is that with international capital mobility and with truly integrated national financial markets, national savings and national investment are no longer interdependent. This follows directly from the fact that for open economies $S - I$ is not necessarily zero. With international capital mobility, national savings and national investment can be decoupled. This is an important observation because it provides us with a direct test of the degree of international capital market integration.[2] Without international capital mobility, S and I must by definition move in unison whereas at the other extreme of perfect capital mobility and perfect capital market integration there is no longer a need for a correlation between national savings and national investment. Particularly for a small country, national investment will not be constrained by a lack of national savings: it is *world savings* that matter. Similarly, one expects to find in this case that national savings are aimed at the worldwide capital market so that it has no direct relationship with national investment.

Based on these observations, the seminal study by Martin Feldstein and Charles Horioka (1980) found, surprisingly, that the correlation between national savings and investment ratios was typically very high. For their sample of OECD countries they found this correlation to be almost equal to 1. They concluded that the degree of international capital market integration, and hence of international capital mobility, was still rather limited. This finding is puzzling because it is in contrast to the popular

---

[2] Here we shall make the simplifying assumption that changes in (the volume of) international capital mobility are indicative of changes in the degree of international capital market integration; the reader should keep in mind that, as we explained in chapter 6, changes in capital flows are not always indicative of the degree of capital market integration.

Table 7.1 Correlation between national savings and investment, 1960–1999

	1960–9	1970–9	1980–9	1990–9
Australia	0.64	0.52	0.35	0.74
Austria	−0.07	0.64	0.88	0.49
Belgium	0.86	0.59	0.46	−0.49
Canada	0.61	0.34	0.76	0.04
Denmark	−0.25	0.79	0.81	0.82
Finland	0.43	0.53	0.62	0.25
France	0.70	0.73	0.82	0.72
Germany	0.33	0.94	−0.49	0.04
Italy	0.72	−0.15	0.85	−0.38
Japan	0.80	0.92	0.23	0.93
Netherlands	−0.74	−0.95	−0.94	−0.96
Norway	0.44	−0.68	−0.68	0.79
Spain	0.66	0.83	0.64	0.47
Sweden	0.16	0.62	0.19	0.53
Switzerland	−0.70	0.95	0.85	0.84
United Kingdom	0.51	−0.67	−0.62	0.32
USA	−0.47	−0.88	0.00	−0.79
Average	0.27	0.30	0.28	0.26

Source: Ostrup (2002), based on OECD, *National Accounts.*

conviction that the world is highly globalized and that capital markets are highly integrated. Their result became known as the Feldstein–Horioka puzzle.

Many studies have corroborated the main finding of Feldstein and Horioka for different periods and groups of countries. So, by this yardstick, the degree of international capital market integration is still far from perfect. We illustrate these findings in tables 7.1 and 7.2. The main message from these tables is that national *S-I* correlations are still clearly significant, although (slightly) decreasing. In table 7.1, and in line with the Feldstein–Horioka study, we present the correlation coefficient between national savings *S* and investment *I*, both scaled by national GDP (denoted by *Y*) for seventeen OECD countries in the period 1960–99. Table 7.1 shows that the correlation coefficients differ markedly between countries (even in sign!) but that on average the positive correlation coefficient has fallen (although not by much).

Table 7.2 presents more conclusive evidence by going beyond mere correlations. Table 7.2 shows the results of a pooled estimate for a large set of countries of the equation

$$\frac{I}{Y} = \alpha_0 + \alpha_1 \frac{S}{Y} \tag{7.4}$$

Table 7.2 The Feldstein–Horioka test (see (7.4))

Period	α_0	α_1	Explained variance (R^2)
1960–4	7.02 (1.50)[a]	0.70 (3.75)	0.50
1965–9	8.78 (2.07)	0.65 (3.90)	0.50
1970–4	5.93 (1.96)	0.74 (6.62)	0.74
1975–9	6.47 (1.45)	0.78 (4.17)	0.54
1980–4	12.17 (4.36)	0.48 (3.81)	0.49
1985–9	10.41 (3.91)	0.54 (4.57)	0.58
1990–4	10.26 (5.88)	0.53 (6.46)	0.74
1995–7	7.83 (2.93)	0.56 (4.74)	0.58

Source: see Table 7.1.
Note: [a] t-statistics in brackets.

for the period 1960–97. Here, stronger evidence is found of increasing capital market integration. As we explained in chapter 6, 1980 is often considered as a watershed year, in the sense that after this year international capital mobility on average gradually increased compared to the period 1945–79. Table 7.2 illustrates this. The α_1-coefficient in the period after 1980 is lower than in the period 1960–80, which suggests that international capital mobility and international capital market integration increased.

To put the recent drop of the α_1-coefficient, and thus the alleged increase of the degree of international capital market integration, into historical perspective, a similar regression analysis for the period 1870–1914 is illustrative. We know from chapters 1 and 6 that this period was the heyday of the first 'wave' of international capital mobility and that net capital flows between countries were even larger than they are today. The Feldstein–Horioka test corroborates this conclusion. On average the α_1-coefficient was much lower during this period than it is has been since then. Based on the work of O'Rourke and Williamson (1999, table 11.3), the α_1-coefficient was lower than 0.5 in the period 1872–1917 on average.

7.4 Does capital flow in the wrong direction?

The Feldstein–Horioka finding in section 7.3 is puzzling in the sense that most people expect capital markets to be more integrated than the empirical findings indicate. This is not the only empirical puzzle surrounding capital market integration. Figure 7.1 shows that countries can gain from international capital mobility when their savings and/or investment schedules differ. The actual benefits may not be as clear-cut as the analysis in section 7.2 suggests. We can show this with the help of

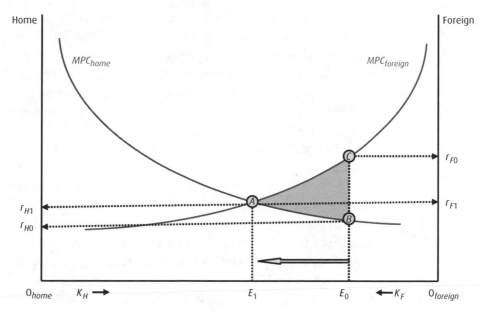

Figure 7.2 Capital re-allocation between Home and Foreign

figure 7.2, which demonstrates the importance of the assumption of diminishing *MPC*. Assume that Home and Foreign differ in their initial level of capital stock, with the Home country being capital-rich: $K_H > K_F$. In other respects (including saving rates), the two countries are alike. The length of the horizontal axis in figure 7.2 is equal to the total world capital stock. It is initially divided between Home (K_H) and Foreign (K_F) as indicated by the point E_0. Given the 'worldwide' capital stock and only two countries, any increase (decrease) in K_H must correspond to a similar decrease (increase) of K_F.

The vertical axis on the left-hand side depicts the marginal product of capital in Home, MPC_H, and the vertical axis on the right-hand side depicts the marginal product of capital in Foreign, MPC_F. We have drawn two downward-sloping MPC curves for both countries; for Home relative to the left-bottom origin and for Foreign relative to the right-bottom origin. Given the initial distribution of capital indicated by point E_0, these curves determine the respective interest rates, r_{H0} and r_{F0}, as indicated in figure 7.2.

With interest rates r_{H0} and r_{F0}, we start with a relatively capital-rich (Home) and capital-poor (Foreign) country in the absence of capital mobility. By allowing next for international capital mobility, agents may act upon the fact that the return on capital is higher in the capital-poor country, Foreign. Again, it is beneficial to re-allocate capital from Home to Foreign. The size of the re-allocation of capital, from Home to Foreign, is indicated by the distance between E_0 and E_1. The re-allocation process stops at point A, where the marginal product of capital is the same in the two countries – $MPC_H = MPC_F$ – and therefore the interest rates are equal – $r_{H1} = r_{F1}$. The world economy is better off when capital mobility is allowed for because world output increases due to the re-allocation of capital from Home to Foreign. The net output gain is given by the shaded area A, B, C. To see this, note first that the area under the MPC curve gives the level of output. For every level of the capital stock, the resulting output level will be given by the area in figure 7.2 under the MPC curve to the left (right) of the level of the capital stock for Home (Foreign). The re-allocation of capital and the corresponding fall (rise) of the interest rate in Foreign (Home), once we allow for capital mobility, means that Foreign will increase its output and that Home will have to decrease its output. The fact that the output increase in Foreign more than offsets the output decrease in Home is due to the fact that the part of Home's capital stock that is transferred to Foreign is put to a more productive use in Foreign because of the higher MPC in Foreign. In terms of figure 7.2, the output gain for Foreign is given by the area E_0, E_1, A, C whereas the output loss for Home is denoted by the area E_0, E_1, A, B. The net output gain is therefore given by the shaded area A, B, C.

This example suggests that when we look at the data we should observe that capital flows from capital-rich to capital-poor countries. We should even observe a convergence of (*per capita*) capital stocks between rich and poor countries over time. In chapter 6 (see table 6.3), we illustrated that for the group of the developing countries as whole there is indeed a net capital inflow, corresponding to a net capital outflow from the capital-rich countries. There are, however, large country differences in the size and composition of these inflows that do not seem consistent with the idea illustrated in figure 7.2.[3] Furthermore, taking a more historical perspective gives an interesting insight into what is happening to the direction of capital flows.

Compared to the first era of globalization at the turn of the twentieth century, the composition of international capital flows is markedly different. In the first era of international capital mobility (1870–1914) capital flows were mainly long-term, whereas an important feature of the second era of international capital mobility (1980–present) is that short-term capital flows have become relatively more important than long-term capital flows. In the period 1870–1914 capital flows were indeed as figure 7.2 suggests: predominantly from capital-rich countries (mainly Europe) to capital-poor counties. FDI and long-term (bond) financing were far more important than short-term flows. This has changed. The recent increase in international capital mobility is much more due to the increase of *short-term flows* between developed

---

[3] Since capital growth is a main determinant of output growth, we should also observe convergence of GDP or income levels between countries once we allow for capital mobility (see chapter 11).

countries. Currently, international capital mobility is mostly a North–North phenomenon.

To get an idea about the relative magnitude of the capital flows to developing countries over time, Obstfeld and Taylor (2004) show that, compared to a hundred years ago, relatively less capital is flowing from 'North to South'. This is a real puzzle because the potential return on investments in the 'South' (the capital-poor countries) is higher because the MPC is higher. This conclusion holds not only when we look at capital *flows* but also for financial *stocks* (for the importance of this distinction, we refer back to chapter 6). Obstfeld and Taylor (2004) show, for instance, that in 1913 about 50 per cent of all international capital, in terms of gross stocks, was directed towards countries or regions with a *per capita* income of 40 per cent, or lower, than that of the USA. In 1997, the picture was very different. About 20–25 per cent of the capital went to these poorer countries, but about 75–80 per cent went to countries with a *per capita* income of 60 per cent or more compared to the USA. This change from 1913 to 1997 is even more striking when one bears in mind that the productivity differences between rich and poor countries were on average smaller in 1913 than in 1997! This means that the potential 'MPC gap' between rich and poor countries is currently larger than in 1913, which makes this change in the direction of capital even more puzzling.

What can account for the fact that capital flows between capital-rich countries instead of from capital-rich to capital-poor countries? Apart from the increased capital market liberalization between 'North–North', three qualifications come to mind. These make it clear that the neo-classical model of figure 7.2 is probably too simple when we try to understand capital flows.

In the first place, the assumption of *diminishing returns to capital* may not be correct. Without this assumption, it is no longer obvious why capital should flow from countries with a relatively high capital stock to countries with a relatively low capital stock. Take, for instance, the case where the MPC is constant for all levels of K_H ($= 1 - K_F$). Now there is no longer an incentive to re-allocate capital between the two countries when capital mobility is introduced, because the marginal product of capital is constant (assuming that a unit of capital cannot become more productive by re-locating it to another country). The notion of a decreasing MPC makes sense only if additional capital is combined with a fixed amount of the other inputs (such as labour). By adding more and more capital to the production process, the additional output per unit of capital has to decrease. Ultimately, the marginal productivity will become arbitrarily small. But this conclusion does not hold if investment, and hence an increase in the capital stock, leads not only to more input of capital goods in the production process, but also to an increase in the overall productivity of the factors of production. The latter can arise if, for instance, the additional capital goes along with positive knowledge or R&D spillovers between firms (see chapter 11).

A second qualification with respect to figure 7.2 is that the potential gains from international capital mobility need not be realized, because the mere introduction of international capital mobility does not mean that *capital market integration* will be perfect. If, for instance, capital taxes differ between Home and Foreign, the return for Home investors on investing in Foreign is different from the *MPC*. Even in the absence of these formal barriers to capital mobility, it is still not obvious that the capital flows will take place. If, for instance, the institutions for the protection of property rights in the capital-poor country are such that the protection of (foreign) shareholders or creditors is inferior to that in the capital-rich country, the introduction of capital mobility may not make any difference. The existence of these additional transactions costs in Foreign for investors from Home may prohibit capital exports altogether (recall (6.1) with $TC > 0$). In chapter 1, we illustrated imperfect *goods* market integration by a *wedge* between export supply and import demand. Such a wedge is, in essence, nothing but the summation of various transaction costs (tariffs, transportation costs, administrative costs, etc.). The same is true for international capital mobility. Restrictions on capital mobility and low-quality institutions all drive a wedge between the actual and the potential return on investment. In terms of figure 7.2 and applied to the Foreign country, such a wedge lowers the marginal productivity (the *MPC* schedule for Foreign shifts to the right). The result could be that Home investors no longer find it profitable to invest in Foreign after capital mobility is introduced.

A third and last qualification is that the overall conclusion as to the fairly limited degree of capital flows to developing countries masks large cross-country differences. It should not lead us to conclude that it is better not to pursue financial liberalization at all. In general, countries with better institutions attract more capital, have a higher degree of financial development and benefit more in terms of economic growth (see box 7.2).

Box 7.2 The importance of institutions for financial development and growth

According to Douglass North, the 1993 Nobel laureate in economics, proper institutions – both formal institutions (e.g. the judicial system and its efficiency) and informal institutions (such as the norms of society or the level of trust) – will lower the transactions costs of market interactions. Leading modern institutional economists such as North or Oliver Williamson claim that without well-functioning institutions a modern market economy cannot exist. Without high-quality institutions the degree of uncertainty pertaining to market transactions becomes so high that transactions may not come about at all, or only at a very low level. This is especially relevant for long-term economic decisions. Without a well-defined system of *property rights* (in which the enforcement of contracts is weak because of political instability, corruption, etc.), long-term commitments suffer. In terms of the model used in section 7.2, the time preference of economic agents will be strongly biased in favour of the present, and the level of savings and investment will be low. The division of labour will also be discouraged. Specialization becomes a risky undertaking in an economy with low-quality institutions so that, as a result, economic growth will be depressed.

All of this may sound rather trivial, but the crucial role of institutions is now widely recognized in academic and policy circles. The empirical evidence that institutions matter for economic growth is strong. Important international policy-makers such as the World Bank and the International Monetary Fund stress the virtues of good institutions, and emphasize that the correlation between good institutions and economic growth is robust. It has taken some time before this insight became widely accepted. The transition from a centrally planned economy (CPE) to a market economy in the CEE countries (a large-scale experiment in institutional change), as well as the large cross-country growth differences between market-friendly countries and others, have brought home the point that well-functioning institutions are a necessary condition for economic development. To give just one example, the IMF (2003, pp. 97–8) shows that both for developed and developing countries there is a significant correlation between GDP *per capita* (levels and growth rates), on the one hand, and the quality of institutions, on the other hand. Showing correlations is not proving causality, but even if one controls for the possible endogeneity of institutions (institutions improve when economic growth is higher), the consensus among researchers is that institutions are extremely important. Research by economists such as Acemoglu, Johnson and Robinson (2001), Easterly (2002) and Rodrik, Subramanian and Trebbi (2002) indicate that cross-country differences in institutions are probably the most important 'deep' structural explanation for the cross-country differences in income *per capita*. Sceptics are referred to the data set on our website.

What is true for institutions and economic development at large is also true for the institutions–financial development nexus. Researchers like La Porta *et al.* (1997, 1998) have painstakingly developed a data set for a large number of countries. They looked, for instance, at the legal origin of countries (common law, French civil law, German civil law and Scandinavian civil law), as well as the efficiency of a country's legal system into account. Data such as these are necessary to test the hypothesis that better legal institutions lead to more financial development. Table 7.3 gives the estimation results for a regression where two indicators of financial development – *MCAP* (stock market capitalization/GDP)

Table 7.3 Institutions and financial development

Variable	Stock market capitalization/GDP	Bank credit to the private sector/GDP
Constant	−0.48 (0.23)[a]	−1.2 (0.34)
$LRGDP^b$	−0.020 (0.038)	0.19 (0.059)
GYP^b	6.4 (2.4)	9.7 (2.8)
$EFJS^b$	0.081 (0.024)	0.028 (0.032)
$ANTI^b$	0.050 (0.021)	
$CRED^b$		0.019 (0.041)
Adj. R^2	0.52	0.54
No. of obs.	41	42

[a] White corrected standard errors between parentheses.
[b] *LRGDP* is the log of real GDP *per capita* in 1976. *GYP* is the average output growth during 1976–93. *EFJS* measures the efficiency of the judicial system. *ANTI* and *CRED* are composite indicators of shareholder and creditor rights, respectively.
Source: own research based on Garretsen, Lensink and Sterken (2004).

and *BPY* (bank credit to the private sector/GDP) are regressed on some of the La Porta *et al.* (1997, 1998) indicators. *ANTI* and *CRED* are two composite indicators of shareholder and creditor rights, respectively. *EFJS* is a variable that measures the efficiency of the judicial system. The estimation results are for (at most) forty-two countries based on annual data for the period 1976–93. The basic data set is taken from Levine and Zervos (1998). *LRGDP* is the log of real GDP *per capita* in 1976 and *GYP* is the average output growth during 1976–93. These last two variables act as control variables. The main conclusion is that better shareholder and creditor rights, and a better enforcement of these rights, go hand in hand with a higher degree of financial development. This conclusion also holds if more informal institutions are included in the set of dependent variables (not shown here).

But does financial development – or, more precisely, that part of financial development that is determined by our La Porta *et al.* (1997, 1998) institutional indicators – also lead to more economic growth? The answer is yes, as research by Ross Levine and his co-authors has shown (see Levine, 1998, for an early example). In what is now known in the literature as the 'legal view' on financial development and growth, it turns out that, once we control for the quality of institutions, financial development boosts economic growth. The result is most clear-cut for bank credit and growth.

7.5 Capital flows and risk diversification

So far, the analysis has been based on a simple macroeconomic model. From the perspective of this book one would like to know more about the *motives* for (international) capital flows from the perspective of the individual portfolio investor or firm. This is the topic of the remainder of this chapter. This section deals with the portfolio investor and the second main benefit of international capital mobility: improved risk diversification.

As we saw in chapter 6, the difference between gross and net capital flows is important. Suppose we permit international capital mobility but still find that $S = I$. Because the current account is in equilibrium there are no *net* capital flows. This does not imply that international capital transactions between residents of this country and the rest of world are absent. It only means that in the *aggregate* the capital inflows and outflows cancel out. Domestic portfolio investors probably have still bought foreign shares and domestic banks have most likely used their funds to provide loans to foreign firms.

In addition, from the national income accounting in chapter 2 we know that national savings S refer only to savings out of current or this year's national income Y. Similarly, investment spending I covers only spending on new investment goods as a part of this year's total spending. These restrictions imply that a large part of the (international) capital flows is not included in savings S or investment I as such. If a Dutch portfolio investor – say, a pension fund – buys shares of American firms and pays for this transaction by drawing on its stock of liquidity accumulated in previous years, this transaction constitutes a capital outflow, but it has no relationship with savings S. From the perspective of the individual portfolio investor this transaction is, however, very much a *savings* decision. As discussed in chapter 2, if a Japanese firm takes over a British firm through the acquisition of the majority of the firm's shares, this is a capital outflow from the perspective of Japan but the take-over does not constitute an investment that will be part of I. For the individual firm, however, the take-over decision is an investment decision. These examples illustrate that the macroeconomic model of the previous section is useful, but it also limits our understanding of international capital flows.

Portfolio investment and risk sharing

International capital mobility also permits a more effective risk sharing or risk diversification. This second main advantage of capital mobility is best understood from the perspective of the individual portfolio investor and from the recognition that financial transactions involve risk. International capital mobility allows for a better risk diversification than is possible in autarky.

To see this, suppose that a portfolio investor can invest her savings in loans to firms in Home and to firms in Foreign. Suppose also that in both countries the interest rate is r and that both countries do not differ in their country risk with respect to, for instance, political uncertainty. Finally, assume that the exchange rate between the two countries is irrevocably fixed. Based on the macroeconomic approach of section 7.2, it would seem that investors are indifferent between supplying funds to firms in Home or Foreign. This is not the case. Financial transactions are risky and the degree of risk between these two types of loans may still differ. Risk-averse investors can reduce their total risk by investing in Home as well as in Foreign.

Why might the degree of risk differ? If Home and Foreign are specialized in the production of different goods, the associated risks of lending to firms in Home and Foreign will most likely be different. Suppose that the loan demand in Home comes exclusively from car manufactures and in Foreign exclusively from wine producers. If the risks associated with these two sectors are not synchronized over time, investors can achieve a better degree of diversification and reduce their risk by being able to lend to firms in both countries. That is, they can benefit from the introduction of international capital mobility.

The diversification argument can also be used to explain why international capital mobility has the potential to reduce the impact of domestic economic shocks for individual agents. Without international capital mobility, economic agents can trade only in domestic assets. Suppose that the only available assets are the stocks of domestic firms. If Home is hit by a negative shock, such as a downturn in the overall business cycle, and the value of the stocks decreases, the investment portfolio of these agents decreases, too. This *country-specific risk*, due to the existence of the business cycle, cannot be reduced by diversification. With international capital mobility, however, there is a possibility for risk diversification if the national business cycles are not synchronized over time. If every time that Home is hit by a negative economic shock, Foreign is hit by a positive economic shock of the same order and magnitude, investors in *both* countries can clearly benefit if they can buy stocks from Home as well as Foreign firms. Here, international capital mobility – or, in other words, the trade in financial assets – has the potential to provide insurance against (income) shocks. Box 7.3 provides a numerical example of this insurance argument.

The diversification argument is, of course, also valid when it is applied to trade of *financial assets* within the same country. As long as domestic assets differ in their risk profile and outlook, the diversification or 'do not put all your eggs in one basket' argument makes sense. The risk argument in favour of *international* capital mobility is simply that it *increases* the possibilities for risk diversification as long as the economic structure of the rest of the world and its asset composition is not a mere

Box 7.3 Insurance against shocks through portfolio diversification[a]

Suppose we have two countries, Home and Foreign, and that residents from each country own one asset, land, which yields an annual harvest of apples. The yield is, however, uncertain. There is a 50 per cent chance that the yield will be 1,000 apples (a good harvest) and a 50 per cent chance that it will be only 500 apples (a bad harvest). Whenever Home has a good harvest, Foreign will have a bad harvest. On average, each country will thus have a harvest of $(1/2) \cdot (1,000) + (1/2) \cdot (500) = 750$ apples. But each year the harvest will either be 1,000 or 500. How can the inhabitants of these countries benefit from the introduction of international capital (the cross-country trade in shares of land)? Suppose that the inhabitants are risk averse, that someone who owns 5 per cent of the shares of land receives as a return 5 per cent of the harvest and that apples cannot be stored.

With international capital mobility, the result will be that Home people will buy 50 per cent of the Foreign land and Foreign people will buy 50 per cent of the Home land.[b] To see why this is the optimal risk diversification strategy, recall that each inhabitant in Foreign and Home knows that whenever the harvest is good in Home it will be bad in Foreign, and vice versa. This means that by owning 50 per cent of the land share in both countries, the inhabitants of Home and Foreign now get a *certain* return of 750 apples. For the world as whole (the Home and Foreign harvest combined) the total harvest of apples is 1,500 every year; only the distribution can differ between Home and Foreign. By owning 50 per cent of the land in Home as well as 50 per cent of the land in Foreign, each country and its inhabitants know that the return on the share investment will invariably be 750 apples. Given the fact that inhabitants are risk averse, this is clearly an improvement over the uncertain annual return (either 1,000 or 500) that they get when there is no international capital mobility. On average and in the long run, the average return is the same before and after international capital mobility, but in the latter case there is no longer any risk involved.

[a] Taken from Krugman and Obstfeld (2003, p. 639).
[b] Any individual portfolio consisting of both Home and Foreign land will yield an average return of 750, but it is only with a 50–50 per cent portfolio split that the average return of 750 is risk-free.

replication of its domestic counterpart. The potential for improved risk sharing and insurance through international financial markets is substantial. Returning to our macroeconomic perspective, it is true for almost every country that the domestic factors of production derive their income by and large from domestic production (see chapter 1). Without international capital mobility and assuming that the only financial assets available are firms' stocks, the factors of production can invest their savings only in domestic stocks. This amounts to saying that if we look at a national economy as if it were a single firm, the firm's production factors not only derive their income from the firm but also have to invest their savings into this 'firm'. In terms of risk diversification, this is a situation that can be improved upon by allowing for international trade in stocks.

If country-specific shocks are not perfectly correlated between countries, this line of reasoning suggests that if a country has a share of, for instance, 15 per cent in world GDP, its investors should invest about 15 per cent of their savings into domestic financial assets, and 85 per cent abroad. Certainly, by this standard, the actual degree of cross-country risk diversification turns out to be rather limited. For almost every developed country it is true that its residents hold a very large share of their wealth in domestic assets. This empirical finding is also known as the 'home-bias puzzle'. It implies that for most countries considerable unexploited gains exist from international portfolio diversification. For most countries, especially the large ones such as Japan, the UK or the USA, the home bias in equity and bond investments is huge. There are a number of possible explanations for the home-bias puzzle. An obvious explanation is that capital mobility has increased in recent times, but is still far from perfect. If the transaction costs of investing abroad are positive, domestic bonds and equity holdings are typically over-represented in a portfolio. One important implication is that the insurance example in box 7.3 is over-stating the issue. In this example there is 100 per cent insurance against (harvest) shocks, such that the consumption levels in both countries are constant over time even though there are country-specific shocks. An easy test is to look at the across-country correlation of consumption and output. The insurance argument predicts that the cross-correlation for consumption should be higher than that for output shocks. It turns out, however, that correlation for consumption is not only very low but also often found to be lower than the correlation for economic shocks (see Obstfeld and Rogoff, 1996, p. 323)! In box 7.4, we discuss another example of home bias: ethnic bias in foreign direct investment.

This concludes our discussion of the two main benefits or gains of international capital mobility. As we explained in section 7.2, the first benefit – an improved international allocation of savings and investment – can also be looked upon as a benefit in the sense that it widens the scope for improved inter-temporal trade. By granting the loan, the supplier of the loan gets a claim on the future production of goods. The result will be the same as if the firm had bought capital goods now and paid for them by the instantaneous supply of final goods. What is true for a single firm is also true for a country as whole. International capital mobility can be beneficial for firms or countries that currently have an excess or shortage of net savings. If this potential gain of international capital mobility were of overriding (and growing) importance for countries, the data should reveal substantial (and increasing) net positions – that

Box 7.4 Ethnic bias in FDI[a]

Many – if not all – Western countries host significant *diaspora communities* from (former) communist or Third World countries. One may assume that such diaspora communities still have a preference for investing in their original homeland if the latter opens up to the outside world. There may be different reasons for such a homeland bias. For instance, the emigrants may want to contribute to the restoration of their original homeland, they may still benefit from network ties in their country of origin, or they may simply feel altruistically and emotionally committed to the country where they were born. During the 1990s, many countries that were, for a long time, hostile to foreign investors, opened their borders in order to stimulate domestic economic growth. Gillespie *et al.* (1999) study the determinants of diaspora interest in homeland investment for four emigrant communities in the USA: Armenians, Cubans, Iranians and Palestinians.

Among other potential determinants of homeland interest, they estimate the impact of *ethnicity*. A questionnaire was distributed among US citizens of Armenian, Cuban, Iranian and Palestinian origin. In total, the sample consisted of 166 Armenian, 111 Cuban, 78 Iranian and 40 Palestinian Americans. Controlling for such variables as the respondents' age, education, income and self-employment status, the analysis produced clear support for the homeland interest hypothesis. Not only had members from the four communities a significant preference for investment in their original homeland, but apart from that they were more willing to bear the barrier of business impediments in their homeland. From their responses to the questionnaires, it became clear that the typical emigrant investor tended to perceive a so-called 'ethnic advantage', believing that they were better positioned to reap the benefits in their original homelands than other ethnic groups were.

[a] Based on Gillespie, Riddle, Sayre and Sturges (1999).

is, countries having (widening) *S–I* gaps and corresponding net capital inflows or outflows. This is, however, not the case. In fact, as we showed at various points in chapter 6 and this chapter, these net positions are in most cases nowadays (still) smaller than they were a century ago, during the first wave of globalisation. This suggests a less prominent role for the first increase in international capital mobility. Indeed, the post-1980 increase in international capital mobility is to a large extent due to the second potential gain, improved risk diversification. As has become clear in this section, risk diversification is not a one-sided affair in terms of capital flows. The basic idea is that countries benefit from international capital mobility by allowing capital to flow from Home to Foreign, and vice versa. Capital flows motivated by risk diversification do not show up as net capital flows but their importance can be grasped by looking instead at *gross flows or stocks*. And the evidence here (see chapter 6: compare tables 6.1 and 6.5, for instance) is clear-cut. In gross terms, international capital mobility has increased strongly and has surpassed the 1900–13 period. In net terms, the difference with this earlier period is not significant; in fact, in net terms, today's degree of international capital mobility seems still more limited than it was at the beginning of the twentieth century.

7.6 Firm investment and asymmetric information

The value of the macroeconomic model of section 7.2 is limited not only when we look more thoroughly at the motives for international savings, as we did in section 7.5, but also when we turn to investment *I*. Figure 7.1 suggests that firms, when they seek funds to finance the expansion of their capital stock, face a supply of funds that looks like the macroeconomic savings function *S*. This is not the case. First of all, national savings are used to buy all kinds of assets (shares, government bonds, bank deposits and the like) and the supply of funds to finance firm investment is only a subset of the uses to which savings are put. Households and the government also engage in investment plans (e.g. durable consumption goods, housing, and infrastructure) to which part of the savings will be directed. The macroeconomic savings function is therefore not suited to describe the supply of funds curve that an individual firm faces.

What does the supply of funds curve look like? Recall that financial transactions are risky. This is certainly true for investment projects; these projects are often large and in many ways unique. This risk is not the kind of risk that can (in principle) be reduced by diversifying, as we explained in section 7.5. It is the type of risk that is associated with *incomplete information*. Both the firm and the supplier of funds have imperfect information about the return on the investment, but the supplier of funds typically has less information compared to the firm. Information is thus not only incomplete but also *distributed asymmetrically*. All suppliers of investment finance – be it banks, venture capitalists or public capital markets – want to be compensated for the risks involved in the financing of firm investment. These risks are ultimately due to informational deficiencies. This is illustrated in figure 7.3 by the fact that the supply of funds curve, beyond I^*, has a positive slope.

The F_d curve gives the demand for funds. It is the translation of the macroeconomic investment function *I* to the firm level. Here, too, the rationale for the downward slope is the decreasing marginal productivity of capital. For $I < I^*$, the supply of funds curve is completely flat. This reflects the well-established preference of firms to finance their investment with internal financing (retained profits) because of the

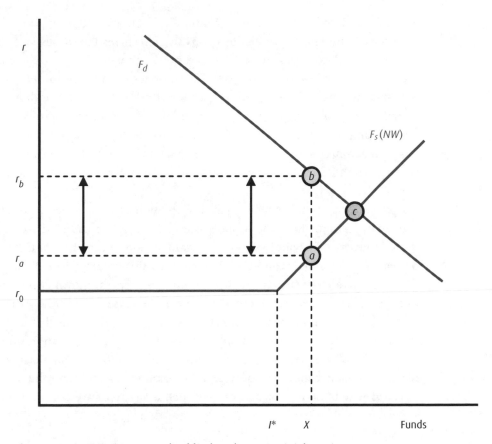

Figure 7.3 Firm investment, supply of funds and asymmetric information

lower costs of capital. The implicit cost of internal finance is the risk-free rate of interest r_0. This is implicit, because it reflects the opportunity cost for a firm of this investment in relation to a risk-free investment in US government bonds that yields a return of r_0. It is only when firms run out of internal finance that they seek external (debt or equity) finance. In a hypothetical world of complete information, the supply of funds curve would be flat for all levels of investment. Incomplete, asymmetric information results in a lower level of investment.

The other main difference with the macroeconomic savings function is that the *positioning* of the supply of funds curve depends on the extent of the asymmetric information problem. So, not only does the positive slope of this curve represent the existence of incomplete information, but the positioning of the curve also depends on the extent of the informational deficiencies faced by a supplier of funds. The problem of asymmetric information can be divided into the so-called *adverse selection* and *moral hazard* problem:

- The *adverse selection* problem refers to the situation where the supplier of external finance through its own actions ends up with firms that it wishes to avoid. The supplier of external finance can discriminate only imperfectly between high-risk and low-risk investment projects. The suppliers want to be compensated for this and they may increase the interest rate or ask the firms for additional collateral. The problem is that the firms with less risky investment projects may as a result drop out of the pool of the applicants for funds because they will not pay a higher interest rate or put in more collateral. This problem can be reduced through an efficient screening of applicants, but screening is costly and never perfect.

- The *moral hazard* problem refers to the information issue that, after the funds have been granted to the firm, the supplier can observe only in an imperfect manner if the funds are being put to good use. Again, actions on the part of the supplier or changes in economic conditions may increase this problem. Monitoring of the firm's actions after the funds have been granted reduces the information problem, but again is costly and can never be perfect in the sense that it 'solves' the asymmetric information problem completely. Nevertheless, it is clear that a financial system in which screening and monitoring is conducted relatively more efficiently is plagued less by these two asymmetric information problems. Financial intermediaries – notably banks – are specialized in monitoring and screening activities, which is why these intermediaries play such a key role in the overall financial system.

The supply of funds and international capital mobility

The adverse selection and moral hazard problems show up in figure 7.3 through the dependence of the F_s schedule on a firm's *net worth* (NW). Net worth is the difference between the firm's assets and liabilities. A fall in net worth signals an increase in both information problems. The adverse selection problem gets worse because the fall in net worth means that if the firm enters into financial trouble there is less to reclaim for the supplier of funds, such as a bank that has supplied a loan to the firm. Suppliers of funds may, as a result, cut back their lending or apply even more stringent borrowing conditions. The more risky firms will signal that they can meet those stringent claims, which only increases the problem for the supplier of funds. The moral hazard problem also increases if net worth falls, because for firms there is now less of their own money at stake, which induces more risky behaviour. In our analysis of financial crises (chapter 9), we shall discuss in greater detail how changes in net worth may impact on the supply of funds schedule. Here, we stress the fact that changes in net worth *shift* the supply of funds schedule, which further illustrates why our macroeconomic savings function is of limited use when we deal with the financing of firm investment.

What is the relevance of international capital mobility for firm investment using the supply of funds schedule F_s? First of all, the access to international capital markets increases the availability of external funds. This implies a shift of the supply schedule to the right. This effect is of particular relevance for firms who see their investment plans constrained by a lack of a domestic supply of finance. In addition, the access to international capital mobility may increase the efficiency of the supply of external finance. In many developing countries the efficiency of the financial system is low. This certainly holds for the efficiency of the banking system. Operating costs and a lack of competition imply that the costs of financial intermediation are relatively high. In figure 7.3, for a level of funds denoted by X, the costs of financial intermediation are given by the distance between points a and b. The corresponding interest rates are r_a and r_b. The difference (or wedge) between r_a and r_b indicates that the supplier of funds receives a gross return of r_b but after deducting the cost of financial intermediation the net return is only r_a. The firm has to pay the interest rate r_b. A decrease in these costs – or, in other words, a decrease in the wedge between the firm's cost of capital and the funds' supplier's net rate of return – would clearly boost both the supply of funds and the level of investment. When the wedge has become zero the financial system in our example is efficient. This occurs at the intersection of the F_s and F_d curves (point c in figure 7.3). Allowing the relatively more efficient foreign banks access to finance domestic firms, or allowing firms to seek finance on well-established foreign financial markets, are two ways through which international capital mobility might lower the cost of financial intermediation (see box 7.5 and figure 7.3). However, allowing for international capital mobility is not necessarily always good news, in the sense that it lowers the costs of external finance or makes external finance more readily available for firms. This will be a central topic in chapter 9.

As with figure 1.11 in the case of international trade in goods and trade costs, the wedge between the costs of external and internal finance may also be the result of restrictions on international capital mobility. If, in the absence of domestic savings, the F_s curve represents the foreign supply of funds, a tax on capital inflows may explain the wedge. This also indicates that, as in the goods trade case, an increase in the volume of international capital flows is not necessarily a sign of increased international capital market integration. This increase (here, a rightward shift of the F_s curve) may come about at an unchanged *wedge* – that is, without interest rate convergence. This last observation nicely sums up the central theme of this chapter and chapter 6: international capital mobility has increased in recent years but the degree of capital market integration is still far from perfect.

Finally, international capital mobility is also relevant for the sensitivity of the supply of funds curve for changes in NW and hence for changes in the problems

Box 7.5 The financing of firm investment and the external finance premium[a]

So far, we have not provided empirical evidence as to the financing of investment at the individual firm level. In doing so, we would like to know if, and if so: how, the relevance of figure 7.3 can be tested. To start with, there is overwhelming evidence that internal finance is more important than external finance for firm investment. When firms do resort to external finance, they prefer debt over equity. This suggests that there is an *external finance premium* (although direct evidence on this premium is hard to come by, because both firms and the suppliers of funds are normally not willing to make the firm-specific cost of funds public knowledge). As a source of finance for firm investment, internal finance in most countries makes up the bulk of the supply of funds.

When one analyzes the net sources of finance for Germany, Japan, the UK and the USA, one finds that internal funds make up at least 70 per cent of total finance. Apart from internal funds, the only other external source of funds that is of quantitative importance is bank lending (between 10 and 25 per cent). Bond and equity issues are on average negligible as a source of funds. Of course, there are large, established firms that do have access to the public capital market, and for them bond and equity financing is relatively more important, but for the aggregate of firms it is *internal finance* that matters, with bank lending as a distant second. The strong preference for internal finance suggests that there is indeed a positive external finance premium.

In order to learn whether an external finance premium really exists, and how this premium could vary across firms because of firm-specific characteristics, we want to find out whether figure 7.3 makes sense. Assuming that the easy option of measuring the firm-specific cost of funds directly is not available, three issues have to be tackled:

- First, we have to infer the *investment opportunities* of the firm – that is, the positioning of the F_d curve.
- Second, we have to come up with firm-specific indicators for the firm's *NW position* that provide information as to how the supply of funds curve F_s shifts when net worth changes. As we explained, shifts in *NW* have an impact on the asymmetric information problem.
- Third, we want to be able to discriminate between firms as to the size of their external finance premium. This premium is firm-specific; this amounts to saying that the *slope of the F_s curve is firm-specific.*

Following the seminal study by Fazzari, Hubbard and Petersen (1988), there has been a vast amount of research for various countries trying to tackle these three issues by estimating the following simple investment equation:

$$\left(\frac{I}{K}\right)_{i,t} = c_0 + c_1 \left(\frac{X}{K}\right)_{i,t} + c_2 \left(\frac{CF}{K}\right)_{i,t} + \varepsilon_{i,t} \tag{7.5}$$

where I, K and CF are investments, the capital stock and cash flows, respectively; X is a variable measuring the profitability of investment; i and t are firm and time indices; ε is the error term; and c_0, c_1 and c_2 are coefficients to be estimated.

By estimating this simple reduced-form investment equation the above-mentioned three issues can be dealt with as follows. The profitability of investment, and hence of a (marginal) addition to the capital stock, are dealt with by the X-variable(s). In most studies, this is the growth of sales or Tobin's q (Tobin, 1969). The latter measures the market value of equity and debt divided by the replacement value of the capital stock (the idea is that with $q > 1$ the firm has an incentive to expand its capital stock). Cash flow (CF) is an approximation for the NW of the firm. With perfect capital markets (and complete information) we expect $c_2 = 0$, but if we find that $c_2 > 0$, this sensitivity of firm investment to cash flow is taken as evidence that firms are liquidity-constrained and that they prefer internal finance (here, cash flows) over external finance. The last issue – the fact that the slope of the F_s-curve is firm-specific – is dealt with by subsampling of the firms. These subsamples, based on the size or age of the firm, dividend policies, or the ties between firms and banks, are indicative of the degree of the asymmetric information problem and hence of the size of the external finance premium. Large, well-established firms are thought to face a relatively low external finance premium. Firms with close ties to banks are also expected to have a smaller wedge between their costs of external and internal finance than firms that do not have these close ties with banks.

So, with regard to the simple investment equation, we would like to know whether or not c_2 is significant and positive and whether or not this coefficient varies across firms in a way that the sorting criteria suggest. The answer to both questions is affirmative. This is important for our present purposes, because it backs up the analysis on which figure 7.3 and chapter 9 is based. For a survey of the empirical results and alternative estimation strategies, we refer to Chirinko (1997), Hubbard (1998), or Lensink, Bo and Sterken (2001). For a critical assessment of the Fazzari, Hubbard and Petersen (1988) methodology, please consult Kaplan and Zingales (1997). Fazzari, Hubbard and Petersen (2000) provide a rebuttal. For an application to a transition economy, see Budina, Garretsen and de Jong (2000)

[a] Based on Garretsen and Sterken (2002).

of asymmetric information. If foreign suppliers of external finance are relatively more efficient in the screening and monitoring activities and if these suppliers are more diversified than domestic suppliers, any given change in the NW of firms has relatively less impact on the foreign suppliers. This means that the slope of the F_s schedule will decrease. A flattening of the supply curve is, all other things equal, beneficial because it increases the equilibrium level of firm investment. If access to international capital markets eliminates the problems of asymmetric information altogether, the supply of funds curve will become perfectly interest elastic at the 'risk-free' interest rate r_0. In chapter 9, we shall make this point time and again. More generally, figure 7.3, and the underlying analytical framework, will be used as a starting point for the analysis of financial crises in chapters 8 and 9. It is to these potential costs of international capital mobility that we now turn.

Investors, exchange rates and currency crises

KEYWORDS

exchange rates   currency crises   investors

risks and hedging   characteristics of crises   first-generation models

second-generation models   coordination   herd behaviour

speculation   efficiency   frequency

measurement   contagion   central bank

8.1 Introduction

In chapter 7 we focused on the potential gains from international capital mobility. We now turn to the analysis of financial markets and international capital mobility when things go wrong. This is clearly relevant, as in today's global economy international capital mobility is often looked upon as the main determinant of financial fragility and financial crises. This was listed as the second potential cost of international capital mobility in section 6.3 (the first cost of international capital mobility, the loss of policy autonomy, was dealt with in chapter 6).

To understand the relationship between financial crises and international capital mobility, we first have to analyse the role of **exchange rates** and of the determinants of exchange rate mayhem – that is, of currency crises. The analysis of currency crises in this chapter serves as an important input for our explanation of financial crises in an open economy in chapter 9. We shall argue there that in an open economy with international capital mobility, a currency crisis and the change in capital flows that come with such a crisis are the crucial links between a domestic financial crisis and the global economy.

Before we begin, a few remarks are needed on what this chapter is *not* about. In discussing exchange rates and currency crises, we should keep in mind that this is a means to an end. The end is to arrive at a better understanding of the potential drawbacks of international capital mobility. This chapter is, therefore, not about exchange rate economics as such. We shall not, for instance, deal with the organization and functioning of the foreign exchange market (either spot or forward), nor with the various pros and cons of flexible and fixed exchange rate regimes. Nor do we devote

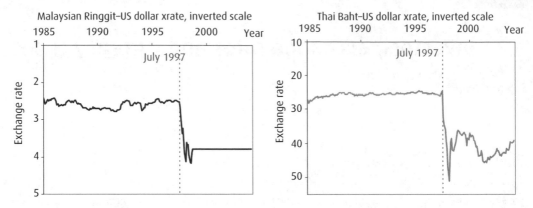

Figure 8.1 The Asian crisis: rapid drop in the value of some currencies, 1985–2002
Sources: IMF, *International Financial Statistics*; noon New York exchange rate, monthly.

much attention to the analysis of exchange rate determination (unless this is helpful for explaining currency crises). Also, we shall not spend much time on the question of how the exchange rate regime influences the effectiveness of macroeconomic policy. On the latter, see section 6.4 and our discussion of one of the costs of international capital mobility: the loss of policy autonomy.[1]

8.2 What is a currency crisis?

At first glance, the answer to this question seems easy. We all know an exchange rate or currency crisis when we see one, don't we? Well, yes and no. If investors lose confidence in an economy and its currency (and hence in the current exchange rate, which is the 'going price' of that currency against other currencies), they might start to sell their investments denominated in that currency. If this is done on a large scale by investors within a short period of time, this amounts to a *speculative attack* on that currency and its going exchange rate against other currencies. If the attack succeeds, the value of the currency relative to other currencies will decrease. The extent of exchange rate depreciation can be really substantial. To give just one example, the currency crisis that hit a number of Southeast Asian economies during 1997 resulted in exchange rate depreciations (against the US dollar) of more than 50 per cent within a few months after the attack took place (see figure 8.1). The example provides us with the archetypical currency crisis that hardly needs any further introduction:

---

[1] Good introductory textbooks on this are Krugman and Obstfeld (2002), Caves, Frankel and Jones (2003) and Husted and Melvin (2003).

- First, there is a mounting pressure on the existing exchange rate to depreciate for some reason (and it really does not matter at this point what the reason is).
- Investors then collectively start to sell their investments denominated in the currency under pressure.
- Initially, the authorities (particularly the central bank) try to defy depreciation of the currency by supporting the present exchange rate, either by raising interest rates or by selling part of their foreign exchange reserves (and thus buying the local currency).
- As the speculative attack continues, the authorities at some point have to give in and the currency starts its (steep) decline.

Just like situations such as a bank run or a stock market crash, the speculative attack on the currency is largely *self-fulfilling*, because the actions undertaken by the investors vindicate their own doubts that started the attack in the first place.

There is, however, more to currency crises than a successful attack and a subsequent exchange rate depreciation. There are aspects of a currency crisis that are less obvious and do not immediately meet the eye. We mention two of them:

- First, there is the category of *un*successful attacks that nonetheless constitute a currency crisis, particularly when the authorities fend off the attack. Abstaining for the moment from the possibility of introducing exchange rate controls, the authorities might ward off the attack by raising interest rates and/or selling part of their foreign exchange reserves against the local currency. Higher interest rates might sufficiently re-assure investors that the 'doubts' about the local economy and its currency are unjustified. Similarly, the willingness of the authorities to sell foreign exchange reserves might signal a commitment to the current exchange rate that also re-assures investors. Even if mounting pressure on the exchange rate does *not* lead to a large depreciation, there is still a currency crisis in this case if the authorities are forced to raise interest rates strongly or to significantly deplete their foreign exchange reserves.
- A second hidden aspect of currency crises is the fact that a perceived weakness of a local economy can sometimes lead to a currency crisis, whereas in other cases the same weakness can cause not even a slight hiccup in the exchange rate. In analysing currency crises it is not only important to understand the crises that did actually occur but also the reasons why crises did *not* occur in otherwise seemingly similar circumstances. As will be discussed in more detail in sections 8.4 and 8.5, the self-fulfilling nature of a currency crisis applies also to situations where a crisis does *not* occur. If investors believe the current exchange rate to be the right one for the local currency, their beliefs can turn out to be self-fulfilling irrespective of the economic conditions that prevail.

In models of currency crises there are two key players: private (portfolio) investors and the local authorities (the central bank). To bring out the dynamics of currency crises most clearly, it is helpful to assume that the authorities care about the level of the exchange rate – that is, they want to maintain a fixed exchange rate. With a flexible exchange rate, there can also be a considerable depreciation of a currency within a short time-span, but this is less interesting for our present purposes. As we shall see in chapter 9, currency crises are at their most 'damaging' in igniting or propagating a full-blown financial crisis when there is initially a fixed exchange rate and economic decisions have been made under the assumption that this fixed exchange rate will be maintained in the future. With a flexible exchange rate, sudden swings in the relative price of a currency can also be a nuisance, but their impact is more limited because – as with price fluctuations on other markets – market participants are aware of these fluctuations and can insure themselves against them on the forward foreign exchange market if so desired (see box 8.1). Regarding a currency crisis and its possible relevance for explaining financial crises, we are interested in the impact of an exchange rate depreciation extending beyond the currency market as such. To achieve this objective, it is useful to start with a situation where at least some economic agents are 'banking on' maintaining the fixed exchange rate.

Box 8.1 Foreign exchange risk, hedging and multinational firms

Foreign exchange risk arises when the value of a firm's transactions may somehow change if exchange rates change. *Hedging* is the action the firm undertakes to cover this risk fully or partially. There are various types of foreign exchange risk:

- One type of risk comes about when a firm agrees today to a certain transaction to be carried out in a foreign currency in the future at the then prevailing exchange rate. So, for example, an American firm agrees today to buy inputs from a German firm, to be paid in euros in three months time against the then prevailing US dollar–euro exchange rate. It is clear that the American firm faces foreign exchange risk, particularly since the US dollar–euro exchange rate is a flexible exchange rate. This is called *transaction risk*.
- The other main type of foreign exchange risk comes about when the American firm has some of its assets or liabilities denominated in foreign currencies. While the firm, for instance, is preparing its annual accounts, it needs to convert all assets and liabilities denominated in foreign currency into US dollars. This valuation is subject to change if the underlying exchange rates are varying. This is called *translation risk*.

There are various ways in which foreign exchange risk can be hedged. One way to do this is to go to the forward exchange market, where contracts are made to guarantee the delivery of foreign currency at a specified exchange rate on a specific date. So, if the American firm at time t wants to make sure that it does not need to pay more for its inputs in three months' time $(t + 3)$ in case the US dollar depreciates against the euro, the firm can purchase a contract on the forward exchange market ensuring delivery of euros at $t + 3$ against the exchange rate prevailing at time t. If every economic agent is always fully covered against foreign exchange risk, currency crises would not be a real problem. However, full and complete economywide foreign exchange risk coverage does not exist. Hedging is costly, so firms or other economic agents will hedge only if the risks and the amount of funds involved pass a certain threshold level. The perception of risk depends, of course, very much on the expectations about future exchange rates. These expectations can be wrong, which is especially troublesome if many agents are wrong at the same time. Moreover, even if a firm thinks that it has covered its own risks, this concerns only the risks on its own transactions. This still leaves open the possibility that it will be affected by exchange rate changes indirectly, because other economic agents it is dealing with encounter difficulties as a result of *their* exchange rate exposure.

If financial hedging strategies fail to be effective, a multinational firms's profit may suffer from unexpected devaluations or revaluations of currencies, increasing its costs and/or decreasing its revenues. For example, if a European firm reports its US profits in euros in its consolidated profit or loss account, it will clearly be harmed by the increasing strength of the euro *vis-à-vis* the dollar, *ceteris paribus*. If DaimlerChrysler, say, makes, a $600 million profit on its US operations, then it matters a lot for its consolidated euro profit whether the euro's exchange rate *vis-à-vis* the dollar is US$1.10 or 1.40. However, some firms will be more exposed to this type of risk than others. Miller and Reuer (1998) is an example of an international business study that tries to estimate the determinants of a multinational's exposure to foreign exchange rate movements.

Miller and Reuer examined 1992 OECD trade data for fifteen major trade partners of the USA, focusing on manufacturing industries. A factor analysis revealed three clusters of countries, each sharing a similar exchange rate exposure: (1) Belgium, France, Germany, Italy, the Netherlands and the UK from Europe, as well as Japan and Singapore; (2) Canada and South Korea; and (3) Hong Kong and Mexico (note that, in 1992, Canada, Japan and Mexico were the USA's largest trading partners, one country from each cluster). Clearly, using a single (weighted) foreign exchange rate exposure index, as is often done in the literature, does hide substantial heterogeneity among different clusters of countries. The estimation results revealed that about fifteen per cent of US manufacturing firms, in 1992, were exposed to foreign exchange rate movements. Moreover, FDI significantly reduces this exposure, so a firm can use its international investment strategy to reduce the risk of exchange rate losses.

In dealing with currency crises, where does international capital mobility fit in? Without international capital mobility – and, in particular, exchange rate convertibility – it is hard to imagine how a currency crisis can occur at all. If investors cannot switch between currencies, or only at large (transaction) costs, a currency crisis is ruled out by assumption. This is one of the reasons why some economists and policy-makers (and most of the anti-globalization protesters) have called for the re-introduction of restrictions on international capital mobility in one form or another, particularly in reaction to the surge of currency crises towards the end of the twentieth century. A case in point is Malaysia where, in the aftermath of the currency crisis in 1997 that led to a very sharp fall of the local currency (the ringgit) against the US dollar (see figure 8.1), the authorities decided to re-instal exchange rate controls to stabilize the exchange rate. It was clear that the Malaysian authorities, notably their former prime minister Mohamad Mahathir, blamed the currency crisis on the purely speculative behaviour of (foreign) investors and not on the intrinsic, fundamental weaknesses of the Malaysian economy. In rationalizing a restriction on international capital mobility it matters a great deal whether one thinks that speculative investors or the fundamentals of your domestic economy are to blame. If the fundamentals are to blame, the introduction of restrictions on capital mobility makes far less sense. In chapter 10 we shall return to these and other policy implications of currency and financial crises.

8.3 Characteristics of currency crises[2]

Currency crises and international capital mobility are related through the fact that a currency crisis typically brings about a *reversal of capital flows*. This is particularly true for emerging market economies, which are much more prone to a currency crisis than developed countries. From chapter 7 we know that emerging market economies have a relatively low level of domestic savings and offer a (potentially) relatively high return on investment. This is why international capital mobility can be beneficial for both emerging market economies and developed counties. Emerging markets that were hit by a currency crisis typically had a substantial net capital inflow (and hence a current account deficit) before the crisis. A currency crisis is very much like a large-scale withdrawal of capital. In the build-up and the wake of a currency crisis, countries frequently experience an enormous capital outflow, resulting in the reversal of the net inflow into a net outflow and the need to run a current account surplus. This is illustrated for the Asian crisis in figure 8.2, which is discussed further below.

---

[2] See also section 8.8.

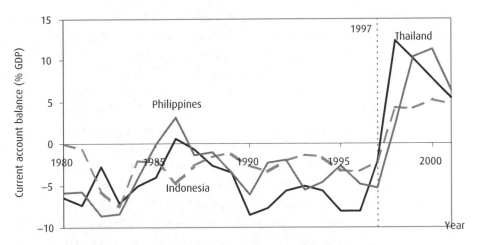

Figure 8.2 The Asian crisis: current account balance, 1980–2000, per cent of GDP
Source: World Bank (2003a).

First, a word on the notation that we shall use. Just as in chapter 6, where we introduced the UIP condition to discuss the policy trilemma, a rise in the exchange rate E implies a depreciation of the local currency, while a fall implies an appreciation. The exchange rate E is defined as the price of the local currency per unit of foreign currency. So, if we take the euro as the local currency and the US dollar as the foreign currency, a rise in the exchange rate from 1.1 to 1.2 indicates that Europeans had first to pay 1.1 euros to purchase 1 dollar whereas they now have to pay 1.2 euros. The price of the dollar has gone up, and the purchasing power of the euro has gone down. The euro has therefore *depreciated* in value.

The role of the exchange rate is essential when we want to understand why international capital flows, and sudden reversals in these flows, play such a key role in many financial crises. It is important to stress again that this holds in particular for countries that are trying to maintain a fixed exchange rate. Prior to their respective recent financial crises Mexico (1994–5), Southeast Asia (1997–8), Brazil (1999), Turkey (2001) and Argentina (2002) all had a surge in their capital inflows while maintaining a fixed exchange rate. The currency crisis went along with a reversal of capital flows so that these countries had to give up their fixed exchange rate. Interest rates are typically higher in an emerging market economy such as Thailand or Argentina than in, for instance, the USA. As long as the exchange rate between the currencies of these emerging markets and the US dollar was thought to remain fixed, this positive interest rate differential boosted capital inflows. It also stimulated borrowing in a foreign currency such as the US dollar, using these funds for investments denominated in the local currency. However, once doubts started to arise (for whatever reason) about the state of the economy and the sustainability of the fixed exchange rate, the supply of funds sharply decreased. This ultimately led to the collapse of the fixed exchange rate as foreign investors tried to pull their money out of these countries since they were no longer willing to extend or roll over their loans. On the currency market, the resulting capital outflow implied a very large excess supply of the national currency. In many cases, a devaluation of the currency became inevitable.

It is important to emphasize here, as we did in the introduction to this chapter, that the reversal in capital flows and the accompanying exchange rate devaluation may potentially contribute strongly to a financial crisis and an ensuing economic downturn for a number of reasons (see Mishkin, 1999; IMF, 2002b). The ways in which a currency crisis and the accompanying shift in capital flows interact with a financial crisis is the subject of the second part of chapter 9. Here, we show only some relevant channels based on section 7.3, where we discussed a firm's demand for investment funds and the corresponding supply of funds curve if there is asymmetric information.

To start with and in line with our discussion of international capital mobility in chapter 7, a sharp decrease in capital inflows means that fewer funds will be available to finance domestic investment. In terms of the discussion in section 7.3, a leftward shift of the supply of funds schedule implies a drop in the volume of investment. It may also lead to a less efficient financial system. In addition, from our balance of payments and income accounts in chapters 1 and 2 we know that for the economy as a whole the current account – or, equivalently, the difference between total savings (S) and total investment (I) – is also affected by the change in capital flows. A net capital outflow has to be matched with a current account surplus and hence by an excess of savings over investment (see also figure 8.2). Furthermore, with many loans denominated in foreign currencies such as the US dollar, a devaluation of the local currency means that domestic firms and banks are confronted with an increase in the *real* value of their debt. In this case, a devaluation has a similar impact on the real debt burden to a fall in the domestic price level. As we shall discuss in chapter 9, debt deflation via exchange rate devaluation increases problems of asymmetric information on financial markets and thus contributes to the financial crisis. Finally, in an attempt to defend the fixed exchange rate and to persuade foreign investors to continue to invest in their economy, the monetary authorities have to raise interest rates. In line with our analysis in chapter 7 on firm investment and asymmetric information, the interest rate increase means that the problems of adverse selection and moral hazard get worse, undermining the efficiency of the financial system.

Table 8.1 illustrates the change in real GDP growth for a few emerging market economies where a capital account crisis emerged during the 1990s. According to the IMF (2002a, p. 128), a capital account crisis is said to occur when there is a 'sudden cessation or reversal of capital flows that forces a large current account adjustment together with a large depreciation of the exchange rate.' Even though there is usually

Table 8.1 Real income growth and capital account crises

Country	Crisis year	Previous year	Crisis year	Following year
		Real GDP growth		
Argentina	1995	5.8	−2.8	5.5
Brazil	1999	0.2	0.8	4.2
Indonesia	1998	4.5	−13.1	0.8
Korea	1998	5.0	−6.7	10.9
Mexico	1995	4.4	−6.2	5.2
Philippines	1998	5.2	−0.6	3.3
Thailand	1998	−1.4	−10.8	4.2
Turkey	1994	7.7	−4.7	8.1

Source: IMF (2002a).

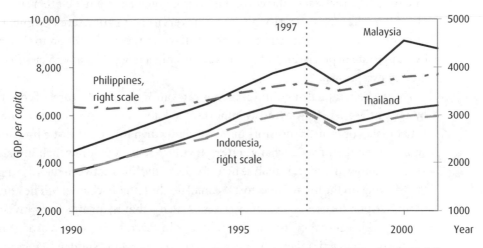

Figure 8.3 The Asian crisis: developments of GDP *per capita*, 1990–2002, PPP in current US dollars
Source: World Bank (2003b).

a sharp rebound in GDP growth in the following year, the contraction in real GDP growth in the crisis year is substantial, suggesting that capital account reversal and the corresponding exchange rate depreciation are potentially important elements of the GDP collapse. The sharp decline in income as a result of a currency crisis is also illustrated in figure 8.3 for some Southeast Asian economies during the Asian crisis.

For the cases reported in table 8.1, the median real GDP growth was −4 per cent in the crisis year. Let *t* denote the crisis year for the same group of countries. Table 8.2 reports the median values for the private capital flows and the current account (both as a percentage of GDP) relative to the crisis year *t*. It clearly shows the reversal of fortunes. In the crisis year, there is a marked change in private capital flows and

Table 8.2 Median changes in private capital flows and current account

Year	% of GDP	
	Private capital inflows (+)	Current account deficit (−)
t-3	4	−3
t-2	4.5	−3.5
t-1	2.0	−3.0
Crisis year $= t$	−2.5	2.5
$t+1$	−0.5	2.0
$t+2$	0.0	1.5
$t+3$	1.2	−0.5

Source: IMF (2002a).

the current account. Private capital flows shift from a net inflow to a net outflow, mirrored by a reversal of the current account, going from a deficit to a surplus (see also figure 8.2). Not surprisingly, these 'reversals of fortune' are accompanied by large depreciations of the currency. As we stated in the introduction to this chapter, exchange rate depreciations of 50 per cent within a few weeks after a crisis occurred are not exceptional.

If changes in capital flows and exchange rates are important features of countries hit by a financial crisis, it is obviously important to know how these changes come about. What makes optimistic investors quite suddenly turn into pessimistic investors who 'attack' a country's fixed exchange rate by trying to sell or withdraw their investments? Once we know this, we can analyse in more detail the links between these changes and the workings of the financial sector: We shall do the latter in chapter 9. The remainder of this chapter focuses on currency crises as such – that is, on attacks by investors on a fixed rate because they lose their confidence in this rate for some reason. Knowing how a currency crisis might occur can help us to understand sudden swings in capital flows and exchange rates, such as shown in table 8.2 and figure 8.1.

8.4 First-generation models

Models of currency crises can be classified along two basic dimensions:
- The first dimension concerns the role that *international investors* play in bringing about the crisis. Do they merely react to a changed outlook for the exchange rate or do they themselves determine what this outlook looks like?
- The second dimension is the *rationale* for the crisis. Is the currency crisis due to inherent flaws in the domestic economy that render a currency crisis inevitable or are the fundamentals of the economy sound and is the attack on the currency a purely speculative one?

In the earliest models of currency crises, as developed by Krugman (1979) and Flood and Garber (1984), investors play a rather passive role and the currency crisis is totally due to bad fundamentals – that is, domestic economic conditions are incompatible with the fixed exchange rate. To grasp the basic workings of the model, consider (8.1)–(8.3)

$$P = m(\overset{+}{M}) \tag{8.1}$$

$$P = E_f P^* \quad \text{with} \quad P^* = E_f = 1 \tag{8.2}$$

$$dM = dF + dR \tag{8.3}$$

Equation (8.1) states that domestic price level P is a positive function of domestic money supply M. The rationale for (8.1) can be found in the idea that most economists believe that in the long run changes in money supply lead only to changes in the price level and, following a famous dictum by the American economist Milton Friedman, that inflation (dP) is in the end always a monetary phenomenon. Equation (8.2) shows that in the long run PPP holds (see chapter 1). With the exchange rate fixed at $E_f = 1$ and assuming that the foreign price level is and will remain fixed at $P^* = 1$, the PPP assumption implies that the domestic price level P also has to equal 1. If the domestic price level exceeded 1, (8.2) informs us that, as long as the foreign price level remains unchanged, the exchange rate has to increase (that is, to depreciate) in order to maintain PPP. To prevent a rise in the domestic price level and to maintain the fixed exchange rate, the money supply cannot increase. Finally, equation (8.3) states that this country finances its government budget deficit F in a rather crude manner, namely by borrowing from the central bank, which increases money supply. (Equation (8.3) can be looked upon as representing the balance sheet of the central bank with loans to the government F and the foreign exchange reserves R as the assets and money supply M as the liability.)

An increase in the government budget deficit, $dF > 0$, and the resulting increase in the money supply would increase the domestic price level and world thereby make it impossible to stick to the fixed exchange rate. This is a clear case where domestic economic conditions are incompatible with the fixed exchange rate. The monetary authorities might, however, prevent the government budget deficit from increasing money supply by counteracting the pressure on money supply by selling off part of its foreign exchange reserves R to the public in exchange for the domestic currency. As a result, money supply contracts because there is less money in circulation in the private sector of the economy. As long as $dF = -dR$, money supply does not increase and the country can stick to its fixed exchange rate. The problem is, of course, that the amount of foreign exchange reserves is limited. At some point in the future, the monetary authorities will have to run down their reserves R completely. Once $R = 0$

in combination with an unchanged fiscal policy, money supply will start to increase ($dM = dF$). At that point, the government can no longer stick to the fixed exchange rate and has to devalue it currency: E_f *increases*.

The question arises as to what investors will do in such a situation. If they wait until reserves are depleted ($R = 0$) and thus for the actual currency devaluation to take place, they will lose some of their money as their investments in the domestic economy will be worth less expressed in the foreign currency. Obviously, investors will not want to wait for this moment to arrive and will attack the currency (that is, sell their investments in the local currency) well *before* the reserves are depleted. This means that the currency crisis will occur at some point between the moment the domestic government starts its money-financed expansionary fiscal policy and the moment the monetary authorities have run down their foreign exchange reserves. In this model, investors display *forward-looking* behaviour and understand the workings of the economy – that is, they know and understand the model as expressed in (8.1)– (8.3). The speculative attack on the currency by investors is then inevitable and, if they all act in unison (see below), will be successful.

The model of currency crisis outlined above is known as a *first*-generation model of currency crises. In this model there is only one possible outcome (a devaluation) and investors who attack the currency simply bring home the bad news a bit earlier than would have been the case if the government had had its way. It is also clear in this model that the devaluation – and hence the currency crisis – is due to the fact that domestic economic conditions (that is, the fundamentals of the economy) are at odds with the fixed exchange rate objective. But is it a useful model? It is, in two respects:

- First, most economists think that currency crises are on average at least to some degree the result of *bad fundamentals*. Speculative attacks that provoke a currency crisis are not random. More often than not, for the countries hit by such an attack, the variables emphasized by our simple model signal that there is a tension between the economic fundamentals and the fixed exchange rate. Kaminsky and Reinhart (1999) show, for instance, that on average (compared to episodes when there were no currency crises) in the eighteen months leading up to a currency crisis countries experience a significant fall in their foreign exchange reserves R, just as the model predicts.
- Second, the model explains why a currency crisis can occur quite suddenly and at a time when the authorities still seem to be able to (temporarily) stick to the fixed exchange rate. The abruptness and the timing of the currency crisis also implies a sudden reversal of capital flows. Investors collectively decide that they are no longer willing to invest in the domestic currency because of the *perceived incompatibility* of the fixed exchange rate with the underlying economic conditions.

8.5 Second-generation models

In a number of respects, however, the first-generation model is less than satisfactory. To begin with, both the monetary authorities and the investors behave in a very passive manner: their behaviour is rather *mechanical*. The government is somehow not able to redress its fiscal policy or to use other instruments (such as an increase in the interest rate) to prevent the future devaluation. The government also has no access to the international capital market to finance its deficit, something which might be true for very poor countries but not for developed countries. Investors' react only to the changes in the economic environment, but their behaviour does not shape this environment. Investors' expectations about the sustainability of the fixed exchange rate matter only in determining the timing of the speculative attack; they do not determine whether or not such an attack will take place to start with. Finally, using the terminology of Mishkin (1992, 1999), a currency crisis is, just like a stock market crash, nothing more than a disruption on a financial market. Given the claim made earlier in this chapter that changes in exchange rates and the underlying capital flows are potentially relevant for our understanding of financial crises in chapter 9, one would like to have a model of currency crises that relates currency crisis and the loss of confidence in the fixed exchange rate to the workings of the financial sector at large.

Some of the shortcomings of the first-generation models of currency crises are explicitly addressed in more recent models, in which the expectations of investors (and of policy-makers) determine whether or not a currency crisis takes place. Currency crises then do not depend only on a given set of fundamentals, but also (and crucially) on the *behaviour* of the investors. Depending on the expectations of the investors, a crisis may or may not occur. These so-called *second*-generation models of currency crises display multiple equilibria – that is, both the occurrence and the absence of a speculative attack can be an equilibrium outcome. The expectations of investors are of a self-fulfilling nature and they are no longer passive about the economy. Instead, their behaviour drives the economy. Following Krugman (1996), these second-generation models are based on the following three assumptions (see also Jeanne, 2000, pp. 24–25):

1. *Policy-makers have a reason to give up the fixed exchange rate*   Policy-makers may want to devalue for various reasons – for example, to boost the export sector of the economy or to decrease the debt burden of the private sector. The latter may for instance occur if the devaluation (see (8.2)) permits a more inflationary policy, provided that the domestic firms have not borrowed too heavily in foreign currency. Inflation in principle decreases the real debt burden of domestic firms and banks.

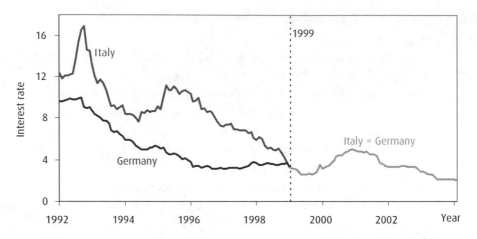

Figure 8.4 Interest rates, Germany and Italy, 1992–2004
Source: IMF, *International Financial Statistics*; three-month interbank interest rates (LDN: BBA).

2. *Policy-makers also have a reason to stick to the fixed exchange rate*   In many cases, policy-makers use the fixed exchange rate to enhance the credibility of their domestic policies (note that we came across this argument in chapter 6, when discussing the loss of policy autonomy). Especially in countries with a traditionally high inflation rate, policy-makers may want to peg their currency to a 'hard' currency such as the US dollar or the euro – that is to say, to a low-inflation country – in an attempt to convince both the domestic private sector and the foreign investors that they are getting serious about fighting inflation. If this strategy succeeds, inflation expectations may come down and the country may have a lower inflation rate as well as a lower nominal interest rate. Giving up the fixed exchange rate therefore implies a loss of credibility.

3. *The costs for policy-makers to hold on to the fixed exchange rate increase if investors expect that at some point in the future the currency will be devalued*   If investors start to doubt the sustainability of the fixed exchange rate, they will ask to be compensated for this perceived increased risk by demanding a higher interest rate. A higher interest rate depresses economic activity and may increase financial fragility if the financial sector is already weak. An interest rate increase therefore raises the costs for policy-makers of sticking to the fixed exchange rate.

Figure 8.4 illustrates an extreme example of the potential benefits for a country of maintaining a fixed exchange rate. Traditionally, Italy has had higher inflation rates in the second half of the twentieth century than Germany, which was keen on fighting even the threat of rapid inflation after the devastating German experience in this respect in the 1920s. Despite the fact that both countries had participated in the exchange rate mechanism of the European Monetary System (EMS) since 1979 (a system of fixed, but adjustable exchange rates), the Italians had to pay higher interest rates to investors to compensate them for the potential risk of an Italian lire devaluation (as occurred, in fact, on several occasions). Only with the formation of EMU, which formally introduced one European currency on 1 January 1999, did the commitment to a fixed exchange rate become fully credible. In the period leading up to the 1 January 1999 deadline, investors became increasingly convinced of Italy's commitment, leading to a rapid reduction of the interest rate differential between Italy and Germany, as illustrated in figure 8.4. Clearly, this saved the Italians billions of dollars (or euros) in interest payments.

The basic mechanism of the second-generation models is quite simple. Assumptions 1 and 2 above imply a trade-off for the domestic policy-maker: there are costs and benefits of sticking to the fixed exchange rate. Assumption 3 establishes that investors determine the position of the policy-maker on this trade-off. If investors start to doubt the fixed exchange rate and ask for a higher interest rate, it becomes more likely that the policy-maker will conclude that the benefits of the fixed exchange rate no longer outweigh the costs. It is easy to understand why these three basic ingredients of the second-generation models give rise to multiple, self-fulfilling equilibria. Suppose, for example, that investors find that the fixed exchange rate is credible (they do not expect a future devaluation). If, given these expectations, policy-makers conclude that the net benefits of sticking to a fixed exchange rate are positive, the currency will not be devalued and the self-fulfilling expectations of the investors will indeed be confirmed. Another outcome is, however, also possible. Suppose that investors, for whatever reason, expect a future devaluation and demand a higher interest rate. The interest rate increase raises the costs of the fixed exchange rate, such that policy-makers may no longer find it worthwhile to stick to the fixed exchange rate and decide to devalue the currency. This is a second equilibrium outcome. If it materializes, we have a case of self-fulfilling expectations, again, on the part of the investors. Box 8.2 provides some more detail on the structure of the second-generation models.

Box 8.2 The second-generation model of currency crises

We briefly explain the main structure of the second-generation models of currency crises (see Krugman, 1996, for more details on the model, and Jeanne, 2000, for a more general, but similar approach). The central equation is the social loss function H given in (8.4) that the policy makers try to minimize

$$H = [a(E_{target} - E_{fixed}) + b(E^{expected} - E_{fixed})]^2 + C; \quad a, b > 0 \qquad (8.4)$$

where E_{target} is the policy-maker's desired 'target' exchange rate, E_{fixed} is the actual, fixed exchange rate, $E^{expected}$ is the investor's expected exchange rate and C is the credibility cost of giving up the fixed exchange rate. This social welfare function contains three arguments corresponding to the three main aspects of the model (see pp. 229–30 in the main text):

- If $E_{target} > E_{fixed}$, the policy-makers have an incentive to give up the fixed exchange rate (recall that an increase in the exchange rate means a depreciation). A positive difference between E_{target} and E_{fixed} indicates that there are welfare costs associated with sticking to the fixed exchange rate.
- Assuming that $C > 0$, this represents the welfare loss of giving up the fixed exchange rate due to a loss of credibility

These first two arguments give the basic trade-off for the policy-maker when she has to decide whether or not to try to maintain the fixed exchange rate. The third argument concerns the role of investors' expectations and their impact on social welfare:

- If investors expect the fixed exchange rate to hold in the future ($E^{expected} = E_{fixed}$), the corresponding argument in the welfare loss function $b(E^{expected} - E_{fixed}) = 0$, having no bearing on social welfare. If, however, investors think that the fixed exchange rate is not credible and expect the policy-maker to abandon the fixed exchange rate at some point in the future to arrive at the target exchange rate ($E^{expected} = E_{target}$), the investors will ask for a higher interest rates thereby increasing the social welfare loss.

To show how this second-generation model can give rise to multiple self-fulfilling equilibria, assume that the following inequality holds

$$a(E_{target} - E_{fixed})^2 < C < (a+b)(E_{target} - E_{fixed})^2 \tag{8.5}$$

What does inequality (8.5) imply? Suppose that the fixed exchange rate is credible, such that $E^{expected} = E_{fixed}$ and thus $b(E^{expected} - E_{fixed}) = 0$. In this case, the first part of the inequality holds: $a(E_{target} - E_{fixed})^2 < C$. This means that the government will not give up the fixed exchange rate and there will not be a currency crisis. If, however, investors do not find the fixed exchange rate credible and $E^{expected} = E_{target}$, we are dealing with the second part of the inequality: $C < (a+b)(E_{target} - E_{fixed})^2$. Now the policy-makers will decide to give up the fixed exchange rate and the expectations of the investors will lead to a currency crisis. Which of the two equilibria will be realized depends on the (self-fulfilling) expectations of investors about $E^{expected}$. For a more advanced treatment of the first- and second-generation models of currency crisis, see Obstfeld and Rogoff, 1996, pp. 559–65, 648–53). For a good survey, we refer to Jeanne (2000).

This brief outline of the second-generation model suffices to show that, in contrast to the first-generation models, expectations are crucial, as in the behaviour of investors and policy-makers. A currency devaluation of the currency because of bad fundamentals is no longer inevitable and what happens to the exchange rate is no longer predetermined. Instead, even though the fundamentals still matter, the interaction between investors and policy-makers is decisive in determining whether or not a currency crisis will take place.

What about the other main drawback of the standard currency crisis model (8.1)–(8.3), the missing link between a currency crisis and the workings of the financial sector? Here, the second-generation model also constitutes an improvement, albeit a limited one. One can think of the trade-off (assumptions 1 and 2 above) for policy-makers as being partly determined by the implications of a change in the exchange rate for the workings of the financial sector (see the motivation for assumption 1). This link is, however, at best implicit and there is certainly room for improvement, which is exactly what the so called 'third-generation' models of currency crises attempt do. In these models, the role of the financial structure and the self-fulfilling nature of currency crises take the centre stage. In chapter 9 we shall deal with this latest addition to the class of currency crisis models.

8.6 Coordination

From the perspective of this chapter, the discussion of the two basic models of currency crises neglects a number of issues and contains one big loose end. Chapter 9 takes care of the loose end: the interaction between currency crises and international capital mobility, on the one hand, and financial crises, on the other hand. Here, we focus on three important issues with respect to currency crises that are not covered by our discussion of the two generations of currency crises models above:
- The coordination of the actions of individual investors
- The efficiency of currency markets
- The empirics of currency crises.

We shall deal with the coordination issue in this section. The other two issues will be dealt with in sections 8.7 and 8.8, respectively.

So far, we have treated individual investors as a homogeneous group, and have thus implicitly assumed that in attacking a currency investors coordinate their actions in such a way that they act as one. This is not an innocent assumption because a speculative attack can succeed only if a sufficiently large number of investors decides to sell the currency in a given time period. The following example, based on Obstfeld (1996), nicely illustrates this point.

Suppose there are two investors and a central bank. The latter can use its foreign exchange reserves R to defend the fixed exchange rate and is willing to use a certain amount of the reserves for this purpose – say, up to $R = 10$. This amount reflects, in a very simple manner, the commitment of the central bank to the fixed exchange rate. Each of the two investors has funds to the amount of 6 at her disposal (expressed in the domestic currency). Both investors now have to decide either to keep these funds and

Table 8.3 Coordination of a speculative attack

Pay-off matrix		Investor 1	
(investor 2, investor 1)		Sell	Hold
Investor 2	Sell	(3/2, 3/2)	(−1, 0)
	Hold	(0, −1)	(0, 0)

to do nothing (option *hold*) or to sell their funds to the central bank (purchase foreign currency) in exchange for reserves R (option *sell*). If both investors use the *sell* option, we call this a speculative attack. Suppose that, if the speculative attack succeeds, the central bank has to devalue the domestic currency by 50 per cent, creating a capital gain for the investors since they sold their funds (denominated in domestic currency) for foreign exchange reserves R and the foreign currency increases in value because of the devaluation. Finally, assume that each investor faces transactions costs of 1 if she decides to exchange her funds for reserves.

Table 8.3 illustrates that coordination of the investors' decisions is needed for a currency crisis to occur. The model is essentially a non-cooperative game in which the players (here, the two investors) have two strategies at their disposal (*sell*, *hold*), for which table 8.3 gives the corresponding pay-off matrix. Left (right) cells in each of the four pay-offs give the pay-off for investor 2 (investor 1).

If both investors choose *hold*, there will be no transaction with the central bank, and hence no speculative attack, so that the exchange rate will remain fixed. Given the commitment of the central bank to put up $R = 10$ of its reserves to defend the currency, it is also clear that a *single* investor cannot launch a successful speculative attack because each investor has only a total of 6 funds at her disposal. In addition, if one of the investors chooses the strategy *sell* while the other chooses *hold*, the former will actually lose money because of the transaction costs involved in buying the reserves from the central bank. The outcome that both investors opt for *hold* is an equilibrium outcome in this set-up of the game; given that the other investor chooses *hold* it is optimal also to choose *hold*. However, from the pay-off matrix it is clear that both investors would be better off if they both decided to *sell*. In this case, there will be a successful speculative attack as the sources of central bank ($R = 10$) fall short of the combined sources of the investors ($6 + 6 = 12$). As a result, the central bank has no option but to devalue the currency by 50 per cent. This is good news for the investors who are now in possession of the reserves and enjoy a capital gain of $10 \times 50\% = 5$, which is 5/2 for each investor. The net gain for each investor after the transactions costs of 1 is then $(5/2) − 1 = 3/2$. If both investors sell their funds to the central bank, this also yields an equilibrium outcome; given that the other investor chooses *sell* it is optimal to also choose *sell*.

The game depicted in table 8.3 thus has two equilibria. A currency crisis will occur only if the individual investors somehow manage to coordinate their actions. The example illustrates that if the investors have more means at their disposal in total than every single central bank, this is not a sufficient condition to launch a speculative attack even if the underlying economic conditions are at odds with the fixed exchange rate. The question then becomes how investors actually manage to coordinate their beliefs. Two basic possibilities exist. First, the state of the economy and the perceived willingness of the central banks to defend the fixed exchange rate produce a focal point for individual investors. Here, the fundamentals of the economy provide a signal to investors that they can use to coordinate their actions. The commitment by the central bank to stick to the fixed exchange rate in our example is $R = 10$. If this level of reserves is perceived to be low, it may set off an attack. This first possibility is in line with the first- and second-generation models of currency crises.

The second coordination possibility is that investors use information as a focal point that is not necessarily related to the actual economy. Given that the currency market, like the stock market or any other speculative market, is prone to herd behaviour, any piece of information that moves the market (herd) in a certain direction might do the trick. One example is that the alleged decision to sell investments in a particular currency by a large, single investor with a good reputation among other investors (think of larger-than-life investors such as George Soros or Warren Buffett) might be enough to lead other investors to do the same. In this case, speculative attacks can be of a purely self-fulfilling nature, in which the fundamentals of the economy are not an issue. Here, the speculative attack becomes very much like a bank run in which the expectations about a devaluation or a bank collapse materialize precisely because investors or bank deposit holders act upon their expectations. As we shall see in chapter 9, the idea that currency crises can be of a purely self-fulfilling nature may have important implications for the way a currency crisis acts as a determinant of a financial crisis. In our example, the central bank can always successfully defend the exchange rate by committing at least $R = 12$ of its foreign exchange reserves. In reality, the reserves of a single central bank are typically smaller than the combined means of the investors. Another line of defence is, therefore, that central banks coordinate their actions. Given the structure of our example, suppose we only have two countries. If the domestic and foreign central bank pool their resources (that is, combine their reserves) it is less likely that the attack will succeed. This is why countries engaging in a system of fixed exchange rates are often obliged to offer support of this kind when one of the currencies is under attack.

8.7 Efficiency

Quite remarkably, in both the first- and the second-generation models of currency crises, investors never get it wrong. That is, a currency crisis never catches them by surprise and once the crisis occurs their initial expectations about the incompatibility between the fixed exchange rate and the economic fundamentals turn out to be correct. The currency market on which the selling and buying of currencies takes place is, in other words, an *efficient market* where there is no room for surprises. Clearly, these are rather strong assumptions to make. In contrast, there is ample evidence to suggest that the currency market is, just like the stock market, not as efficient as the models of currency crises suggest. To start with, table 8.3 has already indicated that what really matters is the information that investors use to coordinate their beliefs about the sustainability of a particular exchange rate. Any kind of information might do the job, also information that is unrelated to the economic fundamentals. This opens up the possibility of currency crises that are of a wholly self-fulfilling nature.

Empirical evidence on currency crises (see below) shows that these self-fulfilling crises are not the rule, but they still can occur. There is, however, even more convincing evidence that questions the alleged efficiency of the currency market with respect to currency crises. First, once a currency crisis arises, the evidence shows that it is often not until very late that investors see the crisis coming. Second, once the crisis has materialized policy-makers can behave differently from what was expected before the crisis. To start with the first issue, in case of the Mexican peso crisis of December 1994 and the Thai baht crisis of June 1997, professional exchange rate forecasters still thought until three months before the crisis occurred that the respective exchange rates (peso–US dollar and baht–US dollar) would not change at all in December 1994 and June 1997, respectively (see Goldfajn and Valdes, 1998)! Similar evidence can be found for other currency crises. Also, when one uses the UIP condition discussed in chapter 6, we know from section 6.4 that the implicit exchange rate forecast in the UIP condition is a rather poor predictor of the actual exchange rate. It is generally not true that, say, the three-month interest rate differential between Home and Foreign provides a good forecast of the actual exchange rate between Home and Foreign three months ahead. Remember that according to the UIP condition it should be the case that $r_{home} - r_{foreign} = dE$. The fact that the UIP condition does not hold up very well empirically is important, because it shows that future changes in the exchange rate (and thus also future currency crises) are hard to predict.

After the currency crisis has taken place and the domestic currency has had to be devalued, domestic policy-makers and fundamentals sometimes behave differently than was expected before the crisis. That is to say, the *a priori* beliefs of investors are certainly not always vindicated. Take the second-generation models of currency crises. In the summer of 1993, investors started to doubt the fixed exchange rate of the French franc against the German Mark. Officially, in the Exchange Rate Mechanism (ERM) of the then operative EMS, the French Franc was pegged to all other participating currencies. *De facto*, however, the EMS worked very much like a German mark system in which the currencies were effectively pegged to the German mark. In 1993,

France was in a recession and investors believed that at some point in the near future the French authorities might want to devalue the French franc, allowing the French economy to have lower interest rates to boost the economy. To be compensated for this perceived increased exchange rate risk, investors started to ask for a higher inter-est rate on their French franc investments. In terms of the second-generation models, this shifted the trade-off for the French authorities: a higher interest rate made it even more costly to stick to the fixed exchange rate. In August 1993, the mounting pressure led to a devaluation of the French franc. To the surprise of investors and in contrast to what the second-generation models predicted, the French policy-makers did *not* lower interest rates in the aftermath of the devaluation. They decided to maintain interest rates at the pre-crisis level so as to make clear that they still preferred to keep the French franc fixed at its pre-crisis level against the German mark. Apparently, the French authorities attached more importance to the exchange rate objective than investors thought. It took about six months before investors had *learned* that they got it wrong, so that at the beginning of 1994 the French franc–German mark exchange rate had almost returned to its pre-crisis level (see Garretsen, Knot and Nijsse, 1998). Notions like 'mistakes' and 'learning' are not at home in the models of currency crises discussed in this chapter, though.

8.8 Frequency and measurement

At the beginning of this chapter we defined a 'currency crisis' in rather general terms as an attack by investors on a fixed exchange rate that came about because investors lost their confidence in the fixed exchange rate. This definition is too vague for empirical purposes. Eichengreen, Rose and Wyplosz (1995) developed a widely used *currency crisis indicator* for empirical research in which a currency crisis does not only occur when there is a forced change in the fixed exchange rate. If we limited ourselves to these changes, only successful attacks would be taken into account. Consequently, Eichengreen, Rose and Wyplosz's index of exchange rate pressure is based on changes in the exchange rate, changes in short-term interest rates and official foreign exchange reserves. When a country successfully defends its fixed exchange rate by (temporarily) raising its interest rates or by drawing upon its reserves, this can therefore also qualify as a currency crisis.

Based on this indicator, Bordo *et al.* (2001) analyse whether currency crises have become more frequent over time – by comparing, for instance, the most recent period with the Bretton Woods period, or the period of the gold standard. To answer this question, they define for each period the *probability* of a crisis as the total number of crises in a period divided by the total number of country-year observations during that period, subdivided into banking crises, currency crises and twin crises (that is,

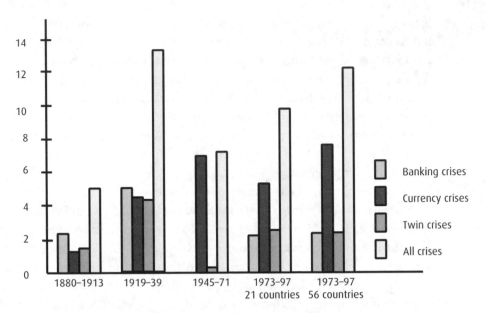

Figure 8.5 Crises frequency, percentage probability per year
Source: Bordo *et al.* (2001).

banking crises combined with currency crises) (see figure 8.5). It turns out that the frequency of *currency* crises has increased when one compares the periods 1880–1913, 1919–39, 1945–71 and 1973–1997 (taking the larger fifty-six country sample in figure 8.5 as the most appropriate estimate). In the heyday of the gold standard (1880–1913), the probability of a currency crisis was about 1 percent compared to more than 7 per cent in the most recent period. As for banking crises or twin crises, there is no such increase. Bordo *et al.* (2001) attribute the increased frequency of currency crises, which is largely due to currency crises in emerging markets, to the increase in international capital mobility.

As to the *causes* of currency crises, the bulk of the empirical research concludes that on average these crises can be attributed to economic fundamentals being at odds with the fixed exchange rate objective. As was stated above, for instance, Kaminsky and Reinhart (1999) show that on average (compared to episodes when there were no currency crises) in the eighteen months leading up to a currency crisis countries experience a significant fall in their foreign exchange reserves R, just as the first-generation models of currency crises predict. Based on the indicator of currency crises outlined above, Kaminsky and Reinhart (1999) analyse sixteen macroeconomic variables or fundamentals just before and just after a crisis took place, based on a sample of seventy-six currency crises in twenty countries in the period 1970–95. Apart from the falling reserves R, countries that are hit by a currency crisis have on average (compared to tranquil times) excessive money and credit growth rates, a high

Table 8.4 The incidence of global contagion, 1970–1998

Other countries with crises (share, %)	Unconditional (A)	Probabilities (%)	
		Conditional (B)	Difference: (B) – (A)
0–25	29.0	20.0	–9.0
25–50	29.0	33.0	4.0
50 and above	29.0	54.7	25.7

Source: Kaminsky and Reinhart (2000).

current account deficit (and thus a high capital outflow) an overvalued currency (in real terms) and lower output growth. After the currency crisis, these trends are often reversed within a few months.

The fact that currency crises tend to be associated with weak fundamentals does not imply that self-fulfilling expectations have no role to play, or that currency crises cannot be of a purely self-fulfilling nature. Evidence that might substantiate the role of self-fulfilling expectations is to be found in studies looking for *contagion* in currency crises. Kaminsky and Reinhart (2000, p. 147) define contagion as 'a case where knowing that there is a crisis elsewhere increases the probability of a crisis at home.' Using the same data set as in Kaminsky and Reinhart (1999), they investigate the incidence of contagion of currency crises for a large number of countries. Their results are summarized in table 8.4 in terms of unconditional and conditional probabilities. The unconditional probability indicates the chance at time *t* that a country will be hit by a currency crisis within the next twenty-four months which is defined as (the total number of crises in the sample period $\times$ 24) divided by the total number of observations. The *un*conditional probability of a currency crisis turns out to be 29 per cent. The element of contagion is introduced in the next column of table 8.4 by calculating the *conditional* probability of a currency crisis – that is, the probability of a currency crisis at home when there is a currency crisis elsewhere. Table 8.4 is based on the entire sample and thus provides information on the relevance of global contagion. It turns out that the conditional probability is clearly larger than the unconditional probability only if at least 50 per cent of the countries experience a currency crisis, in which case it is almost twice as high. This provides some evidence in favour of global contagion. The evidence gets stronger when only regional contagion is taken into account – that is, if the conditional probability is based on a currency crises occurring elsewhere in the *region* (e.g. Europe, Asia, or Latin America), excluding the rest of the world (not shown).

Evidence of contagion does not mean that currency crises are self-fulfilling due to herd behaviour on the part of investors. After all, contagion can also be explained by the fundamentals when the country that is hit by a crisis is linked to other countries via international trade or finance. If firms from developing countries A and B, both with initially a fixed exchange rate against the US dollar, compete on the same export markets and country A has to devalue its currency thereby (temporarily) improveing its competitiveness, this implies a deterioration of the relative competitiveness position for country B. The latter constitutes a weakening of the fundamentals of country B and might thus provoke a currency crisis. Similarly, if firms in both countries A and B borrow from the same group of foreign creditors, a currency crisis in country A might weaken the financial position of these creditors, leading them to re-assess their lending policies with respect to country B as well. The capital flow to country B might come to a halt, followed by a currency crisis for country B. These two examples are cases of so-called 'fundamentals-based contagion'. It is only when contagion cannot be traced to this kind of economic interdependence between countries that one speaks of 'pure contagion' – that is, of contagion that is of a purely self-fulfilling nature. As to the empirical verdict on fundamental versus pure contagio, the jury is still out, but it is fair to say that not all cases of contagion can be traced back to country linkages in fundamentals. In chapter 9 we shall see that the proponents of the view that *financial* crises are due to the speculative behaviour of (international) investors call upon pure contagion to back their claim.

8.9 Looking ahead

International capital mobility is a prime feature of our modern global economy and therefore figures prominently in this book. In chapter 7, we emphasized the gains from international capital mobility. One of the alleged drawbacks of international capital mobility is the increase in financial fragility and associated economic vulnerability, by making countries subject to swings in their capital flows. The central variable that acts like a pressure-cooker with respect to international capital flows to or from a particular country is a country's exchange rate. In this chapter we have dealt with so-called currency or exchange rate crises, a situation in which individual investors (perhaps quite suddenly) lose their confidence in a currency and its underlying economy and collectively head for the exit. We have not elaborated on the foreign exchange market as such, but have focused on understanding currency crises – that is, situations in which a currency is 'under attack' and news about the currency is not only reported on the financial pages but also on the front page of all major newspapers. Exchange rates matter in this part of the book particularly because they clarify how international capital mobility might be relevant in explaining domestic financial crises. The connection between exchange rates, capital mobility, and financial crises will become clear in chapter 9, where the material presented in this chapter will prove to be very useful.

Financial crises, firms and the open economy

KEYWORDS

twin crisis	asymmetric information	disruptions
balance sheets	firms and banks	savings and investment
net worth	external finance premium	third-generation models
real exchange rate	moral hazard	perverse savings
fundamentals	self-fulfilling expectations	vicious circle

9.1 Introduction and terminology

After the work in chapter 8 on currency crises, this chapter focuses on financial crises. Obviously, we need to know what the main differences are between these types of crises. As explained in chapter 8, a *currency crisis* is a disruption on the currency market in which a speculative attack on a currency leads to a devaluation and/or to the monetary authorities defending the exchange rate by depleting their foreign exchange reserves and/or raising interest rates. A *capital account crisis* is the mirror image of a currency crisis, focusing on the sudden reversal of capital flows that accompanies the currency market disruption. As such, a currency/capital account crisis is a potential *external* channel for a financial crisis. Its domestic equivalent is a banking crisis, in which the increased fragility of a country's banking sector, potentially leading to bank runs, forces the government to intervene and/or banks to scale down their business, which is a potential *internal* channel for a financial crisis. It is customary to refer to a 'twin crisis' if a banking crisis and a currency crisis occur (almost) at the same time. The word 'potential' is used in both cases above because not every currency crisis or banking crisis *is* a financial crisis.

A financial crisis, for which a formal definition will be given in section 9.2, consists of disruptions on the financial markets that impair the working of these markets to such an extent that they can no longer perform their main function: the efficient channelling of funds (savings, S) to their most productive uses (investments, I). As a result, a financial crisis leads to a contraction of the real economy in terms of GDP growth (see table 9.1).

Table 9.1 Cost of crises in lost output (relative to trend output)

	No. of crises	Average recovery time (years)	% of crises with output loss	Cumulative output loss per crisis[a]
Currency crises	158	1.6	61	7.1
Industrial	42	1.9	55	5.6
Emerging	116	1.5	64	7.6
Banking crises	53	3.1	82	14.2
Industrial	12	4.1	67	15.2
Emerging	41	2.8	86	14.0
Twin crises	32	3.2	78	18.5
Industrial	6	5.8	100	17.6
Emerging	26	2.6	73	18.8

Source: IMF (1998).
Note: [a] For those crises with an output loss.

As explained in chapter 8, currency crises are measured based on an index of speculative pressure that consists of changes in exchange rates, foreign reserves and interest rates. Banking crises are, in principle, a bit harder to measure, but usually some simple counts of 'bank trouble' are used, such as bankruptcy, (forced) mergers, government assistance, etc. As shown in table 9.1, most currency crises and banking crises occur in emerging markets and are also a financial crisis – that is, they lead to an output loss: namely for 61 per cent of the currency crises and 82 per cent of the banking crises. The costs of restructuring the financial sector for the government are substantial. These costs range from funds and credit injected into the banking system to the fiscal costs of closing down banks. Such costs can amount up to 20 per cent of GDP. Although these costs are already substantial for financial currency crises (about 7.1 per cent), they are substantially higher for financial banking crises (about 14.2 per cent) and even higher for financial twin crises (about 18.5 per cent). From 1980 to the mid-1990s, Caprio and Klingebiel (1996) argue that there were eighty-two banking crises in (mostly) developing and developed countries, where a banking crisis is an episode of major bank insolvencies. Note, finally, that financial crises are not a new phenomenon (see Bordo *et al.*, 2001): the Great Depression of the 1930s can be taken as a prime example.

9.2 An asymmetric information view of financial crises

In our analysis of international capital mobility in chapter 7 we emphasized that financial transactions are special: there is a supply of funds against a mere expectation of a future return or income stream. This feature distinguishes financial transactions from goods transactions and it helps us to understand why the riskiness of financial transactions is such an important issue. This risk associated with financial transactions is primarily due to the existence of incomplete and asymmetric information on the part of the market participants. The asymmetry arises, for instance, because the supplier of funds to a firm is typically less well informed than the firm itself about its investment plans. We have also explained that asymmetric information gives rise to two basic problems, adverse selection and moral hazard and discussed ways to deal with these problems. In a well-developed financial system, the financial intermediaries (banks) specialize in the reduction of the asymmetric information problems through their monitoring and screening activities. Given our aim to analyse financial crises from the perspective of a firm seeking finance for its investment plans, the financial structure of firms will again play a key role in this chapter. We summarize the financial structure using the firm's net worth (NW), as we did in chapter 7. A weakening of the financial structure (that is, a fall in NW) increases the asymmetric information problems and thereby reduces the efficiency of the financial system.

Based on the work of Frederic Mishkin (1992, 1996) and others, we provide a framework for the analysis of financial crises. To this end, we provide the following definition of a financial crisis:

A financial crisis occurs when, due to disruptions on financial markets, the increase of the adverse selection and moral hazard problems is such that the financial system can no longer efficiently perform its main job of channelling funds to the most productive investment opportunities.

A first thing to note about this definition is that not all disruptions on financial markets constitute a financial crisis. A stock market crash, a bust on the housing market, or a currency crisis cause a financial crisis only if, through their impact on the asymmetric information problems, the financial system cannot any longer perform its main task. It is also clear that this definition is not watertight, because it is somewhat arbitrary to decide whether or not the financial system has stopped functioning in the way the definition implies. Having said this, from the introduction to this chapter it is clear that financial crises can have severe implications in terms of output loss. In macroeconomic terms, our definition of a financial crisis means that it can be looked upon as a negative supply shock to the economy. Just like a breakdown of a country's physical infrastructure, a crisis in a country's financial infrastructure or transactions technology also limits future investment and growth opportunities.

9.3 Disruptions and asymmetric information

Our definition of a financial crisis refers to what the IMF (1998) describes as a *systemic financial crisis*. Both internal and external factors may lead to a disruption in financial markets. We will distinguish between the following five categories of disruption:

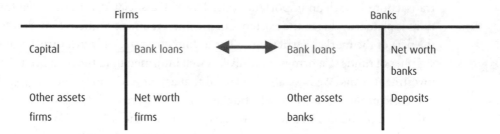

Figure 9.1 Stylized balance sheets of firms and banks

1. An interest rate increase
2. An increase in uncertainty
3. A decrease in asset prices
4. Deflation
5. A bank panic or bank run.

In each case, the crucial question to ask is how these disruptions increase the adverse selection or the moral hazard problem. Suppose we are dealing with a firm that finances its activities though bank loans. Moreover, let us assume for the moment that we are dealing with a closed economy, leaving the international context to be added on p. 247. In doing so, our basic framework in this section refers to a 'banking crisis turned financial crisis.' As we will demonstrate below, the same framework also applies in an international context. When thinking about disruptions 1–5 above, it is useful to keep the two simple balance sheets of figure 9.1 in mind, where as usual entries on the left-hand side refer to *assets* and entries on the right-hand side refer to *liabilities*.

Regarding disruption 1, an increase in the interest rate, this increases the adverse selection problem for banks because the pool of loan applicants will contain relatively more risky clients after the interest rate increase, since firms willing to take on higher risk will still be asking for a bank loan whereas more risk averse firms will no longer ask for such loans. Since the bank can discriminate only imperfectly between more and less risky firms, banks may decide to cut back their supply of loans, as a result of which sound firms may also suffer because they can no longer carry out their investment plans. The moral hazard problem also rises because the interest rate increase will stimulate firms to engage in more risky behaviour after the loan has been granted.

An increase in uncertainty has similar effects in that it makes it hard for the supplier of funds to distinguish between more and less risky investment projects. A decrease in asset prices, such as a fall in stock prices or other firm assets, decreases the *NW* for the owners of these assets. As we know from chapter 7, a drop in *NW* signals to banks that it has become more risky to supply funds to the firms because in case of a default there is less for the bank to recoup. This increases the adverse selection problem. A drop in NW also increases the moral hazard problem because the reduction of funds at stake for the debtor (the firm) stimulates risk-taking. A fall in the non-financial sector NW implies a deterioration in the balance sheets of this sector. This also has an impact on the balance sheet of the bank because if the quality of its loan portfolio is reduced as a result of the reduced NW of its clients, the NW of the bank itself will also fall. In this case, the balance sheet of the bank will also deteriorate.

Deflation – that is, a fall in the general price level – has similar effects as a fall in asset prices. Deflation implies an increase in the *real* value of debt, which reduces the NW of firms and indirectly also of banks, worsening the balance sheets of both firms and banks. Finally, in the extreme case that in our example the bank's deposit holders rightly or wrongly start to doubt whether the bank's financial position has deteriorated to such an extent that the bank might not be able the repay its deposit holders, they may ask for their money back. If most deposit holders try to do this simultaneously, we shall have a bank panic or bank run. These bank runs are not a thing of the distant past but were an important element of the financial crises in Russia (1998), Turkey (2001) and Argentina (2002). Here, too, the role of asymmetric information is crucial because deposit holders are only imperfectly informed about the dealings of their bank; they use (expected) changes in the *bank's NW* to determine whether it is still safe to hold on to their deposits. If the banking system collapses and the system of financial intermediation breaks down, the efficiency of the financial system is seriously reduced.

9.4 A financial crisis framework

We need not be concerned here with all the details of the disruptions described in section 9.3. The important point to note is that these examples show how the two basic problems of asymmetric information may increase. In chapter 7, we have discussed from the perspective of the individual firm how the supply of funds (F_s) and the demand for funds (F_d, or firm investment) can be derived in a world of asymmetric information. Building on this framework, figure 9.2 shows how the above disruptions on financial markets may develop into a financial crisis, hurting investment and affecting the real economy.

Assume, for the sake of simplicity, that the supply of funds schedule that the firms face reflects the supply of bank loans as far as external finance is concerned. From chapter 7, we know that with complete information – that is, in a risk-free world – the economy will find itself at point 1 in figure 9.2 at the interest rate r_0. With incomplete and asymmetric information, the supply schedule is no longer perfectly

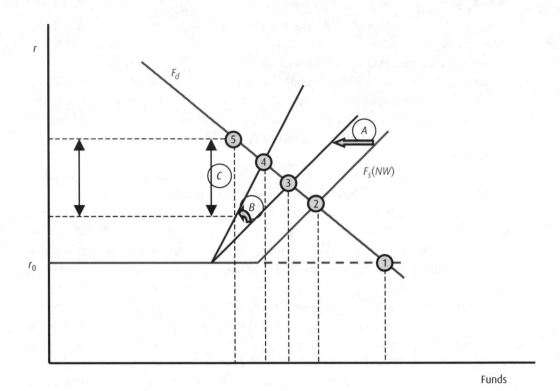

Figure 9.2 Financial crisis in an asymmetric information framework

interest-elastic and, beyond the point where a firm can finance its investment by its own means, its position depends on the NW of the firm. As explained above, changes in NW reflect changes in the degree of the asymmetric information problem. Assume that the economy initially finds itself at point 2 in figure 9.2. We know that various disruptions on financial markets may cause a fall in the NW of firms. This will shift the supply schedule to the left as shown by arrow A in figure 9.2, taking us to point 3. Banks will cut back their supply of loans, depressing investment as fewer investment projects now meet the requirement that their return has at least to equal the cost of capital (recall that the demand for funds or investment schedule reflects the MPC and the interest rate r is the cost of capital).

In addition, the disruption on the financial markets may imply that the slope of the supply schedule F_s becomes steeper (arrow b in Figure 9.2), which may take the economy to point 4. For any *given* level of NW banks may find that it has become riskier to lend money to firms because of an increase in overall uncertainty. Remember that we explained the upward-sloping part of the F_s schedule by stating that this reflects the risk involved in supplying funds. A steeper slope, therefore, implies that the suppliers of funds (here, the banks) perceive the risk to have increased; for any level of supply a higher return is now asked by the banks – that is, a higher interest rate. Finally, if the system of financial intermediation breaks down because of bank runs, firm investment may fall even further. Without a properly functioning banking system, the efficiency of the financial system is reduced, as illustrated in figure 9.2 by the positive *wedge* (as visualized by arrow *C*) between the cost of capital for firms (point 5) and the actual return for the suppliers of funds (banks). At point 4 in figure 9.2, the costs of financial intermediation or the transaction costs are still zero. The size of the wedge reflects the transaction costs of channelling funds to firms seeking to finance their investments. In case of a bank panic, the screening and monitoring costs that make up the transaction costs rise. Without a well-functioning system of financial intermediation both the adverse selection and moral hazard problem increase, leading to higher transaction costs.

Note that in this financial crisis framework, numbers 2 and 5 of the five categories of disruption described in section 9.3 (an increase in uncertainty and a bank panic, respectively) do not lead to a drop in NW, and thus do not shift the F_s curve, but affect its slope and create a wedge, as illustrated by arrows B and C in figure 9.2. We will now extend this simple framework of financial crises to incorporate the international dimension.

9.5 Financial crises in an open economy

We have defined a financial crisis as a situation in which, due to increased problems of asymmetric information, the financial system can no longer ensure an efficient allocation of funds. Various disruptions on financial markets can increase the adverse selection and moral hazard problems to such an extent that a financial crisis will be triggered. As discussed in section 9.4, the most important of these disruptions is the deterioration of the balance sheets of both the financial and non-financial sector of the economy (recall the role of NW). In this view of financial crises, the primary source of a financial crisis is the intrinsic weakness of the *domestic* financial system. Financial crises can, of course, occur in a closed economy, but by allowing international capital mobility and exchange rates to play a role, a number of *additional* channels come into play through which disruptions on financial markets may occur.

If (foreign) investors lose their confidence in an economy, this may lead to a currency crisis and a reversal of capital flows (see chapter 8). The data on capital flows to developing countries indeed show that such a reversal of capital flows can take place (see also chapter 8). Table 9.2, for example, illustrates the dramatic decrease in private capital flows to developing countries that occurred in the late 1990s. Private capital flows remain subdued, so that the developing countries as a whole are now 'forced' to run a current account surplus. Table 9.2 shows the external financing for

Table 9.2 Developing countries: external debt and equity financing, 1997–2003, billion US $

	1997	1998	1999	2000	2001	2002	2003
Current account balance	−91.4	−113.6	−10.7	61.9	27.6	48.3	26.2
Financed by:							
Net equity flows	196.0	181.9	194.3	186.7	177.6	152.3	158.0
of which net FDI	169.3	174.5	179.3	160.6	171.7	143.0	145.0
Net debt flows	102.1	57.4	13.9	−1.0	3.3	7.2	5.0
of which: private creditors	89.1	23.3	0.5	5.1	−24.8	−9.0	5.0
of which: banks	43.1	51.4	−5.9	2.6	−11.8	−16.0	–
of which: short term debt	5.0	−64.2	−21.4	−9.4	−16.2	−6.1	–

Note: – = no data.
Source: World Bank (2003a).

all developing countries for the period 1997–2003. During this period, the fall in net equity flows is very small compared to the decrease in net debt flows. With respect to the latter, the debt supplied by banks as well as the short-term debt flows went from an inflow to a net outflow (repayment of outstanding debt exceeded the new debt inflows).

We now know why a currency crisis might occur, but how does it link up with our incomplete information analysis of financial crisis as outlined in section 9.4? There are various channels through which such a link can be established. To start with, if a substantial part of international lending to domestic firms is either directly or indirectly (e.g. by domestic banks having US dollar liabilities) denominated in the foreign currency, the resulting currency depreciation increases the real debt burden of banks and firms. This deterioration of balance sheets increases the adverse selection and moral hazard problems in the same manner as a fall in the domestic price level does. Figure 9.3 illustrates the US dollar exposure for five emerging markets by giving the share of outstanding debt denominated in US dollars. Three of these countries, namely Korea, Indonesia and Thailand, were hit by a currency-cum-financial crisis in 1997–8. As a benchmark, we also show the corresponding data for Brazil and Argentina, two countries with their own history of financial fragility, for the same period. Both countries were relatively trouble-free in the years considered, although Brazil had a currency crisis at the beginning of 1999 and Argentina had a full-blown currency and financial crisis in 2002. Since typically the degree of exchange rate depreciation against the US dollar was very substantial for those countries that were hit by a currency crisis (see chapter 8), the debt burden in *local* currency terms skyrocketed. We focus on the years 1996 (pre-crisis), 1997(start of crisis) and 1998 (full-blown crisis). Figure 9.3 clearly shows that the share of US dollar-denominated debt of the three Asian countries increased sharply in 1997 and 1998.

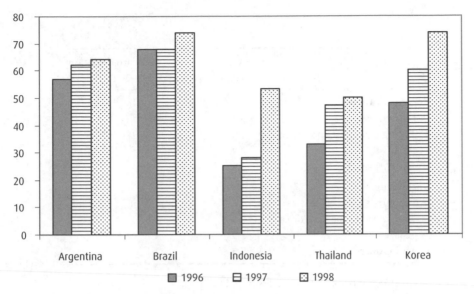

Figure 9.3 Share of $US-denominated debt 1996–1998, selected countries, per cent
Source: IMF (2002).

An increase in interest rates, which might be needed to prevent a plunging currency and to stop capital outflows, increases the asymmetric information problem. If domestic investment is to a large extent financed by foreign lending (because of a lack of domestic savings), the currency crisis and the corresponding decrease in capital inflows also mean that the volume of funds available to finance investment falls. For a number of countries that were part of the financial crisis episode in the late 1990s, the interest rate spread against the USA increased sharply. The *spread* gives the difference between the domestic and (in this case) the US interest rate. In 1997, before the financial crisis in Southeast Asia began to infect many emerging market economies, the Emerging Market Bond Index (EMBI) spread was around 5 per cent. So on average long-term interest rates in emerging markets were 5 per cent higher than corresponding interest rates in the USA. In 1998, the spread rose to about 17 per cent (!), before dropping to about 10 per cent in the years 1999–2001 (see IMF, 2000). Clearly, such a hike in the interest rate spread as a result of financial turmoil puts a severe strain on the economies involved and hampers the workings of the domestic financial system. The rise in the interest rate spread reflects both the increased risk attached by international investors to lending to these emerging markets as well as tight monetary policies. The latter indicates that following the exchange rate depreciation, domestic interest rates were not lowered or were even increased to stop a further fall of the currency and to put an end to the capital outflow. In the sequel of this chapter, we discuss a critique of this policy approach.

Table 9.3 Profitability of non-financial firms in emerging markets, 1992–2001, per cent

	Average 1992–2001	Standard deviation 1992–2001
Income to assets:		
All countries	3.1	0.9
Emerging Europe and Africa	5.9	2.3
Asia	2.2	1.3
Latin America	3.5	1.0
Income to sales:		
All countries	4.6	1.2
Emerging Europe and Africa	6.7	2.8
Asia	2.9	1.7
Latin America	7.5	2.1

Source: World Bank (2003a), table 5.1, p. 114.

Finally, if domestic banks get into trouble because of the currency mismatch on their own and/or their domestic client's balance sheets, the quality of financial intermediation may decrease. The latter also happens if *foreign* sources of finance, which are thought to be relatively more efficient, become less readily available, either directly (through the withdrawal of foreign banks) or indirectly (through the reduced access to international capital markets).

Ultimately, by allowing for currency crises and international capital mobility, we have found additional channels of financial crises in our basic asymmetric information framework, as already illustrated in figure 9.2. In terms of figure 9.2, the currency depreciation and the decrease in capital inflows are foreign channels through which:

(a) the supply schedule F_s shifts to the left

(b) the slope of this schedule increases, or

(c) a wedge between the gross and net return on savings develops.

As a result of (a), (b) and/or (c), investment falls and the economy suffers. The decrease in capital inflows implies a leftward shift in the supply of funds schedule. The exchange rate depreciation and the interest rate increase amplify the problems of asymmetric information, also leading to the leftward shift of the F_s schedule. In line with our earlier analysis, both the exchange rate depreciation (through its effect on the real debt burden) and the interest rate increase imply a drop in the NW of firms. Also, for any given level of NW, international suppliers of funds may find it riskier to supply funds, which increases the slope of the schedule. Finally, the problems in the banking sector trigger a lower efficiency of financial intermediation. This increases the transaction costs and therefore the wedge between the return on funds for the

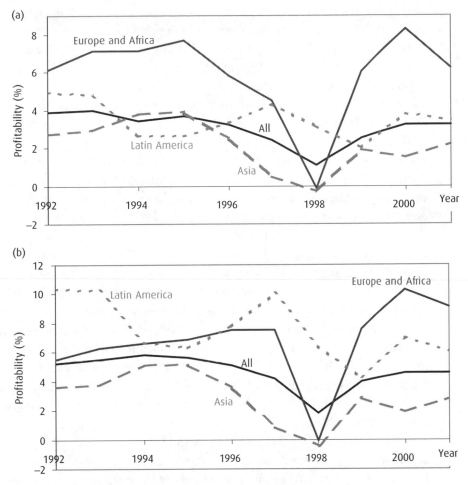

Figure 9.4 Profitability of non-financial firms, emerging markets, 1992–2004, per cent
a   Income to assets, b   Income to sales
Source: See table 9.3.

suppliers of external finance, on the one hand, and the cost of acquiring funds for the firms, on the other hand.

The importance of changes in NW can also be grasped in a more direct manner. The World Bank (2003a) shows how corporate profits of non-financial firms in emerging markets have steadily declined in the period 1992–2001. In terms of figure 9.2, this not only means that less internal finance is available for investment (the horizontal segment of the F_s schedule is shortened), but also that the NW of firms falls. This makes it more difficult to find external finance, which with a relatively low level of domestic savings has to come predominantly through the supply of foreign equity or debt. Table 9.3 presents two indicators of profitability for emerging markets: the net income/assets ratio and the net income/sales ratio. The details in table 9.3 for the individual years 1992–2001 are illustrated in figure 9.4.

Both indicators signal a steep fall in profitability in the late 1990s. The fall in profits thus signals a drop in firms' NW, implying that fewer means are available for internal finance of investment projects. It also implies that the conditions under which the external suppliers of funds will be willing to put their money in a firm becomes less favourable. The external cost of capital will go up.

To answer the question whether or not the contraction in the supply of funds (savings) and the demand for funds (investment) are inevitable, one needs to know if the underlying economic conditions are unsustainable to start with, and if these conditions create *over-investment*. We develop the view that for both foreign lenders and domestic borrowers the financial fragility – and hence the over-investment – are the result of the fact that the *level of private risk* has become too low. In terms of figure 9.2, a lower degree of private risk means that the F_s schedule becomes more interest-elastic. If private risk is no longer taken into account, we are back at a flat savings schedule. With a flat supply of funds schedule, the level of investment will be too high compared to the case where risk is taken into account.

How can the level of private risk be too low? One possibility is that the governments in lender and borrower countries and international financial institutions (IFIs) such as the IMF take over these risks by giving too many implicit or explicit guarantees that they will bail out lenders or borrowers if they get into trouble. Once lenders and borrowers know this, they will undertake more risky behaviour, an example of the *moral hazard* problem.

A second possibility is that both lenders and borrowers are simply too optimistic about the future prospects of the economy: current account deficits are seen as reflecting growth-enhancing investment (and not as the result of too much spending) and fixed exchange rates are thought to remain fixed forever. Based on figure 9.2, we shall discuss a simple model based on McKinnon and Pill (1997) and Krugman (1998) that shows how the interplay between moral hazard behaviour (due to unlimited deposit insurance) and the unlimited access to the international capital market at a supposedly 'risk-free' interest rate r_0 can lead to over-investment (see box 9.1).

9.6 Wake-up call and perverse savings

When foreign creditors start to doubt whether the domestic government will always be willing and able to fully guarantee the banks' liabilities, it is no longer the case that the savings schedule is completely flat. The riskiness of the lending decision will now be an issue and the savings schedule will have a positive slope. This renders over-investment less likely because even if the banking firms in box 9.1 tried to behave

Box 9.1 Moral hazard and over-investment: an example

Assume that, due to a lack of internal finance as well as domestic external finance, we are dealing with a firm seeking to attract foreign funds to finance the purchase of capital goods. These capital goods are needed for the future production of the firm's output. For the sake of simplicity, think of this firm as being a bank. So the bank has to acquire the funds, as well as to buy the capital goods and undertake the manufacturing production. For many emerging markets this is not a far-fetched assumption because of the interdependencies between manu-facturing firms and banks in countries such as South Korea (the *Chaebol* system) or Chile (the industrial–financial conglomerates called *grupos*). To bring out the implications of the moral hazard problem we assume that all bank liabilities are fully guaranteed by the government (so if the bank goes bust all creditors are fully repaid by the government) and that the owners of the bank have not invested any money of their own into the 'bank firm' (if they did, this would limit the moral hazard problem).

To make the model as simple as possible, assume that the banks operate under conditions of perfect competition so that bank profits are zero. To bring out the implications of a flat supply schedule, assume that the bank can borrow in the international capital market against a given interest rate r_0. So, no matter how much the bank wishes to borrow and invest, the interest rate does not change. The supply of funds schedule is perfectly interest-elastic (see the horizontal line in figure 9.2). Moreover, assume that $r_0 = 0$.

Against this background, two simple equations suffice to show why this econ-omy suffers from over-investment. Equation (9.1) gives the production function

$$Q = (A + u)K - BK^2 \tag{9.1}$$

Production of the good Q is realized, given the state of the technology A, through the input of capital K. The variable u reflects the fact that production takes place under conditions of uncertainty. Two possibilities exist: $u = 1$ (a good state of the world) or $u = 0$ (a bad state of the world). Before production can take place, the capital goods have to be purchased, represented by the term $-BK^2$.

What is the amount of investment that will be realized? From chapter 7, we already know that the investment schedule represents the MPC. Investment will take place until MPC equals the cost of capital r_0

$$r_0 = MPC = dQ/dK = A + u - 2BK \tag{9.2}$$

The crucial variable here is u. Suppose that there is a 50 per cent chance that $u = 1$ and thus also a 50 per cent chance that $u = 0$. In this moral hazard situation, banks will behave *as if* only $u = 1$ can occur. They will also base their borrowing on this false assumption. Why? If $u = 1$, in the good state of the economy, banks benefit because they can produce more according to (9.1). If, however, $u = 0$ materializes and banks have based their borrowing on the assumption that this will not occur, they will have a problem because they will now have borrowed too much. Banks do, however, not bear the costs of this over-borrowing because the government has guaranteed to re-pay all creditors if things go wrong with the bank, while the bank-owners have no financial stakes of their own in the bank. In other words, banks do not take the riskiness of their investment into account, but neither do the foreign lenders. They have no incentive to monitor the bank's activities.

To illustrate the example with some numbers, assume that $r_0 = 0$, $A = 2$ and $B = 0.5$. Using (9.2) it can easily be checked that in the moral hazard case (where banks behave as if u is always equal to 1) the equilibrium level of the capital stock is $K = 3$. If, in the absence of the moral hazard problem, banks (and their creditors) based their decision on excepted returns, it follows from (9.2) that the equilibrium capital stock will be lower, namely $K = 2.5$. The behaviour of the banks clearly results in over-investment.

as if there were no uncertainty, creditors would ask for a higher interest rate if the banks wanted to expand their investment, thus limiting investment expansion. This conclusion is line with figure 9.2 if we compare the equilibrium outcomes 1 and 2. But what if, due to over-optimistic foreign lenders and over-guaranteed domestic banks, the economy has really ended up at point 1 in figure 9.2? Any doubts on the part of the foreign lenders about the financial position of the banks might not only take the economy from point 1 to point 2, but it might also lead to a full-blown financial crisis for the reasons discussed earlier in this chapter. A fall in the capital inflow (arrow A) depresses savings; a currency depreciation and an interest rate rise increase information problems through their impact on the borrowers' NW (arrows A and B); and the (partial) withdrawal of relatively efficient foreign creditors decreases the efficiency of the financial system (arrow C).

In addition to the effects summarized in figure 9.2, our example in box 9.1 suggests two other possible negative effects. First, the investment schedule might also shift to the left when the government guarantees are in doubt and domestic banks and firms base their investment decisions on expected returns. To grasp this, note that if in (9.2) it is taken into account that $u = 0$ with a probability of 50 per cent, investment falls. The MPC is lower in this case. In terms of figure 9.2, this means that the investment schedule shifts to the left, which further depresses the economy. This happens because for all levels of investment the MPC schedule will be lower when risk is properly accounted for.

The second additional effect concerns the impact of an interest rate increase on savings. A higher interest rate depresses borrowers' NW and thereby increases the

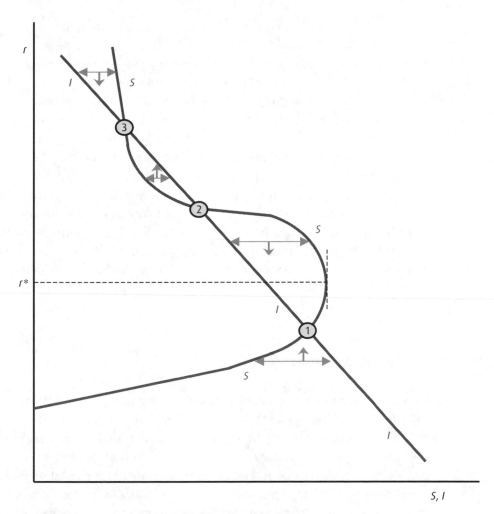

Figure 9.5 Perverse savings and the backward-bending savings curve

problems of asymmetric information. In general, people will save more (and hence supply more funds to firms) when the interest rate increases. But what happens to savings if the interest rate increase implies such a substantial additional burden for the borrowers that the total return on savings falls? This can happen if the borrowers (here, the firms who want to invest) were not able to repay their loans after the increase in the interest rate. In this case the suppliers of funds could be worse off if the interest rate increases and they would therefore be inclined to save less. On the basis of this possibility, an interest rate increase might actually *depress* total savings in the economy which means that the savings schedule will have a *negative* slope. This 'perverse' savings effect of the interest rate is more likely to occur when interest rates are already at a relatively high level. In figure 9.5, this possibility is illustrated for *economywide* savings and investment by assuming that if $r > r^*$ the savings schedule has a negative slope.

This depiction of the savings schedule as a backward-bending curve is at the core of the argument of those critics of the IMF who claim that the IMF's advice not to lower interest rates after a currency crisis may be counter-productive, notably Joseph Stiglitz (2002). Not lowering, or even increasing, interest rates when the country is on the brink of a financial crisis can make matters worse if the economy finds itself in the backward-bending part of the savings schedule. Suppose increasing financial fragility has meant that the economy is at point 2 in figure 9.5. At point 2 we have an unstable equilibrium. Immediately to the right of point 2 a slightly lower interest rate stimulates both savings S and investment I, and the same is true for a slightly higher interest rate to the left of point 2. A slight increase in the interest rate will therefore take the economy from point 2 to point 3. The latter is a stable equilibrium at which savings and investment have become very low. The response by the IMF to this criticism by Stiglitz of their policy prescriptions is that the lowering of interest rates is very often not an option because it will imply further capital outflows and currency depreciations.

9.7 Evidence about twin crises

The analysis in this chapter suggests that by adding the international perspective to the asymmetric information framework of financial crises, the weaknesses in the domestic financial sector may be *reinforced* by (quite sudden) changes in capital flows and by a currency crisis leading to a depreciation of the domestic currency. In this view, the weaknesses in the financial sector are not the result of changes in capital flows and exchange rates but the financial sector is intrinsically weak, and movements in capital flows and exchange rates only add to the problem. Almost all the recent financial crises have occurred in emerging markets, where the domestic financial sector is dominated by the banking sector in its role as financial intermediary in the process of channelling funds to investment opportunities. Financial crises are, in this case, mainly banking crises. Mishkin (1999) argues that a banking crisis *precedes* a currency crisis. If a country experiences both a banking crisis in the domestic financial sector and a currency crisis, this is called a *twin crisis*. Using the asymmetric information framework of a financial crisis, a typical modern financial crisis, as experienced in many emerging markets in recent years, develops (see figure 9.6).

The question is, of course, if this sequence of events can be backed up with empirical evidence. Two main issues are at stake. First, is it true for twin crises that banking crises typically precede the currency crises and that currency crises deepen banking crises? Second, are the underlying economic conditions to blame for

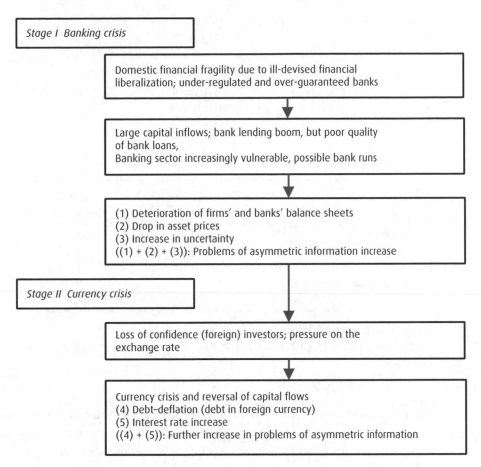

Figure 9.6 The unfolding of a financial crisis

both the banking and currency crisis – that is to say, are these crises the result of *bad fundamentals*?

Graciela Kaminsky and Carmen Reinhart (1999) provide evidence supporting the view that banking crises precede currency crisis, suggesting that by and large the fundamentals are to blame. We encountered their research strategy in chapter 8 on currency crises. Kaminsky and Reinhart use data for the period 1970–95 for twenty countries on seventy-six currency and twenty banking crises and compare the behaviour of sixteen macroeconomic and financial variables in the months leading up to a crisis and in the months just after the banking or currency crisis hit the economy. As a benchmark, they use for each country a period of 'tranquil' times when no crisis occurred. It turns out that in the build-up to a crisis there is an excessive growth of bank credit (as a percentage of GDP) and money supply. In line with the analysis of currency crises in chapter 8, there is also an over-valuation of the currency, a

Table 9.4 Possible relationships between signals
and crises

	Crisis	No crisis
Signal	Possibility *A*	Possibility *B*
No signal	Possibility *C*	Possibility *D*

Table 9.5 Percentage of crises accurately called

Indicator:	Banking crisis	Currency crisis	Twin crisis[a]
Domestic credit/GDP	73	59	67
Money supply	75	79	89
Exports	88	83	89
Real exchange rate	58	57	67
Foreign exchange reserves	92	74	79
Output	89	73	77

Source: Kaminsky and Reinhart (1999).
Note: [a] Twin crisis: A banking crisis is followed by a currency crisis within forty-eight
months.

fall in foreign exchange reserves and an excessive capital inflow. In the months after
the crisis these trends are reversed: credit growth falls, there is a depreciation of the
currency, the current account improves and capital inflows dwindle.

Kaminsky and Reinhart (1999) also investigate whether their set of sixteen variables can be used as indicators to provide early warning signals of an upcoming
banking and/or currency crisis. A variable gives a signal when it passes a specific
threshold value. No signal means that the variable indicates that there will not be a
crisis. Table 9.4 shows that there are four distinct possibilities with respect to these
signals.

Indicators would be perfect signals if only outcomes *A* and *D* were realized. In that
case, the so-called noise-to-signal ratio is zero. In reality, indicators at times provide
false signals (cases *B* and *C* in table 9.5). Nevertheless, table 9.5 shows for some of
the sixteen variables that in the majority of crises the early warning signals accurately
called the crisis (the score for cell *A* in table 9.4). Above all, table 9.4 provides further
evidence that financial crises are at least partly the result of problems in the underlying
economic conditions. For the twin crises, for almost 60 per cent of these crises 10–13
indicators out of a total of 16 gave a correct signal, predicting the onset of a twin
crisis.

9.8 Bad fundamentals or malicious investors?

The illiquidity approach

In our analysis so far, financial crises have been seen to be at least partly the result of weaknesses in the underlying domestic economic conditions, particularly of the domestic financial sector. Empirical research provides support for this view. Especially for financial crises in emerging markets, the fragility of the domestic sector is deemed to be the main driving force of financial crises. Banking crises are thought to precede currency crises that, in this view, are at least to some extent grounded in bad domestic economic fundamentals. To use an analogy with firms that are in financial trouble, financial crises are essentially *solvency crises* (with possibly negative NW). This view is, however, not undisputed. Inspired by the financial crises in Southeast Asia in 1997–8, Radelet and Sachs (1998) and Jeanne (2000, p. 38) put forward a view of financial crises in which there is initially not much intrinsically wrong with domestic economic conditions. In their view, the main determinants of the financial crisis are the self-fulfilling expectations of international investors who, for whatever reason, 'attack' a currency, as in the bank run-type of example of currency crises discussed in chapter 8. In this view, therefore, financial crises are not crises of insolvency but are the consequence of a *liquidity shortage* created by investors.

To back up their claims, proponents of the illiquidity approach point to the fact that contagion of financial crises is widespread and that the phenomenon of contagion (discussed in chapter 8) cannot always be explained by economic fundamentals. They continue to show that for particular crises the macroeconomic fundamentals did not justify a crisis. In this view and in line with our game-theoretic example of chapter 8, portfolio investors withdraw their funds for no good reason other than to try to make a speculative gain. As a result, there is a currency crisis and a capital outflow. Investors can succeed in bringing down a currency because their means outstrip those of the monetary authorities. The vulnerability of a country to an 'attack' by international investors is particularly high when a country's short-term debt is larger than its reserves. In this case, a collective withdrawal of short-term debt means trouble. For the case of the financial crisis in Southeast Asia beginning in the summer of 1997 with a currency crisis of the Thai baht, Radelet and Sachs (1998) use the ratio of a country's short-term debt to foreign exchange reserves to illustrate the vulnerability to a speculative attack, as illustrated in table 9.6. We now illustrate how financial crises can be looked upon as merely liquidity crisis. Section 9.9 presents a synthesis between the insolvency and illiquidity view using a simple figure.

Table 9.6 Ratio of short-term debt to total debt and to reserves, June 1997

Country	Short-term debt to total debt	Short-term debt to reserves
Indonesia	24	160
S. Korea	67	300
Malaysia	39	55
Philippines	19	66
Thailand	46	107
Argentina	23	108
Brazil	23	69
Chile	25	44
Colombia	19	57
Mexico	16	126

Source: BIS and IMF *IFS*, taken from Radelet and Sachs (1998).

Financial crises as liquidity crises

To give an example of how a financial crisis may be nothing other than the creation of a shortage of funds by speculative international investors, think of an emerging market economy in which firms invest in this period (period I) for a total amount of 500. The investment will yield a return only in the next period (period II). Given the lack of domestic savings, the investment in period I must be fully financed by international investors. Assume also that this loan has already been granted in the past (period 0) and that the firms need to re-finance this loan in period I, so that international investors have to agree to roll over the debt for a total amount of 500 in period I. The domestic firms must pay back the new loan at the end of period II. The investment that is undertaken in period I yields a *certain* return of 750 in period II. The firms in this economy are thus solvent (if we take all periods into consideration), but they face a potential liquidity problem in period I. Insolvency is not an issue because the return on investment in period II is clearly larger than the outstanding debt. The liquidity problem may arise because firms need to roll over their debt *before* the investment has paid off.

Suppose that individual international investors are relatively small – that is, they can each contribute only 5 of the required amount of 500. To prevent the liquidity problem, at least 100 investors must be willing to re-finance the loan at the end of period I. This creates a *coordination problem* very similar to the game-theoretic example of a speculative attack in chapter 8. Just like the two investors who had to decide whether or not to sell their funds to the central bank, here too the decision by each investor depends crucially on what she thinks other investors will do. A single international investor is only willing to make her contribution to the new loan if it is clear that at least 99 other investors will do the same. If individual investors somehow doubt that this will be the case, the new loan will not be granted. This is an example with multiple (self-fulfilling) equilibria: for each single investor both the decision to supply a new loan and the refusal to do so are equilibrium strategies. If the international investors cannot come up with the required 500 of new loans, the liquidity crisis develops into a financial crisis. Firms have committed themselves by buying the investment goods, but they now lack the finance to back up this investment. Their NW will suddenly become negative, which will set in motion the (domestic) chain of events discussed above (recall figure 9.2).

9.9 Synthesis and conclusions: the vicious circle

According to the liquidity view of financial crisis, self-fulfilling expectations of international investors are a necessary condition for a crisis to occur. When investors do not extend their loans or sell their investments in a particular country we observe a capital outflow and a depreciation of the currency. In terms of figure 9.6 we have now arrived at stage II, which in this case becomes the *first* stage of the financial crisis. We know that a currency depreciation and higher interest rates (to stop the depreciation and the capital outflow) will be bad news for the balance sheets of the banks and the firms, leading us to stage I in figure 9.6. The economy may end up with weak economic fundamentals. In a nutshell, then, in this view figure 9.6 is turned *upside down*!

The obvious question is: who's right, the 'fundamentalists' who blame weak domestic economic and financial conditions, or the 'self-fulfillers' who blame the self-fulfilling expectations of investors? Krugman's (2000) answer is: both are correct. Figure 9.7 illustrates how aspects of both views can be reconciled in a synthesis leading to a vicious circle. The idea is simply that the main difference between the two views is where to start on the circle. Once the economy moves (clockwise) along the circle, the essential differences between the two views disappear. The circular line of reasoning is as follows. Suppose we start with a loss of confidence on the part of investors → leading to a capital outflow → leading to a sharp real depreciation of the domestic currency required to arrive at a current account surplus → leading to a worsening of firms's balance sheets (with loans or banks deposits denominated in foreign currency) → leading to a fall in NW → leading to a drop in investment and output → leading to a further loss in confidence, etc.

If we take the fragility of the domestic financial sector as our starting point in this circular reasoning, instead of the loss in confidence, the starting point would be different, but the analysis would be the same. So does it matter where you start on the vicious circle? Yes, it does. The policy implications are quite different. In case

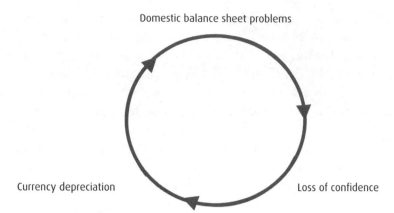

Figure 9.7 The vicious circle of financial crises
Source: Krugman (2000).

you adhere to the self-fulfilling expectations view and start with the loss of confidence, international capital markets are the culprits, providing a possible rationale for restricting international capital mobility. However, if you start on the circle with the domestic balance sheet problems, you would probably call for policies that remedied the regulatory and other weaknesses in the domestic financial sector. In chapter 10, we shall deal with these policy implications.

Finally, note that in the vicious circle approach the crucial variable is the real exchange rate. A change in the real exchange rate has two opposite effects. On the one hand, there is the standard effect that a depreciation improves competitiveness and thereby stimulates net exports, which is necessary because the capital flow calls for a current account surplus and hence for a boost in net exports. On the other hand, the depreciation increases the real value of debt denominated in foreign currency. When we look at the current account and capital account data for developing countries, we can identify both effects of the exchange rate change. For the group of developing countries as a whole, the current account deficit in 1998 was still $68 billion, whereas in 2000 this had turned into a current account surplus of $67 billion. To achieve this turnaround on the current account, currencies in the countries involved had to depreciate substantially. At the same time, the private capital flows to developing countries dwindled, which was especially true for private debt flows. Since 2000 there has been a net debt *out*flow as banks and firms in developing countries seek to repay the now very expensive debt denominated in foreign currency (see IMF, 2003; World Bank, 2003a, ch. 5).

This synthesis between the 'fundamentalists' and the 'self-fulfillers' has been characterized as the *third*-generation model of currency crises. The differences from the second-generation model discussed at the end of chapter 8 are twofold:

- First, there is a larger and more direct role for self-fulfilling expectations in the third-generation model. In the second-generation model, self-fulfilling expectations are also possible but only insofar as these expectations influence the trade-off for the domestic policy-makers between the costs and benefits of a fixed exchange rate. It is up to the domestic policy-makers to decide whether or not to give up the fixed exchange rate. In the models underlying the vicious circle, there is a more direct impact of investors' loss of confidence on the exchange rate.
- The second main difference is that the interaction between the exchange rate and the domestic financial sector is explicitly analysed only in the third-generation model, which makes the vicious circle model particularly well suited to analyse twin crises – that is, the occurrence of both a banking crisis and a currency crisis. In other words, it is a useful model to analyse modern-day financial crises. Note, however, that theorizing about financial crises is influenced by the latest round of crises and the days of the third-generation models as the 'new kid on the block' will no doubt be limited to the arrival of the next type of empirical crisis requiring an adequate explanation.

Part IV

Policy, dynamics and organization

Trade and capital restrictions

KEYWORDS

tariffs and welfare

efficiency versus stability

Harberger triangles

preferential trade agreement (PTA)

(non-) market based regulation

trade policy

pricing of risk

Most Favoured Nation

(MFN)

capital restrictions

Ad valorem

trade-off

UDROP

10.1 Introduction

The policy advice derived from the theory of international trade in part II of this book is simple: open up the borders! This advice is not based only on the static gains from trade – that is, on the re-allocation of production factors to those sectors in which a country has a comparative advantage. It is also a consequence of the dynamic gains from trade arising from the increased competition and R&D investments needed to maintain a competitive edge on the world market. The evidence on the positive effects of trade openness on welfare is strong. As explained in part III of this book, a similar open-doors policy advice holds in principle for international capital mobility, as free capital flows enable a country to achieve a more efficient allocation of savings and investment and allows for improved risk diversification. But the case for free international capital mobility is less clear-cut than the case for free trade, because free capital mobility might lead to financial fragility or instability (see chapters 8 and 9).

Despite the obvious advantages of free trade flows and a gradual reduction of trade barriers since the 1980s, there are still many policy-induced impediments to trade, such as tariffs, quotas and minimum standards. In fact, as discussed below, this constitutes the rationale for the existence of the World Trade Organization (WTO), as trade impediments are very unlikely to be overcome without such institutions. Similarly, the degree of international capital mobility has clearly increased recently (see chapter 6), although many countries still have capital restrictions in place or consider (re-)installing them when confronted with financial mayhem. The main question we address in this chapter is why trade and capital restrictions exist if theory often dictates that they should not. In answering this question, we may come to a better understanding of the pleas for trade and capital restrictions. We shall conclude that it is by and large welfare-decreasing to give in to these pleas. As summarized in the final section (10.13), this holds in particular for trade restrictions (see sections 10.2–10.6), while for capital restrictions (see sections 10.7–10.12) a more nuanced conclusion emerges.

10.2 Welfare effects of trade restrictions: a tariff on imports

Figure 10.1 reveals the most important effects of trade restrictions by analysing the economic consequences of imposing a tariff on imported goods. The figure shows for a single country a standard upward-sloping supply curve and downward-sloping demand curve for some homogeneous product under perfect competition – that is, consumers in this country look only at the price of the commodity and are indifferent as to the origin of the goods. An increase in the domestic price level causes an increase in the quantity supplied domestically and a decrease in the quantity demanded. The difference between these quantities is imported from abroad at the market-clearing price. With free trade, the world market price is equal to p_0 (which is lower than the autarky equilibrium price p_2), such that imports are equal to $q_4 - q_0$. What happens if the country imposes an *ad valorem* tariff on imports t?[1] Most importantly, the tariff drives a wedge between the price that foreign producers receive for their imports (which falls to p_1, see below) and the price on the domestic market (which rises to $(1 + t) p_1$). We analyse the consequences for four different economic agents, namely (i) domestic consumers, (ii) domestic producers, (iii) the domestic government and (iv) the rest of the world.

   (i) *Domestic consumers*   Domestic consumers are confronted with higher prices and therefore reduce the quantity demanded by the amount $q_4 - q_3$. From introductory microeconomics we know that the associated welfare loss, measured by the reduction in consumer surplus, is equal to the reduction of the area under the demand curve, as indicated by the area $D + E + F_1 + G$ in figure 10.1. Consumers therefore suffer a *welfare loss*.

  (ii) *Domestic producers*   Domestic producers perceive less competition from abroad, so that they are able to increase the price they charge to $(1 + t) p_1$ and increase the quantity supplied by $q_1 - q_0$. Again, from microeconomics we know that the associated welfare gain, measured by the increase in producer surplus, is equal to the area D in figure 10.1. Producers therefore enjoy a *welfare gain*.

 (iii) *The domestic government*   The domestic government receives the proceeds of the tariff. The total tariff revenue is equal to the difference between the import

---

[1] In contrast, a *specific* tariff increases the price by a specific amount: $p + t$.

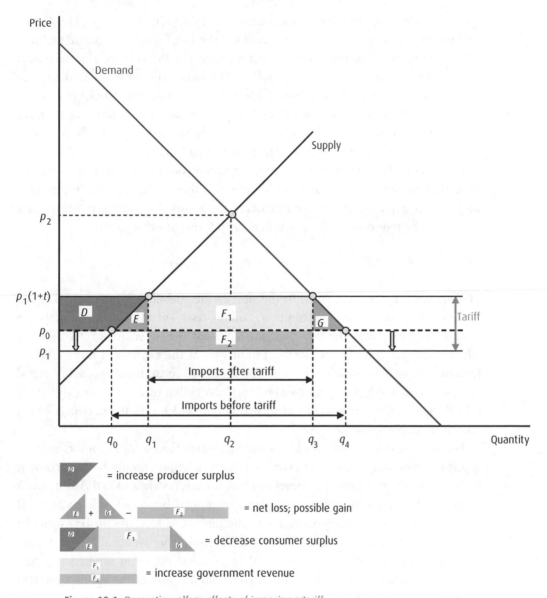

Figure 10.1 Domestic welfare effects of imposing a tariff

price p_1 and the domestic price $(1 + t)\,p_1$, multiplied by the amount of imports (at the price inclusive of the tariff), that is $q_3 - q_1$. The total government revenue is thus equal to the area $F_1 + F_2$.

(iv) *The rest of the world* By comparing imports before the tariff ($q_4 - q_0$) with imports after the tariff ($q_3 - q_1$), it is clear that foreign producers are confronted with a reduction in demand. If this reduction in demand is substantial enough on a global scale – that is, if the economy imposing the tariff is 'large' – the world price for this good will fall, as indicated by the two downward-pointing arrows in figure 10.1 and the associated drop in price from p_0 to p_1. This terms-of-trade change is welfare-enhancing for the tariff-imposing country as it is able to import goods at a lower price; effectively, the area F_2 of government revenue is paid for by foreign suppliers. Obviously, this terms-of-trade change is welfare-reducing for the rest of the world, as it now receives less for its exports. Note that this terms-of-trade effect disappears if the country imposing the tariff is 'small', implying that it is not able to influence the world price level. In that case $p_0 = p_1$ in figure 10.1 so that the area F_2 disappears.

The total welfare change for the tariff-imposing country can now easily be calculated by adding the individual welfare effects – that is, the increase in producer surplus and government revenue (including the terms-of-trade gain), on the one hand, and the reduction of the consumer surplus, on the other hand

$$D + (F_1 + F_2) - (D + E + F_1 + G) = F_2 - (E + G) \tag{10.1}$$

The *net* effect is therefore equal to the sum of the so-called 'Harberger triangles' $E + G$ (a negative welfare contribution) and the terms-of-trade gain F_2 (a positive welfare contribution). The two triangles represent the 'waste' of protection: less efficient domestic producers increase production at the expense of more efficient foreign competitors, which is paid for by domestic consumers who suffer a real income loss due to higher price (see box 10.1). Note that there is no terms-of-trade gain if the country imposing the tariff is small, in which case the net effect of the tariff is unambiguously negative.

At this point, one might wonder what the effects are of imposing an import quota (a quantity restriction) rather than a tariff (a price restriction). Somewhat surprisingly, perhaps, the difference between these two types of trade restrictions in this framework is limited. In fact, if the government restricts imports by imposing a quota equal to $q_3 - q_1$ and sells the import rights to the highest bidder, the proceeds for the government and the effects for the domestic economy are identical for producers, consumers and prices as with the tariff! In practice, the main difference is that the import rights are not sold to the highest bidder, so that the tariff-equivalent government revenue $F_1 + F_2$ represents a formidable lobbying incentive.

Box 10.1 The costs of protection[a]

Many studies have looked into the costs of protection. Estimates of the Harberger triangles $E + G$ shown in figure 10.1 indicate that these costs are probably quite small. A complete removal of protectionist measures by the EU would 'only' amount to an increase of 0.3 per cent of GDP. This even over-states the gains of trade liberalization because it assumes that all restrictions are completely removed, which is seldom the case. Similar estimates of the welfare gains from trade liber-alization for the USA range from 0.01 to 0.1 per cent of GDP.

Various reasons have been put forward to explain the seemingly small estimates of the welfare gains of liberalization based on these Harberger triangles:

- First, estimates such as these are static. The dynamic effects of liberalization are not dealt with. More foreign competition might force firms to invest in R&D, which stimulates productivity in the long run.
- Second, the Harberger triangles can be measured only if products are actually present in the economy and of a given quality. This assumption can seriously under-estimate the true costs of protection: if protection results in fewer prod-ucts of lower quality than would otherwise exist, the associated consumer sur-plus and income will be much lower. Some exploratory simulations suggest that these costs are quite substantial, being in the double-digit range as a percentage of GDP.
- Third, estimates of the Harberger triangles assume that goods are homogeneous. In reality, we know that most trade is of the intra-industry type where goods are not homogeneous. This implies that Harberger triangles can be estimated for only a limited range of goods. Estimates dealing with intra-industry trade suggest that liberalization in the EU could increase trade by some 25 per cent.
- Finally, all types of estimates under-estimate the true cost of trade restrictions because they ignore the transactions costs of protection – in particular, the time and effort spent by special interest groups in lobbying for protectionist measures, which could have been used for producing goods and services.

One should bear in mind, however, that reducing trade barriers also involves costs – for example, the costs of adjustment for firms and workers in dealing with the new situation without protection. This includes unemployment payments to workers in some sectors and training costs to re-employ them elsewhere. Such costs will also have to be considered in giving a balanced account of the gains of liberalization. Kym Anderson (2004) calculates that the ratio of benefits to costs of trade liberalization for the Doha trade round of the WTO (see box 10.3, pp. 277–8) lies somewhere between 24 and 29, with a present value of the benefits ranging from $11,520 to 23,040 billion (depending on the success of the final outcome of the Doha trade round). Based on a similar all-encompassing approach, it is argued that the American economy is about $1 trillion a year better off because of its participation in international trade, which amounts to an annual gain of $9,000 for each American household. This positive welfare effect is expected to rise when future measures to boost trade liberalization materialize.

[a] Based on Brakman and van Marrewijk (1996), Anderson (2004), *The Economist* (2004).

10.3 World welfare effects of trade restrictions

The fact that the introduction of an import tariff might lead to a terms-of-trade gain for the tariff-imposing country implies that the rest of the world suffers from a terms-of-trade loss. This raises the question of what the welfare effect would be of a tariff for the world as a whole. The answer is provided in figure 10.2, which shows the effects of a tariff for the tariff-imposing country as well as for the rest of the world. The upward-sloping foreign export supply curve represents the difference between quantity produced and consumed for different prices in the rest of the world. It thus combines information on the foreign supply and demand curves. Similarly, the domestic import demand curve represents the difference between quantity demanded and supplied domestically for different domestic prices, as already shown in figure 10.1. This implies that the trade volumes in figures 10.1 and 10.2 can be compared – that is, $trade_0 = q_4 - q_0$ and $trade_1 = q_3 - q_1$.

We can now briefly repeat the analysis on the welfare effects of imposing trade restrictions. In this case the tariff-imposing country is large enough to affect world prices, which fall from p_0 to p_1. The letters in figures 10.1 and 10.2 indicate the same areas – that is, $F_1 + F_2$ is the tariff revenue for the government and $E + G$ represents the sum of the two Harberger triangles, where the import demand curve combines the domestic demand and supply curves. This also helps to explain why area D in figure 10.1 is absent in figure 10.2: this part of the consumer surplus cancels out with the producer surplus, such that only $E + F_1 + G$ remains.

So what are the welfare effects for the rest of the world? As a net supplier of the good on the world market, the prices p_0 and p_1 are *above* the autarky equilibrium price for the rest of the world. Repeating the welfare analysis along the lines of section 10.2 shows that the net welfare effect for the rest of the world is equal to the area in between the prices p_0 and p_1 up to the Foreign export supply curve – that is, $F_2 + H$.

We are now in a position to determine the change in world welfare caused by the tariff. It is the sum of the welfare loss for the domestic producers and consumers (the area $F_1 + E + G$), the welfare loss for the foreign producers and consumers (the area $F_2 + H$) and the welfare gain for the domestic government (the area $F_1 + F_2$). The net welfare effect for the two countries combined is thus a welfare *loss* equal to the area $E + G + H$. The difference with the domestic analysis of section 10.2 is evident: for the world as a whole, the welfare effects of a tariff are always negative because part of production is shifted from efficient foreign producers to less efficient domestic producers, the tariff creating an artificial wedge between domestic and foreign prices. At the world level, any potential domestic welfare gain cancels with a welfare loss for the rest of the world, so that the total welfare effect is just the decrease in domestic consumer surplus $E + G$ plus the decrease in foreign producer surplus H.

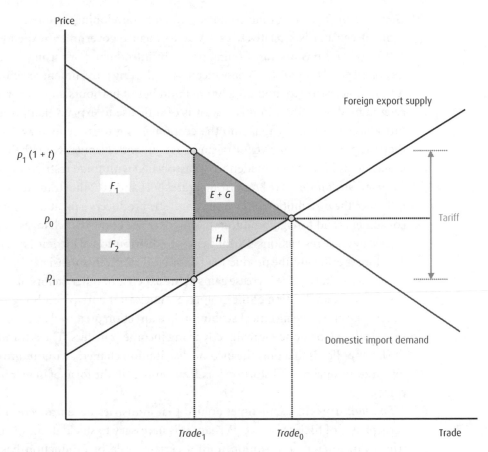

Figure 10.2 The world welfare effects of a tariff

10.4 More on protectionism

The partial equilibrium welfare analysis of the effects of tariffs yields a fundamental insight into the general welfare effects of protectionism: *for the world as a whole, protection reduces welfare.* Usually, although not necessarily so, the same will be true for individual countries, which raises the question why countries do resort to trade restrictions. One answer is, of course, that even if the *net* effect of imposing trade restrictions is negative, the *distributional* impact of the tariff will benefit specific interest groups such as domestic producers or the government. There are, however, additional reasons for imposing trade restrictions. We briefly discuss five of these: (i) government finance, (ii) income distribution, (iii) infant industry protection, (iv) employment considerations and (v) strategic behaviour on imperfect markets.

(i) *Government finance*   Some countries, notably developing countries, impose tariffs because it is a relatively easy way to finance government expenditures. If the tax system is not functioning properly, introducing or raising a tariff on imported goods is a relatively easy means of collecting government revenue; it is, for example, easier to monitor a limited number of harbours and airports than each individual citizen. In this case, it is of little use to explain that protection introduces price distortions into the economy, as governments may find that they lack a valid alternative for raising government revenues. Nonetheless, it is crucial to point out the (hidden) costs associated with trade restrictions.

(ii) *Income distribution*   We know from figures 10.1 and 10.2 that trade restrictions influence the distribution of income: domestic producers gain at the expense of consumers (and foreign producers). Moreover, we know that changes in prices caused by trade restrictions also influence the distribution of income (see chapter 3). More specifically, the production factor used relatively intensively in the sector experiencing a price increase gains at the expense of other factors of production (a direct application of the Stolper–Samuelson theorem). Although tariffs can indeed affect the income distribution in a direction preferred by the government, this can be done more directly using income transfers. The advantage of the latter policy is that only the income distribution changes, without introducing an additional price distortion for all consumers in the form of higher import prices.

(iii) *Infant industry*   It is sometimes argued that industries need protection in the early phases of their existence. Perhaps it is necessary to shield domestic industries from foreign competition until a certain scale of production has been reached, after which domestic firms become competitive on world markets. This argument is therefore based on increasing returns to scale – for example, due to high fixed set-up costs. The domestic industry can initially survive only if foreign competition is reduced by using trade restrictions. Alternatively, the cost of production may fall as a result of learning-by-doing, as seems to be the case, for example, in the aircraft industry.

   Although it may be tempting in cases such as this to resort to trade restrictions, there are two main problems with the infant industry argument:

- First, it is not easy to identify infant industries. Undoubtedly, individual sectors are tempted to argue that they fall into this category. Identifying industries that could temporarily benefit from protection has sometimes been compared with performing acupuncture with a fork.
- Second, if identifying infant industries were possible, why would government support in the form of protection be necessary? The private sector could do the same as profit-seeking banks could give credit to these firms. If firms are profitable in the long run they should be able to repay their debt. This is a

preferred option because consumers will not be confronted with higher prices caused by imposing trade restrictions.

- In addition, firms in the protected industry quite easily get 'addicted' to the trade protection, while governments may find it difficult to decrease the level of protection.

(iv) *Employment considerations*   Protecting an industry raises production and thus employment in that industry. Obviously, this increase in employment comes at the cost of decreased employment elsewhere (the relative price of all other goods decreases). Nonetheless, trade protection is frequently justified on the basis of employment arguments. Even so, the question remains whether this is the best method for influencing employment. In general, the answer is no, as a tariff creates an unnecessary distortion in the consumption of importable goods. This distortion can be avoided by using other policy measures, such as a subsidy on labour. This also avoids possible retaliation by other countries, which is likely if tariffs are imposed. Clearly, retaliation affects the welfare analysis of sections 10.2 and 10.3. If the foreign country reacts by imposing a tariff on goods for which the Home country is a net exporter, we may end up with a tariff war where all countries suffer a welfare loss (see Box 10.2).

Box 10.2 The EU–USA steel conflict

In March 2002, US steel producers were finally successful in their lobby to protect the US market from (EU) imports. Steel firms are concentrated in the states of Ohio and Pennsylvania, both of which were important in George Bush's re-election campaign. American steel producers are in general less efficient than their EU counterparts because the latter were forced to reorganise their production process as a result of the abolition of various EU subsidies. In March 2002, President Bush invoked 'safeguard' tariffs of up to 30 per cent on foreign steel. This was America's single most protectionist act since the 1980s. Two months later he also increased government support for American farmers under the US Farm Bill, claiming that these measures were compatible with WTO rules. Even if this were the case, negotiating trade barrier reductions in the WTO's Doha round (see box 10.3) is not made easier by protecting steel producers and increasing farm subsidies. The Bush administration, however, claimed that these measures would somehow force the EU to reduce their subsidies to farmers, which in the end would contribute to more free trade.

In any case, in reaction to EU complaints (joined by Brazil, China, Japan, Korea, New Zealand, Norway and Switzerland) the WTO did not agree with this line of reasoning by the US administration. The American steel tariffs have been declared illegal by the WTO on a number of occasions, which allowed the EU to raise tariffs of up to $336 million worth of American products in retaliation. The Japanese government also threatened to raise tariffs on $5 million worth of American goods, putting the world trade community on the slippery slope of tit-for-tat protectionism.

The Bush administration gave in to this foreign pressure on 4 December 2003. Robert Zoellick, the US trade representative, of course insisted that the President had based his decision on an analysis showing that the steel industry was already recovering and needed no further protection. In a briefing in the White House press room, President Bush said that while the benefits of the tariff to the US economy had outweighed the costs at first, continued imposition would cost more than the benefits:

Today I signed a proclamation ending the temporary steel safeguard measures I put in place in March 2002. Prior to that time, steel prices were at 20-year lows, and the US International Trade Commission [ITC] found that a surge in imports to the US market was causing serious injury to our domestic steel industry. I took action to give the industry a chance to adjust to the surge in foreign imports, and to give relief to the workers and communities that depend on steel for their jobs and livelihoods. These safeguard measures have now achieved their purpose. And as a result of changed economic circumstances, it is time to lift them. The US steel industry wisely used the 21 months of breathing space we provided to consolidate and restructure. The industry made progress, increasing productivity, lowering production costs, and making America more competitive with foreign steel producers.

Remarkably, all of this was realised by the US government just days before the EU retaliation measures would have become effective.

(v) *Strategic behaviour*   A final argument for trade restrictions is based on shifting profits from foreign firms to domestic firms. As discussed in chapter 4, in imperfectly competitive markets an export subsidy to a domestic firm (also a form of protection) could induce a foreign firm to cut back its output, so that the market share of the domestic firm increases at the expense of the foreign firm. At the same time, profits are shifted from the foreign firm to the domestic firm. Most surprising in this analysis is the fact that sometimes the mere threat of a subsidy could be sufficient if the foreign competitor immediately reduced sales (or its price) to anticipate the trade policy. Rents are shifted from foreign to domestic firms without the actual policy being imposed. This is known as *strategic trade policy*.

Although initially very tempting for governments, analyses such as these also have many drawbacks:

- First, it is well known that the optimal type of policy crucially depends on the type of competition between rivals. If firms compete in prices rather than quantities, taking the other firm's price level rather than the quantity level as given, the optimal policy is to impose an export tax rather than give an export subsidy (because the rivals will increase their price as a consequence).
- Second, not only is detailed knowledge on the type of market competition necessary, but also knowledge regarding production costs, demand, etc. Again, applying some arbitrary policy because it might work is comparable to acupuncture with a fork.
- Finally, as with the infant industry argument, one wonders why, if these opportunities are present, the private sector cannot provide this support and why this should be a task for the government.

10.5 Trade agreements

The central aim of the WTO, known as the General Agreement on Tariffs and Trade (GATT) before 1995, is to promote free trade. It tries to achieve its objective, for instance, by organizing so-called *trade rounds*, eight of which have been completed. The ninth 'Doha' (Qatar) round started on 14 October 2001. These trade rounds typically last many years, during which countries negotiate trade barrier reductions. Previous rounds have been remarkably successful. Tariffs on non-agricultural imports into developed countries have been lowered substantially, but some important tariffs remain, especially directed to the labour-intensive manufactured goods that are important for developing countries and which also compete with labour-intensive manufactures in developed countries. Negotiating these and other trade-related issues is very difficult, leading to ever-longer trade rounds (see box 10.3).

Box 10.3 WTO and GATT trade rounds

Several WTO/GATT trade rounds have been completed successfully. As table 10.1 shows, each round is aimed at *reducing trade barriers*. Increasingly, however, special topics needed to be addressed at the talks. In conjunction with the increasing number of participants, this leads to ever-longer trade rounds, as illustrated dramatically in figure 10.3, which depicts the number of participants, on the one hand, and the duration of the trade rounds, on the other hand. A simple regression line on the basis of this plot suggests that the current Doha round would not be finished at the planned 1 January 2005 deadline, but rather in April 2010.

Table 10.1 GATT and WTO rounds, 1947–

Round	Start	Duration (months)	Principal concern	No. part.[b]
Geneva	Apr. 1947	7	Tariffs	23
Annecy	Apr. 1949	5	Tariffs	13
Torquay	Sep. 1950	8	Tariffs	38
Geneva II	Jan. 1956	5	Tariffs, admission of Japan	26
Dillon	Sep. 1960	11	Tariffs	26
Kennedy	May. 1964	37	Tariffs, anti-dumping	62
Tokyo	Sep. 1973	74	Tariffs, NTBs[a]	102
Uruguay	Sep. 1986	87	Tariffs, NTBs, services, dispute settlement, textiles, agriculture, WTO	123
Doha	Nov 2001	?	Tariffs, NTBs, labour standards, environment, competition, investment, transparency, patents	141

Notes: [a] NTBs = Non-tariff barriers.
          [b] No. part. = Number of participants.
Source: Neary (2004).

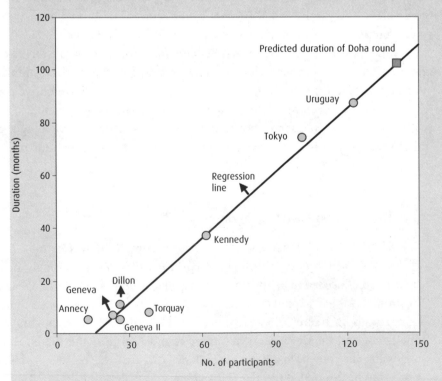

Figure 10.3 'Predicted' duration of the Doha round
Data source: See table 10.1.

The Most Favoured Nation (MFN) principle is central in the WTO negotiations. It implies that all member countries should be treated alike. If a country grants a tariff reduction to another country, it should apply the same reduction to all other members of the WTO. This principle increases the efficiency of the negotiations enormously, because time-consuming bilateral talks are no longer needed.

Preferential Trade Agreements (PTAs) between groups of countries are, however, an important exception to the MFN principle. A group of countries may decide to reduce tariffs between group members, but still apply tariffs to imports from the rest of the world. This can take various forms:

- A group of countries can abandon all tariffs internally, but maintain their own tariff with regard to the outside world (this is a free-trade area or FTA).
- It might also abandon all internal tariffs, and have identical tariffs against the rest of the world (this is a customs union).

Various other types of agreements can be distinguished, but the central principle is always the same: members of the club grant each other preferential trade conditions that outsiders do not receive.

Over 250 PTAs have been notified to the WTO, of which 130 were notified after 1995 and 170 are presently in force. PTAs appear to be becoming ever-more popular. According to the WTO, their total number could rise to over 300 by the end of 2005. Some of the best-known PTAs are:

- European Union (EU)
- European Free Trade Association (EFTA)
- North American Free Trade Agreement (NAFTA)
- Southern Common Market (MERCOSUR)
- Association of Southeast Asian Nations (ASEAN)
- Common Market of Eastern and Southern Africa (COMESA).

Arrangements such as these are permitted by the WTO even if they are a clear violation of the MFN principle, as member countries of the arrangement are treated favourably relative to outsiders, which might include WTO members. The WTO allows these arrangements as basically a first step towards the complete elimination of tariffs. Because arrangements such as these are only partial reductions in trade barriers they can have more complicated welfare consequences than global tariff reductions. An implication of the welfare analysis in section 10.4 is that for the world as a whole the abolition of tariffs is unambiguously welfare-increasing. The question now becomes: is a partial reduction of tariffs between a subgroup of countries also unambiguously welfare-increasing?

To answer this question is a bit more complicated than the analysis in sections 10.2 and 10.3 because there are at least three countries involved – say, Australia, Brazil and China (indexed by A, B and C, respectively). We assume that Australia may form a trade agreement with Brazil. Initially (that is before the agreement),

Australia imposes a specific tariff t on imports from both countries. We assume that Australia is a small country, unable to influence the price level in the other countries. Import prices, inclusive of the tariff, from Brazil and China are $p_B + t$ and $p_C + t$, respectively. Our welfare analysis has to deal with two possible situations – namely if Brazil is the most efficient supplier and if China is the most efficient supplier.

Brazil is the most efficient supplier: trade creation

First, we assume that Australia forms a customs union with Brazil, such that it eliminates tariffs with respect to imports from Brazil (but not with respect to those from China), while Brazil is a more efficient supplier of the product – that is, $p_B < p_C$. As illustrated in figure 10.4, which depicts Australia's domestic demand and supply curves as well as the horizontal supply curves for Brazil and China before the formation of the customs union, Australia imports $q_3 - q_1$ units from Brazil, the most efficient supplier (at a domestic price of $p_B + t < p_C + t$). After the formation of the customs union, Australia imports a larger quantity ($q_4 - q_0$) from Brazil (at a domestic price p_B) because the tariff with respect to Brazil has been eliminated. The increase in imports is labelled *trade creation*. As long as the Chinese price for the product is higher than the Brazilian price, China is not relevant in this case: it does not deal with Australia either before or after the formation of the customs union.

The welfare analysis in this case is simply the *reverse* of our analysis in section 10.2. The reduction of the tariff now *reduces* producer surplus by the area D because of increased foreign competition which reduces domestic prices. The reduction in prices also implies that consumer surplus increases by the area $D + E + F + G$. Moreover, the abolition of tariffs reduces government revenue by the area F, because imports are now free of tariffs. The net welfare effect from the formation of the customs union is therefore $(D + E + F + G) - D - F = E + G > 0$. There is an unambiguous welfare gain for Australia when it forms a customs union with Brazil, which is the most efficient supplier. The increase in imports represents a positive *trade creation* effect.

China is the most efficient supplier: trade diversion

Figure 10.5 illustrates what happens if Australia forms a customs union with Brazil, while China is the most efficient supplier ($p_C < p_B$) and the difference in efficiency is smaller than the tariff (so that $p_B < p_C + t$). Before the formation of the customs union Australia imports $q_3 - q_1$ from *China*, the most efficient supplier. After the formation of the customs union Australia imports a larger quantity ($q_4 - q_0$) from *Brazil*, not because it is the most efficient supplier but because it receives preferential treatment as a member of the customs union (so that no tariffs are levied).

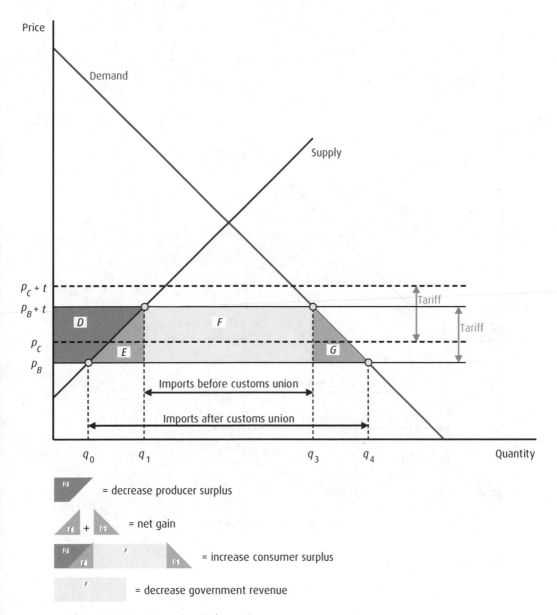

Figure 10.4 Customs union: trade creation

As before, the formation of the customs union increases the level of imports and thus has a trade-creation effect. In this case, however, there is also a supplier switching effect, because imports previously came from China and now come from Brazil. This is known as the *trade-diversion* effect of a customs union. The welfare effects are similar, as before. The reduction of the tariff reduces producer surplus by the area *D*, because domestic producers face increased foreign competition, which reduces

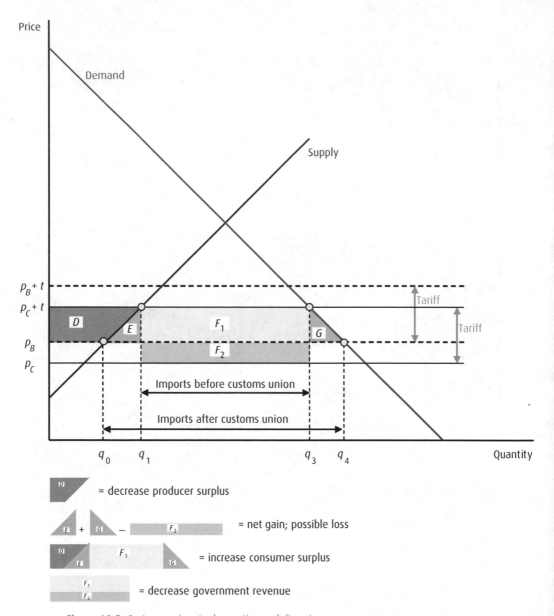

Figure 10.5 Customs union: trade creation and diversion

the prices level. Note, however, that the reduction is not all the way to the most efficient price level! The reduction in prices implies that consumer surplus increases by $D + E + F_1 + G$. Again consumers pay less and import more. The abolition of tariffs now reduces government revenue by $F_1 + F_2$, which includes the extra term F_2, reflecting a decrease in government revenue not compensated by an increase in consumer surplus. The negative term F_2 is thus caused by the trade-diversion effect, as imports no longer come from the most efficient supplier. The net welfare effect for Australia is equal to $(D + E + F_1 + G) - D - (F_1 + F_2) = E + G - F_2$. The extra term F_2 introduces an ambiguity: it is no longer certain that the formation of a customs union will increase welfare. More specifically, welfare increases only if the trade-creation effect $(E + G)$ is larger than the trade-diversion effect (F_2).

This above analysis indeed shows that the formation of PTAs might be a first step towards free trade, but this does not imply that along the way welfare always increases. The argument that trade agreements such as the formation of EU and NAFTA are a stepping stone towards free trade therefore implicitly assumes that the trade-creation effect is stronger than the trade-diversion effect. As the trading bloc expands, it becomes increasingly attractive for outsiders to join. According to the so-called 'domino theory', the world may thus end up as one large trading bloc, so that preferential trade agreements eventually lead to free trade (box 10.4).

Box 10.4 The politics of free trade zones: how many trade blocs?

Paul Krugman (1993) has taken the politics of regional free trade arrangements a step further than we have analysed so far. Once a FTA has been established, the next question is how such a bloc will behave *vis-à-vis* the rest of the world. Krugman argues that world welfare and the number of trading blocs are inter-related issues. More specifically, the relationship between welfare and the number of blocs shows a U-shaped relation, with a welfare minimum at three trading blocs (such as the EU, NAFTA and the rest of the world). Although Krugman's numerical exercise depends on special assumptions, the argument can be based on our tariff analysis. Small countries cannot influence their terms of trade, so that their optimal policy is to set the tariff level at zero. Large countries, however, can influence their terms of trade, so that with uncoordinated actions large trading blocs set tariffs to maximize welfare. Powerful trading blocs, such as the EU or NAFTA, will thus impose high tariffs, which will influence world welfare negatively. In Krugman's numerical analysis the welfare-*minimizing* number of trading blocs is three. Although abstract, the model shows why large trading blocs may threaten to launch protectionist measures if they do not agree with the trade behaviour of other (large) trade blocs; if they impose tariffs no one can ignore the consequences (see also Box 10.2 on the US–EU steel conflict).

10.6 Evaluation of the demand for and supply of trade protection

Our analysis above allows us to draw a few important conclusions regarding the ever-present demand for more protection. First, and foremost, protection is bad news for consumers as they are always hurt by protectionist measures. They should, therefore, welcome free trade. The opposite holds for domestic producers in specific protected sectors. Protection reduces foreign competition and provides consumers with extra profit opportunities. They therefore welcome protectionist measures and have an incentive to actively lobby for protectionism. Considering this conflict of interest, who has the upper hand? It is quite obvious that producers are more vocal or visible in their demand for protection than consumers are in voicing their interests. Studies in political economy show that relatively small special interest groups (producers) are better at organizing themselves than large, less well-organized groups (consumers in general). The gains for small special interest groups are more directly linked to protection, which facilitates the organisation of the group. They are thus capable of making themselves heard in policy circles. The producers' cause is strengthened by pointing at the supposed gains in domestic employment caused by protection (resulting from increased domestic production). The fact that free trade may boost employment in other sectors is more ambiguous. It leaves some consumers in a difficult position; as consumers they welcome free trade, unless they might lose their job.

Most calculations regarding the costs of protection ignore the fact that lobbying is itself costly. These costs can be substantial: estimates suggest that they are in the range of 10–40 per cent of GDP for all possible lobby activities in the economy. Magee, Brock and Young (1989, pp. 216–20) conclude that these costs differ vastly between countries, ranging from about 7 per cent of GDP in India to an enormous 40 per cent of GDP in Kenya. Lobbying for protection is a substantial part of these costs. Estimates for Turkey indicate that lobbying costs for protection alone – leaving aside all other lobby activities – constitute about 15 per cent of GDP.

To summarize, governments of large countries in particular might be tempted to introduce protectionist measures because of the terms-of-trade effect. If the price reduction on world markets is large enough to counterbalance the efficiency loss (Harberger triangles), the net effect for the economy is positive.[2] In practice, this argument is of only academic interest. To our knowledge, no government has introduced a protectionist measure for this reason. Governments are more likely to introduce protectionist measures for domestic or special interest purposes, to increase or protect domestic production and employment. The incentive for governments to do so is limited because other governments might retaliate. This can even put pressure on the largest economy of the world (see box 10.2). In practice, the balance between the pro- or anti-protection forces seems to favour more free trade as opposed to less free trade in the longer run. Tariffs have declined steadily since the Second World War. This is not a painless process, as illustrated by the WTO experience. If history

---

[2] The 'optimal' tariff maximizes the terms-of-trade effect minus the Harberger triangles.

teaches us a lesson, it is that special interest groups will always try to influence trade policies to their own benefit.

10.7 Capital restrictions: the trade-off between efficiency and stability

In chapter 6, we listed the main benefits and costs of international capital mobility:
- Benefit I: improved allocation of savings and investment (see chapter 7)
- Benefit II: improved risk diversification (see chapter 7)
- Cost I: loss of policy autonomy (see chapter 6)
- Cost II: increased financial fragility (see chapters 8 and 9).

It is difficult to compare these costs and benefits. There is no single measure or index that adequately deals with each of the four components. Moreover, the benefits focus on improvements in *efficiency*, whereas the costs mainly relate to the increased *instability* of the economy. These effects do not neatly add up, which makes it difficult to compare costs and benefits. In fact, according to most economists there is a fundamental *trade-off* between efficiency and stability. In order to maximize the benefits of international capital mobility one is inclined to argue that the countries involved should opt for the unhindered working of market forces: get rid of all restrictions on international capital mobility. This maximizes the benefits from international risk diversification and the international allocation of savings and investment. From an efficiency point of view, everything short of full and complete international capital mobility implies a welfare loss, resulting in suboptimal international allocation and risk diversification. In chapters 8 and 9, however, we learned that the variability of international capital flows is a key ingredient in the analysis of currency and financial crises. Especially if one is inclined to think that these crises are also caused by the speculative behaviour of international investors, and not only by 'bad' domestic fundamentals, unhindered international capital mobility is less attractive. Some restrictions on international capital flows may seem 'inevitable' to ensure financial stability. Focusing only on financial stability, one might conclude that international capital immobility is to be preferred. This would, however, completely neglect the efficiency gains from international capital mobility.

In practice, efficiency as well as stability matters. Policy-makers need to be concerned with both issues separately but, given the trade-off, also with their interdependence. Take the benefits, and thus the efficiency argument, first. There is not much controversy about the large benefits; cross-country differences in savings and investment imply that international capital mobility is to be welcomed. Similarly, the possibilities for risk diversification improve once we allow for international capital mobility. It is only when countries are identical in terms of the rates of return on financial transactions and the risk associated with these transactions that nothing is to be gained from introducing international capital mobility. Whether the potential benefits actually materialize is a different matter. In chapter 7, we explained how malfunctioning institutions can drive a *wedge* between the rate of return on savings and investment. Ill-defined property rights, insufficient supervision of banks and a lack of enforcement of shareholder or creditor rights all increase the required rate of return for international portfolio investors. In a nutshell, *malfunctioning institutions increase transaction costs.* Without proper functioning institutions, international investors have to put more effort into screening and monitoring their domestic clients. This implies an increase in the costs of foreign funds for domestic firms or households and a decrease in the effective return for the international investors, the rate of return minus the transaction costs. With these transaction costs, the size of capital flows is smaller than with properly functioning institutions.

In a world of incomplete, asymmetric information, the transaction costs that come with international capital mobility are not only the result of the fact that the supplier of funds is relatively less informed about an investment project (this is also true for within-country capital flows); it follows also from the international aspect. The supplier of funds (the principal) from one country has to deal with two agents in another country – namely the borrower and that country's national government. This so-called 'dual agency' problem implies that the potential benefits from international capital mobility can come about only if minimum standards are met regarding auditing, accounting, banking supervision and creditor and shareholder rights (see Tirole, 2002). The policy implications are relatively straightforward. The benefits from international capital mobility can be reaped only if the transaction costs of international capital flows are not too high. Policies that lower these costs help to stimulate international capital mobility. We use figure 10.6 to illustrate the welfare implications. As the reader may note, this figure is similar to figures 1.11 and 10.2. This is not a coincidence, as will become clear below.

Suppose there are two countries, namely Home (H) and Foreign (F). The upward-sloping curve in figure 10.6 is the net supply of funds by Foreign, whereas the downward-sloping curve is the net demand for funds by Home. Analogous to figure 10.2, net supply gives the difference between Foreign's supply and demand schedules, whereas net demand gives the difference between Home's demand and supply schedules. Note that the rate of return that the lender (supplier) receives at point A is lower than the associated interest rate the borrower (demander) has to pay at point A'. The difference AA' is equal to the transaction costs in between the supply and demand schedules. Figure 10.6 shows that the volume of international capital flows can increase for two reasons (note the similarity with figure 1.11 for the case of international trade in goods). First, a rightward shift of either the demand or supply curve increases capital flows. This is illustrated for a shift in the demand curve (see the arrows labelled 1), which moves the equilibrium to points B and B',

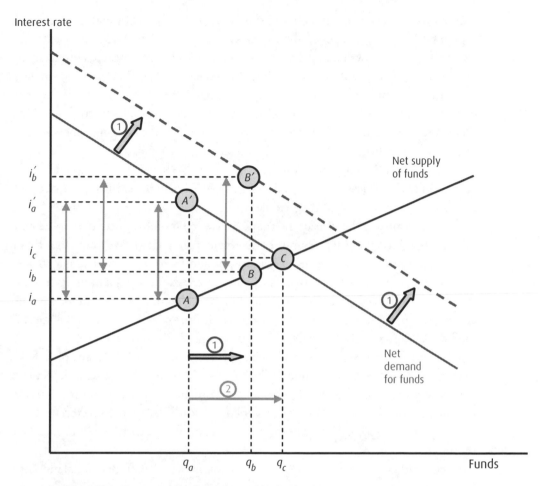

Figure 10.6 The net supply of and demand for funds

with the same transaction costs (the vertical distance AA' is equal to BB') and higher volume (the increase from q_a to q_b). The volume of capital flows and the degree of capital mobility can, however, also increase when transaction costs are lowered. This benefits both the suppliers and demanders of funds. To see this, note that transaction costs are zero at point C, where both the lenders and borrowers are better off. The net return for the suppliers of funds rises from i_a to i_c while the costs for the demanders of funds fall from i_a' to i_c. Welfare is therefore maximized at point C.

10.8 The welfare effects of a tax on capital inflows

There is far less consensus among economists regarding the size of the main costs of international capital mobility (the loss of policy autonomy and increased financial fragility). This holds not only for the actual costs but also for the question as to what policy-makers can do about these costs. First, take the argument that international capital mobility reduces policy autonomy. Our analysis of the 'incompatible triangle' in chapter 6 shows that international capital mobility reduces the autonomy of domestic (monetary) policy-makers. But is this really a problem? The answer depends upon how effective these domestic monetary policies are to begin with. If they are ineffective anyway (that is, unable to influence domestic output and employment), there is not much lost by a reduction of policy autonomy. Changing beliefs in this respect helps us to understand why European countries participated in the EMU in 1999 and not during earlier attempts in the early 1970s, when national monetary and fiscal policies were believed to be more effective in stabilizing output and employment than is now considered likely.

Second, regarding the costs of international capital mobility in terms of increased financial fragility, there are also rather divergent policy views. We know that these costs can be substantial in terms of lost output and fiscal costs (see chapters 8 and 9). However, the crucial policy issue is whether international capital mobility is to be 'blamed' for financial crises. Most economists think that the domestic fundamentals are at least partly to blame for the majority of crises, with international capital mobility adding mainly to the depth and duration of the financial crisis (recall the vicious circle argument at the end of chapter 9). Accordingly, the focus of policy-makers in trying to prevent a financial crisis should be on domestic fundamentals and the regulation and supervision of the domestic financial sector. Restrictions on international capital mobility may be useful if the domestic financial sector, through insufficient domestic regulation or supervision, cannot cope with these international capital flows.

Fischer (2003) argues that a temporary restriction of international capital mobility (through, for instance, exchange rate controls) can be a useful response to a crisis. To the extent that international capital mobility is looked upon as the main *cause* of financial crises, restrictions on international capital mobility quickly become the principal (and sometimes only) policy option to prevent or solve a crisis. In addition, if international capital mobility is the root of the problem, (re-)introducing restrictions on international capital mobility may not suffice and an overhaul of the international financial architecture may be called for.

Section 10.9 elaborates on restricting international capital mobility and its role in preventing or solving financial crises. For the moment, we want to emphasize that a tax on capital inflows increases the wedge between the net return for international investors and the interest rate faced by the domestic economy. To illustrate this, a slight variation on the analysis underlying the tariff on imported goods (see figure 10.2) is useful. In fact, the line of reasoning in the case of a tax on capital inflows is *identical* to the tariff analysis in section 10.2. Our discussion is based on figure 10.6.

Suppose that, before the introduction of the tax on capital flows, the domestic economy is at point C, facing interest rate i_c (the same for borrower and lender). If Home is a large country the capital tax will lead to a lower international interest rate i_a, while the domestic interest rate will increase to i_a'. The capital tax is therefore equal to the difference between i_a' and i_a. The welfare analysis is identical to the case of a tariff on goods. The capital tax drives a *wedge* between the Home and Foreign interest rate. The domestic demanders for funds face a welfare loss, while the domestic suppliers of funds receive a welfare gain. The net welfare loss for Home and Foreign combined is given by the triangle $AA'C$. If Home is a small country, Foreign's supply curve is horizontal, so that the tax will not affect the world interest rate, leading to a smaller combined welfare loss.

10.9 The pricing of risk and the role of policy

Capital restrictions

Capital restrictions, such as a tax on capital inflows, are not introduced for efficiency reasons but to enhance financial stability. Whether such restrictions are effective remains to be seen. We address that question in section 10.10. For the moment, we assume that capital restrictions effectively enhance financial stability, which implies that we are back to square one for policy-makers: how to deal with the trade-off between efficiency and stability? It is only when we look at the benefits as well as the costs of international capital mobility that the tension between these two objectives becomes clear. In essence, this tension is the same for international and national capital flows. For policy-makers to arrive at a reasonably efficient and stable financial system, it is crucial to ensure that the pricing of *risk*, a crucial component of financial transactions, is neither too low nor too high. The ultimate question for the efficiency–stability debate is how much of the risk should be borne by the private investors and how much by the government. The answer to this question is also crucial for the policy stance on the degree of international capital mobility. After answering this question, we shall return to the international capital mobility issue itself.

If all of the risk associated with financial transactions is borne by the private sector, the resulting level of savings and investment will be too low from a social welfare point of view (as the suppliers of funds are confronted with high transaction costs). Imagine a financial system with no banking regulation or with no supervision of the financial system at large – or, even more extreme, with no financial intermediation at all. For an individual economic agent with excess savings it then becomes very risky, and thus rather costly, to engage in financial transactions since she has to bear all the risks of the transaction and also all the costs that are usually at least partly covered by financial intermediaries and the associated supervision and regulatory authorities. In such a world, the price of risk is too high and as a result both the level of savings and investment will be too low.

Deposit insurance

The opposite situation needs to be avoided as well. If the government bears too much of the risk, savings and investment will be too high. This holds for both the volume of savings and investment as well as for the price of financial transactions. The former has already been illustrated in chapter 9, where we showed how over-investment can occur if an over-guaranteed financial system (e.g. unlimited deposit insurance) results in moral hazard behaviour by banks (box 9.1). The prospect of a full and complete bail-out by the government when things go wrong encourages excessive risk-taking by the private parties engaged in the financial transaction (box 10.5).

Box 10.5 Asset/price inflation

To show how the *under*-pricing of private risk may lead to the *over*-pricing of financial assets – that is, to *asset-price inflation* – the following example is illustrative (see Krugman 1998). Suppose we have a 100 per cent deposit insurance scheme where the domestic banks and their (international) deposit holders are always fully bailed out by the government whenever the investments made by the banks do not pay off. We now have a banking system characterized by *moral hazard*. To see this, assume that foreign deposits are the only source of funds for the banks, that all banks are alike, that there is perfect competition in the banking sector and that a bank can attract foreign deposits at the fixed interest rate of, say, 0 per cent. Moreover, a bank can invest its funds in real estate yielding a return of 25 with 2/3 probability and a return of 100 with 1/3 probability. How much will the bank pay for the real estate? A risk-neutral bank would base its offer on the expected return

$$(2/3) \times 25 + (1/3) \times 100 \approx 50$$

that is, it would pay a price of (at most) 50. A 'moral hazard' bank, on the other hand, will base its offer on the assumption that the highest possible return will materialize, and is therefore willing to pay 100. This is how asset-price inflation may develop.

In order to be able to pay 100 the bank has to attract funds (here, bank deposits) of 100 as well. If the owners of the bank are not hurt by a collapse of the bank (which is the case here: the only funds are deposits; there is no equity at stake), one can understand why the bank itself is willing to pay 100. This need not be a problem if the deposit holders do their monitoring job properly and enforce prudent banking behaviour. The foreign deposit holders, however, do not take the probability of a 'bad' return of 25 into account. As a result of the generous deposit insurance scheme they have no incentive to monitor the bank's investment plans. When things go wrong (that is, if the banks pay 100 but the return is 25), the government is expected to come to the rescue anyway: the bank is *insolvent* (net worth is $25 - 100 = -75$), but the deposit holders do not lose their money as the government bears all the risk.

Box 10.5 discusses how the under-pricing of risk (in this case, banks and deposit holders act as if there is no risk at all) leads to over-investment and asset-price inflation. What would be a preferred policy in this case? At first glance, it seems that the financial system would be better off with no deposit insurance. Can adequate supervision of banks not be provided by the financial system itself? Indeed, when the potential (foreign) deposit holders are large institutional investors, they may have the motives and the means to engage in adequate supervision, which may then be left to market forces. But many deposit holders are small, and they do not have the motives or the means to engage in effective supervision. To channel sufficient savings to the banks and to prevent bank runs (chapter 9), some deposit insurance is necessary.

Consequently, almost every country offers limited deposit insurance to individual deposit holders. The example also illustrates that in the efficiency–stability trade-off there is no optimal or first-best policy solution. The reason for government intervention (here, the deposit insurance scheme) is ultimately due to a market failure arising from incomplete information. In the absence of government intervention both efficiency (a suboptimal level of savings and investment) and stability (an excessive level of systemic risk) suffer. The difficult policy question is how much government intervention is needed: too much leads to the under-pricing of risk by the private sector; too little leads to the over-pricing of risk by the private sector (box 10.6).

Box 10.6 Policy options and moral hazard behaviour

In the asset-price inflation example (box 10.5), banks display moral hazard behaviour to an extreme extent, since they are not required to finance trans-actions with at least some of their own funds (equity) and there is an unlimited deposit insurance scheme (which removes the incentive for deposit holders to monitor the bank). As a result, banks have no incentive to take the inherent risk-iness of their transactions into account. In reality, banks do, of course, take the riskiness of their transactions into account, if only because deposit insurance schemes are limited. In addition, various other policy options are possible to limit the risk-taking behaviour of banks and the associated moral hazard problems. Policy-makers can, for example, leave banks in the dark as to the precise conditions under which they will come to the rescue once a bank gets into trouble. This will probably encourage prudent behaviour. More generally, policy-makers and the monetary authorities supervising the banking sector employ various forms of *regulation* to limit risk-taking due to moral hazard behaviour by the banks. The objective is to safeguard the stability of the financial system while at the same time taking efficiency considerations into account, which brings us back to the efficiency–stability trade-off. From the point of view of efficiency, it is part of the normal business of a market economy that a bank can go bust, but this is unwarranted from a stability perspective. Banking regulation basically comes in two flavours: market-based and non-market-based regulation:

- *Non-market-based regulation* occurs when banks are restricted in the kind of activities in which they can engage. We give three examples:
  - First, the distinction between commercial and investment banks in the USA, where the former are retail banks and the latter only do portfolio investment.
  - Second, the restriction of the degree of competition in the banking sector, which allows incumbent banks to make large enough profits to construct sufficiently large buffers against bad times (a clear example of the tension between stability and efficiency). In the Netherlands, for instance, the market share of the three largest banks in the retail banking market is over 80 per cent. On any other non-financial market such a degree of market power (and the implicit collusion that may go with it) would not be appreciated by the competition authorities.
  - A third example of non-market-based regulation is the idea of 'narrow banking', where the government applies deposit insurance only to banks investing in liquid assets. The idea is that deposit insurance should be limited to banks with assets that are as liquid as the liabilities (the deposits). For banks that want to engage in (riskier) long-term, illiquid assets, the government under the system of narrow banking does not give any deposit insurance, thereby providing a strong incentive to the deposit holders of those banks to engage in active monitoring themselves.

More regulation is not the only way to bolster financial stability, however. In some cases *de*regulation might actually improve stability and simultaneously stimulate efficiency. This occurs, for example, when foreign banks are allowed to enter a fragile, inefficient domestic banking market. This happened in the CEE transition countries, where foreign banks have gradually been allowed to enter since the early 1990s. Nowadays, foreign banks dominate the banking sector in these countries. Research shows that their (management) expertise and superior risk diversification have led to an increase of both efficiency and stability in the banking sector (see de Haas and van Lelyveld, 2004).

• The emphasis in banking supervision has recently shifted away from non-market-based regulation to *market-based regulation*. The best (and most relevant) example of the latter is the *capital adequacy ratios* as developed and used by the Bank for International Settlements (BIS) located in Basle, Switzerland.[a] The central banks of the world gather at the BIS to discuss and devise policies to improve the stability of the international financial system. Under the so-called 'Basle I' agreement that went into effect in the 1980s, private banks are obliged to have a minimum amount of capital or equity (their own capital should be at least 5 per cent of their total, risk-weighted assets). In the terminology of our book (see chapter 9), banks are obliged to have a minimum amount of *NW*. The idea is that capital requirements not only create a (solvency) buffer for banks, but also boost financial stability by limiting moral hazard behaviour. This also reduces the problems of asymmetric information (see chapter 9). The 5 per cent minimum is, however, a rather crude rule of thumb. In recent years a new capital adequacy system has been devised by the BIS, the so-called 'Basle II' system, whereby private banks are allowed to devise what might be called 'bank-specific capital adequacy schemes' in an attempt to increase their efficiency. A major instrument in this respect is the *value-at-risk* model, which provides the bank with sufficient information as to its own riskiness (and required capital ratio). The actual application of the Basle II system has turned out to be rather difficult and to be beset with problems (this is an under-statement).

[a] See the website www.bis.org for more information on the BIS.

10.10 Two examples of capital restrictions: preventing crises

Despite enhancing the efficiency of the allocation of both savings and investment, international capital mobility is thus not without its problems, as we saw in chapters 8 and 9. For this reason, various proposals have been introduced to somehow restrict capital mobility, either as a means to prevent financial crises or as a cure for them. This section briefly discusses two proposals that have been put forward to prevent crises.

The first example is the so-called *Tobin tax*, named after James Tobin, the 1981 Nobel laureate for Economics, who first developed the idea for this tax in the 1960s. The Tobin tax (Tobin, 1978) stipulates that all foreign exchange transactions should be taxed (a tax rate of 0.5 per cent of the value of the transaction is often suggested).

The purpose of such a tax is to discourage short-term international capital flows (every time a foreign exchange transaction takes place, the tax has to be paid). The assumption is that short-term capital flows are often of a speculative nature, thereby increasing financial fragility. With every major currency or financial crisis, there is renewed talk of the introduction of a Tobin tax. In policy circles (and among the critics of international capital mobility in general), it is the most 'talked-about' proposal to restrict international capital mobility. So far, the Tobin tax has never been introduced, primarily for reasons of its dubious effectiveness. To be effective, the tax should be introduced on a global scale. This not only requires a substantial amount of international policy coordination, it also implies that, once introduced, individual countries will have a strong incentive not to comply with the tax in an attempt to attract foreign funds. Moreover, the tax is probably too general, in that it discourages all foreign exchange transactions.[3]

The second example of a restriction on international capital mobility, and one that has actually been introduced, is the so-called *Chile tax*. This tax is named after a set of measures that the government of Chile took in 1991 to discourage short-term capital *in*flows. The part of the Chile tax that has received most attention is the requirement for domestic banks to hold a certain percentage (20 per cent in 1991) of their foreign funding for a specified period as an unremunerated deposit at Chile's central bank. Such a non-interest bearing deposit (reserve requirement) effectively constitutes a *tax on capital inflows* for the Chilean banks. Crucially, the tax rate is higher when the maturity of the capital inflow is shorter. If r^* is the international interest rate (the opportunity cost of the reserve requirement), λ is the proportion of foreign funds that has to be deposited at the central bank and ρ is the time period during which the deposits have to remain at the central bank, we can write the tax equivalent of foreign funds that stay at a bank in Chile for k months (see Edwards, 2001) as

$$\text{implicit tax for } k \text{ month deposits} = r^* \left(\frac{\lambda}{1 - \lambda} \right) \left(\frac{\rho}{k} \right) \qquad (10.2)$$

The implicit tax rate on capital inflows therefore increases when the interest rate increases (rising opportunity cost r^*), when more of the foreign funds have to be deposited (λ increases) and with a rise in the duration to maturity (ρ increases). Most importantly, however, the tax rate decreases with a longer maturity (k increases): a longer maturity of the capital inflow will make it relatively less costly for the bank to deposit part of the funds for some period at the central bank. The Chile tax thus stimulates domestic banks to attract funds with a longer maturity. The Chilean government changed the key parameters in (10.2) on a number of occasions. In the late 1990s (in the wake of the Asian financial crisis, see chapter 9), Chile

---

[3] See Eichengreen, Wyplosz and Tobin (1995) and also Buiter (2003), on Tobin's view on his much-cited, but ill-understood idea to 'throw some sand in the wheels' of international capital flows.

Table 10.2 Gross capital inflows to Chile, 1988–1997, million US $

Year	Short-term flows	% of total	Long-term flows	% of total	Deposits[a]
1988	916.6	96.3	34.8	3.7	–
1989	1452.6	95.0	77.1	5.0	–
1990	1683.1	90.3	181.4	9.7	–
1991	521.2	72.7	196.1	27.3	0.58
1992	225.2	28.9	554.0	71.1	11.4
1993	159.5	23.6	515.1	76.4	41.3
1994	161.6	16.5	819.7	83.5	87.0
1995	69.7	6.2	1051.8	93.8	38.7
1996	67.2	3.2	2042.4	96.8	172.3
1997	81.1	2.8	2805.8	97.2	331.6

Source: Edwards (2001, table 2).
Note:[a] = Deposits held at Banco Chile, due to reserve requirements.

was confronted with capital outflows and a reluctance on the part of international portfolio investors to supply funds to emerging markets. The Chilean government then reduced the duration ρ to zero, thereby effectively reducing the tax to zero as well.

Has the Chile tax been a success? After its introduction in 1991, the composition of capital inflows did change. As table 10.2 shows, the short-term capital inflows almost came to a halt, whereas the long-term inflows increased. Table 10.2 also shows that the total capital inflows increased as well, indicating that foreign investors were not put off by this restriction on international capital mobility (an argument often put forward by the opponents of restrictions on international capital mobility). The fact that in 2000 the tax rate was effectively zero shows that it is difficult to stick to this kind of restriction on capital mobility when the capital inflows dry up.

The Chile tax also has its drawbacks. As with most government restrictions on the behaviour of private agents, Chilean banks found ways to evade the tax, which gradually made it less effective. More importantly, from the perspective of preventing massive capital *out*flows to ensure financial stability, the tax does not put a brake on them. So, when the Asian crisis in 1997–8 made international investors jittery about their investments in emerging markets, Chile was confronted with a substantial capital outflow. This prompted the Chilean government to reduce the effective tax rate to zero in an attempt to stimulate the inflow of capital. However, the major international financial institutions (IMF and WB) acknowledge that a Chilean-style capital restriction might be used cautiously and temporarily to make a country less dependent on short-term capital inflows (see Fischer, 2003). From the perspective of the multinational firm that thinks about investing in a certain country, the prospect of being subject to capital restrictions once the investment has been made is a very relevant one and can be seen as an example of political risk (see box 10.7).

Box 10.7 Political risk and the multinational firm's investment strategy[a]

A large literature explores the Vernon type of stages model of internationalization (cf. chapter 12), arguing that firms internationalize in *clear sequential stages*, moving from export to investment-based international entry modes over time (Vernon, 1966). Another literature argues, however, that operating abroad may be subject to political risks (e.g. because domestic governments may decide to nationalize foreign investments or raise taxes on foreign operations). Combining both literatures, one might argue that there is a link between a firm's *internationalization experience* and the *political risk* it is willing to face. A firm that is just starting to explore opportunities outside its domestic market might well be less willing to take political risks than an MNE with a large portfolio of international activities in an array of countries. If this argument held true, then considerations of political risk would operate as entry deterrents for one group of firms, but not for another.

Delios and Henisz (2003) study this issue, using a sample of 3,857 international expansions of 665 Japanese manufacturing firms in the period 1980–98. Their main finding is that 'firms that have followed a sequential process of international expansion exhibit a lower sensitivity to the deterring effect of political hazards' (Delios and Henisz, 2003, pp. 1161–2). The reasons for this may be manifold. Take the following two examples:

- First, by operating a wide array of international activities in a large number of countries, multinationals can spread the risk of political hazard across their international portfolio. Political losses in one country are then more likely to be compensated by political windfalls elsewhere in the world.
- Second, such MNEs learn how to deal with political risk over time. For instance, the multinational's senior management might develop relationships with local authorities that can help them to avoid the downsides of political manoeuvring. From the perspective of a multinational, this suggests that developing experience in many international directions can be instrumental in building the capabilities required for political hazard mitigation.

[a] Based on Delios and Henisz (2003).

10.11 Capital restrictions as a cure for crises

Both the Tobin tax and the Chile tax are examples of capital restrictions trying to *prevent* an increase of financial fragility or a financial crisis. As explained above in our discussion on the efficiency–stability trade-off, there are costs associated with capital restrictions. Whether policy-makers opt for a restriction on international capital mobility therefore also depends on the effectiveness of the policy alternatives, such as a move towards flexible exchange rates, improved supervision and regulation and the use of an early warning system (see chapter 9). How about restricting international capital mobility once a crisis has occurred, such as by the introduction of foreign exchange controls? This implies that the exchange rate is no longer determined by market forces but by the government (buying and selling of foreign exchange occurs at rates determined by the government). To understand why a government might be tempted to resort to such a drastic action, consider the following version of the UIP condition from chapter 6

$$r_{home} = r_{foreign} + dE \qquad (10.3)$$

Suppose that Home is hit by a currency and financial crisis. As a result of the former, Home is confronted with capital outflows and a depreciating exchange rate (an increase in E), while the latter implies that the domestic financial and non-financial sectors suffer from an excessive debt burden. Initially, there is perfect international capital mobility. Home now faces a policy dilemma. Assuming that $r_{foreign}$ is fixed, the exchange rate depreciation goes along with an interest rate increase in Home. In order to stabilize the exchange rate, the interest rate in Home thus has to increase. But this will also increase the debt burden of the domestic financial and non-financial sector. To decrease the debt burden, the policy-makers in Home would prefer to lower the interest rate! With the introduction of exchange controls, Home could cut through this dilemma. These controls would, almost by definition, stabilize the exchange rate and they would enable Home to lower its interest rate. In effect, the exchange controls would imply that the UIP condition no longer holds. Malaysia provides a prime recent example of a temporary (re-)introduction of exchange controls. In the wake of the Southeast Asian financial crisis, the Malaysian government, led by President Mahathir, decided in the autumn of 1998 to instal a regime of exchange controls. Mahathir blamed international investors for the crisis and the Malaysian government decided that, at least temporarily, the benefits of international capital mobility did not outweigh the costs. At the time, the decision of the Malaysian government was criticized by the IMF because exchange controls have a number of drawbacks:

- To start with, even though these controls are meant to be temporary, countries can stick with them for too long, thereby postponing domestic policy adjustments (of course, Mahathir argued that adjustments were not necessary because international investors were to blame for the crisis).
- Secondly, the introduction of exchange controls might scare off (future) international investors, so that once the controls were lifted the risk premium of investing

in the economy would increase, implying higher interest rates (actually, this did not appear to happen in Malaysia).

- Finally, exchange controls are costly to administrate because every foreign exchange transaction now has to be handled by government officials.

10.12 Changing the international financial system?

The Tobin tax, the Chile tax and exchange controls are all examples of 'sand in the wheels of international finance', and as such are not attempts to change the functioning of the international financial *system* (the 'wheels' are left unchanged). Following the spur of currency and financial crises in the last decade of the twentieth century, various proposals have been put forward to change the workings of the international financial system. These proposals to change the rules of the game are stimulated by a number of (interdependent) issues that lie at the heart of every modern financial crisis:

- The distinction between liquidity and solvency crises
- The distribution of risk between the private and the public sector
- The handling of 'severe' (solvency) crises once they have occurred.

In chapter 9, we saw that financial crises can be divided into *liquidity* and *solvency* crises. Even though one should be careful to apply the framework normally reserved for individual firms to (sovereign) nation-states, this division helps to understand why (ideally) the international financial system should not allow for liquidity crises. In the case of a solvency crisis one could say that a crisis is 'inevitable' because of intrinsic problems with the fundamentals of the economy concerned. This is not the case with a liquidity crisis. How can we prevent a liquidity crisis? One interesting proposal has been put forward by Willem Buiter and Anne Sibert (1999), namely to ensure that all loans made in a foreign currency contain a so-called *debt rollover option with a penalty*. Such an option gives a country the right to rollover – that is, to extend – a loan for a limited period (say, three–six months). When a country exercises this right, it pays a penalty because the interest rate exceeds the market interest rate. The penalty ensures that countries use the option only when they face liquidity problems – that is, when they face serious difficulties in acquiring new foreign loans under the prevailing market conditions. The rollover option thus provides a temporary buffer when international investors are no longer willing to grant new loans for no apparent reason – that is, when the fundamentals of the economy are sound and the reluctance of international capital markets is of a short-term nature. The Buiter–Sibert scheme does not work for countries with a solvency problem, because the rollover of loans does nothing to solve the problem: it would, at best, postpone the crisis.

Borrow until UDROP?

Still, in a world of incomplete information, one could argue that private creditors have no incentive to agree to the inclusion of the rollover option in the debt contract as long as they can only imperfectly discriminate between future illiquid debtors and insolvent debtors. If insolvent debtors also exercised the rollover option (to postpone the crisis) this would run counter to the main objective of the scheme. Moreover, debtors might not be willing to ask for the inclusion of the debt rollover option in the contract if they thus signal to creditors an expectation of running into refinancing problems when the loan expires. This is why Buiter and Sibert call for a *universal* debt rollover option with a penalty – or UDROP, for short. To achieve this, the option should be enforced by governments via international policy coordination. As with the introduction of the Tobin tax, this seems quite a daunting task. The allocation of responsibilities to the private and the government sector in the case of a financial crisis leads us to a second crucial issue: the distribution of risk between the private and the public sector. Too much involvement of the private sector leads to under-borrowing whereas too little involvement of the private sector leads to over-borrowing.

The allocation of risk associated with financial transactions between the private and the public/government sector is also central to the proposals to re-design the international financial system (or architecture). This holds in particular regarding 'severe' (solvency) crises once they have occurred. The adjective 'severe' refers to the possibility of a default by the country in question. In the international financial system, as opposed to a national financial system, there is no well-developed framework for dealing with these crises. In a national setting, most countries have a bankruptcy law providing the institutional framework to deal with firms that go into default and with the ensuing restructuring of firms. The lack of such a framework at the international level implies that international institutions such as the IMF have to deal with (potential) default crises, such as Turkey in 2001 or Argentina in 2002, on an ad hoc basis. Most of the recent proposals to change the international financial architecture are about devising mechanisms to change this situation. Stanley Fischer (2003), the former Vice-President of the IMF, argues that the costs of restructuring – that is, the costs when things have gone wrong – are too high because of the lack of a framework to deal with possible default situations.

New rules of the game?

So, what can be done? One option, proposed by Anne Krueger (Fischer's successor as Vice-President of the IMF), is to arrive at an international sovereign debt restructuring mechanism (SDRM), whereby legal arrangements are put in place to deal with payment delays and the restructuring of debts. This would be like an international bankruptcy law. The main objective is to lower the costs of restructuring for all parties involved once a 'severe' crisis has occurred. For the SDRM proposal to work, the incentives for both creditors (the international lenders) and debtors (the borrowing countries) have to be right. If debtor countries find it relatively easy to fall back on international 'bankruptcy' procedures at the first hint of trouble, creditors will be at a disadvantage and increase their interest rates for loans to these countries.[4] As a result, international capital flows may decrease. Debtors may not be very willing to support such a mechanism to start with.

Another idea to lower the costs of financial restructuring and to increase private sector (creditor) involvement in the aftermath of a crisis also carries the danger of 'throwing the baby out with the bathwater'. The idea is to increase the use of so-called 'collective action clauses' (see Eichengreen, 2002, pp. 85–92). These clauses try to overcome coordination problems on the part of the creditors. As we saw in our example of liquidity crises in chapter 9, the incentive for an individual creditor whether or not to grant or extend a loan or to contribute funds in the restructuring process depends on the expected actions of other investors. Even if creditors are collectively better off not to 'walk away', this does not mean that it is the best option for individual investors.

Collective action clauses try to cut through the underlying coordination problem by specifying in the debt contract procedures in the case of a refinancing/restructuring problem. The involvement of creditors in the restructuring process increases if, for instance, they appoint a representative to negotiate with debtors or the IMF on their behalf, and by stipulating that individual creditors are bound by majority voting, In fact, debt contracts with a collective action clause already exist. Bond contracts issued in London are, for instance, obliged to carry such a clause. Contrary to the SDRM proposal, the debtors are less likely to welcome a mandatory, worldwide application of these clauses. The reason is that they fear that creditors will require compensation for these clauses, and will demand higher interest rates.[5]

10.13 Rounding up the restrictions

This chapter has discussed the pros and cons of restrictions on international trade and capital mobility. In both cases, a reduction of protection, transaction costs and other

---

[4] The phrase 'bankruptcy' is put between quotation marks to remind the reader that sovereign states, unlike firms, cannot go bankrupt in a technical sense.

[5] See also Eichengreen (2004) for these and other solutions to tackle financial instability.

barriers to trade is typically welfare-enhancing. From a welfare point of view for the country as whole, it is therefore difficult to defend trade and capital restrictions, and hence policies to limit the degree of globalization. Nonetheless, there are numerous examples of actual measures to restrict trade and capital mobility, and of pleas to do so. Three remarks can help to understand this discrepancy between theory and practice:

- First, the proponents of restrictions often base their conclusions on a partial equilibrium analysis, failing to see that trade or capital restrictions have ramifications above and beyond the more obvious direct, first-round impact. A tariff on imported goods may protect domestic firms and employment, but at the cost of domestic consumers and production in other sectors. Similarly, a tax on capital inflow may be good news for domestic suppliers of finance, but it depresses the overall level of savings and investment and thereby hurts future economic growth.
- Second, the proponents and beneficiaries of restrictions are usually well organized. This means that policy-makers often cater too much to the needs of special interest groups that favour trade or capital restrictions, specifically because consumers, the ultimate winners of free trade and capital mobility, are not well organized at all.
- Third, and in line with our discussion on exchange and financial crises in chapters 8 and 9, the case for free trade is stronger than the case for unhampered capital mobility (see also Bhagwati, 1998). More conditions have to be fulfilled to reap the benefits of capital mobility than those of free trade. Without sufficient regulation and supervision of the domestic financial sector, financial liberalization (international capital mobility) might turn out to be counter-productive. An ill-timed or premature introduction of international capital mobility might require the (temporary) introduction of a restriction on international capital flows, as discussed in this chapter.

As financial transactions involve claims on future income, they differ fundamentally in terms of the degree of riskiness from goods transactions. The associated riskiness implies that the case for the unhampered working of international financial markets is less clear-cut than for international trade. It is therefore not surprising that empirical research has found it easier to establish a positive effect for trade liberalization on economic growth as compared to financial liberalization. Most importantly, however, the positive growth effects seem to be strongest if trade liberalization is combined with financial liberalization (see box 10.8). This leads us to the issue of the determinants of economic growth and development, as analysed in chapter 11. We return to the arguments levelled against international trade and capital mobility in chapter 13.

Box 10.8 Trade, financial liberalization and economic growth[a]

The consensus view among economists is that by and large more trade leads to more economic growth. In a seminal (and also much-criticized) study, Sachs and Warner (1995) conclude that both developed and developing countries benefit from trade openness in terms of their economic growth rates (see table 10.3).

Table 10.3 Annual growth rate 1970–1989

	'Open' economy	'Closed' economy
Developed countries	2.29	0.74
Developing countries	4.49	0.69

Source: Sachs and Warner (1995).

Critics of the Sachs – Warner study point out several problems (see also chapter 13):
- Is causality running from openness to growth or are better-performing economies simply more prone to open up to trade?
- Are their findings robust if one controls for other variables affecting economic growth?
- Is the distinction between open and closed economies based on trade or on other variables, such as the domestic political situation?

Even with these caveats in mind, most economists probably support the claim that trade openness boosts economic growth. It is more difficult to establish a growth bonus of increased capital mobility or financial openness, though (see IMF, 2003). This holds in particular for developing countries that have only fairly recently (post-1980) begun the process of financial liberalization. Typically, the growth bonus of capital mobility for these countries arises only when the analysis is restricted to FDI and growth. Given the link with financial crises it is not surprising that the empirical connection between growth and financial openness is weaker than between growth and trade openness.

Tornell and Westermann (2004) study the combined impact of trade and financial liberalization on economic growth. They establish the following four stylized facts:
- Trade liberalization typically precedes financial liberalization
- Both trade and financial liberalization boost *per capita* growth, provided that the functioning of financial markets meets certain minimum standards
- Financial liberalization is a bumpy process characterized by booms and busts . . .

- ... but countries with bumpy credit paths have grown faster than countries with smooth credit paths.

  Ultimately, the question as to the (combined) impact of trade and financial liberalization on economic growth is part of a larger question: what are the net benefits of globalization for the countries participating in the globalization process? This question will be taken up in chapter 13.

[a] Based on Tornell and Westermann (2004).

Globalization and economic growth

KEYWORDS

catching-up	growth projections	capital accumulation
Total Factor Productivity (TFP)	Solow model	technology
stylized facts of growth	endogenous growth	research and development
knowledge spillovers	new goods	innovation

11.1 Introduction

Chapter 10 argues that, in general, imposing trade and capital restrictions reduces economic prosperity for various reasons. Other things equal we should therefore expect that open economies tend to be wealthier than closed economies. This chapter analyses the theoretical and empirical links between 'globalization', by which we mean the extent to which an economy is open to outside influences, and economic prosperity and development in the long run. It will confirm the basic arguments on the positive relationship between openness and prosperity laid down in previous chapters.

As the core of this chapter is dynamic in nature, we start by giving some insight into the degree to which differences in economic growth rates translate into differences in income levels. Next, we discuss the fundamentals of economic growth in a closed economy, focusing on the importance of human and physical capital accumulation, labour inputs and technology improvements. After a discussion of some stylized empirical facts, we turn to the importance of innovation by firms and entrepreneurs, knowledge accumulation, knowledge spillovers and market power for bringing about the technology improvements that ultimately increase our standard of living. Finally, we discuss the various ways in which open economies are better able to achieve human and physical capital accumulation, reach a more stable economic environment and benefit from access to foreign (incorporated) knowledge. To conclude this discussion, we present two Asian case studies, namely a brief review of the economic developments in Japan since about 1500 and a discussion of China's experience in the second half of the twentieth century.

Table 11.1 GDP *per capita*, 1990–2000 growth projections[a]

Country	GDP *per capita* in 1990	2000	Growth rate 1990–2000(%)	Year in which GDP *per capita* exceeds USA 2000	USA in that year
China	1,858	3,425	6.31	2035	2051
India	1,309	1,910	3.85	2072	2146
USA	23,201	28,129	1.95	–	–

Data source: Maddison (2003).

Notes: [a] Projections based on 1990–2000 average compound growth rates; data are in 1990 international Geary–Khamis dollars, a sophisticated aggregation method of calculating PPPs, which facilitates comparing countries with each other, see the statistical definition at the UN site: http://unstats.un.org/unsd/methods/icp/ipc7_htm.htm.

– = Cannot be computed.

11.2 Catching-up

It takes time to overtake, particularly if the target is moving. It appears that this simple observation, which also holds in economic terms if one country is trying to catch-up with another, is sometimes forgotten. After correcting for purchasing power, the GDP *per capita* in 2000 was $1,910 in India, $3,425 in China and $28,129 in the USA (see table 11.1). The average American is therefore much better off than the average Chinese or Indian. In the last decade of the twentieth century, however, the economic growth rate was higher in China and India than in the USA: as illustrated in table 11.1, the average compound 1990–2000 annual growth rate was 6.31 per cent for China, 3.85 per cent for India and 1.95 per cent for the USA. This information, combined with the fact that in 2000 there were about 1,264 million Chinese, 1,007 million Indians and only 282 million Americans, made firms and the media at the turn of the millennium all over the globe excited about the enormous market potential of China and India. Companies are dreaming: 'if only we could sell a box of Kellogg's cereal to every Chinese', or 'if only we could sell a Volkswagen to one out of every 100 Indians'. Yes, if only that were the case, you would make a killing. Consequently, we read about all sorts of production activities being moved from Europe, Japan and the USA to China and India. But purchasing a box of Kellogg's cereal still represents a substantial share of the annual budget for the majority of Chinese, who might prefer to eat rice anyway, while being able to afford a Volkswagen is simply out of the question for the large majority of Indians. Nonetheless, China and India are thought of as the places to be. Their economies will become more important as a consequence of high growth rates combined with large populations. They will soon dominate the world economy. But when?

Table 11.2 GDP*ᵃ per capita* growth rates per decade, 1960–2000

Country	Average annual compound growth rate of GDP *per capita* (%)			
	1960–70	1970–80	1980–90	1960–2000
China	1.53	3.14	5.70	4.15
India	1.43	0.78	3.39	2.35
USA	2.87	2.14	2.25	2.30

Data source: Maddison (2003).
Note: ᵃ GDP measured in 1990 international Geary–Khamis dollars.

How long does it take for the average Chinese or Indian to be as rich as the average American?[1] Table 11.1 gives a first indicative answer based on 1990–2000 growth projections. Suppose we make the heroic assumption that American, Chinese and Indian GDP *per capita* will henceforth grow by the 1990–2000 average (1.95, 6.31 and 3.85 per cent per year, respectively). Below we give an indication of how heroic this assumption is. Despite these very high growth rates for China and India, it still takes thirty-five years before the average Chinese income level is equal to the American income level in *2000*. American income, however, is also rising, so that in *2035* Chinese *per capita* income would still be only about 53 per cent of American income. It would actually take fifty-one years before Chinese *per capita* income exceeded American *per capita* income. Similarly, it would take seventy-two years before Indian *per capita* income reached the USA's 2000 level, and no less than 146 years before Indian *per capita* income exceeded American *per capita* income. Apparently, catastrophes aside, if you are lucky enough to live in a high-income country and do not emigrate, you can rest assured that you will very likely continue to live in a high-income country for the rest of your life.

Table 11.2 illustrates why we called our 1990–2000 projections 'heroic'. Table 11.2 lists the average annual compound growth rates per decade from 1960 to 1990, as well as the annual growth rate for the period 1960–2000. Chinese and Indian growth rates per decade vary widely, certainly compared to the stable developments in the USA. Over a somewhat longer time horizon of forty years, Indian *per capita* growth is virtually equal to American *per capita* growth. Both are about 1.8 per cent below Chinese *per capita* growth. Table 11.3 repeats Table 11.1's growth projection exercise, this time using the period 1960–2000 as a basis. In this case, it takes fifty-two years before Chinese *per capita* income is equal to the USA's 2000 level, while it takes 118 years before Chinese *per capita* income exceeds American *per capita* income.

---

[1] In chapter 13, we shall see that the choice of comparing China and the USA is special, as China is one of the most rapidly growing developing countries.

Table 11.3 GDP *per capita* 1960–2000 growth projections[a]

Country	Per capita GDP in 1960	Per capita GDP in 2000	Growth rate 1960–2000 %	Year in which GDP per capita exceeds USA 2000	Year in which GDP per capita exceeds USA in that year
China	673	3,425	4.15	2052	2118
India	753	1,910	2.35	2116	7113
USA	11,328	28,129	2.30	–	–

Data source: Maddison (2003).
Notes: [a] Projections based on 1960–2000 average compound growth rates; data are in 1990 international Geary–Khamis dollars.
– = Cannot be computed.

Similarly, based on these projections, India does not reach the USA's current *per capita* income level in the twenty-first century and would have to wait more than 5,000 years to surpass it.

Neither the projections in table 11.1 nor the projections in table 11.3 should be taken as an indication of what is likely to happen in the twenty-first century. Again, barring catastrophes, we can be fairly confident of the likely developments in the USA, which have been very stable over a long time period (see below). For what it is worth, we view table 11.3 as a best-case scenario in the twenty-first century for China and as an attractive scenario for India, as a country that manages to sustain a growth rate of 2 per cent or more per year for a century is rapidly improving its standard of living. Both countries could do much worse than the projections of table 11.3, while India has the potential to do much better. The remainder of this chapter gives an indication of the underlying forces playing a role in this respect.

11.3 Production, capital and investment

In chapters 6–9 we have already discussed several factors that can influence a firm's investment decisions. There can be many different types of investment in many different types of physical, human and knowledge capital (see van Marrewijk, 1999). For simplicity, we lump all these investments together under the heading 'capital'. Similarly, there are many different types of labour, such as janitors, farmers, brain surgeons and engineers. Again, we lump all of these together under the heading 'labour'. Neither simplification is crucial for the arguments below. Pioneered by Nobel laureate Robert Solow (1956), economists emphasize the importance of *capital accumulation* for the economic growth process. This is explained in box 11.1

Box 11.1 Growth accounting and growth modelling

In this chapter we make use of a technique called 'growth accounting,' which looks at the fundamental sources of economic growth. The breakdown starts by analysing the following standard production function

$$Y = F(T, K, L) \tag{11.1}$$

where Y is output, T is the level of technology, K is the capital stock and L is the labour force. Y is characterized by constant returns to scale with respect to capital and labour; this enables us, for example, to write $\dfrac{Y}{L} = F(T, \dfrac{K}{L}, 1) = f(T, k)$, with $k = K/L$. As we are often interested in *per capita* variables, this is an important equation.

From (11.1), we immediately see that growth can come only from the growth of factors of production or technology. Totally differentiating (11.1), dividing the resulting equation by Y, we can rewrite the outcome as

$$\frac{dY}{Y} = \frac{F_T T}{Y}\frac{dT}{T} + \frac{F_K K}{Y}\frac{dK}{K} + \frac{F_L L}{Y}\frac{dL}{L} = g + s_K \hat{K} + s_L \hat{L} \tag{11.2}$$

where F_K, F_L are the marginal products of capital and labour, implying that

$$\frac{F_K K}{Y}$$

equals the share of capital in national output, indicated by s_K. Similarly, s_L equals the share of labour in national output,

$$\hat{X} = \frac{dX}{X}$$

which indicates the growth rate of a variable. Growth due to technological progress equals g. The value of g is known as the Solow residual (SR), or as total factor productivity (TFP) growth: even if factors of production remain constant an economy can grow due to technological progress.

With the help of (11.2), we can make a breakdown of growth into the components that contribute to this growth. This is called growth accounting. Each component can be analysed separately:

- *TFP growth*

$$g = \frac{F_T T}{Y}\frac{dT}{T}$$

is the most difficult variable. That is why it is often assumed to be exogenous. Nevertheless, in empirical research many variables are assumed to be related to g – R&D expenditure, schooling rates, the number of patents and similar variables. They are all assumed to contribute to technological progress in a country, at least in empirical studies.

- *Population growth*   It is often assumed that population growth

$$n = \hat{L} = \frac{dL}{L}$$

is exogenous and is determined by demographic factors.
- *Growth of the capital stock*   The increase of the capital stock equals investment, I, minus depreciation of the capital stock, δK, which gives $dK = I - \delta K$. Assuming that investments are equal to national savings, S, which is a share, s, of national output, Y, this equation can be rewritten as $dK = sY - \delta K$. It is interesting to take a closer look at this part of the growth equation. Start by dividing both sides of $dK = sY - \delta K$ by L. This gives

$$\frac{dK}{L} = sf(k) - \delta k$$

where the small letters indicate *per capita* variables.[a] Note that the right-hand side of this equation is a function of k only. It would be convenient if the whole equation could be in terms of k only. So look at the left-hand side

$$\frac{dK}{L}$$

We like to rewrite this in terms of k. A little trick does this for us. Totally differentiating

$$k = \frac{K}{L}$$

gives

$$dk = \frac{dK}{L} - \frac{K}{L}\frac{dL}{L} = \frac{dK}{L} - k.n$$

using rules of differentiation and the definition of population growth. We already have an expression for

$$\frac{dK}{L}$$

If we use this, we get $dk = sf(k) - (n + \delta)k$. This is one of the most fundamental equations of growth theory. It says that the stock of capital *per capita* increases only if *savings are large enough to compensate population growth and*

---

[a] Note that we should have written $f(T, k)$ instead of $f(k)$, but we take T as a constant for now.

capital depreciation. Turning to

$$\frac{Y}{L} = f(k)$$

which is income *per capita* as a function of k for a given level of technology. We immediately see that income *per capita* can increase only if $dk > 0$, or $sf(k) > (n + \delta)k$. Now see figure 11.2 (p. 311), where the curved line represents $sf(k)$ and the straight line represents $(n + \delta)k$.

In essence, Solow argued that output – the production of goods and services – is a function of three inputs: capital, labour and an input which we label 'Total Factor Productivity' (TFP). An increase in any of these inputs will raise output, as indicated by the + signs below:

$$Output = F(\underset{+}{TFP}, \underset{+}{Capital}, \underset{+}{Labour}) \quad \text{or} \quad Y = F(\underset{+}{T}, \underset{+}{K}, \underset{+}{L}) \qquad (11.3)$$

Increases in the labour force are ultimately determined by increases in the population level, albeit with a time lag of fifteen–twenty years. Solow took the population growth rate as given and focused instead on changes in output *per capita*, obtained by dividing (11.3) by the number of labourers and analysing the capital/labour ratio.[2] Taking the level of technology as given, increases in output *per capita* can then be reached only by increasing the capital stock per worker – that is, the capital/labour ratio. This is explained in the last part of box 11.1. As explained in chapters 6–9, many

---

[2] Formally, this requires that production exhibits constant returns to scale in capital and labour.

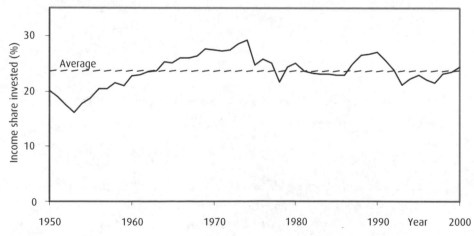

Figure 11.1 France, share of income invested, 1950–2000, per cent
Data source: *Penn World Table Version 6.1* (October 2002).

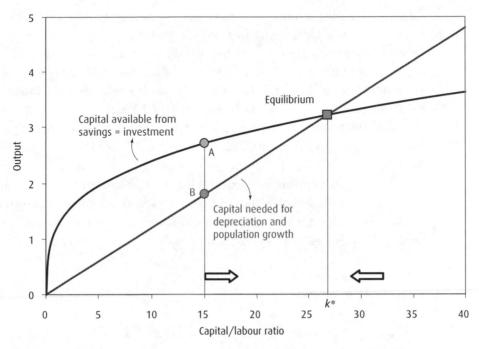

Figure 11.2 Income levels and capital accumulation (Solow)

factors influence a firm's decision to invest in capital, certainly in an internationally connected world. Here, again, Solow took a short cut by analysing a closed economy, so that domestic savings is equal to domestic investment, and assuming that a constant share of income is saved and invested in each time period. As illustrated in figure 11.1 for France in the period 1950–2000, the share of income actually invested fluctuates – in this case, from a minimum of 16.1 per cent in 1953 to a maximum of 29.2 per cent in 1974. Average investments over the period as a whole for France were 23.6 per cent, with relatively minor deviations after 1975, making the Solowian assumption of a constant savings rate acceptable as a first approximation.

   Figure 11.2 illustrates the evolution of the capital/labour ratio as a consequence of capital accumulation. As the capital stock per worker increases, output per worker rises since each worker has more tools and equipment available to work with. The increase, however, is less than equiproportional: output rises, say from 7 to 10 (3 'units' increase), if you have a computer available, but it rises by less if you have an additional computer available, say from 10 to 12 (2 'units' increase). Since Solow assumed that a constant share of income is saved and invested, the capital available for investment also rises less than equiproportionally as the capital/labour ratio increases. This is illustrated by the curved line in figure 11.2. What is available for investment in the capital stock has to be compared to what is needed to maintain the current capital/labour ratio. Two forces are important in this respect: *depreciation* and *population growth*. Newly purchased capital regularly depreciates – say, at 10 per cent per year. To maintain a given capital/labour ratio therefore requires equiproportional replacement of depreciated capital. Similarly, if the labour force regularly increases as a result of population growth, the new labourers would cause the capital/labour ratio to decline. Equiproportional investments are therefore required to maintain the same capital/labour ratio. Combining these two effects gives rise to the straight line in figure 11.2. Suppose the initial capital/labour ratio is 15. As indicated in figure 11.2, the capital available for investment (point *A*) is higher than the capital needed for depreciation and population growth (point *B*). Consequently, the capital/labour ratio will rise, as indicated by the right-pointing arrow. Similar reasoning for other points in the diagram shows that the capital/labour ratio will evolve over time to a steady state indicated by k^* and the point *Equilibrium* in figure 11.2.

11.4 Empirical implications

Several important empirical implications follow from the capital accumulation model outlined in section 11.3. As illustrated in figure 11.2, the capital/labour ratio evolves, other things equal, to a constant ratio k^*. This would imply, once this ratio is reached, that output per worker does not change as well. Obviously, this does not hold empirically as output per worker has generally been rising ever since 1800. Also other stylised facts are at odds with this simple model. One implication of figure 11.2, for instance, is that countries with low k ratios have high returns to capital compared to countries that have high k ratios. One expects capital to flow from countries with high k ratios to countries with low k ratios. As we saw in chapter 7, this is not the case. To remedy these shortcomings, the model needs some extensions: in particular, the level of TFP must rise to explain rising output per worker levels (see also box 11.2):

Box 11.2 TFP and school enrolment in developing countries

As explained in section 11.4, accurately measuring (changes in) TFP is not an easy task, as it requires a careful use of statistics and econometrics. In a paper following up on an earlier study for the OECD countries, Coe, Helpman and Hoffmaister (1997) analyse the relationship between TFP, education and trade openness for seventy-seven developing countries in the period 1971–90. Their structural analysis focuses on five-year averages, but in the boxes in this chapter we focus on averages for the period as a whole and changes during the period.

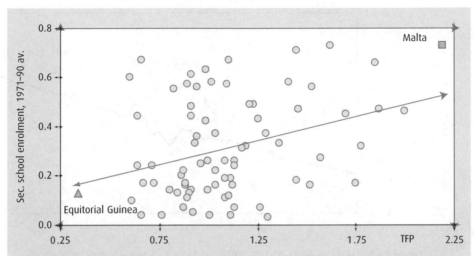

Figure 11.3 Education and TFP in developing countries, TFP ratio, 1990/1971 and secondary school enrolment, 1971–1990 average

Data source: Coe, Helpman and Hoffmaister (1997).

Note: The thin line is a trend line.

Figure 11.3 illustrates the relationship between changes in TFP during the period and the average education level. Obviously, we expect a country's productivity increase to depend on the quality of the labour force, either directly through a more productive workforce or indirectly by attracting FDI or incorporating technical advances in other countries. In the absence of more suitable data on the quality of human capital in most developing countries, we take the share of the population enjoying secondary school enrolment as a proxy for human capital. There is, indeed, a positive association between education levels and TFP growth, as indicated by the trend line in figure 11.3. The worst performance was in Equatorial Guinea, where the 1990 TFP level was only 34 per cent of the 1971 level and on average 13 per cent of the population enjoyed secondary education. The best performance was in Malta, where TFP was more than twice as high in 1990 than in 1971 and on average 73 per cent of the population enjoyed secondary education. As we will see in chapter 13, other factors, such as climate or the quality of institutions, are equally important.

- Rising *per capita production levels ultimately require rising TFP levels*.
  Solow was aware of the importance of TFP. Contributing TFP changes solely to technological improvements, he therefore assumed *exogenous* technological change, resulting in a steady increase in TFP (2 per cent per year, say) that is not explained within the model but imposed. As a consequence, the economy

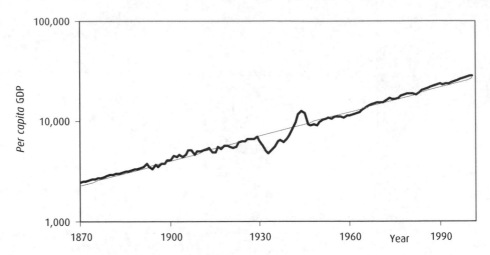

Figure 11.4 USA: GDP *per capita*, international 1990 Geary–Khamis dollars, log scale
Data source: Maddison (2003).
Note: The thin line is a trend line.

converges to a *balanced-growth* path in which capital and output per worker ultimately increase at the same rate as the assumed increase in TFP.

- *Steady TFP growth implies convergence to a balanced-growth path.*

Figure 11.4 depicts the evolution of *per capita* GDP in the USA (1870–2001). Noting
that the vertical axis is a logarithmic scale and recalling from box 1.2 that the slope
of such a graph represents the growth rate, figure 11.4 illustrates that a balanced-
growth path characterizes the developments in the USA since the 1870s fairly well.
The only noteworthy deviations from the steady trend line are the trough during
the Great Depression in the 1930s and the peak at the end of the Second World
War. For the period as a whole, *per capita* GDP increased steadily at a rate of 1.87
per cent per year, implying a doubling of American *per capita* income levels every
thirty-eight years.

If all countries have access to the same technology and are alike in all other
respects apart from the fact that they initially have different capital/labour ratios,
figure 11.2 predicts that in the long run all countries should end up in the same
equilibrium k^*. Since rich (poor) countries typically have relatively high (low)
capital/labour ratios, this would mean that in the long run poor countries would
catch-up with rich countries. This hypothesis of so-called 'unconditional convergence' is not borne out by the facts. One reason may be that not all countries
have access to the same technology and that they differ in other crucial aspects
(see chapter 13). Another reason may simply be that not all countries are on a
balanced-growth path to start with.

Figure 11.5 depicts the evolution of *per capita* GDP in Japan and Indonesia (1870–2001). It illustrates quite clearly that both countries are *not* on a

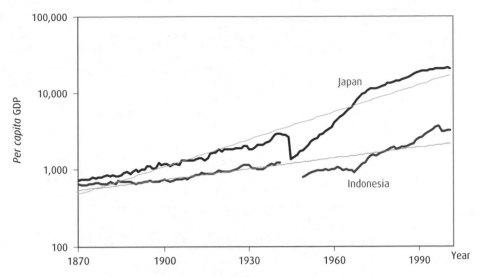

Figure 11.5 Japan and Indonesia: GDP *per capita*, international 1990 Geary–Khamis dollars, log scale
Data source: Maddison (2003).
Note: The thin lines are trend lines.

balanced-growth path for the period as a whole: in both cases there are substantial deviations from the trend lines, which give a poor impression of the actual evolution of these economies over time. This holds particularly for Japan, where the trend line grossly under-estimates actual GDP *per capita* in the period 1870–95, is more or less accurate in the period 1900–40, grossly over-estimates GDP *per capita* in the period 1944–64 and under-estimates it from 1968 onwards. The figure clearly illustrates the enormous growth spurt of Japan from 1945 to 1973. In short, we can conclude that:

• *Not all economies can be characterized by balanced-growth paths.*
  Equation (11.3) is also useful for explaining economic growth rates, and therefore deviations in balanced-growth paths. If capital and labour involved in the production process are both paid the value of marginal product under the conditions of section 11.3, it can be shown (see box 11.1) that (11.3) implies

Output growth = Growth TFP + Capital share × Capital growth

$$+ \; Labour \; share \times Labour \; growth \qquad (11.4)$$

As already argued above, output increases with increases in the capital stock the labour force, or the level of TFP. Since statisticians all over the world are gathering detailed information about increases in production, the capital stock and the labour force, the relationship above can be used to estimate the degree of TFP growth, which is virtually impossible to estimate directly. To do this properly is not an easy exercise and clearly beyond the scope of this book (see, for example, Young, 1995 for details). We can, however, get a rough indication of the empirical importance of TFP growth,

Table 11.4 European output and TFP growth, 1870–2001[a]

Country	Annual growth rate (%)			Country	Annual growth rate (%)		
	Output	Population	TFP		Output	Population	TFP
Austria	2.67	0.45	1.48	Netherlands	3.01	1.13	1.25
Belgium	2.21	0.53	1.12	Norway	3.00	0.73	1.52
Denmark	2.77	0.79	1.32	Sweden	2.57	0.57	1.34
Finland	3.17	0.82	1.57	Switzerland	2.71	0.77	1.29
France	2.47	0.34	1.42	UK	1.96	0.49	0.98
Germany	2.73	0.57	1.44	Portugal	2.81	0.64	1.45
Italy	2.70	0.55	1.43	Spain	2.80	0.69	1.41

Data source: Maddison (2003).
Note: [a] Calculations based on (11.4) using average growth rates and a labour share of two-thirds; see the main text for details.

as summarized in table 11.4 for a selection of European countries. In an influential contribution, Nicholas Kaldor (1961) listed six stylized facts of economic growth, one of which was

Steady capital/Output ratios over long periods (11.5)

In essence, Kaldor argues that over long time periods the growth rate of capital is approximately equal to the growth rate of output. Substituting that information in (11.4) and realizing that

labour share + capital share = 1
implies

TFP growth ≈ Labour share × (Output growth − Labour growth) (11.6)

where ≈ should be read as 'is approximately equal to'. We make two more short-cuts to arrive at our estimates of TFP growth in table 11.4. First, we assume that the labour force growth is equal to the population growth. Over long time horizons, the delay between population growth and entry into the labour force is less relevant. This procedure tends to over-estimate labour growth in view of the declining number of hours worked, whereas it tends to under-estimate labour growth in view of the increased participation of women in the labour force. Second, we assume that labour's share in output is two-thirds. This follows Mankiw, Romer and Weil's (1992) rule of thumb (see also Wilson and Purushothaman, 2003). In general, this rule of thumb tends to under-estimate labour's share in output. As illustrated in figure 11.1, for example, France's capital share in the period 1950–2000 was about 23.6 per cent, so that labour's share was about 86.4 per cent. Consequently, table 11.4 tends to *under-estimate* the contribution of TFP growth to output growth.

As summarized in table 11.4, TFP growth represents a very important contribution to economic growth, ranging from 0.98 per cent per year for the UK to 1.57 per cent per year for Finland. Its contribution usually 'explains' about half of a country's increase in output. In view of the above, we obviously need some understanding of the underlying forces for increases in TFP:

• *A substantial share of output growth can be attributed to TFP growth* (see box 11.3).

Box 11.3 TFP and imports of machinery and equipment in developing countries

Almost all global R&D activity is concentrated in the high-income countries. This high concentration of development of new products, materials, technologies and manufacturing techniques raises the question whether, and how, new break-throughs in one country are of importance for raising another country's TFP. One potential channel is, of course, by purchasing machinery and equipment that incorporates the technical improvements from the innovating country. Although operating new technology usually requires some type of training and learning, this is rarely up to the point where one has to understand the new technology completely. A manager using a Motorola mobile phone to do business in the back seat of a taxi, for example, does not have to understand all the new technology that has gone into making this telephone, but has merely to get used to the smaller buttons!

Figure 11.6 depicts the relationship between changes in TFP levels and the extent to which a country imports machinery and equipment from the industrial countries (twenty-one OECD countries plus Israel), where most R&D takes place. The relationship is only rather weakly positive; (see, however, box 11.4). TFP levels more than doubled in Malta, which spends a substantial share of its income on importing machinery and equipment (on average about 18 per cent in the period 1971–90). TFP levels fell by about 25 per cent in Rwanda, which spends some 3 per cent on imports of machinery and equipment. As an outlier, Singapore is not visible in figure 11.6. It spends a larger share of income on imports of machinery and equipment (38 per cent of GDP) than any other country, while its TFP level increases by 'only' 41 per cent. Considering the prominent role of Singapore as a trade hub, this could be due to re-exports of initially imported machinery and equipment. A detailed study of TFP growth in Singapore is provided by Young (1995).[a]

---

[a] Although presently not classified as such, Singapore was a developing economy in 1971.

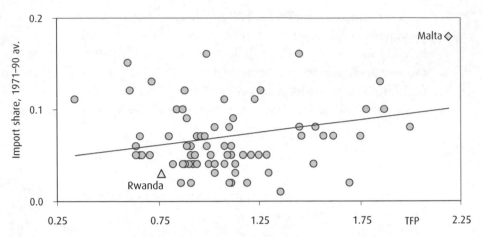

Figure 11.6 Machinery imports and TFP in developing countries; TFP (ratio 1990/1971) and import
share of machinery and equipment (relative to GDP, 1971–1990 average)
Data source: Coe, Helpman and Hoffmaister (1997).
Note: The thin line is a trend line.

11.5 Technology, knowledge, innovation and TFP growth

As outlined in sections 11.3 and 11.4, TFP is a catch-all term for any increase in output
that cannot be directly attributed to a change in the capital stock or employment.
Its contribution remains important even if we can identify many different types of
capital and many different types of labour. Although many issues play a role in TFP
growth, we need to highlight briefly three such issues:
- Endogenous R&D efforts
- Knowledge, quality and new goods
- Innovation and market power.

Endogenous R&D efforts

Robert Solow associated rising TFP levels with increases in 'technology'. But why
does technology increase? It certainly is not an automatic process – that is, it does
not suffice to assume we have exogenous technological change. Mankind cannot sit
back idly, waiting for increases in technology to raise our standard of living by 2 per
cent per year. Instead, the 'endogenous growth' revolution initiated by Paul Romer
(1986, 1990), with important contributions from Aghion and Howitt (1991) and
Grossman and Helpman (1992), emphasizes the endogenous nature of technological
progress, not only by arguing that such progress is the consequence of considerable
R&D efforts by individuals and firms investing large sums of money and time in
improving technology, but also by arguing that any economic growth model trying

to explain our standards of living will have to model R&D efforts endogenously. It is widely acknowledged that both nations and firms have a role to play in R&D efforts:

- *Nations* (governments and government agencies) play a primary role in *fundamental* R&D – that is, research which increases our understanding of the world we live in and the extent of our knowledge, without direct immediate practical applications. Obviously, given time, fundamental research may turn out to have very important practical applications, perhaps even in areas that appear to be initially not even remotely related. Who would have thought, for example, that inventing the square root of minus one would turn out to be so useful in so many different areas? Most fundamental research is done at universities and in national research institutes.

- *Firms* play a primary role in *applied* R&D – that is, research that can be directly applied in new goods and services, together with process and product development actually to bring these new goods and services to the market. Successful firms can finance their investments in applied R&D from their market sales (see below). It should be pointed out that the distinction between fundamental and applied R&D is not always crystal clear, as many large firms are active in both types of research, or in research areas very close to the cutting edge of fundamental research, while universities regularly engage in applied work.

Knowledge, quality and new goods

If successful, the R&D efforts described above increase our knowledge level and presumably ultimately our TFP level as indicated in (11.1). In this respect, 'knowledge' is a remarkable input, quite unlike the use of capital and labour in (11.1). The latter are *rival* inputs – that is, inputs that can be used only by one person at the same time. I can sit on a chair and work at my desk, and so can you. But we cannot both sit on the same chair and work at the same desk simultaneously. Desks and chairs are rival goods, as are computers, photocopiers, cars, etc. Knowledge, however, is in general a *non-rival* input. The fact that I use particular knowledge in my work, such as addition or subtraction, in no way affects your ability to apply these same principles in your work. In combination with a replication argument for rival inputs (if I double the amount of capital and labour used in production I also double the output), non-rival knowledge as an input into the production process leads to increasing returns to scale.

For newly created knowledge to be noticeably useful in output requires that it is actually applied. This could be in the shape of improvements in organization that increase productivity, such as Ford's conveyor belt for producing model T cars, or reduce the required amount of inventory, such as Toyota's JIT delivery system. It could be in the shape of increases in productivity associated with new types of capital goods, such as ASML's chip-making machines, or quality improvements of existing technology for intermediate goods, such as Intel's increased speed of its pentium processor (from 2.6 to 3.0 GHz). If measured appropriately, it could also be in the shape of newly created final goods, such as Philips' CD players, or quality improvements in existing services, such as the better sound delivered by Nokia's newest mobile phones. In short, there are many different ways in which newly created knowledge can lead to quality improvements, and to new goods and services.

Innovation and market power

Scientific and technical inventions require daring and imagination to be discovered by scientists and engineers. As emphasized by Joseph Schumpeter (1912), however, these inventions amount to nothing unless they are *adopted*, which requires as much daring and imagination from dynamic innovating entrepreneurs as the discovery itself. Schumpeter gave a pivotal role to entrepreneurs and firms to achieve technical progress and a positive rate of profit on capital. In so doing, Schumpeter distinguished between *invention* (the act of discovery by scientists and engineers) and *innovation* (the act of implementing the inventions by entrepreneurs and firms).

Innovation does not only mean bringing new goods and services to the market, but also activating new sources of supply, new forms of industrial and financial organization and new methods of production. Schumpeter emphasized that successful innovations cannot take place without firms exercising some form of *market power*. Firms and entrepreneurs incur high R&D costs. To make innovations worthwhile, they need a way to recoup these costs – that is, once they have successfully innovated they should be able to exercise some market power – for example, by patents, licences, trade marks and the like – that allows them to earn an operating profit and sell their products at a mark-up over marginal production costs. Innovations by firms and entrepreneurs cannot take place without private market power: in the light of our discussion in section 11.4, the economy would ultimately stop growing in the absence of some form of private market power.

11.6 Open economies, TFP and economic growth

In previous chapters we have emphasized the importance of open economies for increases in a country's (*per capita*) prosperity levels. In section 11.3 we argued that capital accumulation and TFP are both crucial aspects of increases in prosperity. Without endeavouring to be comprehensive, this section briefly reviews some of the main arguments for a positive association between open economies, TFP levels and economic growth.

Open economies can specialize according to comparative advantage

For a variety of reasons – related for example to technology, climate, or factor abundance – countries may have a *comparative advantage* for producing certain types of goods and services. In the absence of international trade, such goods tend to be cheap at home and expensive abroad. By granting mutual access to the markets of other countries, open economies give themselves the opportunity to benefit from international arbitrage opportunities. This allows them to gain easy access to the goods and services that they can produce only at very high cost (or not at all), in exchange for exports of goods and services that they can produce more easily.

Open economies benefit from efficiency gains created by competitive advantage

In many cases, industrial or service sectors are characterized by *increasing returns to scale*, frequently implying that a minimum efficient scale of production is required for economic viability. Under autarky, then, these sectors are either dominated by one or two firms exercising their market power, or production is not economically feasible. By letting foreign firms enter the domestic market, open economies can benefit from efficiency gains from increased competition. Alternatively, by having access to foreign markets, which effectively increases the extent of the market, firms in open economies may be able to reach the required minimum efficient scale to initiate production and sell their goods and services.

Open economies have access to various financial sources and destinations

An autarkic economy, on the one hand, by definition has only domestic savings as a source of financing for its domestic investments. This makes *intertemporal savings and investment adjustments* very difficult. Open economies, on the other hand, may also finance their investments from foreign sources, ranging from bank loans to FDI. Alternatively, open economies may allocate their savings to a range of foreign destinations, generally trying to direct them to those places where they can reap the highest yield. In both cases intertemporal savings and investment adjustments are made much easier. This is illustrated for Singapore in the period 1972–2001 in figure 11.7. Initially – that is, up to the year 1985 – Singapore had a large current account deficit (close to 20 per cent of GDP in 1974), implying large inflows of foreign funds to finance the high-yield investments in the Singapore economy. During the process of rapid development, the Singapore economy started to repay its foreign debts and was increasingly looking for suitable destinations for its domestic funds, leading to large current account surpluses from 1988 onwards (up to 24 per cent of GDP in 1998).

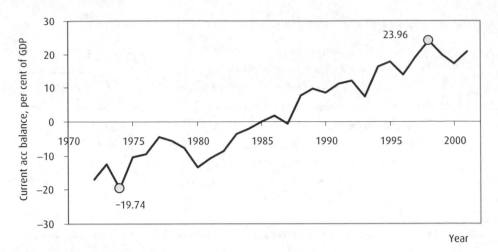

Figure 11.7 Intertemporal adjustments in Singapore, 1972–2001, current account balance, per cent of GDP
Data source: World Bank (2003).

Two caveats are in order here:

- First, in chapters 8 and 9 we saw that intertemporal savings and investment adjustments are not always as smooth as the case of Singapore suggests. The experience of many emerging economies of a sudden reversal of capital flows and the associated risk of a currency and financial crisis in recent years shows that financial openness may also have a downside.

- Second, and again keeping figure 11.2 in mind, given that the return on investment is higher for countries with a low capital/labour ratio one might expect that the excess savings of rich countries would flow to poor countries to be invested there so as to increase the capital/labour ratio and thereby economic growth in the poorer countries. In reality, however, the capital flows from rich to poor countries are quite small. This suggests that the benefits to poor countries of financial openness are not as large as theory predicts. In chapter 7, we discussed several arguments for this tension between theory and fact.

Open economies can benefit from risk sharing

The discussions above on international access encapsulate the ability of open economies to benefit from *international risk sharing*. This holds both for the ability to spread financial sources and destinations over a wide range of countries as well as the ability to have access to various foreign sources and destinations in case of catastrophe or rapidly changing circumstances. In 1958, for example, Mao Zedong introduced a new economic programme called the Great Leap Forward during a largely autarkic period in China. Although the intention was to raise industrial and agricultural production by forming large cooperatives and building 'backyard factories', the related market disruption and poor planning resulted in the production of unsaleable goods and very low food production, leading to massive starvation in the early 1960s. The deaths of millions of Chinese might have been avoided if China had had adequate access to foreign food supplies at the time. The other side of the coin is, of course, that open economies are to some extent more affected by disruptions in other countries, as explained in chapter 9.

Open economies have access to incorporated foreign knowledge

International trade enables a country to increase the range of intermediate capital goods and services in its production processes or to increase the quality level of such intermediate inputs, and thus raise the *productivity of its resources*. In essence, this allows a country to use scientific breakthroughs and knowledge created abroad incorporated in machinery and equipment imports effectively (see also box 11.2). In most cases, it is not necessary fully to comprehend the scientific knowledge used to fabricate the equipment before it can be used effectively. It is now relatively easy, for example, to use powerful portable computers with wireless internet access in most large cities around the world, without understanding the physical process underlying the creation of hyper-speed new computer chips or the sophisticated techniques of data compression associated with wireless internet access. A large share of the costs of trade restrictions may actually be associated with the costs of *not* introducing a foreign good on the domestic market – that is, by denying the economy the chance to benefit from incorporated foreign knowledge, as illustrated in sections 11.7 and 11.8.

Open economies can benefit from knowledge created abroad

In open economies, international trade and capital flows provide a means to communicate with the outside world. This stimulates *cross-border learning* in a variety of ways, concerning production methods, market conditions, product design and organizational methods. Moreover, by imitating foreign technology, a widespread phenomenon around the world, international contacts enable a country to adjust foreign technology to better suit its domestic purposes. These indirect means of benefiting from knowledge created abroad to increase domestic productivity are not available in a closed economy (which relies only on its domestic ingenuity for scientific discovery). Coe, Helpman and Hoffmaister (1997) provide empirical evidence for the importance of direct and indirect international contacts with the industrial countries (twenty-one OECD countries plus Israel) for seventy-seven developing countries regarding increases in TFP productivity (see boxes 11.2–11.4).

Box 11.4 Foreign R&D and TFP in developing countries

As argued in the main text, open economies have access to knowledge created abroad primarily through their international trade and capital flows. These channels operate both directly (through imports of machinery and equipment) and indirectly (through various forms of interaction and contacts). Here, the role of FDI and multinational firms is clearly important. The extent to which a country benefits from foreign knowledge therefore depends on the openness of the economy. This can be measured, for example, by constructing a 'Foreign R&D capital stock' on the basis of the share of income spent on the import of machinery and equipment and a country's trade pattern (using the size of trade flows with its trading partners as weights to calculate the impact of that partner's R&D stock).

Figure 11.8 illustrates the positive association between TFP growth and changes in the foreign R&D capital stock for a given period. On average, TFP grew by 10 per cent and the foreign R&D stock grew by 111 per cent. Both were higher in Taiwan, where TFP increased by 87 per cent and the foreign R&D stock increased by 133 per cent, indicating that Taiwan was able to take advantage of foreign

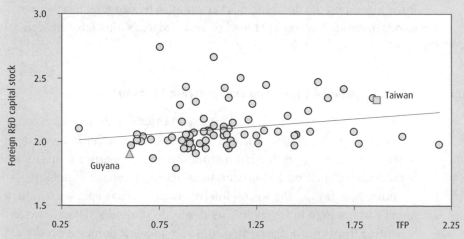

Figure 11.8 Foreign R&D capital stock and TFP in developing countries, ratio 1990/1971
Data source: Coe, Helpman and Hoffmaister (1997).
Note: The thin line is a trend line.

knowledge effectively. The opposite held for Guyana, which failed to benefit from foreign knowledge. After a detailed structural analysis based on five-year average periods, Coe, Helpman and Hoffmaister (1997, p. 148) feel confident enough to conclude that:

Even allowing for the margins of uncertainty that are inherent in any empirical work, it seems clear that developing countries derive important and substantial benefits from research and development performed in industrial countries.

11.7 An historical example: Japan[3]

In this section and section 11.8, we shall briefly discuss two examples that illustrate the usefulness, as well as the limitations, of the growth theories discussed in the first part of this chapter. The two examples are Japan (yesterday's growth miracle) and China (today's growth miracle). The growth experience of both countries suggests that, as emphasized by growth theory, variables such as capital accumulation, TFP growth or openness are indeed important, but it also indicates that this experience is very much country-specific and, in line with one of the main themes of our book, determined by history.

Take Japan first. From the seventh century, China served as the main source of inspiration for Japan, which imitated its writing, clothing, calendar and rice culture. These developments, evolving more slowly than in China, lasted until about 1550 when the old regime collapsed after a civil war that had begun in 1467. Tokugawa Ieyasu, the last of three ruthless military dictators, succeeded in unifying Japan by force and established a long-lasting peace after 1603. That marked the beginning of the Togukawa shogun era which ended with the Meiji Restoration in 1868. There were four distinct classes in a strictly hierarchical system in Japanese society (in declining order of social status): samurai (the warrior class), farmers (particularly rice), crafts-people (sword-makers, carpentry, sake-brewing, etc.) and traders (wealthy, but at the bottom of the social hierarchy as a result of the Confucian belief that merchants did not produce anything).

Portuguese sailors landed on the South Japanese island of Tanegashima in 1543, followed six years later by the Spanish Jesuit Francisco Xavier, who started a successful Christian mission in Japan, leading to about 300,000 converts. The Japanese were afraid that the Spaniards would take control of the country, as they had done

---

[3] Information sources for this section are: Maddison (2001), the International Institute of Social History website (particularly www.iisg.nl/exhibitions/japaneseprints) and the website of the Global History Consortium (particularly http://loki.stockton.edu/~gilmorew/consorti/1ceasia.htm).

in the Philippines, and started trading with the Dutch and English who had no religious/colonial ambitions. The first Dutch contacts were in 1600 when the ship *Liefde* (*Love*) entered Usuki Bay in Kyushu with twenty-four half-starved men on board,[4] the survivors of an expedition of five ships which had left Rotterdam two years earlier. For more than two centuries (from 1641 to 1854) the Dutch were the only westerners allowed to trade with Japan; their stay was confined to Deshima, a small artificial island in the harbour of Nagasaki, where they were visited by traders, translators and prostitutes. Usually two Dutch ships arrived per year, and the Japanese were impressed by Dutch knowledge and craftsmanship (see figure 11.9).

As a consequence of these crucial but still limited contacts with foreign technology and the stability of the Tokugawa era, which made it attractive to bring new land under cultivation, the Japanese economy prospered. Agricultural production rose rapidly as a result of land reclamation, new techniques, the introduction of fast-ripening seeds, double harvests and fertilizers, as well as new cultures such as cotton, sugar, tobacco, oil seeds and silk. This enabled a rapid migration from rural to urban areas, which in turn led to rising production of manufactures and services. After an initial period of about 100 years of fairly rapid growth, the disadvantages of the rigid Japanese structure and the limitations of the trading monopoly for the Dutch became apparent.[5] The economy was still growing, but not as fast as the world economy. The limited foreign contacts, not very profitable for the Dutch once the Japanese banned the export of precious metals and insisted on fixing the prices at which the Dutch could sell their goods, did not suffice to accommodate technological breakthroughs elsewhere. In 1853, an American fleet commanded by Matthew Perry forced the Japanese to enter negotiations which resulted in the treaty of Kanagawa in 1854. Other countries followed suit, leading to the end of the Dutch trade monopoly.

A new era of prosperity began with the Meiji Restoration of 1868. The power of the emperor was restored and there was institutional change in many areas to limit the gap with the Western world. A democratisation process began to erode the barriers between the social classes, and the education system was reformed after the French and later the German model. A draft was introduced and the military was reformed after the Prussian, and the navy after the British example. Japanese scientists were sent abroad to study languages and foreign technology to set up an industrial base in Japan; foreign experts taught in Japan. The transport and communication system was improved and business was supported, particularly the powerful *Zaibatsu*. International contact with the outside world – through trade, education, technology and investment – was stimulated. Again, we can see that openness was a crucial

---

[4] Seven of these twenty-four men died soon afterwards.

[5] As a vivid example: for (shogun) safety reasons very few bridges were allowed and vehicles with wheels were prohibited. Needless to say, this made transportation very costly.

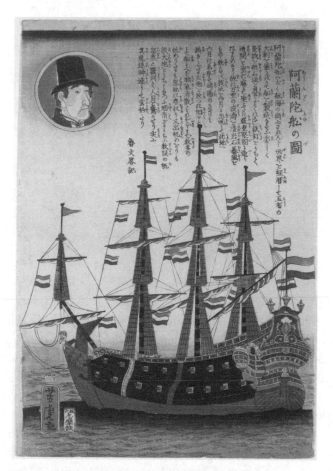

Figure 11.9 A Dutch ship in Nagasaki, 1859

Text (right to left): A long time ago the Dutch already were very skilled in navigation, and Dutch ships sailed around the world. The Dutch were very well versed in shipbuilding and of how to use ships profitably for foreign markets. They chose good materials and worked like when building up stone walls; they used iron nails and filled up cracks with tar and hemp.

In the fourth month they sailed from their country (from Indonesia, the journey from Indonesia lasted much longer) and in the sixth month they arrived here.

When (the ship arrives) in Nagasaki and the cannons, which are placed side by side, are fired, clouds appear and make the ship invisible. When the smoke has risen, the sails that had been visible in large numbers suddenly appear to have been rolled up.

Upon departure they also fire cannons, and before the smoke has risen they have already hoisted the sails, astonishing the spectators.

Their manoeuvring is truly miraculously fast and mysterious.

Oranda fune no zu, 1859. Artist, Yoshitora; Publisher, Yokohama, Shimaya, 36.5 × 25.5 cm. Inv.nr.: NEHA SC 477 nr. 31, IISG.

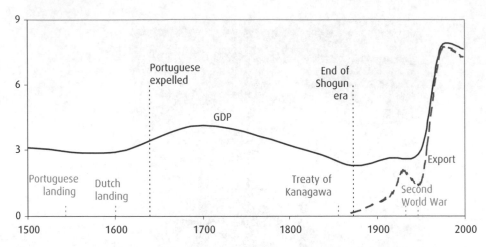

Figure 11.10 The Japanese economy, 1500–1998, GDP and exports, per cent of world total
Data source: Maddison (2001).

determinant for the surge in Japanese economic growth, and that openness was particularly important for the transfer of foreign technology.

Figure 11.10 summarizes the impact of the two main waves of international contact on the prosperity of the Japanese economy. Figure 11.10 shows Japan's GDP as a percentage of world GDP for the period 1500–1998 and Japan's exports as a percentage of world exports for the period 1870–1998. The first period of rising prosperity relative to the world economy in the seventeenth century coincided with an implementation of foreign technology and a period of peace compared with the tumultuous events in the sixteenth century. The Japanese economy was in relative (but not absolute) decline in the period 1700–1870, as its limited contact with the outside world and rigid structures precluded the economy from keeping up with developments in the world economy. This was a prime example of the ultimate decline in relative terms of an almost autarkic economy. The Meiji Restoration drastically changed Japan's focus on the world economy, leading to increased contacts, rapidly rising international trade flows, a significant organized exchange of knowledge and imitation of foreign technology. The result was a drastic increase in relative economic power as a result of a catch-up with developments in the rest of the world, but with a notable interruption in these developments during the Second World War.

The entire history of Japan since 1500 thus illustrates the importance of open economies for prosperity through the various channels discussed in section 11.6. Box 11.5 discusses how in the process of opening up to international trade in countries such as Japan, international business was already playing a part in the seventeenth century! The growth experience of Japan, as summarized by figure 11.10, is also a reminder that economic prosperity cannot be taken for granted and that from a

Box 11.5 VOC: the world's first multinational[a]

In chapter 5, we introduced multinational firms, and we shall return to the role played by these firms in the global economy in chapter 12. Box 11.5 shows that multinational firms are not a recent invention but that as far back as the seventeenth century international business was playing a role in the world economy.

The opening of the sea route to India by Vasco da Gama in 1499 established the colonial power of Portugal in the Indian Ocean. The initial motivation was the spice trade, soon followed by other commodities (figure 11.11). When Spain and Portugal united in 1580, the sea route to Asia remained closed to other European nations. In 1594, nine merchants who thought it would be very profitable to break the Portuguese spice monopoly got together in Amsterdam. Using Portuguese information and maps, they started the 'Compagnie van Verre' that sent four ships (and 240 men) to Asia, of which three ships (and eighty-seven men) returned in early 1597. The endeavour hardly made a profit, but demonstrated that the route around the Cape of Good Hope was viable.

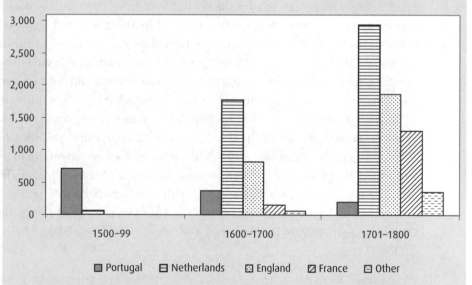

Figure 11.11 Rapid growth in Europe–Asia trade, 1500–1800, no. of ships sailing from Asia to Europe
Data source: Maddison (2001).
Note: 'Other' refers to ships of the Danish and Swedish trading companies and the Ostend company.

Eight 'compagnies' sent out sixty-five ships in fifteen fleets in the period 1595–1601. Due to strong competition, prices fell and profits were low. This prompted the merchants to join forces, after difficult negotiations initiated by Johan van Oldenbarnevelt, and form the Verenigde Oostindische Compagnie (VOC, United

East India Company) on 20 March 1602. The VOC was given monopoly rights for all Dutch trade in Asia and was the first and soon the largest worldwide dominant trading company.

The VOC was a joint-stock company: to raise its huge capital of more than 6 million guilders access was given to a wide public to purchase tradable shares at a nominal value of 3,000 guilders. There were no certificates issued; instead, shares were entered in the company's share register. Purchases and sales were also entered in this register, which made the VOC the 'first stock exchange in the world'. The subscribed capital had to be produced in four part-payments between 1603 and 1606. Proof of a 1606 payment still exists and is now known as the 'oldest share in the world' (see http://batavia.ugent.be/B@taviaE.htm for a picture and documentation).

The VOC, which had authority to establish military outposts and negotiate with foreign rulers, owned and built all its own ships, about 1,500 during a period of almost 200 years. All ships would visit the Cape of Good Hope in South Africa on their trips to and from Asia. The company flourished and soon dominated Europe–Asia trade, taking over the leading role from Portugal, as illustrated in figure 11.11. The VOC had 7,700 employees in 1625; it would grow to multi-national proportions with establishments in dozens of countries worldwide and 36,000 employees in 1750, of whom 20,000 were working in offices in Europe. The Dutch were heavily involved in pepper and spices (cloves, nutmeg and mace), but its scope for expansion was limited and the composition of trade flows changed. This is illustrated in figure 11.12 for Portuguese state trading (the *Estado da India*, with headquarters in Goa), the Dutch VOC and the English East India Company (EIC). The trade in Bengali textiles, silk, coffee and tea became more important, and the English were in a better position to deal with these changes. Together with management problems associated with the sheer size of the company, this eventually led to the downfall of the VOC. After 198 years of existence, the most significant company in the history of world trade was dissolved on 31 December 1799.

[a] Information sources for box 11.5 are: Maddison (2001), the University of Ghent (Belgium) Batavia website, http://batavia.UGent.be and the Think Quest website http://library.thinkquest.org/26488.

long-run perspective economic growth will be characterized by leaps and fallbacks. Take the post Second World War period in Japan. As figure 11.10 clearly shows, GDP growth really took off after 1945, which was a prime example of export-led growth. In a few industries (e.g. automobiles, consumer electronics) Japan gradually gained a very strong export position, first by copying and imitating (US) technology but

a

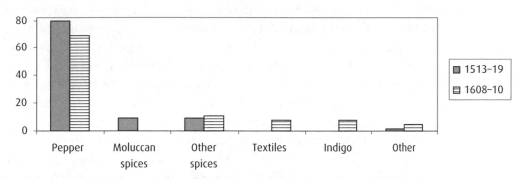

b

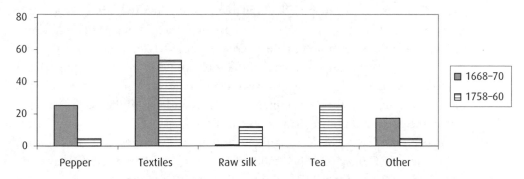

c

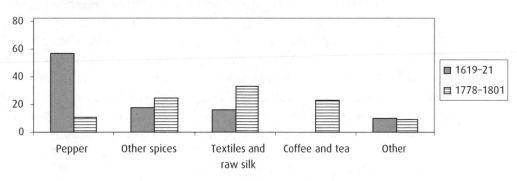

Figure 11.12 Multinational trade composition, Portugal, the Netherlands and England
Data source: Maddison (2001).

as the country moved ever closer to the *technology frontier* for their export goods, it also succeeded in developing new products on its own, and it even took the worldwide technological lead in some sectors. Japan's economic success even prompted fears in the USA and Europe that Japan would soon start to 'dominate' the world economy. In particular in the 1980s, when Japan's success story seemed to go on forever, many books and publications were published warning managers in the USA and Europe that their days were effectively over and that soon 'Japan Inc.' would rule the world economy. But things turned out differently. Japan went into a deep recession in the 1990s and it became clear that at least some of the country's alleged economic strength was more apparent than real. In fact, the 1990s were a prime example of the kind of financial crisis that was the topic of chapter 9. Around 1990, economic growth in Japan was increasingly founded on a 'bubble' in housing and share prices. With the benefit of hindsight we can say that at that time the financial sector (notably, the Japanese banks) was not doing a good job in channelling savings to the most productive investment opportunities. In our growth model, this implies that instead of the $S = I$ condition we could write $\varphi S = I$, where the parameter φ $(0 < \varphi < 1)$ signals the quality of financial intermediation. In Japan in the 1990s this parameter turned out to be significantly smaller than 1, which meant that only a relatively small part of savings ended up in financing productive investments. In terms of figure 11.2, this implied that the curved line shifted down, lowering economic growth.

11.8 A recent example: China[6]

We now turn from yesterday's talk of the town among trendwatchers of the international economy to this year's much-talked-about model: China. At present, China is the most populous nation on earth. There were about 1,262 million inhabitants in the year 2000. As indicated by some of the tools found in north and central China left behind by *homo erectus*, the history of China dates back some 1.3 million years, but we shall focus on the developments in the second half of the twentieth century (when the population more than doubled). China has been under communist rule since 1949 and has eventually managed to replace Taiwan (where the Nationalist government of Chiang Kai-Shek took refuge) in most international organizations (the UN in 1971, and the IMF and the WB in 1980), although both countries are a member of the WTO. The British occupied Hong Kong, which was barren, rocky and sparsely settled, during the Opium War (1839–42). Hong Kong returned to China in 1997, when it became a special administrative region (SAR): 'one country, two systems'.

---

[6] Adapted from van Marrewijk (2002, ch. 17) and Hinloopen and van Marrewijk (2004).

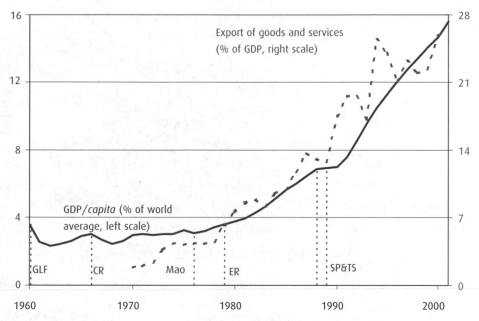

Figure 11.13   Developments in Chinese income and trade flows, 1960–2001
Data source: World Bank (2003).
Notes: GDP *per capita* measured in constant 1995 US dollars. GLF = Great Leap Forward, CR = Cultural
Revolution, Mao = Mao's death, ER = Economic Reform, SP&TS = Student protests on Tiananmen
Square.

Figure 11.13 depicts the evolution of the Chinese economy relative to the world
economy in the period 1960–2001 in terms of production (GDP *per capita* as a
percentage of the world average) and in terms of trade openness (exports of goods
and services as a percentage of Chinese GDP). It is clear that after 1980 both relative
GDP growth and export growth accelerated.

In 1958, the communist leader Mao Zedong broke with the Soviet model and
started the *Great Leap Forward*, a new economic programme with the intention of
raising industrial and agricultural production by forming large cooperatives and
building 'backyard factories'. The result, however, was market disruption and poor
planning, leading to the production of unsaleable goods and starvation during
the famines of 1960–1. The impact of the Great Leap Forward is demonstrated in
figure 11.13 as a deterioration of China's living standards from an already low 3.62
per cent in 1960 to an even lower 2.32 per cent in 1962 (a relative decline of 33 per
cent). In 1966, just when the Chinese economy had almost recovered from the consequences of the Great Leap Forward, thanks to Liu Shaoqi's and Deng Xiaoping's
pragmatic economic policies (Chinese *per capita* GNP had bounced back to 3.01 per
cent of the world average), Mao started the *Cultural Revolution*, a political attack

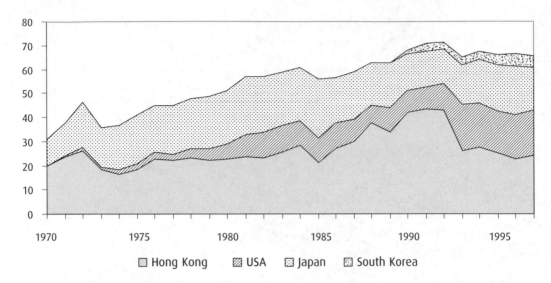

Figure 11.14 China: geographic export market composition, four highest export-markets, 1997, per cent of total

Data source: Hinloopen and van Marrewijk (2004).

on the 'pragmatists' who were trying to drag China back toward capitalism. The Red Guards (radical youth organizations) attacked party and state organizations at all levels. Again, the results were disastrous for the Chinese standard of living, which dropped to 2.42 per cent of the world average in 1968 (see figure 11.13, this time 'only' a relative decline of 20 per cent). The Chinese political situation stabilized after some years, which also raised Chinese living standards to slightly above 3 per cent of the world average. Deng Xiaoping was reinstated in 1975, but stripped of all official positions only a year later by the *Gang of Four* (Mao's wife and three associates).

Mao's death in 1976 led to the arrest of the Gang of Four and the reinstatement of Deng Xiaoping. In December 1978, the new leadership adopted *Economic Reform* policies to expand rural incentives, encourage enterprise autonomy, reduce central planning, open up to international trade flows with the outside world, establish FDI in China and pass new legal codes (figure 11.14). As already suggested by figure 11.13, the Chinese standard of living increased dramatically as a result of the open economy policies: from 3.58 per cent in 1979 to no less than 15.61 per cent in 2001 (a relative increase of 350 per cent in twenty-two years). There was a period of temporary stagnation in 1988–90 (see *Student Protests and Tiananmen Square* in figure 11.13) when party elders called for greater centralization of economic controls for fear of social instability. Eventually, this stopped the reform process only temporarily as younger, reform-minded leaders began their rise to top positions and Deng Xiaoping renewed his push for an open, market oriented economy.

The importance of Deng Xiaoping (who died in 1997) for the increase in Chinese prosperity can hardly be over-estimated. As with Japan, the opening up of China to international trade and capital flows contributed to the recent economic success story of China. But more than in the case of Japan, the catching-up of China was also significantly due to institutional changes and market oriented reforms. Given its enormous potential in terms of its labour force and other (natural) endowments, the withdrawal from the ineffective economic policies of the 1960 and 1970s almost inevitably resulted in high growth rates. In terms of figure 11.2, China is still clearly in a situation where capital accumulation stimulates growth. Ultimately, however, figure 11.2 and more recent growth theories tell us that economic growth *per capita* requires *TFP growth*: in fact, in the long run, TFP growth drives economic growth *per capita*. Here, too, China might benefit from openness. The process of fragmentation (see chapter 5) or slicing-up-the-value-chain that characterizes the current wave of globalisation means that many Western firms have moved part of their production to China and in doing so have transferred knowledge. Increasingly, these are not only the low-cost parts of the production process but also more skill-intensive activities. As with Japan, openness is and will continue to be a key factor for China. But the example of Japan is also a reminder that a country's economic fortunes can change abruptly. It is very much an open question as to whether China will be plagued by the same structural weaknesses (notably in the financial sector) as Japan. Finally, at the beginning of this chapter we showed that even with the high growth figures of recent years, convergence to US or EU GDP *per capita* levels will still take quite some time. To close this chapter and to present some counter-arguments against the idea that, as the examples of Japan and China suggest, all countries benefit from openness, box 11.6 discusses the possibility that, by participating in the world economy, developing countries suffer in terms of their terms of trade. In chapter 13 we shall return to this theme.

11.9 Conclusions

According to the growth theory that has been the subject of this chapter, in the long run 'globalization' – indicating the extent to which an economy is open to outside influences – should be beneficial to a country's economic prosperity and development. This is in line with the basic arguments on the positive relationship between openness and prosperity discussed in previous chapters. Increases in income levels take time to achieve, so it requires several decades of continued high economic growth rates for developing countries to catch-up or overtake currently developed countries.

Box 11.6 The Prebisch–Singer hypothesis

In the 1950s and 1960s many developing countries, particularly in Latin America, became dissatisfied with the existing world order. The developing countries seemed unable to catch-up with the industrial countries. One possible explanation was the *Prebisch–Singer hypothesis*, referring to a secular decline in the prices of primary products relative to those of manufactures. Because developing countries were the main exporters of primary products, they experienced a similar decline in their terms of trade. The change in the terms of trade is defined as the change in the ratio of export prices over import prices: $T = (P_x^t/P_x^0)/(P_m^t/P_m^0)$, where P_x is export price, P_m is import price, and t and 0 are time indices. If the terms of trade decline by x per cent, this implies that a given volume of exports buys only $(100 - x)$ per cent imports compared to the initial period. The first economist to link this idea to the predicament of developing countries was the Latin American economist Raoul Prebisch. The economic rationale behind his hypothesis was based on two key issues:

- *Different income elasticities*   Developed countries have a higher demand elasticity for *manufactured products* than for primary products (their needs for primary products are already satisfied). An increase in income in the developed world would increase demand more for manufactures than for primary products, resulting in relatively increasing prices on manufactured products
- *Different price elasticities*   Primary commodities satisfy basic needs. Once they are satisfied a lower price hardly increases demand. So, demand elasticities for *primary products* are lower than for manufactures. Combined with a relatively high elasticity of supply of primary products, this might result in secular declining prices of primary products. A special case emerges if the export supply price elasticity is less than unity: a fall in export prices results in a fall in export revenue. This is known as 'immiserising growth'.

Subsequent empirical research by Prebisch, Singer and others provided evidence for this idea. Prebisch's work was, however, heavily criticized. He took, for example, British exports as FOB and imports as CIF. As we saw in chapter 5, the difference between CIF and FOB prices is an indicator of *transportation costs*. The fall in transportation costs in the period under consideration in Prebisch's study is interpreted by him as a worsening of the terms of trade of developing countries. Recent research, however, has not found clear-cut evidence that developing countries face a worsening of their terms of trade. The modern literature on development issues looks at other possible explanations for the failure of developing countries to catch up.

Box 11.7 A multinational's experience and performance in transition economies[a]

In the 1990s, many former communist countries, after decades of isolation, opened up to investors from the Western world. In the future, this may happen to other, still rather closed, economies. From the perspective of an MNE, such transition economies offer opportunities and threats: *opportunities*, because of access to new markets and cheap resources; *threats*, because institutional instability may undermine revenues and increase costs. A key question is therefore how MNEs can efficiently and effectively find their way in such new territories. Luo and Peng (1999) explore this issue by focusing on the role of *international learning* by the multinational, in interaction with the nature of the host country's environment. That is, how do the extent and nature of a multinational's experience of expansion in transition economies affect the performance of a new subsidiary in a transition economy, and how is this relationship influenced by the environment's own features (i.e. complexity, dynamism and hostility)?

In their study, Luo and Peng (1999) analyse the answers by 108 multinational subsidiaries operating in China, distinguishing two types of experience. The *intensity* of experience is the number of years a multinational has been operating in China. The *diversity* of experience includes measures of the variety of products, the breadth of markets and the diversity of buyers. Both types of experience are positively associated with the subsidiary's performance in terms of returns and sales. The positive performance impact of the intensity of experience declines over time, though, which is not the case for the diversity of experience. Only diversifying activities in a host transition country seems to have a long-lasting (positive) influence on performance. In hostile environments, the positive effect on the intensity and diversity of experience is even stronger: particularly in hostile transition markets, it helps to be experienced. So, 'the acquisition of country-specific experience clearly represents a critical competitive edge for MNEs operating in transition economies' (Luo and Peng, 1999, p. 288).

[a] Based on Luo and Peng (1999).

Numerous historical examples show that it is possible for countries lagging behind in economic prosperity today to become leaders tomorrow, and vice versa.

Various factors play a role in determining a nation's rate of economic growth. For example, investments in *physical capital accumulation* (determined by the interplay between savings and investments) are an important contributing factor. The same holds for investments in *schooling and human capital accumulation*. Ultimately, however, the state of (organization) *technology*, which determines how efficiently we allocate finite means over numerous ends, appears to be the most important factor for determining our standard of living. Inventions by scientists and engineers, innovation by firms and entrepreneurs, knowledge accumulation, knowledge spillovers and market power are all crucial for bringing about improvements in technology. Open economies seem better able to achieve human and physical capital accumulation, reach a more stable economic environment and benefit from access to foreign (incorporated) knowledge. In this chapter, the case studies of Japan and China illustrate the importance of openness (see box 11.7 for more information as to how multinational firms have to find their way in countries such as Japan or China in the transition phase from a closed to an open economy). Countries opening up to the forces of globalization therefore tend to be more prosperous. In chapter 13, we shall return in more detail to the (hotly contested) hypothesis that, when all is said and done, globalization should be welcomed.

Nations and organizations

KEYWORDS

convergence	corporate governance	cooperation
divergence	cultural differences	competition
multi-domestic strategy	home country effect	game theory
global strategy	shareholder value	institutional differences
transnational strategy	national business system	entry mode choice

12.1 Convergence or divergence?

Cross-national transactions

In the 1990s, one of the authors was dean of a Dutch School of Business and Economics. In that capacity, he needed to negotiate with a German Institute about a joint Masters programme. The German delegation was wearing black suits and tasteful ties; they referred to one another as 'Herr Doktor'. From day one, they proposed a detailed contract in which all contingencies were covered. It was all very well prepared, with concepts in print emerging from their smooth suitcases. The Dutch 'uniform', on the contrary, consisted of jeans and sweaters, and the Dutch delegation used only first names. The Dutch chairman started to make jokes within five minutes, in a failed attempt to break the ice. The Dutch delegation's preparation had been no more than an informal chat of 30 minutes.

After leaving office, this dean moved from the south of the Netherlands (Maastricht) to the north (Groningen). There, too, they liked wearing jeans during official meetings; and there, too, they enjoyed making jokes within five minutes after making acquaintance. In the south, though, he and his family were invited for drinks and cakes by locals all the time. In the north, they are still waiting for the first invitation by local fellow villagers after five years. In the south, people immediately went to the pub after the Catholic mass. In the north, Protestant churchgoers engage in quiet walks on Sundays. In the south, an appointment at 11 am may start at 11:15 am, or 11:30 am, or at whatever pm time that happens to be more convenient. In the north, an appointment at 10 am kicks off at 10:00 am sharp.

Four years later, this former dean was employed by an English university, near the Scottish border. Within a month after his arrival, it became clear that the famous Anglo-Saxon flexibility was translated into an impressive bureaucracy. Each and every move by each and every member of staff was supposed to leave a paper trace to safeguard accountability and to be prepared for potential claims. Forms and guidelines were all over the place. The Dutch attitude, that rules are there to be ignored or sidelined, was received with total incomprehension. His suggestion for bypassing the obligation to engage in double-blind marking by two members of staff of each and every piece of student work by simply agreeing with all the marks of his co-marker, triggered a shock at the other side of the table.

Two regions within one and the same small country, and three neighbouring member states of the EU – they could not be more different. Within the EU, this becomes clear time and again, when government officials try to agree about policy issues. In the business world, *cross-national transactions* – let alone cross-country acquisitions – must be handled with great care. The two examples in box 12.1 tell their own tales. So, how global is the world now, really, in this era of globalization? This chapter deals with this issue. Is the world of international business and economics witnessing a process of *convergence*, where universal national and organizational templates are spreading across the globe? Or does globalization trigger *divergence*, where local identities are made even sharper? Is a 'universal' nation-state institution and way of doing business emerging, or not? Are the differences between nations persistent, or are we witnessing an overall trend towards 'Americanization'?

At the European level, similar questions can be asked. Developments in the EU may well force countries and firms to adopt the same practices, either 'voluntarily' or forced by European Directives. This holds in particular for multinationals, as they must find their way in different institutional and market settings. Up to now, we have analysed the economic differences between nations. This chapter, instead, analyses the *cultural* and *institutional* differences between nations. To illustrate the key issues, we discuss three examples, out of inevitably many more:

- First, we develop our case of the importance of inter-cultural or cross-country differences on the basis of a Prisoners' Dilemma experiment, illustrating how human economic behaviour is affected by individual background variables.
- Second, we explain how multinational or national enterprises design specific human resource management (HRM) practices, and evaluate the home or host-country effect on HRM with reference to national systems of industrial relations.
- Third, we discuss issues of corporate governance, arguing how global hypes are modified to fit with local circumstances.

Box 12.1 Cross-national culture clashes in the business world

As advisors of works councils, three of the authors are regularly involved in the analysis of the strategy changes of multinationals. More often than not, such analyses reveal important *cross-national culture clashes*. Two cases may illustrate this.

First, the British venture capitalist CVC acquired the fibres division (since then called Acordis) from the Dutch firm AKZO Nobel in the late 1990s. As a consequence, Acordis experienced a culture shock. As an Anglo-Saxon venture capitalist, CVC's objective was simply to maximize value by either selling their properties to new owners with a profit or to engage in Initial Public Offerings (IPOs). If needed, they stripped their assets, and sold lucrative bits and pieces separately, or brought them to the stock market one by one. To make the bits and pieces lucrative, high financial targets were set, which offered incentives to management to clean up their balance sheet and to polish up their income statement. All this was quite different from the relative protection offered by a large Rhineland chemical/painting/pharmaceutical conglomerate such as AKZO Nobel, whose long-run perspective was replaced by CVC's short-term pressure. Within Acordis, the ENKA Business Unit produced standard viscose fibres as an intermediate product for the textile industry. With this industry having been in decline for many decades in Western Europe, ENKA was facing tough market conditions. This triggered another culture clash, as the Dutch and German branches of ENKA were engaged in an internal battle, fighting for survival. As a result, Dutch and German managers and units experienced mutual distrust, and productive intra-ENKA cooperation was lacking. In 2002, the German ENKA top management decided to close the one remaining production facility in the Netherlands.

Second, the giant American company General Electric (GE) bought Enron's windmill activities in 2002, in the aftermath of the latter's fatal bookkeeping scandal. Part of the Enron heritage was a production facility in the Dutch town of Almelo, a plant that had been part of Enron for only a short period of time (prior to that it had been a medium-sized independent producer). In 2004, GE announced its intention to close down Almelo's production facility. In the aftermath of this announcement, Dutch managers started to complain about GE's 'American' culture, which was much more top-down than they had been used to. Financial targets were a top priority, implying an emphasis on short-run financial performance. GE imposed a massive bureaucracy on the relatively small Almelo unit, introducing extensive training programmes and piles of formal guidelines. All this happened at the expense of immediate production and product development. One of the Dutch managers indicated that he now had to spend about 60 per cent of his time accounting for whatever had to be accounted for, filling in forms and preparing reports. The 'real' American bosses were far away, not spending much time – if any – talking to their Dutch employees.

Our three examples illustrate the main issue we want to emphasize in this chapter: 'hard' (institutional) and 'soft' (cultural) issues work together to determine the divergent behaviour of multinationals from different home countries, as well as the templates of behaviour that feature in these home countries.

Multinational organizations: modes, motives and strategies

The international business literature is rather eclectic. It tends to borrow freely from a wide array of theories, producing appropriate multidisciplinary prescriptions for the issue involved. Sources of inspiration are the international economics literature (see chapters 3–5), transaction cost studies (Williamson, 1975), research on organizational learning (March, 1991) and business strategy theories (Porter, 1980). A well-known eclectic theory is Dunning's OLI framework, discussed in chapter 3, arguing that a multinational arises only when all three types of advantages (ownership, location and internalization) are realized simultaneously. If the firm cannot benefit from a firm-specific competitive edge it will be out-performed by rivals (ownership-specific advantages); if host countries do not have such advantages, the firm will stay at home (location-specific advantages); and if the firm can increase its performance by outsourcing, it will not engage in foreign activities itself (internalization-specific advantages). This set of advantages relates to the modes, motives and strategies discussed below. For instance, a factor-seeking objective will guide the selection of host countries so that location-specific advantages can be reaped. In box 12.2, we briefly discuss the related example of international outsourcing.

An early contribution to the multinational literature is Vernon (1966), who developed the *lifecycle model* of internationalization:

- In the first stage, new products are initially developed for sale in the domestic market.
- In the second stage, exports start to develop to foreign markets where consumers have the same preferences and incomes as at home. This is known as the Linder (1961) effect.
- In the third stage, as the foreign markets start to grow, the firm might establish a subsidiary abroad to produce closer to the destination markets, implying that exports to those markets will fall.
- Finally, in the fourth stage, as the foreign subsidiaries master the production process and as their costs fall with the increased scale of production, they might begin to export their products to the initial home market, creating re-import of the same product in a later stage. From the perspective of a host country, conversely, initial imports are replaced by FDI, which leads to exports in a later stage.

Box 12.2 International outsourcing

In Europe and the USA, there is a debate about one of the, allegedly, most important economic downsides of globalization: outsourcing by MNEs to low-wage countries. The argument is that this is happening to such an extent that a vulnerable segment of the labour market is being hard hit: after all, such outsourcing is associated with job losses for the lower-educated workers in the multinationals' rich home countries, and these jobs are being re-created elsewhere in the world. This clearly relates to the multinationals' *factor-seeking motive*. By outsourcing those parts of their activities that can be done more cheaply by firms in low-wage countries, they can significantly reduce their cost levels. What is relatively new is that such outsourcing is not restricted to traditional production activities, but now extends to services as well. For instance, the Bangalore area in India offers ample opportunities to outsource ICT-related activities, given the large supply of cheap but highly qualified ICT experts. Another example is call centres for English-speaking countries such as the UK and the USA, which are often located in India rather than the home country of the customers calling such centres.

The question is, of course, how important this phenomenon of international outsourcing really is, and to what extent the rich home countries are indeed negatively affected by this aspect of globalization. Amiti and Wei (2004) show that the current wave of anxiety in the West is partly justified: international outsourcing of services activities has been steadily increasing over time. For instance, the share in GDP of the USA's imports of computing and business services has approximately doubled each decade since 1983. However, this is only part of the story. Taking a full account of what is happening in the area, international services outsourcing leads to a radically different conclusion, for two reasons:

- First, the *absolute* levels of services outsourcing are still very low indeed. In the USA, for example, they only amounted to 0.4 per cent of GDP in 2003.
- Second, the USA is exporting such services much more than it is importing them! Hence, in the aggregate, the positive trade balance in this area is job-*creating* rather than job-destroying.

This example, again, shows that in the heated debate about globalization myths should be carefully distinguished from the actual facts.

Related to the above is the issue of foreign *entry modes* (see table 12.1 for an overview), the analysis of which falls into three main categories (Dunning, 1993). That is, a multinational must:

- Choose between *non-equity* (e.g. exporting, licensing, or franchising) and *equity* (e.g. greenfield investments, acquisitions, or alliances) modes of entry.

Table 12.1 Overview of multinational organizations'
typologies

Modes[a]	Motives[a]	Strategies[a]
Exporting	Risk-spreading	Multi-domestic
Licensing	Factor-seeking	Global
Franchising	(vertical)	Transnational
Alliances	Market-seeking	
Greenfields	(horizontal)	
Acquisitions		

Note: [a]Decisions on modes, motives and strategies are
based on transaction cost theory, international trade
theory and strategic management theory, respectively.

- Investigate the desired *level of ownership* in the case of equity entry – for instance, the choice between a wholly-owned and partially-owned (e.g. JV) foreign entity.
- Analyse the pros and cons of buying an existing foreign entity or establishing a foreign operation from scratch, which is the choice between an *acquisition* and a *greenfield* type of investment.

In all cases, the answer depends on balancing the benefits and costs of each entry mode, which is related to all kinds of organizational and environmental contingencies. The alliance mode, for instance, is associated with advantages in the area of local knowledge and risk reduction, but comes with disadvantages in the domain of knowledge appropriation and shared control. Transaction cost theory plays a prominent role in entry mode research (see, e.g., Caves and Mehra, 1986; Hennart and Park, 1993; and Brouthers and Brouthers, 2000).

The international business literature emphasizes the role of the *motives* (see table 12.1 for an overview) underlying multinational behaviour, including FDI strategies and entry mode choices. Motivations, taking the ultimate objective of profit maximization for granted, can be classified into at least three general categories: risk-spreading, market-seeking and factor-seeking (see Root, 1977, 1994). A traditional motive is risk-spreading, by allocating activities over a diversified portfolio of countries. Market-seeking (or horizontal) FDI follows demand, penetrating foreign markets with a promising sales potential. Factor-seeking (or vertical) FDI includes multinational behaviour aimed at gaining access to raw materials and low-cost locations (see chapter 5 for a discussion of horizontal and vertical FDI).

The most popular classification of multinationals in the international business literature is probably Bartlett and Ghoshal's (1989) typology of *strategic* postures: global, multi-domestic and transnational (again, see table 12.1):

- *Global* companies promote a convergence of consumers' preferences and strive to maximize *standardization of production*, which makes centralization and integration profitable. They benefit from home-country specific advantages and export these abroad by creating 'replicas of the parent company.' Strategic decisions on marketing and production are tunnelled down to the subsidiaries, so that the latter have not much discretion to adapt to local circumstances. Global companies possess firm-specific advantages that are mostly characterized by home-country specificities that do not need to be complemented by the exploration of host-country advantages. These firm-specific advantages are therefore not bound to a particular host location and are efficiently transferable to foreign locations, thus overcoming any natural or unnatural market imperfections in foreign markets.
- *Multi-domestic* firms, by contrast, develop strategies for *national responsiveness*. Due to significant competitive differences between countries, the multi-domestic strategy is determined by cultural, political and social national characteristics. The primary objective is the adaptation of marketing and production strategies to specific local customer needs and government requirements. Products and policies conform to different local demands and the investor's activities are usually tied to the buyer's location, which creates incentives for the development of competitive advantages that are bound to a particular location. Responsiveness to different national markets requires the accumulation of local country-specific knowledge, and the latter's efficient integration into local business networks.
- *Transnational* enterprises (TNEs) finally, operate a *balanced combination of the multi-domestic and global strategies*. Although activities and resources may differ from country to country (decentralization), particular activities are coordinated and executed globally (centralization). For example, a TNE might decide to carry out R&D centrally to reap economies of scale and scope, but to organize tailor-made advertising campaigns locally to guarantee a 'fit' with national circumstances. In their pure form, transnational companies are 'denationalized' (Ohmae, 1995), without any clear dominance by a national origin. They do whatever is thought to be best, irrespective of national origin.

The suggestion in the literature is that the current globalization process comes with an increasing dominance of the 'footloose' multinational, opting for equity modes of foreign entry in the context of a dual-motive (factor and market-seeking) transnational strategy. Box 12.3 reports statistics that, at first glance, seem to support this view. This chapter, however, critically evaluates to what extent such 'globalized' universalism is indeed justified, or rather whether 'nationalized' specificities are in fact still dominant.

Box 12.3 The case for dominant transnationality

A well-known index in the transnationality debate is produced by UNCTAD in cooperation with Erasmus University in Rotterdam. This 'transnationality index' is equal to the unweighted average of three firm-level ratios: foreign assets/total assets, foreign sales/total sales and foreign employment/total employment. The higher this index, the less 'rooted' a multinational is in its home country. An index close to 100 per cent would indicate a really 'footloose' multinational. Table 12.2 lists the top ten transnationals ranked according to this index in 2003.

Table 12.2 Top ten non-financial multinationals, 2003, ranked according to TNI

Rank	Corporation	Home country	Industry	TNI[a]
1	NTL Inc	USA	Telecommunications	99.1
2	Thomson Corp.	Canada	Media	97.9
3	Holcim AG	Switzerland	Construction materials	95.5
4	CRH Plc	Ireland	Lumber and other building materials	94.7
5	ABB	Switzerland	Machinery and equipment	94.5
6	Roche Group	Switzerland	Pharmaceuticals	91.0
7	Interbrew SA	Belgium	Beverages	90.8
8	Publicis Groupe SA	France	Business services	90.7
9	News Corporation	Australia	Media	90.1
10	Philips Electronics	Netherlands	Electrical and electronic equipment	86.8

Source: UNCTAD (2004).
Note: [a] TNI = TransNationality Index.

At least three arguments can be put forward to downplay the claim that the degree of transnationality is high:

- First, as could be expected, there is a clear negative correlation between transnationality and country size: after all, firms from relatively small countries operate from a tiny domestic market; the world's largest firm (General Electric, USA) has a transnationality index of only 40.6 per cent. With the exception of one American and one French firm, the top ten transnationals all originate from small countries.
- Second, the transnationality index of the top 100 multinationals increased only gradually from 51 per cent in 1990 to 57 per cent in 2003; this is not very impressive, particularly in view of the negative correlation between transnationality and country size.
- Third, having a dominant foreign presence does not say anything about the transnational nature of the firm's *strategic* posture, as we shall argue extensively in the main text.

Table 12.3 Firm I–Firm II interaction pay-off matrix (in 1,000 euro)

			Firm II price
(Firm I pay-off, Firm II pay-off)		Low (P_{II}^L)	High (P_{II}^H)
Firm I price	Low (P_I^L)	(−30, −30); cell 1	(600, −600); cell 2
	High (P_I^H)	(−600, 600); cell 3	(300, 300); cell 4

12.2 Game theory: basics and terminology

As a stepping stone for further discussion, we briefly elaborate on some key concepts in game theory (see also chapters 3–5, 8). In general, game theory is the conceptual and mathematical toolkit for the study of *interaction among parties* (or players) with *conflicting interest* (see Morgenstern and von Neumann, 1944). This makes it a natural candidate for the analysis of (international) competition-related issues, both conceptually (e.g. Brandenburger and Nalebuff, 1996) and mathematically (e.g. Gibbons, 1992). We focus on simple games with two organizations that do not explicitly communicate in any way (bargaining does not occur) to review a number of core game-theoretic concepts.

A key concept in game theory is the *Nash equilibrium*, named after Nobel laureate John Nash (1950), a mathematician well known from the movie 'A Beautiful Mind'. A Nash equilibrium is defined (in the two-player context) as the pair of strategies from which neither player deviates because a unilateral change of strategy does not produce a pay-off improvement. That is, each player i's strategy x is her best reply to the rival j's strategy y in the sense that x maximizes i's pay-off, given j's strategy y (where $i, j = 1, 2$ and $i \neq j$). The Nash equilibrium concept can be illustrated using table 12.3, portraying a *Prisoner's Dilemma* in a Bertrand duopoly game.[1]

Firms *I* and *II* operate in the same market. The firms are identical, offering the same homogeneous product and being equally efficient, with neither firm facing a binding capacity constraint. Both firms can choose from two price strategies: setting a low price P^L or a high price P^H. Consumers select their preferred product on the basis of price only and profits depend on the pair of price strategies chosen. Taking, for the time being, the standard economics interpretation of the firm as a *homo economicus* for granted, the assumption is that both firms seek to maximize expected individual profit. The cells in table 12.3 indicate the (negative or positive) profit combinations for firms *I* and *II*. In cell 2, for example, firm *I* offers a lower

---

[1] See any industrial organization (IO) textbook. IO has been heavily dominated by game theory since the 1980s (Tirole, 1988). However, its roots date back to the nineteenth century, when the French economists Bertrand and Cournot applied a game-theoretic logic *avant la lettre*. Recall that Bertrand games are in prices and their Cournot counterparts in quantities (see chapter 3).

price than firm *II*, so that customers prefer to buy from the cheaper firm *I* (which achieves a profit of €600,000, compared to a loss of €600,000 for firm II).

Both firms select their price strategies simultaneously, so that their expected individual profit is maximized. Low prices are associated with *competitive* behaviour and high prices with *cooperative* (in anti-trust jargon: collusive) behaviour. Following the definition provided above, only cell 1 is a Nash equilibrium as neither firm can increase profits by unilaterally moving from a low to a high price. All other cases are associated with instability, as either firm can increase profits by unilaterally changing price. Table 12.3 reflects a Prisoners' Dilemma because the Nash equilibrium that follows from individual profit-maximizing behaviour produces an outcome that minimizes market-level (or collective) profitability: an aggregate loss of – €60,000. Only cell 4 – the (high-price, high-price) outcome – reflects mutually cooperative behaviour, maximizing industry-level profitability: an aggregate profit of €600,000. However, this is not a Nash equilibrium.

Played only once, table 12.3 reflects a so-called *one-shot game*. If a series of similar games is played, a *supergame* emerges, which can be associated with a known (*finite* horizon) or with an uncertain or unknown (*infinite* horizon) series of games. In a finite supergame of known length *t*, the tool of *backward induction* can be applied. That is, the series of Nash equilibria can be found by first determining the Nash equilibrium that emerges in the end game *t*. In table 12.3, this is the (low-price, low-price) outcome. Subsequently, given the last game's Nash equilibrium, the Nash equilibrium for game $t - 1$ can be determined (which again is cell 1 in which both firms opt for the low price). Given the Nash equilibria of games *t* and $t - 1$, the Nash equilibrium in game $t - 2$ is mutual low-price-setting – and so on. This backward-induction logic implies that the finite supergame of Table 12.3 is associated with an equilibrium of mutual low pricing throughout. The backward-induction notion is applicable to *sequential* games, too. In a finite sequential game, a series of different subgames rather than similar games is played. For example, subgame 1 may involve an advertising or R&D decision, followed by the pricing subgame of table 12.3. Backward-induction logic then produces a consistent series of subgame Nash equilibria known as *subgame perfectness*.

In infinite horizon games (super or sequential ones), the backward-induction principle cannot be used since there is no known end game *t* to start the rolling-back argument. In a setting like this, the so-called *Folk Theorem* emphasizes the key role of the discount rate (see Tirole, 1988, pp. 245–7). Intuitively, the argument runs as follows. The discount rate measures a player's *time patience*. A high discount rate reflects an impatient player who prefers to get paid now rather than tomorrow. A low discount rate reflects a more patient player who more easily substitutes future for current payments. In the context of an infinite supergame based on table 12.3, a high discount rate motivates the player to opt for low prices, because this maximizes the

Table 12.4 Reciprocal dumping game

(Michelin pay-off, Goodyear pay-off)		Goodyear strategy	
		Dumping	No dumping
Michelin strategy	Dumping	$(D - C, D - C)$ Reciprocal dumping	$(D - C + P, p - c)$ One-sided dumping
	No dumping	$(p - c, D - C + P)$ One-sided dumping	$(P + p - c, P + p - c)$ Tacit collusion

immediate likelihood of reaping the high profit that comes with unilateral under-bidding, which suits well her impatience.

Reciprocal dumping is an example of a Prisoners' Dilemma, as explored by Brander and Krugman (1983). Take a Bertrand duopoly, illustrated by the Goodyear–Michelin example analysed in van Witteloostuijn (1993). Assume that initially both tyre producers have a market share of 90 per cent in their home market (America and Europe, respectively) and a 10 per cent share in their rival's market. In both countries, a 'peaceful' cartel-like arrangement guarantees high prices and profits, implying tacit collusion between the firms. For simplicity, assume that both markets are equal in size and (potential) profitability. Shipping tyres across the Atlantic costs c. In the 'cartel' case, let P denote profitability for the domestic firm and $p - c$ profitability for the foreign rival. Suppose that either Goodyear or Michelin decides to launch a dumping strategy in the rival's home market, defined here as a strategy of under-pricing the rival in his home market.[2] If the rival decides not to respond, all customers purchase from the cheapest firm, leading to an increase in the dumping firm's profits to $D - C > p - c$ in the export market, where C is the cost of shipping a larger number of tyres across the ocean. The domestic firm does not produce and sell anything at home, leaving only an export profit $p - c$. Alternatively, the domestic firm might decide to retaliate by launching a dumping strategy in the foreign market.[3] Table 12.4 provides the four possible pay-off combinations.

Clearly, at the aggregate level, the tacit collusion case minimizes transportation costs to $2c$, while the reciprocal dumping outcome maximizes transportation costs to $2C$. In general, the low-price dumping profit in the export market is lower than the high-price tacit collusion profitability in the home market: $D - C < P$. In conjunction with $D - C > p - C$, table 12.4 is therefore a Prisoners' Dilemma with reciprocal dumping as the unique Nash equilibrium. Changing the rules of the game

---

[2] Legally, 'dumping' is defined as below-cost pricing. To assess whether a firm has applied a dumping strategy or not, it is necessary to calculate this cost level, which is far from easy (see chapter 2).

[3] For simplicity, we ignore alternative strategies and complications, such as home market retaliation, scale economies, reputation spillovers and efficiency differences. The key message is how game theory can be applied to issues of multinational strategy-making.

may trigger a way out of this dilemma, such as a supergame infinite repetition with low discount rates or multi-market retaliation with credible 'hostage' market shares in the rival's home market (see Pinto, 1986; van Wegberg and van Witteloostuijn, 1992).

12.3 An experiment

To illustrate how inter-cultural differences may influence individual behaviour, we briefly discuss an experiment with table 12.3's Bertrand duopoly Prisoners' Dilemma (see Boone, de Brabander and van Witteloostuijn, 1999). A key issue is the fact that the tacit collusion equilibrium in table 12.3 (cell 4) can be reached if both players decide that the other party can be trusted to play the high price, reaching the highest collective pay-off.[4] Five versions of the Bertrand oligopoly game were played in three Experiments *A*, *B* and *C*, with 42, 182 and 92 Business and Economics students from two Dutch universities. The 92 students in Experiment *C* were a subset of the students in Experiment *B*. The appendix to this chapter (pp. 370–2) describes the experiments in greater detail. A summary of each game's structure is given below:

- *Game I*: one-shot Bertrand duopoly game with incomplete information
- *Game II*: one-shot Bertrand duopoly game with complete information on the rival's past behaviour
- *Game III*: repeated Bertrand duopoly game with complete information and finite horizon
- *Game IV*: repeated Bertrand duopoly game with complete information and infinite (an uncertain random) final period
- *Game V*: repeated Bertrand duopoly game with complete information, finite horizon and increasing pay-offs.

The degree of cooperation or trustworthiness is measured as the average number of high-price choices across the experiment's participants. Figure 12.1 illustrates the results of the various experiments. We first compare the benchmark one-shot versus the infinite horizon games – that is, Games I and IV, respectively. The other games will be discussed later in this section. In Experiments *A* and *C*, there is a clear jump in average trustworthiness from the one-shot to the infinite horizon game, as predicted by the Folk Theorem. However, the rules of the game alone cannot explain all that is going on in the experiments, as is clearly illustrated by the unexpected – at least, from

---

[4] These predictions are analysed in experimental economics, a branch of applied research that has boomed since the 1980s and for which Vernon Smith and Daniel Kahneman received the Nobel Prize in 2002. A stylized fact of the accumulated experimental evidence is that *individual* behaviour often deviates from *homo economicus* (see p. 347), but that the rules of the game lead to outcomes in the direction predicted by modern game theory at the *aggregate* (market) level (see Smith, 2000).

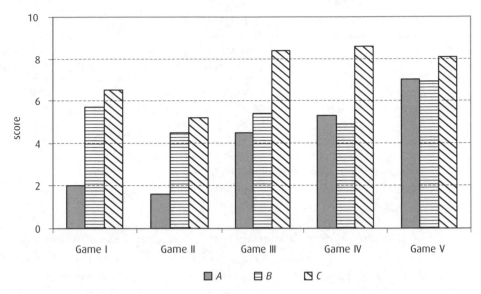

Figure 12.1 Results from three experiments *A, B,* and *C*
Note: 'Trustworthiness' is measured as the average number of high prices (0–12), normalized to a 0–12 scale for the infinite horizon Game IV.

a game-theoretic perspective – decrease in average trustworthiness in Experiment *B*. Another case in point is the fact that the game-theoretic Nash equilibrium outcome of zero high prices (competitive or untrustworthy behaviour throughout) almost never occurs in the one-shot (I and II) and finite horizon (III and V) games.

These simple experiments illustrate a general pattern in experimental economics: the rules of the game matter in ways suggested by formal game theory, albeit imperfectly so. The Folk Theorem, for example, underscores the importance of the discount rate, where a lower rate induces more patience and stimulates trustworthiness. So, a culture of short-termism, such as reflected in US shareholder value capitalism (see below), is bound to produce untrustworthy behaviour, whereas the reverse holds true in cultures of long-termism, such as in Asian types of capitalism, where trustworthy strategies are likely to dominate (see Gordon, 1996). Changes in the rules of the game cannot explain individual differences. Although all players are confronted with identical (changes in the) rules of the game, the variety of behavioural patterns is huge. In Experiment A, for example, the standard deviation in the number of high prices is 3.2 (Game I), 3.5 (Game II), 4.2 (Game III), 4.4 (Game IV) and 4.5 (Game V). As the rules of the game cannot explain such variance, we need a theory that takes individual differences into account.

Table 12.5 therefore illustrates the influence of cultural or ethnic background by comparing the outcome from the Dutch experiment *A* with similar American experiments performed by Cox, Lobel and McLeod (1991), as discussed by Boone and van

Table 12.5 Information, culture and trustworthiness[a]

	Dutch	Anglo-Americans	Hispanic Americans	Asian Americans	African Americans
No feedback	2.1	3.6	4.7	4.9	5.0
Cooperation feedback	1.7	3.1	5.8	7.6	5.3
No. of participants	40	75	19	25	17

Sources: adapted from Boone and van Witteloostuijn (1999, p. 342). The American studies are based on Cox, Lobel and McLeod (1991).
Note: [a] The table reports the degree of trustworthiness.

Witteloostuijn (1999). The *no feedback* case resembles the incomplete information one-shot Game I. Clearly, players with a background from the collectivist cultures of Africa, Asia and Latin America are much more inclined to engage in trustworthy behaviour (cooperative choices) than those from individualist cultures in Europe and North America. In the *cooperation feedback* or complete information scenario, the players were informed that their counterpart had consistently chosen to set a high price in the previous Game I. In this case, the impact of cultural background is even more striking, as players from collectivist cultures *increase* while their counterparts from individualist cultures *decrease* the number of cooperative choices. Hence, 'soft' cultural issues help to explain the behaviour of individual players, next to and on top of the 'hard' rules of the game. Box 12.4 illustrates how the two may work together to produce country-specific competitive templates. We shall argue below in more detail, using two examples, that this holds for real-world nations and organizations as well.

12.4 HRM and cultural diversity

Probably the number one aspect of any international organization where issues of inter-cultural differences are involved is how employees are being treated. At a country level, this relates to issues of *industrial relations*. At the firm level, this pertains to *HRM*. Industrial relations have to do with the way in which the interaction between employees (or labour) and employers (or capital) is organized. Industrial relations differ wildly from country to country, as the contrast between Anglo-Saxon and Continental European industrial relations illustrates (see Rogers and Streeck, 1995). In Anglo-Saxon societies, the capital/labour *conflict* is emphasized, whereas in Continental European countries the focus is on arrangements stimulating employee/employer *cooperation*. In Germany, for example, the obligation to install

Box 12.4 'Hard' institutions and 'soft' cultures: competition or cooperation?

The pay-off structure in table 12.3 shifts in favour of cooperative or collusive Nash equilibria if the profit from opportunism decreases or the benefit from cooperation increases. Governmental regulation, for example, may stimulate competition (e.g. US-style anti-trust law) or promote cooperation (e.g. EU-style innovation programmes: see van Wegberg, van Witteloostuijn and Roscam Abbing, 1994). From an intra-country perspective, this suggests what we should expect – an emphasis on competition or cooperation. It is no wonder, for example, that East Asian countries that emphasize collectivist values, such as Japan and Korea, have produced strikingly cooperative institutional business arrangements, namely the *Keiretsu* and *Chaebol*, respectively. Such arrangements of formally independent organizations are closely tied together through cross-shareholdings, inter-organizational alliances, interlocking directorates and all kinds of informal coordination arrangements.

Similarly, Arrighetti, Bachmann and Deakin (1997) show how such nation-level collectivist versus individualist national cultures are reflected in the ways in which legal contracts are used to back up the formation of inter-organizational relationships in, for example, Germany and Great Britain: in Germany, detailed contracts are an *ex ante* signal of trust; in Great Britain, such contracts are an *ex post* safeguard against opportunistic behaviour. From an inter-country perspective, on the other hand, the issue of international alliances will raise additional issues. From psychology's in-group versus out-group literature, for example, it can be expected that cross-country alliances will face much more difficulty in the area of trust development and maintenance (see Bornstein and Ben-Yossef, 1994). This line of reasoning is well embedded in the international business literature, where the impact of 'cultural distance' is included in the argument as a matter of routine (see Barkema and Vermeulen, 1997). The main argument is that cross-cultural transactions, such as acquisitions and alliances, are less likely to turn into a success, the larger the cultural distance between the partners involved.

works councils at the firm level is formally regulated in national legislation, implying an institutionalized employee participation system (called *Mitbestimmung*, or code-termination). At the macro level, German labour unions and employer associations negotiate about formal agreements over a wide array of labour-related issues. In the USA, in contrast, national industrial relations regulation is very weak. In effect, firms even tend to be proud if they are 'union-free' – that is, without a single employee with a union membership card.

Such nation-level institutional differences have an impact upon the way in which individual firms 'treat' their personnel (see also box 12.1). Gooderham, Nordhaug and Ringdal (1999), for example, report significant and systematic cross-country heterogeneity of HRM practices.[5] Collaborative (or cooperative) practices emphasize the 'soft' model of HRM, with a humanistic focus on codetermination. Calculative (or conflict) practices reflect a 'hard' perception of HRM, focusing on the autocratic treatment of employees. Relatively expensive 'collaborative' HRM practices dominate in Denmark, Germany and Norway. Their relatively cheap 'calculative' counterparts are typical in France, Spain and the UK. Clearly, the type of HRM model adopted by a multinational is heavily influenced by a home-country effect. A German multinational tends to apply works council-type arrangements throughout the organization, whereas an American multinational often prefers to bypass domestic 'codetermination'-type behaviour to the extent this is legally possible.[6]

An interesting question from the perspective of multinationals is to what extent domestic HRM practices can be transferred abroad – i.e. implementing them in foreign subsidiaries. Beechler and Yang (1994), for example, report evidence from an in-depth multi-case study of the transfer of Japanese-style HRM practices to American subsidiaries and observe that: 'Japanese organizations put a primary focus on human resource . . . [which] translates into three principal human resource management practices: (1) an internal labour market; (2) a company philosophy that expresses concerns for employee needs; and (3) emphasis on cooperation and teamwork in a unique company environment' (1994, p. 469). They conclude that the international transfer of HRM practices is constrained by the local environment. For example, quite a few Japanese multinationals were forced by US legislation to adopt American-style HRM practices, emphasizing functional specialization, job classification and career development. The result is therefore often a hybrid HRM system, characterized by a unique mixture of home- and host-country practices.

National culture and multinational behaviour

The classic contribution to the national culture literature is Hofstede (1980, 1991, 2003), who developed four dimensions of national culture on the basis of a large worldwide questionnaire sent to employees of IBM. Hofstede's four dimensions are:

- *Power distance* High power distance implies that hierarchy matters a lot and that employees rely largely on their bosses. With small power distance, consultation

---

[5] The HRM concept as such is Anglo-Saxon. The idea of treating employees as 'resources', just like any other factor of production, is alien to many cultures outside the Anglo-Saxon world.

[6] Obviously, there is intra-country and inter-industry variety as well. Here, we focus on 'averages'.

Table 12.6 International cultural diversity in four dimensions, index scores, 1994[a]

Highest three			
Mexico 81	Belgium 94	USA 91	Japan 95
India 77	Japan 92	Australia 90	Austria 79
Singapore 74	France 86	UK 89	Italy 70
:	:	:	:
Power distance	*Uncertainty avoidance*	*Individualism*	*Masculinity*
:	:	:	:
Denmark 18	Greece 11	Singapore 20	Netherlands 15
Israel 13	Portugal 10	S. Korea 18	Norway 8
Austria 11	Singapore 8	Pakistan 14	Sweden 5
Lowest three			

Source: Hofstede (2003).
Note: [a] Ranking for a subset of thirty countries: Argentina, Australia, Austria, Belgium, Brazil, Canada, Denmark, Finland, France, Germany, Greece, Hong Kong, India, Ireland, Israel, Italy, Japan, Mexico, Netherlands, New Zealand, Norway, Pakistan, Portugal, Singapore, S. Korea, Spain, Sweden, Switzerland, UK and USA.

gains importance and subordinates are more willing to oppose their bosses. Employees are reluctant to accept their supervisor just for the sake of her position.

- *Uncertainty avoidance*   If uncertainty avoidance is weak, people tend to react positively to change, enjoy challenges, emphasize opportunities rather than threats and do not avoid risky adventures. If uncertainty avoidance is strong, people are more likely to avoid ambiguity and risk, thus relying more on the authorities to solve problems and revealing a preference for bureaucracies and routines.
- *Individualism* (versus collectivism)   In individualist societies, people tend to put immediate family and self-interest first and society second.[7] Self-respect and independence are dominant forces, as is a lack of tolerance for opposing viewpoints. In collectivist cultures, people put the group first and group harmony is important, much more so than individual freedom or success.
- *Masculinity* (versus femininity)   Feminine cultures are associated with overlap in gender roles. Men and women are both concerned with tenderness and the quality of life. In masculine societies, traditional macho-type values dominate, implying that men are in charge, revealing more assertive and acquisitive behaviour.

This set of four dimensions and their per-country scores has been used extensively in international business research. Table 12.6 shows the three highest- and lowest-scoring countries on each dimension for a subgroup of thirty countries (complete

[7] As former British Prime Minister Margaret Thatcher said: 'there is no such thing as society'.

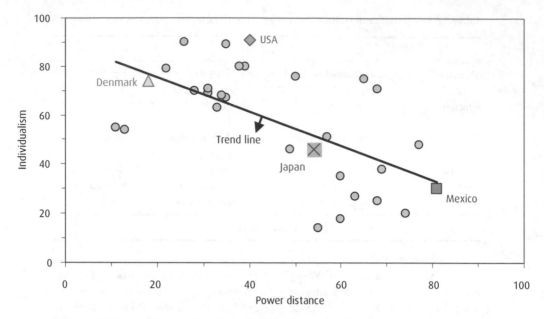

Figure 12.2 Correlation in cultural characteristics
Data source: Hofstede (2003). Note: The figure shows the thirty countries listed in table 12.6.

scores are provided on the website). Cultural variety is large: India is very different from the USA, as is France from Germany. For instance, India scores much higher on power distance than the USA, and France much higher on masculinity than Germany. 'Triangle differences' dominate much of the debate. Indeed, Japan's culture is very different from that of Germany or the USA, scoring high on uncertainty avoidance and masculinity and relatively low on individualism. The forces of globalization have not (yet?) changed these very divergent cultural differences. As figure 12.2 illustrates, cultural characteristics tend to be correlated: countries scoring high on individualism, for example, tend to score low on power distance, and vice versa (see Denmark and Mexico in figure 12.2). Similarly, countries scoring high on masculinity also tend to score high on uncertainty avoidance.

There is a large literature arguing that national culture, next to and in interaction with the institutional context, heavily influences the way organizations behave. For example, Noordin, Williams and Zimmer (2002) tested the hypothesis that career commitment is higher in individualist than in collectivist cultures, using survey data from a sample of 120 Australian and 203 Malaysian managers in 1997. As a key aspect of commitment, *career resilience* is defined as the extent to which a manager is independent from organizations. That is, a career resilient manager will move to another organization if she thinks that this will foster her career. This type of behaviour is expected to be more pronounced in individualist cultures, while in collectivist cultures managers are expected to rely more on the organization they currently work for. Indeed, the Malaysian managers turn out to score significantly lower on career resilience than their Australian counterparts. According to Hofstede (2003), Australia scores much higher on individualism than Malaysia, with scores of 90 (rank 2) and 26 (rank 36), respectively. Box 12.5 illustrates the importance of national culture in relation to the choice of foreign entry mode for a multinational.

The home-country effect on multinational behaviour

From an international business perspective, the key argument is that national cultural roots partly determine a multinational's behaviour. This is true not only for HRM-related issues, but also for more distant 'non-human' aspects of multinationals (see p. 352). This implies that a multinational must take account of the implications of the different cultures in which it operates. After all, as illustrated throughout this chapter, the domestic culture constrains the way in which marketing strategies will be effective, capital can be attracted, and employees have to be treated. Brouthers, Werner and Matulich (2000), for instance, suggest three triad-based 'regional stereotypes' of the price/quality strategies of multinationals, indicating a powerful home-country effect on a key aspect of strategy. This argument runs counter to the globalization rhetoric that the TNE is taking over the world. Brouthers, Werner and Matulich (2000) find evidence for their three stereotypes based on data from 1982 to 1995 for *Fortune 500* firms from four industries – consumer electronics, automobiles, tyres and beverages:

- *American* multinationals tend to focus on lower quality and lower price.
- *European* multinationals tend to pursue a strategy of high quality and high price.
- *Japanese* multinationals tend to focus on a superior-value strategy (higher value and lower price).

Another illustrative study is Neelankavil, Mathur and Zhang (2000). They investigate the differences across American, Chinese, Indian and Philippine managers concerning the perceived determinants of managerial performance. In this study, the potential determinants of managerial performance are (a) planning and decision-making ability, (b) self-confidence and charisma, (c) educational achievements, (d) communication skills, (e) past experience and (f) leadership ability. Clearly, *inter-country differences* are substantial. For instance, educational achievements are considered to be the number one determinant of managerial performance in the Philippines, but is in the bottom position in the USA. In line with what could be expected from known cultural and institutional differences, the two extreme cases are China and the USA, which differ substantially along all dimensions except planning and decision-making ability. For example, Chinese managers consider self-confidence

Box 12.5 Culture distance and foreign entry mode[a]

The impact of cultural diversity or distance on multinational behaviour has been extensively studied in international business. Many works, for example, include cultural distance as one of the explanatory variables when modelling a multinational's foreign entry mode choice, such as the entry of Western multinationals into transition economies such as those in the CEE countries. Cultural distance and its effect on the post-acquisition learning within and integration of CEE enterprises is a complex matter. On the one hand, the system of controlled ideology, a CPE, a hierarchical society and the restrictions and rigidities of the CEE countries cannot yet be fully abandoned and replaced with West European pluralism, market decentralization and democracy after just twelve years of transition. On the other hand, the CEE countries (the Czech Republic, Hungary, Poland, Slovakia and Slovenia) and the Baltic nations (Estonia, Latvia and Lithuania) share a common experience of European history and have historical, cultural and geographical proximity to their neighbouring European states, particularly Austria, Germany and the Scandinavian countries. Moreover, the advanced level of economic and social development that the CEE nations had achieved before the imposition of communism assisted their transition progress. Therefore, organizational learning processes in culturally distant CEE nations might be assisted by such commonalities with Western Europe and by the implementation of Western European training programmes.

At the same time, the lack of Western historical connections in Bulgaria and Romania could seriously obstruct organizational learning: their Ottoman and Tsarist heritage blocked the influence of the shaping events in the rest of Europe and resulted in sluggish political, social and economic transformation. Because of the absence of historical, cultural and geographical ties to Western Europe, the learning processes in firms located in culturally distant Eastern European nations might be difficult to bring about. This, in turn, is likely to discourage potential acquisitions. In line with previous studies that found a positive relationship between cultural distance and the preference for greenfield over acquisition entry, it can therefore be expected that the greater the cultural distance between an investor's home country and the host country, the greater the likelihood of a greenfield investment. After all, with a greenfield investment the multinational can avoid the costs of integrating culturally distant organizations and loss of control over the subsidiary's behaviour.

[a] Adapted from Dikova and van Witteloostuijn (2004). See the website for more references.

and charisma to be very important and past experience to be rather irrelevant, which is totally opposed to the American managers' perception.[8]

12.5 Corporate governance and institutional diversity

The modern enterprise

After emphasizing the home-country effects of multinational behaviour and inter-country differences in such areas as HRM and managerial behaviour as a consequence of national culture differences, this section focuses on corporate governance – the role of capital and institutional diversity. In so doing, we consider issues of ownership and management, particularly focusing on the way in which an organization's owners and managers interact in determining organizational behaviour, strategy and, ultimately, performance. The corporate governance literature is dominated by the question as to whether capital's interests can be protected against the opportunistic behaviour of managers, a danger that became real with the claimed increase of the separation of ownership and management in modern enterprises. In their 1932 classic, Berle and Means (1932) argued that ownership of capital (firms) is dispersed among many small shareholders, at least in the American context. This raises serious issues of control – that is, managers may decide to satisfy their own individual interests, such as income and prestige, rather than that of the owners.

In response to Berle and Means' (1932) diagnosis, a large literature emerged dealing with issues of ownership control over management. The managerial economics literature of the 1960s (see, e.g., Baumol, 1963) was followed by agency theory (see, e.g., Jensen and Meckling, 1976). This triggered many empirical and theoretical studies into the relationship between managers or agents and owners or principals, focusing on incentives and mechanisms that could correct for the opportunism trap associated with the increased separation of ownership and management (cf. the delegation games in box 12.6). Many studies, such as Morck, Shleifer and Vishny (1990), have zoomed in on the antecedents and consequences of top executive rewards. This literature is characterized by a clear Anglo-Saxon bias, which raises the question to what extent this American experience can be extrapolated to other countries, given the large cultural and institutional variety already discussed.

---

[8] In addition, the study provides evidence that differences within the Eastern Asian region are large as well. Another example relates to the way the business system is organized, with more or less emphasis on *Keiretsu*-type network groups in Japan *vis-à-vis* family-based ties in China (see Scott, 1997).

Box 12.6 Delegation games and managerial compensation

Delegation games pertain to changes in the firm's utility function and its influence on the equilibrium economic outcome. Insights from microeconomic agency theory have been merged with industrial organization models to develop a specific type of sequential games, namely a first-stage contract subgame combined with a second-stage competition subgame. Agency theory argues that the principal–owner of a firm must design incentive systems such that the agent–manager acts in the principal–owner's interest (see Holmström, 1989). This problem is highly relevant in the modern epoch of the separation of ownership and management, the argument goes, since a manager's interests tend to be different from the owner's interests, and since managerial input and output cannot be easily measured and monitored. Managers may, for example, strive for sales maximization rather than profit maximization (see Baumol, 1963). In delegation games, such size-related motives enter into the firms' utility functions through an agency mechanism in otherwise orthodox models of (oligopoly) competition.

Principal–owners therefore design compensation contracts for their agent–managers with variable profit- and size-related performance elements, in the context of a two-stage contract competition sequential game, so that the utility-maximizing agent–managers are expected to act in the interest of the principal–owners. In the first stage of the game, principal–owners decide on the design of the compensation contract for their agent–managers, which they expect will trigger managerial behaviour to maximize profits in the second-stage competition game (given the expectations on rival behaviour: see Vickers, 1985; Fersthman and Judd, 1987; Sklivas, 1987). An important finding is that firms headed by agent–managers that seek to reach size-related objectives may perform better than their counterparts aiming at profit maximization only, because the former may turn out to be larger and more profitable than the latter, or may be the only ones to survive (see van Witteloostuijn, Boone and van Lier, 2003). By offering compensation contracts with non-profit elements to their agent–managers in the first stage of the game, the principal–owners maximize their profits in the second competitive stage. This is ultimately in line with the traditional assumption of the profit-maximizing *firm economicus* in neo-classical economics.

In the context of international business, this raises an interesting dual question: to what extent are managerial objectives and compensation schemes different across countries, and what does this imply for the outcomes of international competition? Evidence suggests that inter-country differences are large, even in the current era of stock-market globalization, as is also discussed in section 12.5. Brouthers and Werner (1990), for example, find that success is largely measured by market share in Japanese firms, which differs radically from the Anglo-Saxon emphasis on profit-based or shareholder-driven performance yardsticks. In terms of performance, it may well be that firms that do not give top priority to profit maximization, such as those from Japan (e.g. Toyota), out-perform their 'pure' profit-driven rivals, such as the shareholder value enterprises from the USA (e.g., GM).

Corporate governance diversity

La Porta, Lopez-de-Silanes and Shleifer (1999) report evidence on differences in corporate governance for a sample of twenty-seven countries (see also chapter 7). Analysing the ownership structure of modern corporations, they distinguish the following seven key indicators:

- *Widely held*   Equals one if there is no controlling shareholder, and zero otherwise
- *Family*   Equals one if a person is the controlling shareholder, and zero otherwise
- *State*   Equals one if the (domestic or foreign) state is the controlling shareholder, and zero otherwise
- *Pyramid*   Equals one if the controlling shareholder exercises control through at least one publicly traded company, and zero otherwise
- *Cross-shareholding*   Equals one if the firm has both a controlling shareholder and owns shares in its controlling shareholder or in a firm that belongs to its chain, and zero otherwise
- *Control 20 per cent*   Minimum percentage of the book value of common equity required to control 20 per cent of the votes
- *Anti-director index*   An index aggregating shareholder rights, ranging from 0 (few rights) to 6 (many rights).

As table 12.7 shows, there is a wide variety of corporate structures around the world. Most corporations are widely held in the UK, Japan and the USA, while they are mostly family-controlled in Mexico, Hong Kong and Argentina. State control is high in Austria, Singapore and Italy. Pyramid structures are common in Belgium, Israel and Austria. Cross-shareholding is frequent in Germany and Austria, and so on. Roughly speaking, high-protection regimes can be distinguished from low-protection ones: in the former, contrary to the latter, the corporate governance system is associated with a high protection of shareholders.

Institutional diversity

Related to issues of corporate governance is the extent to which national legislation guarantees employee participation. There is a long tradition in Europe of research into the functioning of works councils, in line with the heavily institutionalized role of the

Table 12.7 Corporate governance around the world, shares

Country	Widely held	Family	State	Control 20 per cent	Pyramid	Cross-shareholding
High protection (high anti-director index)						
Argentina	0.00	0.65	0.15	19.60	0.05	0.00
Australia	0.65	0.05	0.05	20.00	0.14	0.10
Canada	0.60	0.25	0.00	19.36	0.13	0.00
Hong Kong	0.10	0.70	0.05	19.51	0.39	0.05
Ireland	0.65	0.10	0.00	20.00	0.00	0.00
Japan	0.90	0.05	0.05	20.00	0.00	0.00
New Zealand	0.30	0.25	0.25	20.00	0.36	0.00
Norway	0.25	0.25	0.35	18.15	0.13	0.00
Singapore	0.15	0.30	0.45	20.00	0.41	0.10
Spain	0.35	0.15	0.30	20.00	0.38	0.00
UK	1.00	0.00	0.00	20.00	–	0.00
US	0.80	0.20	0.00	19.19	0.00	0.00
Average	0.48	0.25	0.14	19.65	0.18	0.02
Low protection (low anti-director index)						
Austria	0.05	0.15	0.70	19.89	0.47	0.15
Belgium	0.05	0.50	0.05	20.00	0.79	0.05
Denmark	0.40	0.35	0.15	14.87	0.08	0.00
Finland	0.35	0.10	0.35	15.75	0.00	0.00
France	0.60	0.20	0.15	20.00	0.38	0.00
Germany	0.50	0.10	0.25	18.61	0.40	0.20
Greece	0.10	0.50	0.30	20.00	0.11	0.00
Israel	0.05	0.50	0.40	20.00	0.53	0.00
Italy	0.20	0.15	0.40	18.04	0.25	0.00
Mexico	0.00	1.00	0.00	16.45	0.25	0.00
Netherlands	0.30	0.20	0.05	15.00	0.14	0.00
Portugal	0.10	0.45	0.25	20.00	0.44	0.05
S. Korea	0.55	0.20	0.15	20.00	0.33	0.05
Sweden	0.25	0.45	0.10	12.63	0.53	0.10
Switzerland	0.60	0.30	0.00	14.18	0.00	0.00
Average	0.27	0.34	0.22	17.69	0.31	0.04

Source: La Porta, Lopez-de-Silanes and Shleifer (1999).

employee participation bodies in many Continental European countries, particularly concerning the German experience (see Frege, 2002; Addison, Schnabel and Wagner, 2004). Clearly, Continental European works councils are different from their Anglo-Saxon counterparts, as the former are legally institutionalized bodies, unlike the

Anglo-Saxon voluntary labour–management committees. The strong works council tradition in Continental Europe has created a cross-country body of legally protected worker participation in internationally operating enterprises (see Hall *et al.*, 2003). The nation-specific institutional environment thus determines wider issues of how the business world is organized.

More generally, the literature on 'varieties of capitalism' or 'national business systems' is full of detailed descriptions of how countries differ in terms of their institutional arrangements. For example, Sorge (2005) offers a revealing view of the 'inside' of German capitalism, explaining how current Germany can be understood only by carefully analysing historical path dependencies. For instance, the federalist structure of the medieval Holy Roman Empire and the long tradition of medieval-type guild structures are still very influential through the modern system of powerful *Bundesländer* and professional associations, which is also reflected in the German corporate governance regime of codetermination, characterized by formal and powerful positions of labour in works councils and non-executive boards.[9] Another example is Scott (1997), who provides extensive evidence of the very different ways in which the business world is organized in different countries. For instance, the Korean *Chaebol*, Chinese *Quanxi*, or Japanese *Keiretsu* structures are very different from Anglo-Saxon enterprises, with a heavy emphasis on horizontal and vertical network linkages across industries and full of cooperative arrangements. By way of illustration, box 12.7 provides an example of another piece of empirical evidence on worldwide institutional diversity.

Just like cultural differences, *institutional diversity* is a key driver of multinational behaviour. For example, Carstensen and Toubal (2004) argue that the institutional variety specific to transition economies, such as the method of privatization and the level of country risk, are important in explaining FDI inflow into countries in the CEE region. In the early twenty-first century, the FDI stock *per capita* was low in Bulgaria and Romania, and high in the Czech Republic and Hungary. This is in line with what could be expected from the scores on the twelve variables of political risk (see box 12.7). Such measures of country risk are traditionally taken on board in the international business literature as key determinants of the decision whether or not to engage in FDI into a specific country and, if so, which entry mode to use. For instance, MNEs prefer partial-ownership establishments (e.g. JVs) in nation-states that are characterized by substantial institutional instability, so as to minimize the financial risk of the higher failure hazard in such countries.

---

[9] And, related to part III of this book, countries are very different in terms of their financial system as well. For instance, as Sorge (2005) argues, in Germany banks were established to increase access to capital for the poor, whereas British banks were there to provide a money-making machine for the rich. In line with this, Germany developed a bank-based system of corporate finance.

Box 12.7 Institutional diversity

The PRS Group, Inc. publishes a widely used International Country Risk Guide (ICRG), comprising twenty-two variables in three subcategories of risk: political, financial and economic. Table 12.8 provides an example of the degree of institutional diversity for the twelve ICRG political risk components for a selection of countries, illustrated for the association between corruption and social economic conditions in figure 12.3.

The most striking aspect about table 12.8, where higher scores imply less political risks, is the high degree of variation in the various political risk components – such as government stability, external conflict, ethnic tension and degree of corruption. Not surprisingly, these various items tend to be correlated. Social and economic conditions, for example, tend to be

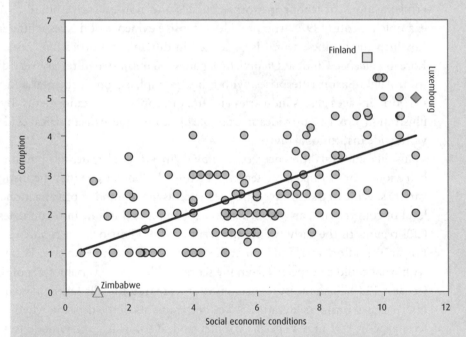

Figure 12.3 Correlation between corruption and social economic conditions
Data source: see table 12.8.

better in the absence of corruption (i.e. a high score on the index), as is illustrated by Finland and Luxembourg in figure 12.3. The opposite also holds, as illustrated by Zimbabwe.

Table 12.8 Political risk diversity, 2003

Dimension[b]	Country (World Bank code)[a]							
	AUS	BRA	CHN	DEU	IND	NGA	RUS	USA
Gov stab	10.0	9.0	10.9	7.8	8.5	7.6	11.5	10.7
Soc ec cond	9.5	5.6	6.6	7.7	3.5	1.5	5.7	7.6
Inv profile	10.4	7.5	7.5	12.0	8.2	4.0	9.0	11.6
Int conflict	10.0	10.4	11.3	11.1	8.0	6.1	8.8	10.3
Ext conflict	10.0	11.0	11.0	10.0	8.8	10.6	9.4	7.1
Corruption	4.5	4.0	1.9	4.2	1.5	1.0	1.3	4.0
Mil in politics	6.0	4.0	2.9	6.0	4.0	2.0	4.5	5.0
Rel in politics	6.0	6.0	4.9	6.0	1.0	1.4	4.6	4.6
Law and order	6.0	1.5	4.5	5.0	4.0	1.5	4.0	5.0
Ethnic tension	3.5	3.0	5.0	4.0	2.0	1.6	2.0	5.0
Dem account	6.0	5.0	1.0	5.0	6.0	3.2	3.8	5.5
Bureau qual	4.0	2.0	2.0	4.0	3.0	1.0	1.0	4.0

Source: International Country Risk Guide, PRS Group, Inc.

[a] Countries are: Australia, Brazil, China, Germany, India, Nigeria, Russian Federation (CIS) and USA, respectively.

[b] Dimensions are: government stability, socioeconomic conditions, investment profile, internal conflict, external conflict, corruption, military in politics, religion in politics, law and order, ethnic tension, democratic accountability and bureaucratic quality, respectively.

12.6 Recent Americanization?

The above discussion should make it clear that home-country cultural and institutional effects are very powerful, and influence managerial objectives, HRM decisions, governance regimes, corporate strategies and much more.[10] However, anti-globalists argue that while this may well have been the case for many centuries, that the current epoch of globalization is different. In particular, the argument goes, the widespread dominance of the American variant of capitalism has triggered an unstoppable process of 'McDonaldization', ever since Ronald Reagan launched his neo-liberal revolution and the Berlin Wall collapsed (marking the end of the Soviet Union, with its communist system, as the world's second superpower), which is manifested in the economic domain through the global diffusion of US institutions (e.g. enterprises driven by shareholder value) and policies (e.g. liberalization and privatization).

Take the following example. According to Sorge and van Witteloostuijn (2004), the global business world is infected by a virus (fed by the management consultancy

---

[10] See, e.g., Borkowski (1999) Gooderham, Nordhaug and Ringdal (1999) and Brouthers, Werner and Matulich (2000).

industry) that induces a permanent need for *organizational change*. Its nature changes frequently, for sure, but it does so on a global level. This makes it into a key aspect of globalization: the universal diffusion of changes in institutional and organizational blueprints, with their roots in the USA. Such change fashions come and go. Eric Abrahamson (1997) concludes that 'soft' hypes succeed 'tough' fads, and vice versa. The period of Taylorism, linked to an expansion of mass markets, was followed by the human relations and human resources movement, linked to saturated markets, rejuvenation of the product lifecycle and customization of products and services. After the 'gentle' 1960s and 1970s came, halfway through the 1980s, a turn towards 'the hard-headed' cost reduction, downsizing and re-engineering fashion at the end of the twentieth century. What will come next?

Organizational change has become the *raison d'être* of the consultancy and management professions. The consultancy world is dominated by large global players with American roots, such as Arthur D. Little, Bain, the Boston Consulting Group (BCG), Deloitte and Touche, KPMG, McKinsey and PriceWaterhouseCoopers. These consultancy giants have offices in Beijing, Berlin, London, New Delhi, New York, Paris, Rio de Janeiro, Rome, Stockholm and in every other big city across the globe, from which they sell the same products to their local clients. The shelves of bookshops are piled with the next generation of management guru bestsellers for tired, bored or frustrated travelling managers, hungry for vision and 'cook book' recipes. The Druckers, Kellys, Peters, Porters and Prahalads explain to a management audience keen on a mix of distraction, expression of gut feelings, surprise, entertainment and elucidation, why the 'old ways of doing business' are a recipe for failure in the (post-) modern era of the information, network or whatever economy. All, or at least by far the majority, of these gurus are working from an Anglo-Saxon home base, mostly the USA. Their 'revolutionary new strategies for fighting competition' then offer a unique way out. Since the lifecycle of 'new' organizational recipes is limited, management hypes tend to come in waves: the business world exhibits 'herd' behaviour.

James O'Shea and Charles Madigan (1997), two American journalists, illustrate the 'consultancy addiction' that pervades the business world. Telecommunications giant AT&T, for example, spent billions of dollars in the 1990s on a range of consultancy projects. The US (virtual) energy mammoth Enron's catastrophic demise in 2002, together with that of Arthur Andersen (Enron's accountants and consultants), provides another example and shows that, in the extreme, consultancy may shade into unethical behaviour, such as corruption and falsification of documents and records. Such tendencies are not restricted to the USA, as the global consultancy giants have beaten their growth record after a profit peak. For instance, the then Andersen Consulting firm employed about 40,000 people worldwide by the end of the 1990s. There is even a market, not yet tapped by many business consultants and guru books, of 'how to handle consultants' – meta-consultancy.

DaimlerChrysler provides a prominent case in point. In the 1980s, Daimler-Benz was a multidivisional, international but very German conglomerate making cars, lorries, aerospace and defence equipment and electronic commodities. It had been constructed following the then current diversification and 'synergy' global hype. Unfortunately, nothing came of the synergy. After dwindling performance and the appointment of new managers, Daimler-Benz sold off the aerospace and electronics components to follow a new global hype: focusing on the core (car) business through the acquisition of Mitsubishi Motor and Chrysler. These acquisitions immediately proved to be loss-making, leading to a predictable response in the canteens: the generals had fouled things up again. It is anyone's guess to which hype Daimler-Chrysler will next fall victim, now that following global management tides is so costly. Box 12.8 provides another example.

Box 12.8 Shareholder value, 'Americanization' and downsizing[a]

A prominent universal hype that spread across the globe ever since the 1980s is *downsizing*, again a fashion with strong American roots (see Gordon, 1996). A series of empirical studies into its effectiveness has revealed that the value added of this management fad is low indeed, however. Table 12.9 provides illustrative empirical evidence from a extensive survey among American managers, asking them to what extent downsizing has *not* been instrumental in reaching a series of organizational objectives

None of the downsizing objectives listed in table 12.9 has been reached by a majority of firms. Even the direct positive effects of downsizing – a decrease in spending and an increase in productivity – are reported by only 46 and 22 per cent of the firms, respectively. Increased product quality, improved innovativeness and technological progress hardly occur. In line with this overall finding, in-depth empirical work is starting to reveal the detailed intra-organizational 'downsides of downsizing'. Amabile and Conti (1999), for example, demonstrated devastating and long-lasting negative consequences of major downsizing operations for shop floor creativity. Nonetheless, the business world still seems addicted to the downsizing diet, as mass lay-off announcements are rewarded with increasing share prices (and thus a fall in the cost of capital). Table 12.10 lists seven examples.

Because the hype of shareholder value has spread across the world, downsizing operations are popular among stock exchange-listed companies, irrespective of the country of origin. For example, van Witteloostuijn (1999) provides evidence

Table 12.9 Effectiveness of downsizing

Objective	Firms *not* able to reach the objective (%)
Reduced spending	54
Increased profit	68
Increased cash flow	76
Improved productivity	78
Increased return on investment	79
Increased competitive strength	81
Reduced bureaucracy	83
Improved decision-making	86
Increased customer satisfaction	86
Increased sales volume	87
Increased market share	88
Improved product quality	91
Increased technological progress	91
Increased innovativeness	93
Avoided acquisition	94

Source: Wyatt, *Wall Street Journal* survey (1991), reported in Cameron (1994).

Table 12.10 Stock exchange reactions to downsizing announcements

Company	Downsizing announcement	Next-day share price change (%)
IBM	60,000	+ 7.7
Sears	50,000	+ 3.6
Xerox	10,000	+ 7.0
US West	9,000	+ 4.6
McDonnell Douglas	8,700	+ 7.9
RJR Nabisco	6,000	+ 4.0
Du Pont	4,500	+ 3.4

Source: Cameron (1994).

of similar behaviour of stock exchange-listed multinationals from four Continental European countries: Belgium, Germany, the Netherlands and Sweden.

[a] Adapted from Sorge and van Witteloostuijn (2004); see the website for further references.

The rhetoric is clear: the international world of business is dominated by American fads and fashions: they may come in waves, but they do originate, time and again, from the USA. However, this rhetoric is again too simple. In the early twenty-first century, the business world was hit by a series of scandals caused by bookkeeping fraud, such as Enron in the USA, Ahold in the Netherlands and Parmalat in Italy. Managerial behaviour, driven by stock-based compensation schemes, is generally considered to be part of the underlying problem. As a consequence, many international firms may turn elsewhere for inspiration, as they did before. For example, in the 1970s and 1980s, Japanese business practices were regarded as the world's best. Perhaps, the 2010s or 2020s will turn out to be the Chinese epoch, in this respect, pushing US-inspired shareholder value hypes into the background. Second, rhetoric is one thing, but practice is quite another matter. As we shall argue in chapter 14, behind the smokescreen of consultancy jargon and managerial peptalk, the actual implementation of fads and fashions that are claimed to be universal is often heavily influenced by local forces that produce local adaptations – and hence wide heterogeneity across countries.

12.7 Conclusions

This chapter's key argument has been that 'hard' (institutional) and 'soft' (cultural) issues work together to determine the divergent behaviour of MNEs from different home countries, as well as the 'behaviour templates' that feature in these home countries. Whatever the current rhetoric about globalization or Americanization, influential home-country influences cannot be denied. The above examples have focused on international business issues. However, this key message can also be illustrated by analysing the role of politics in trade, which is heavily influenced by non-economic motives – varying from cultural preferences and ethnic hostilities to military conflicts and geopolitical strategies. That is, political arrangements play an important role in determining and shaping the size and direction of international trade flows, in addition to the forces analysed in chapters 3–5.

The idea of a *mutual influence between trade and policy* is not new: it dates back at least to the seventeenth- and eighteenth-century mercantilism, which advocated that a country should export more and import less in order to enhance its political power. In later centuries, Marxists and imperialists were well aware of the fact that foreign trade could be an instrument of national power. Hirschman (1945) argued that Germany used the structure of its international trade flows to coerce Bulgaria, Hungary and Romania to support its political objectives. Since the second half of the twentieth century, researchers have measured the relationships between international trade and politics quantitatively. Four arguments dominate this literature.[11]

---

[11] Each argument is supported by ample empirical evidence; see the website for further details.

- First, trade flows are significantly influenced by *political conflict and cooperation between nations* (see Savage and Deutsch, 1960; Pollins, 1989a, 1989b). Trade flows are affected by the decisions of risk-averse agents who wish to minimize the risk of disrupting trade flows. Political conditions are therefore important and must be taken into account when taking decisions. The trade level between two countries will therefore decline if their political relations are strained.
- Second, countries that are *both democratic* will trade more than partners of which at least one is not democratic. Oneal and Russett (1997) argue that it is less likely that a democratic trade partner will use its gains from trade to endanger a partner's security. Accordingly, governments of democratic countries may construct policies to encourage their private economic actors to trade with people in other democratic countries. Moreover, from the perspective of a private actor, trading with a democracy is less risky than trading with an autocracy, not only because of the lower likelihood of conflict, but also because of the confidence inspired by the rule of law.
- Third, *institutionalized political–economic cooperation* increases international trade flows. PTAs, such as free trade areas, customs, unions, or common markets, are important examples of such institutionalized cooperation. As discussed in chapter 10 on the basis of Viner (1953), there is a trade-creation effect for the members of such PTAs, and possibly a trade-diversion effect relative to non-members. Both of these effects turn out to be important.
- Fourth, *military alliances* influence the direction of trade flows (see Gowa 1989, 1994; Mansfield, 1994). The causal relation between military capability and international trade is reciprocal. Trade increases the wealth of both countries. If one country invests these gains in an increase of its military power, the trade partners will also enjoy the benefits from this investment, as long as the military alliance pursues similar ends. Conversely, a country might impede trade with enemy states for fear that the benefits could be used to build up military capability abroad, hence posing a greater threat. Free trade is thus more likely within than across military alliances.

Together, these four arguments suggest that 'hard' and 'soft' country-specific forces have not only a clear impact on the behaviour of MNEs, but also on the size and direction of international trade flows.

Appendix: the Bertrand duopoly experiment

The following instructions were given for the six games, after introducing the general setting along the lines described in the main text (see table 12.3).

- *Game I*   Suppose you are Chief Executive Officer (CEO) of firm *I*. You decide autonomously on the price strategy of your company. You have an agreement with

Table 12A.1 *Firm I – Firm II interaction pay-off matrix, in 1000 euro*

		Firm II price	
(Firm I pay-off, Firm II pay-off)		Low (P_{II}^L)	High (P_{II}^H)
Firm I price	Low (P_I^L)	$(-20, -20)$; cell 1	$(800, -400)$; cell2
	High (P_I^H)	$(-400, 800)$; cell 3	$(600, 600)$; cell 4

your distributor to fix the future price levels for your product. It is a custom in this industry that yearly contracts with distributors are drawn, in which the price level you prefer to set in each month for the coming year is fixed in advance. It is impossible to change the terms of the contract during the year. The CEO of firm *II* will simultaneously determine her price strategy with her distributor (different from yours) for the following twelve months. You do not know the price intentions of firm *II* (and vice versa). Indicate for each month which strategy you prefer (capital *L* indicates a low price and capital *H* a high one). Note that all sequences of low and high prices are feasible.

- *Game II, Condition 1* At the end of the contract, you find out that firm *II* has consistently chosen to set a high price in each month of the previous year. Subsequently, you have to draw a new contract with your distributor for the next twelve months. Indicate, again, which price level you prefer in each month.
- *Game II, Condition 2* At the end of the contract, you found out that firm *II* has chosen to set a high price in eight of the twelve months of the previous contracting period. Subsequently, you have to draw a new contract with your distributor for the next twelve months. Indicate, again, which price level you prefer in each month.
- *Game III* Your information on the past intentions and price strategies of firm *II* becomes irrelevant. The reason is that firm *II* has been taken over by another company, which installed a new CEO. Moreover, the government has decided that contracts in which prices are pre-fixed for more than one month in advance are now illegal. Thus, for the next year you are allowed to fix your price level for only one month; after each month, therefore, you now have to decide again for the next month. Decisions are made simultaneously in each month, by both firm *I* and firm *II*. After each month, you are informed about each other's price level. The sequence of decisions you must make and activities you have to perform is as follows:
  1. At the beginning of each month, the price levels are set simultaneously, and marked on the associated response sheet.
  2. Subsequently, the choices of both firms are exchanged by means of the pieces of paper provided by the game instructor.
  3. With reference to the strategy–profit matrix above (i.e. table 12.3), you determine your own profit, given the strategy of the other firm.

- Except for the exchange of the pieces of paper at the end of each month, no communication is allowed during the experiment. Please keep pace with the game instructor's announcements. She may slow down the pace of the game to allow each and every pair to finish the sequence of activities in time.
- *Game IV*   Repeat Game III for an unknown number of months. You do not know in advance how many times you will have to make a decision on your price level. The game can end at any moment in time after August in the first year. After that, the probability that the game ends is 10 per cent in each month. The game instructor will announce the final month of decision-making.
- *Game V*   In the following period of twelve months, demand has increased substantially, associated with a growth in potential profits and a decline in potential losses. This new situation is reflected in the strategy–profit matrix in table 12A.1. Repeat Game *III*.

Part V

Conclusion

Globalization: is it really happening?

KEYWORDS

global income inequality	international outsourcing	globalization bonus
labour skill bias	technological progress	transnationality
institutional stability	institutional globalization	globalization

13.1 Introduction

As argued in chapter 1, we are interested in the economic consequences of globalization, where this term refers to the growing *interdependency* between nations and firms through international trade and factor mobility. Throughout the book, we have focused on international trade and capital mobility. Although labour migration does occur as well, both other forces are clearly dominant. In box 13.1, we briefly reflect on the labour migration issue. In chapter 3, we concluded that international trade increases welfare. In chapter 7, we reached a similar conclusion with respect to international capital mobility. At the same time, it became clear that globalization does not necessarily make *everyone* better off. In general, there are both winners and losers.

Box 13.1 Globalization and international labour migration

As explained in the preface (p. xxii), labour migration is not a main focus in our analysis of the global economy. In chapter 3 we briefly analysed labour migration. The effects are rather similar to international capital flows (see chapter 7). Still, at least in the public globalization debate, labour migration is a prominent issue, with increased fears in developed countries that domestic labour markets are becoming subject to fierce international competition. Low-skilled workers in particular worry about competition from low-wage countries. The discussion in the main text focuses on the role of trade in final or intermediate goods. This is not the only form in which globalization might affect the position of the low-skilled workers, however; migration can also be a factor.

In fact, as argued in box 3.5, labour migration is a substitute for trade. Since factors of production are incorporated in the traded commodities, it does not really matter from a factor content perspective whether factors of production migrate or whether the goods themselves are traded. Both options can lead to factor price equalization and might result in the same equilibrium. If, however, factor prices are not equalized, migration increases the competition from low-wage countries and increases the supply of labour in the destination countries. To analyse the effects of migration on wages in destination countries it is instructive to look at the motivation for migration. Many studies have found that differences in earnings between the destination country and the source country are the primary motive, corrected for a home bias and direct migration cost.[1]

The *home-bias effect* indicates that people like to stay at home (because of cultural factors, language, friends and family), unless they are sufficiently compensated. *Direct migration costs* relate to the investment needed to migrate to, and integrate in, the destination country, for which the earnings difference should also compensate. Empirical tests for the USA show that a relative decline in income in the destination country reduces migration flows to the USA between 4 per cent (relative to Asia) and 13 per cent (relative to Europe). It is remarkable that Africa, one of the poorest regions in the world, is not the main source of migration flows to developed countries, as Africans potentially have a lot to gain from migration. This is probably caused by (i) migration restrictions in the destination countries and (ii) a poverty trap: migration is costly and below a certain threshold income level, migration is simply not possible. The fact that migration to developed countries is relatively more costly has led to a situation in some African countries where migration is confined to people moving to neighbouring countries, which are often only marginally better off.

[1] See for example Borjas, G. J. (1989, pp. 457–85).

The advocates of globalization argue that the gains outweigh the losses, provided that free trade and financial stability operate under properly functioning international and domestic institutions. The critics of globalization, on the other hand, state that the gains might not outweigh the losses. It is not always clear what the arguments of the opponents to globalization are, but the common factor is a critical attitude towards modern capitalism in general and the MNE in particular.[2] In this view, international competition stimulates a race-to-the-bottom in which the poor have no power to prevent the adverse outcomes of globalization. The main actor in this process is the MNE, which allegedly has the power to 'rule the world'. In addition, the

[2] See Elliot, Kar and Richardson (2004) for an excellent survey of the critique on globalization.

WTO, IMF and World Bank (WB) are criticized for supposedly serving the interests of large international investors and MNCs, rather than the local citizens of (poor) countries.

In this chapter, we shall not review the debate between the proponents and the critics of globalization. Instead, we shall take the globalization process as dealt with in earlier chapters for granted and discuss, for illustrative purposes, the consequences of globalization for economic growth and income inequality (both within and between countries). Along the way we shall show, in line with the title of our book, what is gained by combining insights from the International Economics (IE) and International Business (IB) literature. We argue that the traditional IE analysis of the effects of globalization is too limited, and needs to be complemented with insights from an IB perspective in view of the central role of multinationals. Even though the focus on multinationals is useful, we conclude with a reminder that the power of these 'footloose' firms is often over-stated and that domestic policies and institutions still matter very much (see also chapter 12).

13.2 Income inequality over time

To put the discussion below into a proper perspective, it is instructive to analyse the income statistics for the different countries in the world somewhat more closely. To measure the extent of income inequality we use the *Theil index*, which has the advantage that it can be decomposed into two parts, namely the *between-country* and the *within-country* component (see below and Theil, 1967).[3] The higher the Theil index, the more unequal is the underlying income distribution.

As illustrated in figure 13.1 using data for the period 1820–2000, global income inequality has generally increased since 1820. The rise in global income inequality occurred mainly in two subperiods, namely 1820–1910 and 1960–2000. In the period in between, the Theil index did not increase. We know that the late nineteenth and the second half of the twentieth century are associated with the first and second 'wave' of globalization, respectively. It is thus tempting to conclude that globalization stimulates income inequality. Some critics of globalization indeed assume that the rise in income inequality and globalization are somehow correlated, and have used data such as these to point out that globalization is not always beneficial. As figure 13.1 also shows, it is in particular the *between*-country inequality that has increased over time. It is only recently that a (renewed) relatively modest increase of *within*-country income equality can be discerned. These issues are now addressed.

---

[3] The Theil index is a measure of (income) inequality. If there are n individuals, indexed by i, with income x_i, it is defined as: *Theil* $= (1/n) \sum_{i=1}^{n} (x_i/\mu) \times \ln(x_i/\mu)$, where $\mu = (1/n) \sum_{i=1}^{n} x_i$ is the average income level. It ranges from 0 (= equal distribution) to $\ln(n)$, indicating maximum inequality.

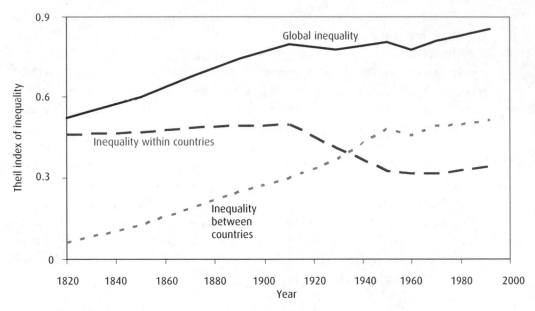

Figure 13.1 Inequality among world citizens, 1820–1992, global income inequality
Data source: Bourguignon and Morrison (2002, table 2).

13.3 Does globalization make the rich richer and the poor poorer?

A first answer to the question posed in the title of this section is given by the seminal study of Sachs and Warner (1995) (see figure 13.2). Figure 13.2 distinguishes between two groups of countries: open economies and closed economies. For both developing and developed countries Sachs and Warner find that open economies have higher growth rates than closed economies. In general, developing countries have more closed economies than developed countries.

Contrary to the convergence hypothesis discussed in chapter 11, however, income inequality increases. To quote Sachs and Warner (1995, p. 37): 'The data suggest that the absence of overall convergence in the world economy during the past few decades might well result from the closed trading regimes of most of the poorer countries.' As most closed economies are found in the group of developing countries, it seems that the critics of globalization are right in the sense that the benefits of openness accrue more to the developed than to the developing countries.

Two qualifications are necessary with respect to the above conclusion, however. First, the distinction between open and closed economies is not as clear-cut as one might assume. Sachs and Warner classified countries as 'closed' if they fulfil *one* of the following five criteria: (1) non-tariff barriers (NTBs) covering at least 40 per cent of trade, (2) average tariff rates of at least 40 per cent, (3) a 'black' market exchange rate depreciated by 20 per cent or more relative to the official exchange rate (on average) during the 1970s or 1980s, (4) a socialist economic system, or (5) a state monopoly on

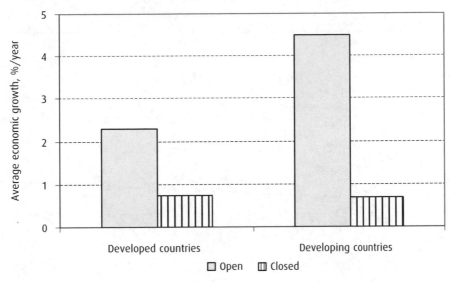

Figure 13.2 Growth rates in open and closed economies, 1970–1989
Data source: Sachs and Warner (1995, p. 36).

major exports. Although these may seem reasonable classification criteria, Rodriquez and Rodrik (1999) show that two of the five criteria suffice to make the distinction between open and closed economies, namely the (3) black market exchange rate criterion and (5) a state monopoly on major exports. All but one of the closed countries are located in sub-Saharan Africa (SSA). This raises the question as to what figure 13.2 is actually telling us. Are the growth rates correlated with openness to global competition, or with some unknown characteristic of sub-Saharan countries, such as the prevalence of infectious diseases? This critique stimulated a large debate on the relationship between openness and growth. Our conclusion is that openness fosters growth (despite the above reservations), although the picture is less clear-cut than figure 13.2 suggests (see also Bordo, Taylor and Williamson, 2003).

The second qualification concerns the *size* of countries. Figures 13.1 and 13.2 are based on country data in which each observation receives the same weight. Luxembourg is then considered as important as the USA, despite the fact that it is a much smaller country in terms of population, size and economy (e.g. 0.44 versus 288 million inhabitants in 2002). The important bias in our perception of economic developments that this may cause was strongly argued by Fischer (2003). This can be illustrated by comparing panels *a* and *b* of figure 13.3.

Figure 13.3a depicts average annual growth rates in the period 1980–2002 (vertical axis) relative to the initial income *per capita* level in 1980 (horizontal axis). The observations for the individual countries are given by squares for SSA countries and by circles for other countries. Figure 13.3a therefore provides information on the degree to which countries that were relatively poor at the beginning of the period

(a)

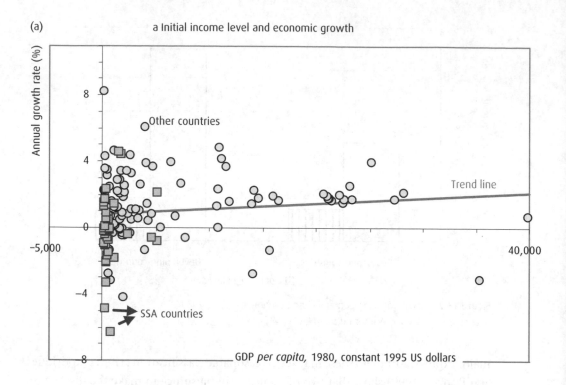

(b)

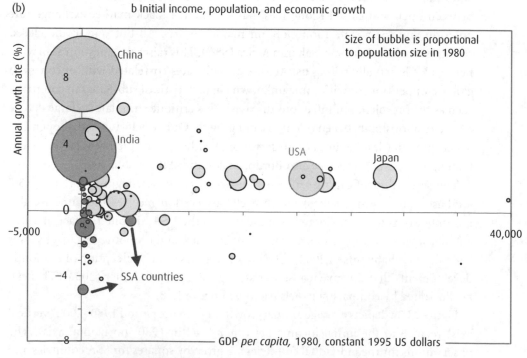

Figure 13.3 Income levels, growth rates and population, 1980–2002
Data source: World Bank (2004).

grew faster or slower than countries that were relatively rich in 1980. Despite wide variation, figure 13.3a and the simple, positively-sloped trend-line suggest that on average initially rich countries grew faster than initially poor countries, which is in line with the conclusion of increasing inequality of figure 13.2. This conclusion, however, is at odds with neo-classical growth theories predicting that poor countries will grow faster than rich countries (see chapter 11).

Panel *b* of figure 13.3 depicts exactly the same information as panel *a*, with one addition: the size of the circle is proportional to the size of the population of the country. Countries such as China, India and the USA thus stand out as large circles, while it will be hard to locate Luxembourg in figure 13.3b. Taking this additional information into consideration, we arrive at a completely different conclusion. China and India were relatively poor in 1980 and showed very high growth rates. These two countries together represent a third of the world population and increasingly participate in the world economy (i.e. can be classified as open economies). Weighing growth rates by population numbers overturns the conclusion of figure 13.1: income inequality between countries actually decreases once we take population size into account![4]

The conclusions of this section are simple: (i) open economies grow faster than closed economies and (ii) income inequality among world citizens has recently declined if we take population size into consideration, mainly due to a few large and fast-growing countries, such as India and China. For the group of developing countries as a whole, the message that openness stimulates growth is relevant. Research indicates that fast-growing developing countries also have a higher rate of poverty reduction (see Easterly, 2002). In this sense, openness is also a good way to reduce poverty. The World Bank (2002) notes, however, that despite the potential benefits of participating in the globalization process, about 2 billion people in the developing world cannot reap these benefits because their native countries are classified as 'closed' in terms of figure 13.2. A simple conclusion seems to emerge: all that countries have to do in order to stimulate economic growth is to open their borders. Is it really this simple? The answer is: no. In section 13.7 we shall argue that openness is a necessary, but not a sufficient condition for economic growth and prosperity.

13.4 Low-skilled labour, trade and within-country income inequality

The discussion above has not made much use of the international business (IB) perspective to explain trends in income inequality between countries. This is no longer the case when we try to explain the relevance of globalization for within-country

---

[4] Readers who are not convinced by looking at pictures should consult Sala-i-Martin (2002).

income inequality. The basic message of the international economics (IE) literature is that free trade is welfare-enhancing. This is not surprising, as globalization is the opposite of protectionism. Specialization according to comparative advantage raises income. Increased globalization and specialization, however, lead to changes in the industrial composition for the trading countries: some sectors shrink while others grow. This raises the question as to what happens to the income distribution within the countries concerned.

The ensuing debate focused on the role of low-skilled workers in the developed world. From 1980 onwards, the low-skilled workers in most developed countries have experienced either (i) that their wage growth lagged behind that of high-skilled workers or (ii) that their unemployment levels have increased (in countries with wage rigidity). Given the simultaneous rise of trade with developing countries, critics of globalization were quick to point to these trade flows as the culprit for the plight of the low-skilled workers. This section reviews this discussion.

To see how trade influences the relative wage of the low-skilled workers we first go back to the factor abundance (Heckscher-Ohlin) model of chapter 3, which has been used extensively in this debate in the 1990s. For a country increasingly participating in the globalization process (moving from autarky towards free trade), the prices of export goods will rise and the prices of import goods will fall. Due to comparative advantage, prices in the export sector are lower in autarky compared to prices in the same sector in the foreign country. This is essentially the reason why this sector becomes the export sector once trade is allowed. Increased foreign demand then raises prices in the export sector. At the same time, the import sector shrinks and domestic demand for this good is redirected to the foreign country, which is able to produce this commodity at lower prices (because it has a comparative advantage in this sector). The growing export sector attracts factors of production (capital, high-skilled and low-skilled labour and entrepreneurship) from the import sector. Are there winners and losers in this model? The answer is, yes there are.

As we explained in chapter 3, a price increase in, say, the high-skilled labour-intensive sector increases the wage rate of high-skilled workers relative to low-skilled workers. The price increase raises the demand for both production factors in the expanding sector. However, in the high-skilled labour-intensive sector the demand for high-skilled labour increases more than the demand for low-skilled labour, which drives up high-skilled relative to low-skilled wages. The supply of the production factors comes from the other sector, which shrinks and releases relatively more low-skilled workers than high-skilled workers, again reducing the relative factor reward for low-skilled workers. This is called the Stolper-Samuelson theorem, named after its inventors. Because it is important in the discussion on the effects of globalization, we state it here explicitly (see chapter 3 for the details):

Stolper-Samuelson theorem: in a neo-classical framework with two final goods and two factors of production, an increase in the price of a final good increases the reward for the factor used intensively in the production of that good and reduces the reward for the other factor, provided both goods are produced.

The theorem immediately explains why we have winners and losers in the globalization process. If countries open up their borders and start trading with each other, the scarce factor of production loses from increased globalization whereas the abundant factor gains. This brings us to the heart of the matter. The discussion on globalization in developed countries centres around workers in import-competing sectors. As a stylized fact, developed countries have a comparative advantage in high-skill-intensive products, whereas the developing world has a comparative advantage in low-skill-intensive products. This implies that increased globalization is bad news for those working in the import sectors in the developed world: they see their wages decline. So, according to the Stolper-Samuelson theorem, increased globalization is indeed bad news for the relatively low-skilled workers in the developed world.

The harm done might even be greater than this effect alone. If the replaced workers in the developed world are not immediately re-employed in the export sector, they become unemployed. This excess labour supply reduces wages in other sectors and thus also influences wages in the non-tradable sectors of the developed countries. Competition from low-wage countries thus has an effect on wages of low-skilled workers in all sectors, even if they do not compete directly on world markets.

In the developing countries the opposite happens. The most abundant factor, low-skilled labour, benefits from trade. These countries have a comparative advantage in the low-skilled labour-intensive sector. Extra demand from the developed world increases the prices of these commodities and, due to the Stolper–Samuelson effect, raises the wages of the unskilled workers. High-skilled workers in the developing countries lose from trade. So, there also are winners and losers here. Although in both types of countries the import sector shrinks while the export sector grows, it is by no means certain that the person who gets a higher-paying job in the export sector is necessarily the one who has lost a job in the import sector. So while theoretically everyone may gain from globalization, it is unclear if all individuals actually do so.

13.5 Low-skilled labour and the irrelevance of trade

Although trade between developed and developing countries has increased since the 1970s, many economists are convinced that only a relatively small part of the rising

Table 13.1 Price changes; manufacturing industries, per cent

	Domestic price change	Import price change
USA (1980–89)		
High-skilled weights	33.1	26.0
Low-skilled weights	32.3	28.1
Japan (1980–90)		
High-skilled weights	-5.60	-18.23
Low-skilled weights	-3.90	-17.29
Germany (1980–90)		
High-skilled weights	23.98	15.24
Low-skilled weights	26.03	17.07

Sources: Lawrence and Slaughter (1993); Lawrence (1994).
Notes: Low-skilled labour = production workers or manual labour. High-skilled labour = non-production workers or non-manual labour.

within-country income inequality in some developed countries can be ascribed to globalization. Why are they so convinced that this is the case? The following reasons are often mentioned:

- First, *international trade flows are simply too small*. The flows between, for example, the USA and the rest of the world or between the EU and the rest of the world were only about 14 per cent of GDP in 2000. These shares are higher than in 1913 or in 1970, but not dramatically higher. For this reason Paul Krugman (1995, p. 331) observes that 'it would be hard to argue that the sheer volume of trade is now at a level that marks a qualitative difference from previous experience.' Imports of manufactured goods from developing countries are also still only approximately 2 per cent of the combined GDP of the OECD countries. The relatively large changes in factor prices are difficult to reconcile with the small changes in trade relative to GDP and also with the small share of developing countries in the total imports of the OECD countries.

- Second, *prices do not behave as we expect according to trade theory*, as illustrated for three countries in table 13.1, which shows industry price changes weighted with that sector's share of either high-skilled or low-skilled labour. The first row for each country uses each sector's share of high-skilled workers in total employment. The second row uses the share of low-skilled workers as weights. Table 13.1 indicates that price changes in sectors that use relatively more low-skilled labour are higher (or decline less, in the case of Japan) than in sectors that use relatively more high-skilled labour. International competition with low-wage countries should have resulted in lower import prices in sectors that make intensive use of low-skilled labour.

- Third, based on the Stolper-Samuelson theorem, we expect not only that wages of low-skilled workers decline relative to wages of skilled workers, but also a *change in the labour skills composition*. As globalization stimulates further specialization, the high-skilled labour-abundant developed country specializes further in the high-skill-intensive sectors. The increased demand for high-skilled labour causes an increase in the relative factor rewards (driving up high-skilled wages). This provides an incentive to reduce the ratio of high-skilled to low-skilled workers in each sector in the developed country. Empirical evidence, however, points in the opposite direction. In the USA, for example, the relative demand for high-skilled labour has increased, despite the increase in the wages of high-skilled workers (see box 13.2).[5]

Box 13.2 A closer look at wage differentials and labour market differences

The trade–wages discussion dominated the globalization debate in the 1980s and 1990s. Table 13.2 shows that for countries with flexible wages, such as the USA and the UK, the relative wage of the low-skilled workers falls during this period, where the level of education is used as a proxy for skill. During this same time

Table 13.2 Wage differentials, by education

	High to low education earnings ratio (men)	
Country	Around 1980	Around 1990
USA	1.37	1.51
UK	1.53	1.65
France	1.66	1.66
Germany	1.36	1.42
Italy	1.60	1.61

Source: Nickell and Bell (1996), cited in Peeters (2001).

period, the wage gap does not widen (or at least not as much) in Continental Europe where wages are less flexible, such as in France, Germany and Italy. In those countries, the change in the relative demand for low-skilled labour shows up by changes in unemployment, as illustrated in table 13.3. For the period under consideration overall unemployment levels rise, but in relative terms the unemployment

---

[5] See also Sachs and Shatz (1996). Feenstra and Hanson (2001).

Table 13.3 Unemployment and labour skills

| | Unemployment (per cent of labour force) | | | |
| | Low-skilled workers | | High-skilled workers | |
Country	1979–82	1991–93	1979–82	1991–93
USA	9.4	11.0	2.1	3.0
UK	12.2	17.1	3.9	6.2
France	6.5	12.1	2.1	4.2
Germany	7.6	10.7	2.0	2.2
Italy	4.8	7.5	12.2	12.5

Source: Peeters (2001).

rate of the low-skilled workers increases in Germany and Italy, but not in the USA and the UK.

If increased trade is not the main cause for the position of low-skilled workers on the labour markets in the developed world, than what is? Probably the best answer is *technological progress*, which may hurt the low-skilled workers in two ways:

(1) Technological progress is biased against low-skilled workers in all sectors of the economy (skill-biased technological change). The increased use of ICT, for example, partially replaces low-skilled labour and at the same time increases the demand for high-skilled workers.

(2) Low-skilled workers are traditionally over-represented in the manufacturing sector, where technological progress is much higher than in other sectors, such as the services sector (sector-biased technological change).

Technological progress is easier to implement in the manufacturing sector than in the services sector. Parts of the production chain might be automated and thus become more capital-intensive and high-skilled labour-intensive. In contrast, not much technological progress takes place in a barber shop or in a symphony orchestra. It still takes about twenty minutes to get a haircut, as it did fifty years ago. Similarly, an orchestra still uses approximately the same time to play a Mozart opera as it did fifty years ago. Technological progress thus reduces the demand for labour in the manufacturing sector relative to that in the services sector, as pointed out in the 1960s by Baumol (1967). In box 13.3, we reflect briefly upon this issue by discussing what is happening inside a typical example of a manufacturing multinational, Philips Electronics.

Table 13.4 illustrates the fact that labour productivity in industry was indeed growing faster than in the service sector in the EU and the USA during the period

Box 13.3 Philips Electronics

In the late 1980s, Philips Electronics was a European electronics giant that had great difficulty facing up to new competition, particularly from Southeast Asia. Firms such as Samsung from Korea and Sony from Japan seemed to be out-competing Philips not only in their home countries, but also in Philips' European foothold. The then CEO of Philips, Jan Timmer, launched a major restructuring programme, called Centurion, and his successor, Cor Boonstra, followed in his footsteps. Apart from a major overhaul of Philips' product portfolio, concentrating activities in a limited number of divisions (from light bulbs and consumer electronics to medical equipment and semiconductors), the Centurion operation and its follow-up programmes were large cost-cutting exercises. As a result, Philips became a much slimmer organization. In 1996, it had about 260,000 employees, worldwide, which already implied a substantial reduction compared to the 300,000-plus employees in the heyday of the 1970s; in 2003, employment had fallen to approximately 165,000.

In addition, Philips was heavily involved in international outsourcing – that is, in slicing-up-its-value-chain. More and more activities are now outsourced to other companies, which may be former Philips units. ASLM, for example – one of the world's leading semiconductor production machinery firms – is a former Philips unit. Other activities have been moved to low-wage countries such as China and Poland. In China, the first joint venture (JV) was established in 1985; in 2004, roughly 18,000 staff were employed by Philips China in thirty wholly-owned enterprises and JVs. As a consequence, one after another Dutch Philips plant was closed, meaning that by far the largest part of Philips' production capacity is now located outside the Netherlands. Currently, Philips management is speculating about the opportunity for moving service-type activities to countries where labour cost is low but labour quality is high. For instance, Philips' Chief Financial Officer (CFO), Jan Hommes, announced in November 2003 that they were planning to move about 600 service jobs to Poland. Indeed, Philips started to invest in the establishment of a Polish services centre in Łódz.

1979–2001. Changes in technology required more high-skilled workers in the industrial sectors. Low-skilled workers did not lose their jobs due to competition with low-wage countries, but simply because they were no longer needed in an increasingly complex and technologically advanced world that required more high-skilled workers.

Not international trade, but technological progress is therefore thought to be responsible for the increased demand for high-skilled relative to low-skilled labour,

Table 13.4 Changes in labour productivity;[a] Europe and USA, 1979–2001, per cent

	1979–90		1990–5		1995–2001	
Sector	EU-15	USA	EU-15	USA	EU-15	USA
Total economy	2.3	1.2	2.4	1.1	1.8	2.2
Industry	3.5	3.2	4.0	3.7	2.9	3.6
Services	1.3	0.6	1.6	0.5	1.4	2.3
Other	3.4	1.7	3.2	0.8	2.1	0.2

Source: Groningen Growth and Development Centre, 60-industry data base, March 2004.
Note: [a] Labour productivity = value added (constant prices) per hour; see http://www.ggdc.net.

and so for the increased income inequality within the major developed countries. In view of the problems associated with the standard IE explanation discussed above, this technology explanation has much going for it. In section 13.6, we shall argue that the globalization processes associated with technological change can be better understood from an IB perspective, particularly in combination with the underlying economic forces as analysed in IE. There is, therefore, much to be gained from combining insights from both disciplines.

13.6 Outsourcing and income inequality

If we take globalization to include only trade in final goods, it is difficult to explain how this can be responsible for the increased income inequality within countries. A recurring theme of our book is that globalization, particularly in the current era, is much more than just increased trade in final goods. One of the crucial, new elements of the current globalization phase is the *fragmentation of the production process* by multinational firms, as touched upon in chapter 5. This implies that the IB perspective is crucial for understanding the powers of globalization. Fragmentation or outsourcing is also the driving force for increased FDI, assisted by the increase in capital mobility, as discussed in chapters 6–9.

As table 13.5 illustrates, international trade increasingly consists of trade in intermediate goods. This is to a large extent caused by *outsourcing*. We know from chapter 5 that outsourcing can be profitable if firms can relocate low-skilled labour parts of the value chain to countries with a relative abundance of low-skilled labour (see also box 12.2). Multinationals play a vital role in this process, provided they have the ability to organize and maintain the increasingly complex production processes in different countries, catering to the needs, social and cultural backgrounds and peculiarities of each of these individual countries. Even if trade flows remain unchanged, outsourcing can have a dampening effect on wages because the demand for low-skilled labour

Table 13.5 Imported intermediate deliveries, industry, 1974–1993

Country	Share of imported intermediates (%)		
	1974	1984	1993
Canada	15.9	14.4	20.2
Japan	8.2	7.3	4.1
UK	13.4	19.0	21.6
USA	4.1	6.2	8.2

Source: Feenstra and Hanson (2001).

declines and the demand for high-skilled, organizational and management labour increases in the outsourcing countries.

Recall table 13.1, which weighs industry price changes by that sector's share of either high-skilled or low-skilled labour. The data from table 13.1 can be put in a different perspective. Some industries are outsourcing parts of the value chain to cheaper countries. It can be expected that this will have an effect on the price of domestic relative to import prices. In this case, one will expect to see domestic prices (say, the price of a computer) increase relative to import prices (say, the price of an imported PC monitor). Comparing column (2) with column (1) in table 13.1, we see that this is indeed the case, suggesting that international trade in the guise of outsourcing might still be relevant.

If the wages of high-skilled workers rise relative to those of low-skilled workers there is an incentive to reduce the ratio of skilled to unskilled workers in all sectors in the skilled-labour-abundant country. In most countries, we observe the opposite, namely a rise in the skill intensity of production. Section 13.5 argued that technological change is thought to be the main underlying reason. But technological change does not fall from the sky; it is a conscious process in which individual firms, under the constant competitive threat of other firms, actively invest in R&D and re-organize their production processes.

The forces of globalization enable restructuring and organization complexities unachievable previously. The fragmentation and outsourcing processes therefore also help to explain the low-skilled labour 'puzzle'. The relocation of the low-skilled labour-intensive parts of the production chain to the low-skilled labour-abundant countries leads to skill upgrading, productivity increases and higher wages in the remaining parts of industry. Recent evidence suggests that outsourcing is indeed an important contribution.[6] To explain the impact of globalization on income inequality

[6] Vanessa Strauss-Kahn (2004) analyses how domestic technological progress and outsourcing have both contributed to the position of low-skilled workers in France. She finds that the 'within-industry shift away from unskilled workers toward skilled workers' is up to 25 per cent caused by outsourcing. See also Feenstra and Hanson (2001) and recent work by Bernard, Jensen and Schott (2002).

within countries we therefore need to supplement the IE analysis with the IB analysis on the role of large multinationals in the world economy.

13.7 Developing countries and the 'globalization bonus'

Using the same line of reasoning that we applied to the developed countries, we find that for the developing countries the net benefits of globalization are supposed to be positive, although not everybody gains. In the developing countries, too, we can identify losers and winners from globalization using a similar methodology to that in section 13.4. Based on the logic of the Stolper-Samuelson theorem, the winners and losers are the mirror image of those in the developed countries. Since the developing countries are abundant in low-skilled labour, their comparative advantage is in low-skilled intensive activities, such as apparel, leather and textile industries. Specializing accordingly, the low-skilled workers gain and the high-skilled workers lose. The discussion on outsourcing also has a mirror image in the developing world.

Outsourcing of parts in the production chain to countries that have a comparative advantage in low-skilled intensive products provides an extra boost in demand for this type of labour. For developing countries, this is an additional bonus to the already large potential gains from specialization due to globalization. Moreover, it is expected that this type of investment will bring additional skills and production experience from the developed world with it. This 'imported' technology also benefits low-skilled income in the developing countries (see chapter 11). The gains from trade are not a zero-sum game between developed and developing countries (or any country, for that matter). All participants gain from trade.[7] But some might gain more than others. Finally, we saw in section 13.3 (recall figure 13.2) that globalization – or, in more general terms, openness – is good for the economic growth of the developing countries.

If the static and dynamic net gains from participating in the process of globalization are clearly positive, why is there so much doubt among the critics of globalization, in both the developed and developing world, that there really is a 'globalization bonus'

---

[7] There are theoretical circumstances in which countries might not gain. Very large countries, for example, might not gain if they dominate the world market, and pre-trade autarky prices are the same as post-trade international prices. Gains from trade are zero, but not negative in this case. Gains from trade can be negative if economies of scale are present. Established firms can have a lower cost per unit than new entrants even if new entrants eventually have lower costs per unit. If countries start trading, the established firm might outbid an (in the long run) more efficient competitor. The world gets stuck in a second-best-outcome.

for the relatively poor countries in our world economy? Are these doubts justified? There are a number of economic arguments that have been put forward as to why the gains of globalization might be smaller than the theory tells us (for non-economic arguments along the cultural, environmental and political dimension, see Klein, 2001).

First, there is the notion of *export pessimism*. The central advice from trade theorists for developing countries is to participate in the global economy. If all developing countries have a comparative advantage in low-skilled-intensive products they cannot, so goes the argument, all gain from globalization. Increased supply from all developing countries at the same time on the world market will drive export prices down. The countries involved suffer terms-of-trade losses that reduce real income. In response, protectionist-type measures have been promoted, as is briefly discussed in box 13.4.

Although compelling, the terms-of-trade argument hardly stands up against the evidence. The exports of the developing world, including Brazil, China, India, Mexico and the Southeast Asian countries, is still only a limited fraction of world exports. It is unlikely that an increase in exports of the developing world will greatly affect prices in world trade. The empirical evidence also points in this direction. In general, the terms of trade do not seem to worsen for developing countries, although for some specific commodities world prices have gone down, so that for some developing countries that are heavily dependent on these products the terms of trade have not improved.

A second often-cited reason why the developing countries would not benefit from globalization is that workers in those countries lack *bargaining power*, and have no union representation. As a result, wages will not increase, and labour conditions do not improve. This, according to some globalization critics, is the main reason why multinational firms invest in these countries in the first place. Evidence, however, points in another direction. On average, the wages paid by foreign affiliates in low-wage countries are twice as high as the average wage in the domestic manufacturing sector in these countries (Graham, 2000). But wages in these countries are on average still lower than in the developed countries. This, however, reflects differences in labour productivity, as we explained in chapter 3.

A third qualification is the lack of *well-functioning institutions* in some parts of the developing world. In a number of countries corruption flourishes, property rights are absent and the legal system functions imperfectly, preventing the poor from benefiting from globalization (see box 12.7). The countries that do not well in this respect are mostly found in Africa. According to a recent survey by the World Economic Forum, Nigeria and Chad have the lowest score in terms of corruption, independence of the legal system from political influences, bribes and nepotism

Box 13.4 Let's dance to the New (International) Order (NIO)

The belief in the terms-of-trade argument became so strong that the developing world in the 1960s proposed a New International Order (NIO), the main reason for setting up UNCTAD. In practice, the consequence of the discussions that took place around that time was that many developing countries introduced a so-called 'import-substitution strategy'. The idea was that the expansion of exports of primary products would lead to immiserizing growth (see chapter 11). Moreover, a change to more profitable manufacturing exports was deemed impossible, because these industries would not be competitive on the international market. The imposition of tariffs could protect the domestic market from outside competition and could give domestic producers time to gain experience with relatively new production techniques in order to become competitive (the infant industry argument). The effects of these policies were at best mixed. Some sectors, such as the automobile industry in Japan, were protected and over time became internationally competitive. For other sectors, the introduction of tariffs raised the cost of intermediate imports and the final goods became more expensive.

Some inefficient industries could survive only because of protection. In addition, the protected manufactured industries were relatively capital-intensive, and did not benefit from the relatively abundant unskilled labour. During this period, many developing countries introduced some form of protection, with mixed results; modern versions of this policy stress export diversification. Some countries, such as Hong Kong, Malaysia, Singapore and Thailand, never used temporary protectionist measures as a main development instrument, but for the 'Asian Tigers' this was a successful strategy. One has to keep in mind, moreover, that the composition of trade is not given. As countries start to develop, the composition of exports changes. Developing countries usually start by exporting primary products, then move on to manufactures and subsequently to high-skilled-manufactures and services. In the 1970s Japan shifted export production towards more high-skilled-intensive production, thus making room for the 'Asian Tigers'. These are now also moving towards more high-skilled-intensive production, making way for China.

(World Economic Forum, *Africa Competitiveness Report*, 2003–2004). This is an important qualification of the supposed benefits of globalization or openness. In fact, opening up your borders to trade or capital flows is a necessary but far from a sufficient condition for a country to benefit from globalization. In order to yield the static and dynamic benefits from increased specialization, minimum standards as to

Table 13.6 Institutions and economic performance, correlation coefficients[a]

Variable	GDP *per capita*	Growth	Volatility	Governance	Property	Constraint
GDP *per capita*	1.00					
Growth	0.65	1.00				
Volatility	−0.53	−0.36	1.00			
Governance	0.86	0.59	−0.61	1.00		
Property	0.76	0.54	−0.62	0.79	1.00	
Constraint	0.72	0.45	−0.64	0.73	0.63	1.00

Source: IMF (2003, p. 98).

Notes: [a] All correlations are significant at the 5 per cent level; GDP *per capita* is in 1995 US dollar; Growth = growth rate of GDP *per capita* (average annual, 1960–98); Volatility = growth volatility of GDP *per capita* (standard deviation, 1960–98); Governance = overall governance measure; Property = property rights; Constraint = constraint on power of executive.

the functioning of domestic institutions have to be met. Protection of property rights, an effective judicial system, a certain amount of mutual trust between citizens and the like are all crucial conditions for a market economy to function at all. Without these and other institutions, participating in the globalization process will not make a country better off. There has been a significant outburst of research in recent years that shows how important well-functioning institutions are for economic development (see Acemoglu, Johnson and Robinson, 2001; Easterly and Levine, 2003; Rodrik, 2003; Rodrik, Subramanian and Trebbi, 2004).

If institutions do their job properly, they reduce transactions costs. And, as we have seen at various instances throughout this book, a reduction of transactions costs or of the wedge between supply and demand prices is trade-stimulating and welfare-enhancing. The relevance of institutions for economic development is not only a hot topic among researchers but at present almost every policy institution emphasizes the relevance of institutions for economic development (see World Bank, 2002; IMF, 2003). Table 13.6 gives for three institutional measures the correlation with economic performance for a large sample of countries. Table 13.6 illustrates that better governance, better protection of property rights and more constraints on the power of the executive are positively associated with a higher GDP *per capita*, a higher growth rate and less growth volatility (for more details, particularly on the measurement of institutional variables, see IMF, 2003).

Correlation, however, is not causality: does higher growth imply better functioning institutions, or vice versa? The recent literature tries to find evidence as to whether or not a positive correlation between economic performance and institutions can be interpreted as causation, in the sense that better institutions lead to improved economic performance. How is this done? Acemoglu, Johnson and Robinson (2001) show for eighty countries that the mortality rates of colonial settlers provide a means to isolate the exogenous part of institutions. The idea is that these mortality rates have a lasting impact on the type of institutions that were introduced by the colonizers. High mortality rates meant that the colonizing powers did not invest much in setting up good institutions themselves, whereas the opposite was the case with low mortality rates. On top of that add the fact that institutions are strongly path-dependent or determined by history and the following estimation strategy can be adopted. By first regressing the quality of institutions on these exogenous mortality rates, and some other exogenous variables, for each country and by subsequently using the part of institutional variation that is explained by these exogenous variables as the main independent variable in a regression with income *per capita* as the dependent variable, one can hope to establish whether the correlation message from table 13.6 is also one of causation: better institutions lead to better economic performance. Based on this strategy, good institutions indeed cause economic growth (according to Rodrik, Subramanian and Trebbi, 2004, 'institutions rule'). In addition, the role of institutions trumps the impact of the two other 'deep' explanations for cross-country differences in income *per capita*: physical geography and trade openness. Acemoglu, Johnson and Robinson (2001) find that a 1 per cent positive shock in the institutional quality leads to a 2.15 per cent increase in income *per capita* for a country.[8]

A final qualification that comes to mind as to why developing countries may not succeed in reaping the benefits of globalization even if their own house 'is in order' is *protectionism*. Trade restrictions do not only hurt the consumers in the rich countries, as we explained in chapter 10, but they certainly also hurt the developing countries. The WTO, for instance, is a strong advocate of reductions in trade barriers between developing countries. On average these are higher than those between developed countries and developing countries. The largest benefits of further trade liberalization can thus be found in the developing world. To sum up, for developing countries, participation in the global economy is beneficial provided that certain requirements are met. We know from figure 13.2 that open economies grow faster than closed economies. Whether or not this growth also 'trickles down' to the very poor in developing countries is another issue. By and large, the evidence suggests that more growth implies less poverty, but this not an automatic process. But if globalization-induced growth does not reach the very poor, one can hardly blame the globalization

---

[8] Not everyone is convinced that institutions are this important. For (rather outspoken) criticism of the 'institutions rule' idea and the methodology employed, see Sachs (2003) and Glaeser *et al.* (2004).

process itself for this shortcoming. National governments remain first and foremost responsible for the domestic income distribution.

13.8 Conclusions

The analysis in section 13.6 on low-skilled labour and the possible role of outsourcing shows that the analysis of the impact of globalization should take the international business perspective into account. To understand what globalization implies for the developing countries, we also need to look at FDI and multinational firms. In fact, many critics of globalization not only acknowledge this but go much further by arguing that multinational firms are the beginning and end of almost every discussion on globalization. Globalization is supposedly good only for multinational firms and high-skilled workers, while the less mobile – that is, the low-skilled workers, national policy-makers and brand-addicted consumers – suffer. Is this the kind of globalization that is really happening?

Those who are internationally mobile tend to do better than those who are not. Rodrik (1997) has stressed that in a globalized economy where some groups are internationally mobile and others are not, those who can move tend to benefit at the expense of those who cannot. As we have seen, capital has become much more mobile since 1950, while labour has lagged behind. Therefore, we can expect some additional tendency for labour to lose, and capital to gain, from globalization. At the same time, it is tempting to over-state the power of multinational firms and other allegedly 'footloose' factors of production, as we observed in chapter 2. Widespread fears that in order to keep and attract these 'footloose' agents within their territory, national governments must engage in a race-to-the-bottom have so far not materialized to the extent that anti-globalists suggest. In chapter 7, we noted, for instance, that no clear downward trend in corporate income taxes is visible. Clearly, globalization is a complicated issue, where a full analysis of what really goes on helps to distinguish facts from myths. In this book, we have tried to offer precisely this: a balanced analysis of globalization, applying tools and insights from both the IE and IB literatures.

While the analysis of nations and firms in the global economy is really better off by combining IE with IB, the addition of the IB literature to the IE literature does not imply that international businesses predominantly shape the world. On the contrary, the allegedly 'footloose' firms often turn out to be less footloose than expected (cf. box 12.3). Both the modern IE and IB literature show us why this is the case. Re-location is costly, not only because new production facilities have to be set up or because positive agglomeration rents associated with the present location would no longer apply, but also because low-wage countries are sometimes also character-ized by less well-functioning institutions. In addition, as emphasized in chapter 12, differences in cultures and institutions between countries (and firms) are still very relevant. These elements together determine whether or not firms might engage in globalization, and whether or not specialization patterns follow comparative advan-tage. In the process, some will turn out to be the winners and some will, regrettably, emerge as the losers. For sure, globalization is happening, but it is a multi-faceted phenomenon that is not in line with the simple observations so often put forward in the public arena.

14

Towards an international economics and business?

KEYWORDS

glocalization   resource-based theory   ceremonial adoption
FDI–trade causality   universal enterprise   multi-level analysis

14.1 Glocalization

When we have analysed the global economy throughout the book we have provided ample empirical information, backed by theory, on the globalization process, to be able to distinguish myths from facts. Indeed, globalization is really happening, as we argued in chapter 13, although its forms and shapes are different from what is often suggested in the public debate – and so are its consequences. In chapter 13, we concluded that at the macroeconomic level, globalization takes place as a process of further integration of the economies of different nation-states, thus raising inter-country interdependencies at the world level. Important as this may be, it does *not* imply that all nation-states develop into clones of a single universal model or global template: cultural and institutional differences still abound. There is no reason to expect that this will change in the near future. In a world that is more and more integrated economically, such diversity can be sustained. In this concluding chapter 14, we focus on another key player in the global economy: the Multinational enterprise (MNE). First, we continue chapter 13's evaluation of the globalization process, but now at the micro level of the MNE (see section 14.1). Second, we return to one of the leading threads in this book in section 14.2: the macro–micro linkages across multinationals and nation-states.

Our starting point is the following observation: it might be that globalization processes at the micro or firm level are even more powerful than those at the macro or country level. After all, countries do not really compete, as we explained in detail in this book, but firms do. The consequences of comparative advantage are very different from those of competitive advantage. In a global economy, the nation-states can all benefit from specialization along the lines of comparative advantage. In the world as a marketplace, firms that suffer from a competitive disadvantage may be expelled from the market altogether by superior rivals. That is, perhaps, global competition forces MNEs to adopt similar best practices, in order to avoid becoming the victim of competitive disadvantages. As a result, a template of *the* MNE will be spread across the globe, as a bundle of universal best practices. If an MNE fails to follow such universal 'guidelines', it will be competed away by those rivals that do not. Throughout the book, we have discussed examples that suggest that this might indeed be the case.

An example is international outsourcing (see chapters 5 and 12). By outsourcing those activities that can be done more cheaply in another country to firms or subsidiaries in that country, an MNE can lower its costs. If a firm fails to deliver on this front, by not slicing-up its-value-chain to minimize its costs, it will simply be under-priced by rivals that are smart enough to do so. Hence, according to standard competition logic, the international outsourcing strategy will start to dominate, either because firms mimic first-movers or because – if they fail to do so – they are forced to exit from the market. Arguments like this may explain why, time and again, universal business fashions seem to spread across the globe. In chapter 12, we briefly discussed the example of downsizing. It may well be that MNEs are 'forced' to downsize, out of competitive necessity. If they ignored this universal fashion, they could not reap the cost reductions necessary to survive in the global marketplace. More generally, if the American version of the MNE, with its emphasis on shareholder value, is out-performing alternative models of running a business, then it is no wonder that the world of multinationals is being 'Americanized'.

Again, as in the case of macro-level globalization (see chapter 13), it is not that simple. The key reason is a theoretical one: a firm cannot, by definition, develop a competitive advantage *vis-à-vis* its rivals by being just like them. By doing so, this firm can only be as cheap or as good as its competitors, at best. By its very nature, a competitive advantage can be developed only by being *different*. A competitive advantage can be achieved only by being unique, along whatever dimension of competition that is important in the market involved. This logic is explored in the *resource-based theory* of the firm (Wernerfelt, 1984; Barney, 1991; Maijoor and van Witteloostuijn, 1996). Competitive advantages are the result of bundles of resources that allow the firm to compete efficiently and effectively. Such resources may be tangible – such as production machineries – or intangible – such as brand names. Often, a competitive advantage is derived from a particular 'synergetic' combination of different resources. To be able to produce a sustainable competitive advantage, though, such resources must be (relatively) rare, valuable, difficult to imitate and costly to circumvent. That is, both the product market (rare and valuable) and the factor market (difficult to imitate and costly to circumvent) must be imperfect. Otherwise, whatever the advantage, it can and will be competed away.

Take the example of perhaps the best-known multinational of the early twenty-first century: Microsoft.

1. *Rare*   If its main product – the Windows operating system – were not rare, but if alternative (perfect) substitutes were offered to the demand side of the markets by many rivals, then Microsoft's high profits would probably be competed away.
2. *Valuable*   Straightforwardly, if Microsoft's products did not represent value for its clients, selling these products is a no-go, leaving Microsoft out of pocket.
3. *Difficult to imitate*   If Microsoft's software packages could be imitated easily because patent protection had been abolished, then entrants would develop substitute products, implying that profits would fall as a result of entry.
4. *Difficult to circumvent*   If alternative technologies were available with which clients could circumvent the use of Microsoft products, then clients would start to use them to avoid Microsoft's high prices, forcing Microsoft to lower its prices.

So, only if *all* four conditions are met can Microsoft sustain, and benefit from, its competitive advantage. Indeed, Microsoft is *different* from all its (potential) competitors, making it into one of the most profitable multinationals in the world.

From the logic of the resource-based theory of the firm, it can be understood that, on many counts, multinationals will be *different*. That is what competition in imperfectly competitive markets is all about. Whatever their similarities, General Motors is different from DaimlerChrysler, which is different from Toyota, which is different from Renault, etc. Paradoxically, increasing globalization forces firms to seek ways to increase their differences; otherwise competitive advantages will fade away, and global markets will turn out to be perfectly competitive. Of course, this is not happening precisely because of the nature of competition among multinationals: just like any other firm, they do not like perfectly competitive markets because, in such markets, profits are zero. Therefore, by their very nature, multinationals continuously search for ways to make their markets imperfect. By definition, this implies a permanent drive, or incentive, to search for uniqueness.[1] This may be called the 'globalization paradox'. In box 14.1, we argue that a similar paradox may operate at the macro level of nation-states as a result of national processes of adaptation, dubbed *glocalization*.

A follow-up question is, of course, to what extent home-country effects do matter in developing and sustaining competitive advantages. After all, it may be that competition among multinationals is 'global' in the sense that, notwithstanding their differences, home-country diversity is no longer a source of competitive differentiation. Again using the logic of the resource-based view of the firm, we believe this not to be the case. Our argument runs as follows. 'Universal' resources are easier to copy. If multinational x finds out that outsourcing to low-wage country y makes perfect

---

[1] Of course, not only differences matter. As a platform (a minimum or necessary condition) from which to build competitive advantages, multinationals might need to adopt similar 'best practices' (e.g. downsizing and outsourcing). The point we want to make here, though, is that this is not enough (i.e. it is not a sufficient condition).

Box 14.1 Glocalization

Sorge (2005) offers a rich and historical analysis of globalization and its counter-forces for Germany. Using impressive evidence from many detailed comparative cross-country studies in such traditions as 'national business systems', 'societal effect studies' and 'varieties of capitalism', Sorge convincingly shows that home-country effects are very persistent, though in subtle ways that change over time. In Germany, for instance, the influence of the way in which society was organized during the Holy Roman Empire is still visible in the German preference for a federal state (with fairly autonomous *Bundesländer*, as successors of the many small former kingdoms) and the prominent role for professional associations (the remnants of medieval guilds). Basically, Sorge's argument is that, in our terminology, home-country effects imply that 'universal practices' are adapted locally so that hybrid templates emerge that may even produce larger differences. Superficially, it may look as if global convergence is taking place, as German institutions and practices are said to be being replaced by American-style ones. At a deeper level, though, path dependencies force such practices to be adapted to local templates (see also box 14.2). As a result, foreign influences trigger local adaptation mechanisms that produce practices that are very different from their initial examples.

In this chapter's context, the case of the multinational is particularly interesting. German multinationals, the popular argument goes, are adopting more and more American-style practices since the late 1980s and early 1990s, in order not to be out-competed by foreign rivals. They are moving away from the German system of codetermination, they flag shareholder value objectives, they call their top bosses CEOs, they move production facilities to China, they downsize their German operations and so on. However, behind this smokescreen of global management talk, actual practices are still very German. For instance, the same multinationals negotiate detailed downsizing deals with the labour unions, they replace foreign managers by German ones in their subsidiaries abroad, they still appoint employee representatives in their non-executive boards, they acquire firms abroad more than they sell parts to foreigners, they work closely together with their German house banks, etc. It is this type of superficial convergence – deeper-level divergence dialectic that has been coined 'glocalization'.[a]

[a] This argument relates to the institutional theory in sociology, which is very popular in the academic (international) business literature. In this theory, scholars try to explain why organizations tend to look so alike within particular so-called organizational fields (e.g. an industry or a profession within a country) with reference to 'isomorphic' forces and processes. A classic contribution is DiMaggio and Powell (1983). In our context, the question is which isomorphic forces are more influential: those that operate globally, or those originating from the firm's local home-country environment? As already said, both forces simultaneously play a role, but there is abundant evidence that the latter cannot be simply put aside, whatever else the globalization rhetoric might be suggesting.

sense, its rival z can easily imitate this type of behaviour. If downsizing turns out to be a profitable strategy, firms can quickly mimic the behaviour of the pioneers. It is precisely home-country resources that are often difficult to imitate, the complexities and subtleties of the imprints of local cultures or domestic institutional practices are not only difficult to observe by foreign enterprises, but they are also (very) hard to copy. As argued extensively in chapter 12, cultural and institutional diversities are very persistent, and have a clear impact upon multinational behaviour. In effect, although many practices seem at first sight to be universal – such as downsizing strategies and performance pay – they tend to be implemented in ways that produce deeper-level home-country differences. In box 14.2, we briefly discuss the related phenomenon of 'ceremonial adoption'.

Box 14.2 Ceremonial adoption

Saying that you adopt this or that new universal practice – be it shareholder value, business process re-engineering (BPE), or anything else – is one thing, but *implementing* it is quite another matter. In chapter 12 and Box 14.1, we argued that talking about such universal best practices more often than not disguises actual practice: it might be that these firms are engaged in 'window dressing'. In the business literature, this is called 'impression management': say that you do what important stakeholders, such as shareholders, want you to do in order to impress them so much that they pay more for your products or shares (or offer higher executive rewards), without bearing the cost of really investing in such so-called best practices. Alternatively, it might be that these firms really believe that they are behaving according to universal best practices, not being aware of the things that actually go on deep in their organizations.

Whatever the interpretation, the outcome is the same: 'ceremonial adoption' of those universal templates. An illustrative study in our context is Kostova and Roth (2002). Drawing on institutional theory (see p. 400), they define ceremonial adoption as the 'formal adoption of a practice on the part of a recipient unit's employees for legitimacy reasons without their believing in its real value for the organization' (Kostova and Roth, 2002, pp. 219–20). They examined the transfer of quality management practices from the headquarters of a large US multinational to its subsidiaries in ten countries in Asia, Europe or elsewhere in the Americas, by analysing questionnaire data. A major finding is that the less 'quality thinking' is part of the subsidiary's local host-country environment, the lower the likelihood that the headquarters' practices will be adopted. Similarly, if the host-country's regulatory system is less favourable to the headquarters' practices, the more the latter's adoption will be in danger. In such circumstances, it is very likely that the subsidiary will be associated with 'ceremonial adoption' only: implementing orders without internalizing them.

14.2 More than macro or micro alone: multi-level interaction

In many respects, the decisions by individual (multinational) firms produce the most important driving forces behind the globalization process, ultimately determining international trade patterns, capital flows and foreign investments. Naturally, these firms react to the conditions of the economic environment in which they operate, which is determined to a considerable extent by national governments and international organizations. MNEs therefore both shape and are shaped by the global environment. In earlier chapters, we gave examples of both types of causalities. Indeed, the analysis of the factors influencing the organizational structure of individual firms is becoming increasingly important in the IE curriculum. We argued, therefore, that it is becoming increasingly clear that the latter type complements the former type. Similarly, the international economic environment in which the (multinational) firms operate is an increasingly important part of the IB curriculum. After all, a good understanding of global and local conditions is a prerequisite for good strategy-making – e.g. selecting the appropriate countries to invest in, while using the appropriate foreign entry modes. Once again, the latter type of analysis complements the former type, which is the reason why we combined these perspectives throughout the book.

To further substantiate our claim that the combined IE and IB perspective will produce value-added, we briefly discuss an example: FDI–trade linkages. From decades of research, it is clear that FDI and trade are closely inter-related. Multinational activity has a distinctive effect on the trade structure of both home and host countries because of the multinationals' ability and willingness to internalize cross-border transactions, thereby affecting the value-added activities both within a country and between countries (Dunning, 1993). By and large, the IB and IE literatures are unanimous on the importance of this link. However, in the real world, the precise nature of the relationships between FDI and trade is a controversial issue, because (a) causalities can run both ways, from FDI to trade and from trade to FDI, and (b) the sign of any FDI–trade linkage is dependent upon the underlying multinational strategies.

The mainstream in the classic theory of international trade in IE views the mobility of goods and factors as substitutes. As part of international integration processes, trade in goods leads to the convergence of product prices, and thus of factor rewards; alternatively, migration or FDI triggers a convergence of factor rewards, and hence of product prices. This is the so-called 'Mundell principle'. The well-known Heckscher–Ohlin–Samuelson–Mundell framework, as discussed extensively in chapter 3, suggests that the international trade in goods can substitute for international movement of factors of production, which includes FDI.[2] Similarly, the other way round,

---

[2] Note, however, that outsourcing or fragmentation might complicate the relation between trade and factor prices, as we explained in section 3.8.

international factor mobility, including FDI, may substitute for trade in goods. In Mundell's words (1957, p. 320):

Commodity movements are at least to some extent a substitute for factor movements . . . an increase in trade impediments stimulates factor movements and . . . an increase in restrictions to factor movements stimulates trade.

The IB literature emphasizes the role of the motives underlying multinational behaviour, including FDI strategies, as discussed above in section 12.2. Market-seeking or horizontal FDI follows demand, penetrating foreign markets with a promising sales potential. Market-seeking or vertical FDI may have a negative impact on the host country's trade balance, since 'the affiliates of foreign firms [in the USA] do show an apparent tendency to export somewhat less and import significantly more than US firms – indeed over two and a quarter times as much' (Graham and Krugman, 1989, p. 67). Factor-seeking or vertical FDI includes multinational behaviour aimed at gaining access to raw materials and low-cost locations. FDI motivated by the quest for raw materials is used to produce goods with natural resources that are lacking or under-supplied in the home country. In general, this type of FDI increases exports from the host nation to the home country, as well as to other third countries (Root, 1994). FDI motivated by low-cost production objectives takes advantage of low-cost factors, such as cheap labour, as part of an overall global sourcing strategy, leading to an ability to export products from the emerging host nation to other countries in the world, including the multinationals' home countries. In this case, the host country is able to increase exports and improve its trade balance (Phongpaichit, 1990).

So, in the business and economic approaches to FDI, trade is considered to be one of the factors that determine the multinational's choice of location for FDI initiatives. On the one hand, a high level of imports in host countries suggests a high level of penetration by foreign companies, which may start off by exporting to the host country, subsequently to switch to FDI once they have established a foothold in these countries. Following this logic, a long-run positive relationship is hypothesized between host-country import and inward FDI (Culem, 1988). On the other hand, in the short run, multinational companies may regard export and FDI as alternative modes of foreign market penetration, which implies a negative relationship. There is therefore uncertainty as to the net effect of the level of the host country's imports on FDI (Billington, 1999). Of course, a multinational's motivation may be complex, implying that FDI is undertaken for more than one reason. Furthermore, regional economic integration and growth of intra-firm trade complicates the prediction of the trade effect of FDI (Narula, 1996). All this explains why unconditional hypotheses about the causality and sign of FDI–trade linkages make no sense. In box 14.3, we illustrate how the net effect of the different forces can be estimated for the case of China.

Box 14.3 FDI and trade in China[a]

In terms of FDI–trade relations, China is an interesting case that has attracted, and still attracts, much attention from both economists and politicians. Using China's provincial data over the 1985–95 period, Wei *et al.* (1999) revealed that provinces with a higher level of international trade attracted more FDI. Using provincial data for 1984–97, Sun (2001) found evidence for a one-way causality from FDI to export in China's coastal and central regions. Using bilateral data for China and nineteen trade partners for 1984–98, Liu *et al.* (2001) indicated that import causes FDI and FDI causes export. Using quarterly data from 1981 to 1997, Liu, Burridge and Sinclair (2002) investigated the causal links between economic growth, FDI and trade, showing that two-way causal connections exist between economic growth, FDI and export.

Zhang, Jacobs and van Witteloostuijn (2004) explore three possible linkages for the 1980–2003 period, in terms of both their size and their causality, given a set of three key variables: export, import and FDI. Their empirical study confirms the interactive causality relationships between China's exports, imports and FDI, as summarized in figure 14.1.

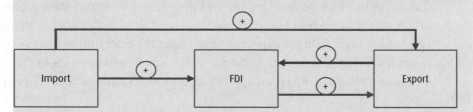

Figure 14.1 China's FDI and trade connections

Their study finds evidence in support of more relationships between the three variables, although the findings are in line with that in the existing literature. In the long run, FDI relates positively to exports and imports, and exports are positively associated with imports. This result implies that MNE investments in China do not substitute for China's exports and imports. In the short run, the study reveals *bi-directional causal links* between FDI and exports, and *one-way causal links* from imports to FDI and from imports to exports.

Clearly, the micro-level FDI behaviour of multinationals has an impact on the macro-level trade performance of a country at large, which in turn influences the multinationals' strategies, etc. The literature on this issue is rapidly growing. It seems, in general, that if horizontal or market-seeking multinationals are involved trade and FDI are *substitutes*, and if vertical or factor-seeking multinationals are involved trade and FDI are *complements*. One might expect that the latter form is more relevant for China than the former, which is consistent with the findings described in this box (see Barba Navaretti and Venables, 2004)

[a] Adapted from Zhang, Jacobs and van Witteloostuijn (2004).

This example offers another illustration of why we need to link insights from the IE tradition with those from the IB literature. In so doing, we can deepen our understanding of the role and performance of both nations and firms in the global economy by developing what may emerge to be a new multi-disciplinary research domain: International Economics and Business.

Bibliography

Chapter 1

Albert, M. (1993), *Capitalism against Capitalism*, London, Vintage

Baldwin, R. E. and P. Martin (1999) 'Two waves of globalisation: superficial similarities, fundamental differences', NBER Working Paper, 6904, Cambridge, MA, NBER

Brakman, S., H. Garretsen and C. van Marrewijk (2001), *An Introduction to Geographical Economics*, Cambridge, Cambridge University Press

Bordo, M. D., A. M. Taylor and J. G. Williamson (eds.) (2003), *Globalization in Historical Perspective*, Chicago, Chicago University Press

Deevey, E. S. (1960), 'The human population', *Scientific American* 203: 195–204

Drucker, P. (1990), *The New Realities*, New York, Mandarin

Eichengreen, B. (2002), 'The globalization wars: an economist reports from the front lines', *Foreign Affairs* July–August

Findlay, R. and J. G. O'Rourke (2001), 'Commodity market integration, 1500–2000', NBER Working Paper 8579, Cambridge, MA, NBER

Fournet, L. H. (1998), 'Diagrammatic chart of world history over the last 5000 years', SIDES, France, Fontenay-sous-bois

Francois, J. F. (2002), 'Globalization and development: do we know anything?', *Tinbergen Institute Magazine* Fall: 7–12

Gourevitch, P., R. Bohn and D. McKendrick (2000), 'Globalization and production: insights from the hard disk drive industry', *World Development* 28: 301–17

Hertz, N. (2001), *The Silent Takeover: Global Capitalism and the Death of Democracy*, New York, Free Press

Keynes, J. M. (1919), *The Economic Consequences of the Peace*, London, Macmillan.

Kremer, M. (1993), 'Population growth and technological change: one million B.C. to 1990', *Quarterly Journal of Economics* 108: 681–716

Krugman, P. R. (1991), 'Increasing returns and economic geography', *Journal of Political Economy* 99: 483–99

Maddison, A. (2001), *The World Economy: A Millennial Perspective*, Paris and Washington, D.C., OECD

McDonald, F. and F. Burton (2002), *International Business*, London, Thomson

Neary, P. J. (2003), 'Globalisation and market structure', *Journal of the European Economic Association* 1: 245–71

Obstfeld, M. and A. M. Taylor (2003), 'Globalization and capital markets', in M. D. Bordo, A. M. Taylor and J. G. Williamson (eds.), *Globalization in Historical Perspective*, Chicago, Chicago University Press

Ohmae, K. (1995), *The End of the Nation State: The Rise of Regional Economies*, HarperCollins, London

O'Rourke, K. H. and J. G. Williamson (1999), *Globalization and History: The Evolution of a Nineteenth-Century Atlantic Economy*, Cambridge, MA, MIT Press

(2002), 'When did globalization begin', *European Review of Economic History* 6: 23–50

Porter, M. E. (1990), *The Competitive Advantage of Nations*, London, Macmillan

Stiglitz, J. (2002), *Globalization and its Discontents*, New York, W. W. Norton

Sorge, A. M. and A. van Witteloostuijn, A. (2004) 'The (non)sense of organizational change: an *essai* about universal management hypes, sick consultancy metaphors and healthy organization theories', *Organization Studies* 25: 1205–31

UN Population Division (2001), World Population Prospects: The 2000 Revision, New York, United Nations

World Bank (2002), World Bank Development Indicators CD-ROM

Chapter 2

American Accounting Association (1966), *Statement of Basic Accounting Theory*, New York

Buijink, W. and M. Jegers (1989), 'Accounting rates of return: comment', *American Economic Review* 79: 287–9

Daniels, J. D. and L. H. Radebaugh (2001), *International Business: Environments and Operations*, 9th edn., Upper Saddle River, NJ, Prentice Hall

De Grauwe, P. and F. Camerman (2003), 'How big are the big multinational companies?', *World Economics*, 4: 23–37

Eiteman, D. K., A. I. Stonehill and M. H. Moffett (2004), *Multinational Business Finance*, 10th edn., Boston, MA, Pearson Addison Wesley

Eun, C. S. and B. G. Resnick (2001), *International Financial Management*, 2nd edn., New York, McGraw-Hill

Hertz, N. (2001), *The Silent Take-Over: Global Capitalism and the Death of Democracy*, London, William Heineman

IMF (1996), *Balance of Payments Textbook*, Washington DC, IMF

Klein, N. (2001) *No Logo*, London, Flamingo

Radebaugh, L. H. and S. J. Gray (1997), *International Accounting and Multinational Enterprises*, 4th edn., New York, John Wiley.

Salamon, G. L. (1989), 'Accounting rates of return: reply', *American Economic Review* 79: 290–3

Stern, R. M. (1973), *The Balance of Payments: Theory and Economic Policy*, Chicago, Aldine

UNCTAD (2004), UNCTAD World Development Report, New York and Geneva, UN

World Bank (2002), World Bank Development Indicators CD–ROM

Chapter 3

Abu-Lughod, J. (1989), *Before European Hegemony: The World System AD 1250–1350*, Oxford, Oxford University Press

Baldwin, R. E. and P. Martin (1999), 'Two waves of globalisation: superficial similarities, fundamental differences', NBER Working Paper, 6904, Cambridge, MA, NBER

Davis, D. R. and D. E. Weinstein (2001), 'An account of global factor trade', *American Economic Review* 92: 1423–53

Deardorff, A. V. (2001), 'Fragmentation across cones', in S. W. Arndt and H. Kierzkowski (eds.), *Fragmentation: New Production Patterns in The World Economy*, Oxford, Oxford University Press

Debaere, P. (2003), 'Relative factor abundance and trade', *Journal of Political Economy* 111: 589–610

Dunning, J. H. (1977), 'Trade, location of economic activity and MNE: a search for an eclectic approach', in B. Ohlin, P. O. Hesselborn and P. M. Wijkman (eds.), *The International Allocation of Economic Activity*, London, Macmillan

(1999), 'Trade, location of economic activity and MNE: a search for an eclectic approach', in B. Ohlin, P. O. Hesselborn and P. M. Wijkman (eds.), *The International Allocation of Economic Activity*, London, Macmillan

(1981), *International Production and the Multinational Enterprise*, London, Allen & Unwin

Feenstra, R. C. (2004), *Advanced International Trade: Theory and Evidence*, Princeton, NJ, Princeton University Press

Findlay, R. and J. G. O'Rourke (2001), 'Commodity market integration, 1500–2000', NBER Working Paper, 8579, Cambridge, MA, NBER

Frank, A. G. and B. Gills (1993) (eds.), *The World System: Five Hundred Years or Five Thousand?*, London, Routledge

Helpman, E. and P. R. Krugman (1985), *Market Structure and Foreign Trade: Increasing Returns, Imperfect Competition, and the International Economy*, Brighton, Harvester Wheatsheaf

Hummels, D. (1999), 'Have international transportation costs declined?', mimeo, University of Chicago

Irwin, D. A. (2002), *Free Trade Under Fire*, Princeton, NJ, Princeton University Press

Krugman, P. R. (1992), *The Age of Diminished Expectations: US Policy in the 1990s*, Cambridge, MA, MIT Press

(1995), 'The end is not quite nigh', *The Economist*, 29 April: 117–18

Neary, J. P. (2004), Cross-border mergers as instruments of comparative advantage', University of Dublin, mimeo

Olson, M. (1982), *The Rise and Decline of Nations*, New York, Free Press

O'Rourke, K. H. and J. G. Williamson (1999), *Globalization and History: The Evolution of a Nineteenth-Century Atlantic Economy*, Cambridge, MA, MIT Press

(2000), 'When did globalization begin?', NBER Working Paper, 7632, Cambridge, MA, NBER

Thurow, L. (1993), *Head to Head: The Coming Economic Battle among Japan, Europe and America*, London, Allen & Unwin.

Trefler, D. (1995), 'The case of the missing trade and other mysteries', *American Economic Review* 85: 1029–46

Chapter 4

Baumol, W. J., J. C. Panzar and R. D. Willig (1982), *Contestable Markets and the Theory of Market Structure*, New York, Harcourt Brace Jovanovich

Chamberlin, E. H. (1933), *The Theory of Monopolistic Competition: A Re-Orientation of the Theory of Value*, Cambridge, MA, Harvard University Press

Davis, D. and D. Weinstein (2002), 'What is the role for empirics in international trade?', in R. Findlay, L. Jonung and M. Lundahl (eds.), *Bertil Ohlin: A Centennial Celebration (1899–1999)*, Cambridge, MA, MIT Press

Feenstra, R. C. (2004), *Advanced International Trade*, Princeton, NJ, Princeton University Press

Frost, T. S. (2001), 'The geographic sources of foreign subsidiaries' innovations', *Strategic Management Journal* 22: 101–23

Grubel, H. G. and P. J. Lloyd (1975), *Intra-Industry Trade: The Theory and Measurement of International Trade in Differentiated Products*, New York, John Wiley

Helpman, E. (1987), 'Imperfect competition and international trade: evidence from fourteen industrial countries', *Journal of the Japanese and International Economies*, 1: 62–81

Leamer, E. E. and J. Levinsohn (1995), 'International trade theory: the evidence', in G. M. Grossman and K. Rogoff (eds.), *Handbook of International Economics*, 3, Amsterdam, North-Holland

Maijoor, S. J. and A. van Witteloostuijn (1996), 'An empirical test of the resource-based theory: strategic regulation in the Dutch audit industry', *Strategic Management Journal* 17: 549–69

Rugman, A. M. and A. Verbeke (2001), 'Subsidiary-specific advantages in multinational enterprises', *Strategic Management Journal* 22: 237–50

The Economist (1997), 'Piece in our time', 26 July, http://www.economist.com

Tsurumi, Y. and H. Tsurumi (1999), 'Fujifilm–Kodak duopolistic competition in Japan and the United States', *Journal of International Business Studies* 30: 813–30

Verdoorn, P. J. (1960), 'The intra-block trade of Benelux', in E. A. G. Robinson (ed.), *Economic Consequences of the Size of Nations*, London, Macmillan

Wernerfelt, B. (1984), 'A resource-based view of the firm', *Strategic Management Journal* 5: 171–80

Witteloostuijn, A. van and M. J. A. M. van Wegberg (1992), 'Multimarket competition: theory and evidence', *Journal of Economic Behavior and Organization* 18: 273–82

Chapter 5

Baldwin, R. E. and P. Martin (1999), 'Two waves of globalization: superficial similarities, fundamental differences', NBER Working Paper, 6904, Cambridge, MA, NBER

Davis, D. R. (1998), 'The home market, trade and industrial structure', *American Economic Review* 88, 1264–77

Driffield, N. and M. Munday (2000), 'Industrial performance, agglomeration and foreign manufacturing investment in the UK', *Journal of International Business Studies* 31: 21–37

Evenett, S. J. (2003), 'The cross border mergers and acquisitions wave of the late 1990s', NBER Working Paper, 9655, Cambridge, MA, NBER

Gallup J. L. and J. D. Sachs, with A. D. Mellinger (1998), 'Geography and economic development', Annual Bank Conference on Development Economics, Washington, DC, World Bank

Hanson, G. (2002), 'The role of maquiladoras in Mexico's export boom', NBER National Bureau of Economic Research, UCSD, La Jolla, mimeo

Harrigan, J. (2003), 'Specialization and the volume of production: do the data obey the laws?', in K. Choi and J. Harrigan (eds.), *The Handbook of International Trade*, Oxford, Basil Blackwell

Hinloopen, J. and C. van Marrewijk (2005), 'Locating economic activity', in S. Brakman and H. Garretsen (eds.), *Location and Competition*, London and New York, Routledge

Hummels, D. (1999), 'Have international transportation costs declined?', University of Chicago, mimeo

Krugman, P. R. and M. Obstfeld (1994), *International Economics: Theory and Policy*, 3rd edn., New York, HarperCollins

Leamer, E. and J. Levinsohn (1995), 'International trade theory: the evidence', in G. Grossman and K. Rogoff (eds.), *Handbook of International Economics, 3*, Amsterdam, North-Holland: 1339–94

Markusen, J. R. (2002), *Multinational Firms and the Theory of International Trade*, Cambridge, MA, MIT Press

Markusen, J. R. and A. J. Venables (1998), 'Multinational firms and the new trade theory', *Journal of International Economics* 46: 183–203

Marrewijk, C. Van (2002), *International Trade and the World Economy*, Oxford, Oxford University Press

Neary, J. P. (2001), 'Of hypes and hyperbolas: introducing the New Economic Geography', *Journal of Economic Literature* 39: 536–61

Radelet, S. and J. Sachs (1998), 'Shipping costs, manufactured exports and economic growth', Harvard University, mimeo

Shatz, H. J. and A. J. Venables (2000), 'The geography of international investment', in G. L. Clark, M. P. Feldman and M. S. Gertler (eds.), *The Oxford Handbook of Economic Geography*, Oxford, Oxford University Press

Shaver, J. M. (1998), 'Do foreign-owned and US-owned establishments exhibit the same location pattern in US manufacturing industries?', *Journal of International Business Studies* 29: 469–92

Shaver, J. M. and F. Flyer (2000), 'Agglomeration economies, firm heterogeneity and foreign direct investment in the United States', *Strategic Management Journal* 21: 1175–93

World Bank (2004), World Bank Development Indicators CD-ROM

Chapter 6

BIS, *Annual Reports*, various issues, Basle, BIS

Brakman, S. and C. van Marrewijk (1998), *The Economics of International Transfers*, Cambridge, Cambridge University Press

CPB (2001), *Capital Income Taxation in Europe: Trends and Trade-offs*, The Hague, CPB

Gillespie, K., L. Riddle, E. Sayre and D. Sturges (1999), 'Diaspora interest in homeland investment', *Journal of International Business Studies* 30: 623–34

IMF (2000), *World Economic Outlook*, September, Washington, DC, IMF
  (2002), *World Economic Outlook*, September, Washington, DC, IMF
  (2003), *World Economic Outlook*, April, Washington, DC, IMF

Kaminsky, G. and S. Schmukler (2003), 'Short-run pain, long-run gain: the effects of financial liberalization', NBER Working Paper, 9787, Cambridge, MA, NBER

Levi-Yeyati, E. and F. Sturzenegger (2002), 'Classifying exchange rate regimes: deeds versus words', Universidad Torcuato di Tella, mimeo, http://www.utdt/edu/~ely/DW2002.pdf
  (2003), 'To float or to fix: evidence on the impact of exchange rate regimes on growth', *American Economic Review* 93: 1173–93

Marrewijk, C. van (2002), *International Trade and the World Economy*, Oxford, Oxford University Press

Obstfeld, M. (1998), 'The global capital market: benefactor or menace?', *Journal of Economic Perspectives* 12: 9–30

Obstfeld, M. and A. M. Taylor (2003), 'Globalization and capital markets', in N. D. Bordo, A. M. Taylor and J. G. Williamson (eds.), *Globalization in Historical Perspective*, Chicago, University of Chicago Press
  (2004), *Global Capital Markets: Integration, Crisis and Growth*, Cambridge, Cambridge University Press

Obstfeld, M., J. C. Shambaugh and A. M. Taylor (2003), 'The trilemma in history: trade-offs among exchange rates, monetary policies and capital mobility', UC Berkeley, mimeo

O'Rourke, K. and J. Williamson (1999), *Globalization and History*, Cambridge, MA, MIT Press

Ostrup, F. (2002), *International Integration and Economic Policy*, University of Copenhagen, manuscript

Shambaugh, J. C. (2004), 'The effects of fixed exchange rates on monetary policy', *Quarterly Journal of Economics*, 119: 301–52

Sinn, H. W. (2002), 'The new systems competition', NBER Working Paper 8747, Cambridge, MA, NBER

Chapter 7

Acemoglu, D., S. Johnson and J. A. Robinson (2001), 'The colonial origins of comparative development', *American Economic Review* 91: 1369–1401

Bordo, M. D., A. M. Taylor and J. G. Williamson (eds.) (2003), *Globalization in Historical Perspective*, Chicago, NBER/University of Chicago Press

Budina, N., H. Garretsen and E. de Jong (2000), 'Liquidity constraints and investment in transition economies: the case of Bulgaria', *The Economics of Transition* 8: 453–77

Chirinko, R. S. (1997), 'Finance constraints, liquidity and investment spending: theoretical restrictions and international evidence', *Journal of the Japanese and International Economics* 11: 185–207

Easterly, W., (2002), *The Elusive Quest for Growth: Economists' Adventures and Misadventures in the Tropics*, Cambridge, MA, MIT Press

Fazzari, S. M., R. G. Hubbard and B. C. Petersen (1988), 'Financing constraints and corporate investment', *Brookings Papers on Economic Activity* 1: 141–95

   (2000), 'Investment–cash flow sensitivities are useful', *Quarterly Journal of Economics* 115: 695–705

Feldstein, M. and Ch. Horioka (1980), 'Domestic savings and international capital flows', *Economic Journal* 90: 314–29

Garretsen, H. and E. Sterken (2002), 'Investeringen en vermogensstructuur', in *Preadviezen van de KVS 2002*, Amsterdam, De Nederlandsche Bank (in Dutch)

Garretsen, H., R. Lensink and E. Sterken (2004), 'Growth, financial development, societal norms and legal institutions', *Journal of International Financial Markets, Institutions and Money* 14: 165–83

Gillespie, K., L. Riddle, E. Sayre and D. Sturges (1999) 'Diaspora interest in homeland investment', *Journal of International Business Studies* 30: 623–34

Hubbard, R. G. (1998), 'Capital market imperfections and investment', *Journal of Economic Literature* 36: 193–225

IMF (2003), *World Economic Outlook*, April, Washington, DC, IMF

Kaplan, S. N. and L. Zingales (1997), 'Do investment–cash flow sensitivities provide useful estimates of financing constraints?', *Quarterly Journal of Economics* 112: 169–215

Krugman, P. R. and M. Obstfeld (2003), *International Economics: Theory and Policy*, 6th ed. Reading, MA, Addison Wesley-Longman

La Porta, R., F. Lopez-de-Silanes, A. Shleifer and R. W. Vishny (1997), 'Legal determinants of external finance', *Journal of Finance* 52: 1131–50

   (1998), 'Law and finance', *Journal of Political Economy* 106: 1113–55

Lensink, R., H. Bo and E. Sterken (2001), *Investment, Capital Market Imperfections and Uncertainty*, Cheltenham, Edward Elgar

Levine, R. (1998), 'The legal environment, banks and long-run economic growth', *Journal of Money, Credit and Banking* 30: 596–620

Levine R. and S. Zervos (1998), 'Stock markets, banks and economic growth', *American Economic Review* 88: 537–58

North, D, (1990), *Institutions, Institutional Change and Economic Performance*, Cambridge, Cambridge University Press

Obstfeld, M. and K. Rogoff (1996), *Foundations of International Macroeconomics*, Cambridge, MA, MIT Press

Obstfeld M. and A. M. Taylor (2004), *Global Capital Markets: Integration, Crisis and Growth*, Cambridge, Cambridge University Press

O'Rourke, K. and J. Williamson (1999), *Globalization and History*, Cambridge, MA, MIT Press

Ostrup, F. (2002), 'International integration and economic policy', University of Copenhagen, manuscript

Rodrik, D., A. Subramanian and F. Trebbi (2002), 'Institutions rule: the primacy of institutions over geography and integration in economic development', NBER Working Paper, 9305, Cambridge MA, NBER

Tobin, J., (1969), 'A general equilibrium approach to monetary theory', *Journal of Money, Credit and Banking* 1: 15–29

Chapter 8

Bordo, M., B. Eichengreen, D. Klingebiel and M. Soledad Martinez-Peria (2001), 'Is the crisis problem growing more severe?', *Economic Policy*, April: 51–75

Caves, R. E., J. A. Frankel and R. W. Jones (2003), *World Trade and Payments: an Introduction*, Reading, MA, Addison Wesley-Longman

Eichengreen, B., A. K. Rose and Ch. Wyplosz (1995), 'Exchange rate mayhem: the antecedents and aftermath of speculative attacks', *Economic Policy* 21: 251–312

Flood, R. P. and P. M. Garber (1984), 'Collapsing exchange rate regimes: some linear examples', *Journal of International Economics*, 17: 1–13

Garretsen, H., K. Knot and E. Nijsse (1998), 'Learning about fundamentals: the widening of the French ERM bands in 1993', *Weltwirtschaftliches Archiv/Review of World Economics* 134: 25–41

Goldfajn, I. and R. O. Valdes (1998), 'Are currency crises predictable?', *European Economic Review* 42: 873–87

Husted, S. and M. Melvin (2003), *International Economics*, New York, Addison Wesley-Longman

IMF (2002a), *World Economic Outlook*, April, Washington, DC, IMF

(2002b), *World Economic Outlook*, October, Washington, DC, IMF

Jeanne, O. (2000), 'Currency crises: a perspective on recent theoretical developments', Special Papers in International Economics, 20, Department of Economics, Princeton NJ, Princeton University

Kaminsky, G. and C. Reinhart (1999), 'The twin crises: the causes of banking and balance-of-payments problems', *American Economic Review* 89: 473–500

(2000), 'On crises, contagion and confusion', *Journal of International Economics* 51: 145–68

Krugman, P. R. (1979), 'A model of balance-of-payments crises', *Journal of Money, Credit and Banking* 11: 311–25

(1996), 'Are currency crises self-fulfilling?', *NBER Macroeconomics Annual 1996*: 347–407, Cambridge, MA, NBER

(1998), 'What happened to Asia?', Cambridge, MA, MIT, mimeo http://web.mit.edu/krugman/www/DISINTER.html

Krugman, P. R. and M. Obstfeld (2002), *International Economics: Theory and Policy*, 5th ed., Reading, MA, Addison Wesley-Longman

Miller, K.D. and J. J. Reuer (1998) 'Firm strategy and economic exposure to foreign exchange rate movements', *Journal of International Business Studies* 29: 493–514

Mishkin, F. S. (1992), 'Anatomy of a financial crisis', *Journal of Evolutionary Economics* 2: 115–30

(1996), 'Understanding financial crises: a developing country perspective', NBER Working Paper, 5600, Cambridge MA, NBER

(1999), 'Global financial instability: framework, events and issues', *Journal of Economic Perspectives* 4: 3–20

Obstfeld, M. and K. Rogoff (1996), *Foundations of International Macroeconomics*, Cambridge, MA, MIT Press

Obstfeld M. (1996), 'Models of currency crises with self-fulfilling features', *European Economic Review* 40: 1037–47

Chapter 9

Bordo, M., B. Eichengreen, D. Klingebiel and M. Soledad Martinez-Peria (2001), 'Is the crisis problem growing more severe?', *Economic Policy*, April

Caprio, G. and D. Klingebiel (1996), 'Bank insolvency: bad luck, bad policy, or bad banking?', in M. Bruno and B. Pleskovic (eds.), *Annual World Bank Conference on Development Economics*, Washington, DC, World Bank: 79–104

Galbraith, J. K. (1954), *The Great Crash of 1929*, Boston, Houghton Mifflin

(1990), *A Short History of Financial Euphoria*, New York, Penguin

IMF (1998), *World Economic Outlook*, April, September, Washington, DC, IMF

(2000), *World Economic Outlook*, September, Washington, DC, IMF

(2002), *World Economic Outlook*, September, Washington, DC, IMF

(2003), *World Economic Outlook*, April, Washington, DC, IMF

Jeanne, O. (2000), 'Currency crises: a perspective on recent theoretical developments', Special Papers in International Economics, 20, Department of Economics, Princeton, NJ Princeton University

Kaminsky G. and C. Reinhart (1999), 'The twin crises: the causes of banking and balance-of-payments problems', *American Economic Review* 89: 473–500

Kindleberger, C. P. (1996), *Manias, Panics and Crashes: A History of Financial Crises*, New York, Wiley

Krugman, P. (1998), 'What happened to Asia?', Cambridge, MA, MIT, mimeo http://web.mit.edu/krugman/www/DISINTER.html

(2000), *The Return of Depression Economics*, New York, W.W. Norton

McKinnon, R. I. and H. Pill (1997), 'Credible economic liberalizations and overborrowing', *American Economic Review, Papers and Proceedings*, May: 189–93.

Minsky, H. P. (1975), *John Maynard Keynes*, New York, Macmillan

Mishkin, F. S. (1992), 'Anatomy of a financial crisis', *Journal of Evolutionary Economics* 2: 115–30

(1996), 'Understanding financial crises: a developing country perspective', NBER Working Paper, 5600, Cambridge, MA, NBER

(1999), 'Global financial instability: framework, events and issues', *Journal of Economic Perspectives* 3–20

Radelet, S. and J. D. Sachs (1998), 'The East Asian financial crisis: diagnosis, remedies, prospects', *Brookings Papers on Economic Activity*, 1: 1–90

Stiglitz, J. (2002), *Globalization and its Discontents*, London, Penguin.

World Bank (2003a), *Global Development Finance*, Washington, DC, World Bank

(2003b), World Bank Development Indicators CD ROM

Chapter 10

Anderson, K. (2004), 'Subsidies and trade barriers', in B. Lomborg (ed.), *Global Crises, Global Solutions*, Cambridge, Cambridge University Press: 541–77

Bhagwati, J. (1998), 'The capital myth: the difference between trade in widgets and dollars', *Foreign Affairs* 77(3): 7–12

Brakman, S. and C. van Marrewijk, (1996), 'Trade policy under imperfect competition: the economics of Russian roulette', *De Economist* 144: 223–58

Buiter, W. H. (2003), 'James Tobin: an appreciation of his contributions to economics', *The Economic Journal*, 113: F585–F631

Buiter, W. H. and A. C. Sibert (1999), 'UDROP: a contribution to the new international financial architecture', *International Finance* 2: 227–47

Delios, A. and W. J. Henisz (2003), 'Political hazards, experience and sequential entry strategies: the international expansion of Japanese firms, 1980–1998', *Strategic Management Journal* 24: 1153–64

Edwards, S. (2001), 'Exchange rate regimes, capital flows and crisis prevention', NBER Working Paper 8529, Cambridge, MA, NBER

Eichengreen, B. (2002), *Financial Crises and What to Do about Them*, Oxford, Oxford University Press

(2004), 'Financial instability', in B. Lomborg (ed.), *Global Crises, Global Solutions*, Cambridge, Cambridge University Press

Eichengreen, B. C. Wyplosz and J. Tobin (1995), 'Two cases for sands in the wheels of international finance', *The Economic Journal*, 105: 162–72

Fischer, S. (2003), 'Financial crises and the reform of the international financial system', *Review of World Economics* 139: 3–37

Haas, R. T. A. de and I. P. P. van Lelyveld (2004), 'Foreign banks and credit stability in Central and Eastern Europe: a panel data analysis', *Journal of Banking and Finance*, forthcoming

IMF (2003), *World Economic Outlook*, April, Washington, DC, IMF

Krugman, P. R. (1993), 'Regionalism versus multilateralism: analytical notes', in J. De Melo and A. Panagariya (eds.), *New Dimensions in Regional Integration*, Cambridge, Cambridge University Press: 58–79

(1998), 'What happened to Asia?', Cambridge, MA, MIT mimeo

Magee, S. P., W. A. Brock and L. Young (1989), *Black Hole Tariffs and Endogenous Policy Theory: Political Economy in General Equilibrium*, Cambridge, Cambridge University Press

Neary, P. J. (2004), 'Europe on the road to Doha: towards a new global trade round?', *CESifo Economic Studies* 50: 319–32

Sachs, J. D. and A. Warner (1995), 'Economic reforms and the process of global integration', *Brookings Papers on Economic Activity*, 1: 1–95

The Economist (2004), 'Trade's bounty', 4 December: 80

Tirole, J. (2002), *Financial Crises, Liquidity and the International Monetary System*, Princeton, NJ, Princeton University Press

Tobin, J. (1978), 'A proposal for international monetary reform', *Eastern Economic Journal* 4: 153–9

Tornell, A. and F. Westermann (2004), 'The positive link between financial liberalization, growth and crises', CESifo Working Paper 1164, Munich

Vernon, R. (1966), 'International investment and international trade in the product cycle', *Quarterly Journal of Economics* 80: 190–207

Chapter 11

Aghion, P. and P. Howitt (1992), 'A model of growth through creative destruction', *Econometrica* 60: 323–51

Coe, D. T. E. Helpman and A. W. Hoffmaister (1997), 'North–South R&D spillovers', *The Economic Journal* 107: 134–49

Grossman, G. M. and E. Helpman (1991), *Innovation and Growth in the Global Economy*, Cambridge, MA, MIT Press

Heston, A., R. Summers and B. Aten (2002), *Penn World Table Version 6.1*, Center for International Comparisons at the University of Pennsylvania (CICUP)

Hinloopen, J. and C. van Marrewijk (2004), 'Dynamics of Chinese comparative advantage', Working Paper 04–034/2, Rotterdam and Amsterdam, Tinbergen Institute

Kaldor, N. (1961), 'Capital accumulation and economic growth', in F. A. Lutz and D. C. Hague (eds.), *The Theory of Capital*, London, Macmillan: 177–222

Luo, Y. and M. W. Peng (1999), 'Learning to compete in a transition economy: experience, environment and performance', *Journal of International Business Studies* 30: 269–96

Maddison, A. (2001), *The World Economy: A Millennial Perspective*, Paris and Washington, DC, OECD

(2003), *The World Economy: Historical Statistics*, Paris and Washington, DC, OECD

Mankiw, N. G. D. Romer and D. N. Weil (1992), 'A contribution to the empirics of economic growth', *Quarterly Journal of Economics* 107: 407–37

Marrewijk, C. van (1999), 'Capital accumulation, learning and endogenous growth', *Oxford Economic Papers* 51: 453–75

(2002), *International Trade and the World Economy*, Oxford, Oxford University Press

Romer, P. M. (1986), 'Increasing returns and long run growth', *Journal of Political Economy* 94: 1002–37

(1990), 'Endogenous technological change', *Journal of Political Economy* 98: S71–S102

Schumpeter, J. A. (1912), *The Theory of Economic Development*, Cambridge, MA, Harvard University Press

Solow, R. M. (1956), 'A contribution to the theory of economic growth', *Quarterly Journal of Economics* 70: 65–94

Wilson, D. and R. Purushothaman (2003), 'Dreaming with BRICs: the path to 2050', Goldman Sachs, Global Economics Paper 99

World Bank (2003), *World Development Indicators* CD ROM

Young, A. (1995), 'The tyranny of numbers: confronting the statistical realities of the East Asian growth experience', *Quarterly Journal of Economics* 110: 641–80

Chapter 12

Abrahamson, E. (1997), 'The emergence and prevalence of employee management rhetorics: the effects of long waves, labor unions, and turnover, 1875 to 1992', *Academy of Management Journal* 40: 491–533

Addison, J. T., C. Schnabel and J. Wagner (2004), 'The course of research into the economic consequences of German works councils', *British Journal of Industrial Relations* 42: 255–81

Aitken, N. D. (1973), 'The effect of the EEC and EFTA on European trade: a temporal cross-section analysis', *American Economic Review* 63: 881–92

Anderson, K. and R. Blackhurst (1993), 'Regional integration and the global trading system: introduction and summary', in K. Anderson and R. Blackhurst (eds.), *Regional Integration and the Global Trading System*, New York, St. Martin's Press: 1–15

Amabile, T. M. and R. Conti (1999), 'Changes in the work environment for creativity during downsizing', *Academy of Management Journal* 42: 630–40

Amiti, M. and S.-J. Wei (2004), 'Fear of outsourcing: is it justified?', CEPR Discussion Paper Series 4719, London, Centre for Economic Policy Research

Arrighetti, A., R. Bachmann and S. Deakin (1997), 'Contract law, social norms and inter-firm cooperation', *Cambridge Journal of Economics* 21: 171–95

Barkema, H.G. and G. A. M. Vermeulen (1997), What differences in the cultural backgrounds of partners are detrimental for international joint ventures', *Journal of International Business Studies*, 20: 845–64

Barney, J. B. (1991), 'Firm resources and sustained competitive advantage', *Journal of Management* 17: 99–120

Bartlett C. A. and S. Ghoshal (1989), *Managing Across Borders: The Transnational Solution*, Boston, MA, Harvard Business School Press

Basu, S. (1995), 'Stackelberg equilibrium in oligopoly: an explanation based on managerial incentives', *Economics Letters* 49: 459–64

Baumol, W. J. (1963), *Business Behaviour, Value and Growth*, New York: Macmillan

Beechler, S. and J. Z. Yang (1994), 'The transfer of Japanese-style management to American subsidiaries: contingencies, constraints and competencies', *Journal of International Business Studies* 29: 457–91

Berle, A. and G. Means (1932), *The Modern Corporation and Private Property*, New York, Macmillan

Bhagwati, J. and A. Panagariya (1996), 'The theory of preferential trade agreements: historical evolution and current trends', *American Economic Review* 86: 82–7

Billington, N. (1999), 'The location of foreign direct investment: an empirical analysis', *Applied Economics* 31: 65–76

Bliss, H. and B. Russett (1998), 'Democratic trading partners: the liberal connection, 1962–1989', *Journal of Politics* 60: 1126–47

Boone, C. and A. van Witteloostuijn (1999), 'Competitive and opportunistic behaviour in a prisoner's dilemma game: experimental evidence on the impact of culture and education', *Scandinavian Journal of Management* 15: 333–50

Boone, C., B. De Brabander and A. van Witteloostuijn (1999), 'The impact of personality on behavior in five Prisoner's Dilemma games', *Journal of Economic Psychology* 20: 343–77

Borkowski, S. C. (1999), 'International managerial performance evaluation: a five-country comparison', *Journal of International Business Studies* 30: 533–55

Bornstein, G. and M. Ben-Yossef (1994), 'Cooperation in intergroup and single-group social dilemmas', *Journal of Experimental Social Psychology* 30: 52–67

Brada, J. C. and J. A. Mendez (1983), 'Regional economic integration and the volume of intra-regional trade: a comparison of developed and developing country experience', *Kyklos* 36: 589–603

Brandenburger, A. M. and B. J. Nalebuff (1996), *Co-opetition*, New York, Doubleday

Brander, J. A. and P. R. Krugman (1983), 'A "reciprocal dumping" model of international trade', *Journal of International Economics* 15: 313–21

Brouthers, K. D. and L. E. Brouthers (2000), 'Acquisition or greenfield start-up?: institutional, cultural and transaction cost influence', *Strategic Management Journal* 21: 89–98

Brouthers, L. E. and S. Werner (1990), 'Are the Japanese good global competitors?', *Columbia Journal of World Business* 25: 5–12

Brouthers, L. E., S. Werner and E. Matulich (2000), 'The influence of triad nations' environments on price–quality product strategies and MNC performance', *Journal of International Business Studies* 31: 39–62

Cameron, K. (ed.) (1994), 'Investigating organizational downsizing: fundamental issues', Special issue of *Human Resource Management* 33: 183 ff

Carstensen, K. and F. Toubal (2004), 'Foreign direct investment in Central and Eastern European Countries: A dynamic panel analysis', *Journal of Comparative Economics* 32: 3–22

Caves, R. E. and S. K. Mehra (1986), 'Entry of foreign multinationals into the US manufacturing industries', in M. E. Porter (ed.), *Competition in Global Industries*, Boston, MA, Harvard Business School Press: 449–81

Cox, T. H., S. Lobel and E. McLeod (1991), 'Effects of ethnic group cultural difference on cooperative versus competitive behavior in a group task', *Academy of Management Journal* 34: 827–47

Culem, C. G. (1988), 'The locational determinants of direct investment among industrialized countries', *European Economic Review* 32: 885–904

Dikova, D. and A. van Witteloostuijn (2004), 'Acquisition versus greenfield foreign entry: diversification mode choice in Central and Eastern Europe', Working Paper, Groningen, University of Groningen

Dixon, W. J. and B. E. Moon (1993), 'Political similarity and American foreign trade patterns', *Political Research Quarterly* 46: 5–25

Driffield, N. and M. Munday (2000), 'Industrial performance, agglomeration and foreign manufacturing investment in the UK', *Journal of International Business Studies* 31: 21–37

Dunning, J. H. (1993), *Multinational Enterprises and the Global Economy*, Wokingham, Addison-Wesley

Fersthman, C. and K. Judd (1987), 'Equilibrium incentives in oligopoly', *American Economic Review* 77: 927–40

Frege, C. M. (2002) 'A critical assessment of the theoretical and empirical research on German works councils', *British Journal of Industrial Relations* 40: 221–48

Gibbons, R. (1992) *A Primer in Game Theory*, New York, Harvester Wheatsheaf

Gooderham, P. N. O. Nordhaug and K. Ringdal (1999), 'Institutional and rational determinants of organizational practices: human resource management in European firms', *Administrative Science Quarterly* 44: 507–31

Gordon, D. (1996), *Fat and Mean: The Corporate Squeeze of Working Americans and the Myth of Managerial 'Downsizing'*, New York, Free Press

Gowa, J. (1989), 'Bipolarity, multipolarity and free trade', *American Political Science Review* 83: 1245–56

  (1994), *Allies, Adversaries and International Trade*, Princeton, NJ, Princeton University Press

Graham, E. and P. R. Krugman (1989), 'Economic impact', in B. Gomes-Casseres and D. Yoffie (eds.), *The International Political Economy of Direct Foreign Investment*, II, Brookfield, VT, Edward Elgar

Hall, M. J., A. Hoffmann, P. Marginson and T. Müller (2003), 'National influences on European Works councils in UK- and US-based companies,' *Human Resource Management Journal*, 13: 75–92

Hennart, J.-F. and Y.-R. Park (1993), 'Greenfield versus acquisition: the strategy of Japanese investors in the United States', *Management Science* 39: 1054–70

Hirschman, A. O. (1945), *National Power and the Structure of Foreign Trade*, Berkeley, CA, University of California Press

Hofstede, G. (1980, 1991), *Culture's Consequences: International Differences in Work-Related Values*, Thousand Oaks, London and New Delhi, Sage; edn. 1991

  (2003), *Comparing Values, Behaviors, Institutions and Organizations across Nations*, Thousand Oaks, London and New Delhi, Sage

Holmström, B. (1989), 'Agency costs and innovation', *Journal of Economic Behavior and Organization* 12: 305–27

Huselid, M. (1995), 'The impact of human resource management practices on turnover, productivity and corporate financial performance', *Academy of Management Journal* 38: 635–72

Jansen, T., A. van Lier and A. van Witteloostuijn (2005), Strategic delegation in oligopoly: the market share case, University of Groningen, mimeo

Jensen, M. C. and W. Meckling (1976), 'Theory of the firm: managerial behavior, agency costs and ownership structure', *Journal of Financial Economics* 3: 305–60

Kagel, J. H. and A. E. Roth (1995), *Handbook of Experimental Economics*, Princeton, NJ, Princeton University Press

Kaplan, S. N. (1994), 'Top executive rewards and firm performance: a comparison of Japan and the United States', *Journal of Political Economy* 102: 510–46

Krueger, A. O. (2000), 'NAFTA's effects: a preliminary assessment', *World Economy* 23: 761–75

La Porta, R., F. Lopez-de-Silanes and A. Shleifer (1999), 'Corporate ownership around the world', *Journal of Finance* 54: 471–517

Linder, S. B. (1961), *An Essay on Trade and Transformation*, New York, John Wiley

Liu, X., P. Burridge and P. J. N. Sinclair (2002), 'Relationships between economic growth, foreign direct investment and trade: evidence from China', *Applied Economics* 34: 1433–41

Liu, X., D. Parker, K. Vaidya and Y. Wei (2001), 'The impact of foreign direct investment on labor productivity in the Chinese electronics industry', *International Business Review* 10: 421–39

Mansfield, E. D. (1994), 'Alliances, preferential trading arrangements and sanctions', *Journal of International Affairs* 48: 119–39

Mansfield, E. D. and R. Bronson (1997), 'Alliances, preferential trading arrangements and international trade', *American Economic Review* 91: 94–107

March, J. G. (1991), 'Exploration and exploitation in organizational learning', *Organization Science* 2: 71–87

Martinez-Zarzoso, I. (2003), 'Gravity model: an application to trade between regional blocs', *Atlantic Economic Journal* 31: 174–87

Morck, R. A., A. Shleifer and R. W. Vishny (1990), 'Do managerial objectives drive bad acquisitions', *Journal of Finance* 45: 31–48

Morgenstern, O. and J. von Neumann (1944), *Theory of Games and Economic Behaviour*, Princeton, NJ, Princeton University Press

Morrow, J. D., R. M. Siverson and T. Tabares (1998), 'The political determinants of international trade: the major powers, 1907–907', *American Political Science Review* 92: 649–62

Mundell, R. (1957), 'International trade and factor mobility', *American Economic Review* 47: 321–35

Narula, R. (1996), *Multinational Investment and Economic Structure*, London and New York, Routledge

Nash, J. (1950), Equilibrium points in N-person games', *Proceedings of the National Academy of Sciences* 36: 48–9

Neelankavil, J. P., A. Mathur and Y. Zhang (2000), 'Determinants of managerial performance: a cross-cultural comparison of the perceptions of middle-level managers in four countries', *Journal of International Business Studies* 31: 121–40

Noordin, F., T. Williams and C. Zimmer (2002), 'Career commitment in collectivist and individualist cultures: a comparative study', *International Journal of Human Resource Management* 13: 35–54

Ohmae, K. (1995), *The End of the Nation State*, London, HarperCollins

Oneal, J. R. and B. M. Russett (1997), 'The classical liberals were right: democracy, interdependence and conflict, 1950–1985', *International Studies Quarterly* 41: 267–94

Shea, J. and C. Madigan (1997), *Dangerous Company: The Consulting Powerhouses and the Business They Save and Ruin*, New York, Times Business

Pelzman, J. (1977), 'Trade creation and trade diversion in the Council of Mutual Economic Assistance: 1954–70', *American Economic Review* 67: 713–22

Phongpaichit, P. (1990), *The New Wave of Japanese Investment in Asia*, Singapore, Institute of Southeast Asian Studies

Pinto, B. (1986), 'Repeated games and the reciprocal dumping model of trade', *Journal of International Economics* 20: 357-66

Pollins, B. M. (1989a), 'Does trade still follow the flag?', *American Political Science Review* 83: 465–80

   (1989b), 'Conflict, cooperation and commerce: the effect of international political interactions on bilateral trade flows', *American Journal of Political Science* 33: 737–61

Porter, M. E. (1980), *Competitive Strategy: Techniques for Analyzing Industries and Competitors*, New York, Free Press

Powell, R. (1991), 'Absolute and relative gains in international relations theory', *American Political Science Review* 85: 1305–22

Remmer, K. (1998), 'Does democracy promote interstate cooperation?: lessons from the Mercosur region', *International Studies Quarterly* 42: 25–51

Rogers, J. and W. Streeck (eds.) (1995), *Works Councils: Consultation, Representation and Cooperation in Industrial Relations*, Chicago, University of Chicago Press

Root, F. (1977), *Entry Strategies for Foreign Markets: From Domestic to International Business*, New York, AMACOM

   (1994), *Entry Strategies for International Markets*, New York, Macmillan

Savage, R. and K. W. Deutsch (1960), 'A statistical model of the gross analysis of transaction flows', *Econometrica* 28: 551–72

Scott, J. (1997), *Corporate Business and Capital Class*, Oxford, Oxford University Press

Sklivas, S. D. (1987), 'The strategic choice of management incentives', *RAND Journal of Economics* 18: 452–8

Smith, V. L. (2000), *Bargaining and Market Behavior: Essays in Experimental Economics*, Cambridge, Cambridge University Press

Sorge, A. M. (2005), *The Global and the Local*, Oxford, Oxford University Press

Sorge, A. M. and A. van Witteloostuijn (2004), 'The (non)sense of organizational change: an *essai* about universal management hypes, sick consultancy metaphors and healthy organization theories', *Organization Studies* 25: 1205–31

Sun, H. (2001), 'Foreign direct investment and regional export performance in China', *Journal of Regional Science* 41: 317–36

Tirole, J. (1988), *The Theory of Industrial Organization*, Cambridge, MA, Harvard University Press

UNCTAD (2004), *World Investment Report*, New York and Geneva, UN

Verdier, D. (1998), 'Democratic convergence and free trade', *International Studies Quarterly* 42: 1–24

Vernon, R. (1966), 'International investment and international trade in the product cycle', *Quarterly Journal of Economics* 80: 190–207

Vickers, J. (1985), 'Delegation and the theory of the firm', *Economic Journal* 95: 138–47

Viner, J. (1953), *The Customs Union Issue*, New York, Carnegie Endowment for International Peace

Wei, Y., X. Liu, D. Parker and K. Vaidya (1999), 'The regional distribution of foreign direct investment in China', *Regional Studies* 33: 857–67

Wegberg, M. J. A. M. van and A. van Witteloostuijn (1992) 'Credible entry threats into contestable markets: a symmetric multi-market model of contestibility', *Economica*, 59: 437–52

Wegberg, M. J. A. M. van, A. van Witteloostuijn and M. Roscam Abbing (1994), 'Multimarket and multiproject collusion: why European integration may reduce intra-community competition', *De Economist* 142: 253–85

Williamson, O. E. (1975), *Markets and Hierarchies*, Englewood Cliffs, NJ, Prentice Hall

Witteloostuijn, A. van (1993), 'Multimarket competition and business strategy', *Review of Industrial Organization* 8: 83–99

(1998), 'Bridging behavioral and economic theories of decline: organizational inertia, strategic competition and chronic failure', *Management Science* 44: 501–19

(1999), *De anorexiastrategie: over de gevolgen van saneren* (*The Anorexia Strategy: About the Consequences of Downsizing*), Amsterdam/Antwerp, Arbeiderspers

(2002), 'Interorganizational economics', in J. A. C. Baum (ed.), *Companion to Organizations*, Oxford, Blackwell: 686–712

Witteloostuijn, A. van, C. Boone and A. van Lier (2003), 'Toward a game theory of organizational ecology: production adjustment costs and managerial growth preferences', *Strategic Organization* 1: 259–300

World Bank (2002), *World Development Indicators*, CD ROM

Yeung, I. Y. M. and K. L. Tung (1996), 'Achieving business success in Confucian societies: the importance of Guanxi (connections)', *Organizational Dynamics* 1: 54–65

Zhang, J., J. Jacobs and A. van Witteloostuijn (2004) 'Multinational enterprises, foreign direct investment and trade in China: A cointegration and Granger-causality approach', Working Paper, Groningen, University of Groningen

Chapter 13

Acemoglu, D. S. Johnson and J. A. Robinson (2001), 'The colonial origins of comparative development', *American Economic Review* 91: 1369–1401

Baumol, W. J. (1967), 'Macroeconomics of unbalanced growth: the anatomy of urban crisis', *American Economic Review* 57: 415–26

Bernard, A. B., J. B. Jensen and P. K. Schott (2002), 'Survival of the best fit: competition from low wage countries and the (uneven) growth of US manufacturing plants', NBER Working Paper, 9170, Cambridge, MA, NBER

Bordo, M. D., A. M. Taylor and J. G. Williamson (2003), *Globalization in Historical Perspective*, Chicago, NBER and University of Chicago Press

Borjas, G. J. (1989), 'Economic theory and international migration', *International Migration Review* 23: 457–85

Bourguignon, F. and C. Morrison (2002), 'Inequality among world citizens: 1820–1992', *American Economic Review* 92: 727–44

Easterly, W. (2002), *The Elusive Quest for Growth: Economists' Adventures and Misadventures in the Tropics*, Cambridge, MA, MIT Press

Easterly, W. and R. Levine (2003), 'Tropics, germs and crops: how endowments influence economic development', *Journal of Monetary Economics* 50: 3–40

Elliott, K. A., D. Kar and J. D. Richardson (2004), 'Assessing globalization's critics: talkers are no good doers?', in R. E. Baldwin and J. D. Richardson (eds.), *Challenges to Globalization*, Chicago, NBER and University of Chicago Press

Feenstra., R. C. and G. Hanson (2001), 'Global production sharing and rising inequality: a survey of trade and wages', NBER Working Paper 8372, Cambridge, MA, NBER

Fischer, S. (2003), 'Globalization and its challenges', *American Economic Review*, 93: 1–30

Glaeser, E., R. LaPorta, F. Lopes-de-Silanes and A. Shleifer (2004), 'Do institutions cause growth?', *Journal of Economic Growth* 9: 271–303

Graham, E. M. (2000), *Fighting the Wrong Enemy: Antiglobal Activists and Multinational Enterprises*, Washington, DC, Institute for International Economics

IMF (2003), *World Economic Outlook*, April, Washington, DC, IMF

Klein, N. (2001), *No Logo*, London, Flamingo

Krugman, P. R. (1995), 'Growing world trade: causes and consequences', *Brookings Papers on Economic Activity* 1: 327–62

Krugman, P. R. and R. Lawrence (1994), 'Trade, jobs and wages', *Scientific American*, April.

Lawrence, R. (1994), 'Trade, multinationals and labor', NBER Working Paper 4836, Cambridge, MA, NBER

Lawrence, R. and M. Slaughter (1993), 'International trade and American wages in the 1980s: giant sucking sound or small hiccup?', *Brookings Papers on Economic Activity: Microeconomics* 2: 161–226

Nickell, S. and B. Bell (1996), 'Changes in the distribution of wages and unemployment in OECD countries', *American Economic Review* 86: 302–8

Peeters, J. J. W. (2001), *Globalisation, Location and Labour Markets*, PhD thesis, University of Nijmegen

Rodrik, D. (1997), *Has Globalization Gone too Far?*, Institute for International Economics, Washington, DC

  (ed.), (2003), *In Search of Prosperity: Analytic Narratives on Economic Growth*, Princeton, NJ, Princeton University Press

Rodrik, D., A. Subramanian and F. Trebbi, (2004), 'Institutions rule: the primacy of institutions over geography and integration in economic development', NBER Working Paper, 9305, Cambridge, MA, NBER

Rodriguez, F. and D. Rodrik (1999), 'Trade policy and economic growth: a scep-
tic's guide to the cross-national evidence', NBER Working Paper 7081, Cambridge,
MA, NBER

Sachs, J. D. (2003), Macroeconomics in the Global Economy, *Journal of Economic Growth* 9:
131–65

Sachs, J. D. and H. J. Shatz (1996), 'US, trade with developing countries and wage inequality',
American Economic Review, Papers and Proceedings 86: 234–9

Sachs, J.D. and A. Warner (1995), 'Economic reform and the process of global integration',
Brookings Papers on Economic Activity, 1: 1–95

Sala-i-Martin. X. (2002), The myth of exploding income inequality in Europe and the world,
in H. Kierzkowski, *From Europeanization of the Globe to the Globalization of Europe*,
London, Palgrave

Strauss-Kahn, V. (2004), 'Globalization and the shift away from unskilled workers', in R. E.
Baldwin and L. A. Winters, *Challenges to Globalization: Analyzing the Economics*, Chicago,
NBER and University of Chicago Press

Theil, H. (1967), *Economics and Information Theory*, Chicago, Rand McNally

World Bank (2002), *Globalization, Growth and Poverty: Building an Inclusive World Economy*,
Oxford, Oxford University Press

Chapter 14

Barba Navaretti, G. and A. J. Venables (2004), *Multinational Firms in the World Economy*,
Princeton, NJ, Princeton University Press

Barney, J. B. (1991), 'Firm resources and sustained competitive advantage', *Journal of Management* 17: 99–120

Billington, N. (1999), 'The location of foreign direct investment: an empirical analysis', *Applied
Economics* 31: 65–76

Culem, C. G. (1988), 'The locational determinants of direct investment among industrialized
countries', *European Economic Review* 32: 885–904

DiMaggio P. J. and W. W. Powell (1983), 'The iron cage revisted: institutional isomor-
phism and collective rationality in organizational fields', *American Sociological Review* 48:
147–60

Dunning, J. H. (1993), *Multinational Enterprises and the Global Economy*, Wokingham,
Addison-Wesley

Graham, E. and P. R. Krugman (1989), 'Economic impact', in B. Gomes-Casseres and D.Yoffie
(eds.), *The International Political Economy of Direct Foreign Investment*, II, Brookfield,
VT, Edward Elgar

Kostova, T. and K. Roth (2002), 'Adoption of an organizational practice by subsidiaries of
multinational corporations: institutional and relational effects', *Academy of Management
Journal* 45: 215–33

Liu, X., P. Burridge and P. J. N. Sinclair (2002), 'Relationships between economic growth,
foreign direct investment and trade: evidence from China', *Applied Economics* 34: 1433–
41

Liu, X., D. Parker, K. Vaidya and Y. Wei (2001), 'The impact of foreign direct investment on labor productivity in the Chinese electronics industry', *International Business Review* 10: 421–39

Maijoor, S. J. and A. van Witteloostuijn (1996), 'An empirical test of the resource-based theory: strategic regulation in the Dutch audit industry', *Strategic Management Journal* 17: 549–69

Mundell, R. (1957), 'International trade and factor mobility', *American Economic Review* 47: 321–35

Narula, R. (1996), *Multinational Investment and Economic Structure*, London and New York, Routledge

Phongpaichit, P. (1990), *The New Wave of Japanese Investment in Asia*, Singapore, Institute of Southeast Asian Studies

Root, F. (1994), *Entry Strategies for International Markets*, New York: Macmillan

Sorge, A. M. (2005), *The Global and the Local*, Oxford, Oxford University Press

Sun, H. (2001), 'Foreign direct investment and regional export performance in China', *Journal of Regional Science* 41: 317–36

Wei, Y., X. Liu, D. Parker and K. Vaidya (1999), 'The regional distribution of foreign direct investment in China', *Regional Studies* 33: 857–67

Wernerfelt, B. (1984), 'A resource-based view of the firm', *Strategic Management Journal* 5: 171–80

Zhang, J. J. Jacobs and A. van, Witteloostuijn (2004), 'Multinational enterprises, foreign direct investement and trade in China: a cointegration and Granger-causality approach', Working Paper, Groningen, University of Groningen

Author index

Subject index